EXECUTIVE JOB-CHANGING WORKBOOK

...the ATTACHE PAGES

JOHN LUCHT

Take advantage of the sophisticated tools executive recruiters use.

This comprehensive search administration system will bring you more and better opportunities faster and more easily.

You'll NETWORK more effectively, INTERVIEW more impressively...and track tax-deductible expenses more efficiently.

THE VICEROY PRESS
NEW YORK

DISTRIBUTED BY HENRY HOLT AND COMPANY, INC.
NEW YORK

 Manufactured in the United States of America. Distributed to the trade in the USA by Henry Holt and Company, Inc., 115 West 18th Street, New York, NY 10011.

Designers: John Charles, Erik Jensen
Editors: Lenka Knowski, Jean Sanders, Monica Becerra
Drawings: Erik Jensen

Better Safe than Sorry!

...and Why Worry?

Yes! There's a ***large*** supply of everything you'll need to manage your search in these ATTACHE PAGES.

No! That doesn't mean that you'll have to use all of them.

Chances are, you'll use only a fraction. Certainly I hope so. But, even though publishing "experts" strongly urged me to, I haven't shortchanged you on materials some folks conceivably may wind up needing, just to make the WORKBOOK "look like less work."

So enjoy plenty of scribbling room...probably lots *more* than you'll need. I just don't want you to run short.

Think of the extra pages as "insurance."

You're taking your umbrella. That way, you can be pretty sure it *won't* rain!

With warmest wishes...and the best help I can provide for a fast, successful search.

Sincerely,

John Lucht

To Help With Your Search...

ATTACHE FEATURES

(STRAIGHT AHEAD IN THE **ATTACHE PAGES***)*

AND THEIR EXPLANATIONS

(FLIP BACK TO THE **WORKBOOK PAGES***)*

The heart of your search administration system is the combination of NETWORKING CONTACTS pages, *KEY* NETWORKING CONTACTS pages, and a chronological INDEX that links all of the components (more than just these three) in a special way. Read all about it in the Networking Chapter of the WORKBOOK (Workbook pages 164-180).

Another powerful information-based tool is the INTERVIEW DE-BRIEFER. You'll find plenty of these, beginning at ATTACHE PAGE 173...and you can read about them toward the end of the Interviewing Chapter of the WORKBOOK (Workbook pages 225-232).

Yet another convenience are your Attache Pages for tracking tax-deductible expenses of your job search. Read about them in the Tax / Expense Chapter of the WORKBOOK (Workbook pages 237-240).

And Now Onward with Your Search!

(PLEASE READ AND USE THE WORKBOOK *BEFORE PROCEEDING)*

PERSON	COMPANY / CONNECTION	PAGE NUMBER

INDEX OF CONTACTS

PERSON	COMPANY / CONNECTION	PAGE NUMBER

INDEX OF CONTACTS

PERSON	COMPANY / CONNECTION	PAGE NUMBER

INDEX OF CONTACTS

PERSON	COMPANY / CONNECTION	PAGE NUMBER

PERSON	COMPANY / CONNECTION	PAGE NUMBER

INDEX OF CONTACTS

PERSON	COMPANY / CONNECTION	PAGE NUMBER

PERSON	COMPANY / CONNECTION	PAGE NUMBER

INDEX OF CONTACTS

PERSON	COMPANY / CONNECTION	PAGE NUMBER

PERSON	COMPANY / CONNECTION	PAGE NUMBER

INDEX OF CONTACTS

INDEX

PERSON	COMPANY / CONNECTION	PAGE NUMBER

Person	Company / Connection	Page Number

ATTACHE PAGE

INDEX OF CONTACTS

INDEX

PERSON	COMPANY / CONNECTION	PAGE NUMBER

PERSON	COMPANY / CONNECTION	PAGE NUMBER

INDEX OF CONTACTS

INDEX

PERSON	COMPANY / CONNECTION	PAGE NUMBER

PERSON	COMPANY / CONNECTION	PAGE NUMBER

INDEX OF CONTACTS

INDEX

PERSON	COMPANY / CONNECTION	PAGE NUMBER

INDEX

PERSON	COMPANY / CONNECTION	PAGE NUMBER

Networking Tools

Please turn the page for an ample supply of the most powerful tools-on-paper that can be applied to an executive job search ...Networking Contacts pages (2 of every 3) and *Key* Networking Contacts pages (1 of every 3).

These tools have their origins in the "S&P" sheets used by the executive recruiting profession. Please read Chapter 4 of the Workbook (page 164) before using them. Success depends on—among other things—skillful use of chrono-indexing. Once you're using these tools, you'll apply the same methods to many areas of your life that extend far beyond job-changing.

NETWORKING CONTACTS

DATES | PERSON: TITLE, COMPANY, ADDRESS, PHONES | COMMENTS & FOLLOW-UP

PHONE

VISIT

LETTER

SOURCE MENTION **YES** ☐ MENTION **NO** ☐

PHONE

VISIT

LETTER

SOURCE MENTION **YES** ☐ MENTION **NO** ☐

PHONE

VISIT

LETTER

SOURCE MENTION **YES** ☐ MENTION **NO** ☐

PHONE

VISIT

LETTER

SOURCE MENTION **YES** ☐ MENTION **NO** ☐

NETWORKING CONTACTS

DATES PERSON: TITLE, COMPANY, ADDRESS, PHONES COMMENTS & FOLLOW-UP

PHONE

VISIT

LETTER

SOURCE MENTION **YES** ☐ MENTION **NO** ☐

PHONE

VISIT

LETTER

SOURCE MENTION **YES** ☐ MENTION **NO** ☐

PHONE

VISIT

LETTER

SOURCE MENTION **YES** ☐ MENTION **NO** ☐

PHONE

VISIT

LETTER

SOURCE MENTION **YES** ☐ MENTION **NO** ☐

KEY NETWORKING CONTACT

Person/Title: ______________________________

Company: ______________________________

Address: ______________________________
TITLE STREET ADDRESS CITY STATE/ZIP

Phones/Fax: #1 (   ) ____-______ ☐ SWITCHBOARD ☐ PRIVATE #2 (   ) ____-______ ☐ SWITCHBOARD ☐ PRIVATE FAX (   ) ____-______ ☐ GENERAL ☐ PERSONAL/SECURE

Assistant(s): ______________ ______________ FAX (   ) ____-______ ☐ GENERAL ☐ PERSONAL/SECURE

Spouse: __________ **Home Address:** ______________________________
STREET ADDRESS CITY STATE/ZIP

Home Phones: #1 (   ) ____-______ ☐ FAMILY PHONE ☐ HOME OFC. #2 (   ) ____-______ ☐ FAMILY PHONE ☐ HOME OFC. FAX (   ) ____-______ ☐ FAMILY ☐ HOME Office

Introduced by: ______________ **Connection:** ______________

NETWORKING

CONTACTS	DATE: LETTER/PHONE/MTG.	WHAT ABOUT?	MY FOLLOW-UP	HIS / HER FOLLOW-UP	DATE THANKED
	1st				
	2nd				
	3rd				
	4th				
	5th				

COMMENTS:

OFFERS OF SEARCH FIRM INTRODUCTIONS:

RECRUITER / FIRM/ CITY ______ RELATIONSHIP WITH RECRUITER ______ FOLLOW-UP / DATE

RECRUITER / FIRM/ CITY ______ RELATIONSHIP WITH RECRUITER ______ FOLLOW-UP / DATE

NETWORKING CONTACTS

DATES | PERSON: TITLE, COMPANY, ADDRESS, PHONES | COMMENTS & FOLLOW-UP

PHONE

VISIT

LETTER

SOURCE MENTION YES ☐ MENTION NO ☐

PHONE

VISIT

LETTER

SOURCE MENTION YES ☐ MENTION NO ☐

PHONE

VISIT

LETTER

SOURCE MENTION YES ☐ MENTION NO ☐

PHONE

VISIT

LETTER

SOURCE MENTION YES ☐ MENTION NO ☐

NETWORKING CONTACTS

DATES PERSON: TITLE, COMPANY, ADDRESS, PHONES COMMENTS & FOLLOW-UP

PHONE

VISIT

LETTER

SOURCE MENTION YES ☐ MENTION NO ☐

PHONE

VISIT

LETTER

SOURCE MENTION YES ☐ MENTION NO ☐

PHONE

VISIT

LETTER

SOURCE MENTION YES ☐ MENTION NO ☐

PHONE

VISIT

LETTER

SOURCE MENTION YES ☐ MENTION NO ☐

 ATTACHE PAGE

KEY NETWORKING CONTACT

Person/Title: ______________________________

Company: ______________________________

Address: ______________________________
TITLE STREET ADDRESS CITY STATE/ZIP

Phones/Fax: #1 (   ) ____-______ ☐ SWITCHBOARD ☐ PRIVATE #2 (   ) ____-______ ☐ SWITCHBOARD ☐ PRIVATE FAX (   ) ____-______ ☐ GENERAL ☐ PERSONAL/SECURE

Assistant(s): ______________ ______________ FAX (   ) ____-______ ☐ GENERAL ☐ PERSONAL/SECURE

Spouse: __________ **Home Address:** ______________________________
STREET ADDRESS CITY STATE/ZIP

Home Phones: #1 (   ) ____-______ ☐ FAMILY PHONE ☐ HOME OFC. #2 (   ) ____-______ ☐ FAMILY PHONE ☐ HOME OFC. FAX (   ) ____-______ ☐ FAMILY ☐ HOME Office

NETWORKING

Introduced by: ______________ **Connection:** ______________

CONTACTS: DATE: LETTER/PHONE/MTG.	WHAT ABOUT?	MY FOLLOW-UP	HIS / HER FOLLOW-UP	DATE THANKED
1st				
2nd				
3rd				
4th				
5th				

COMMENTS:

OFFERS OF SEARCH FIRM INTRODUCTIONS:

RECRUITER / FIRM/ CITY —— RELATIONSHIP WITH RECRUITER —— FOLLOW-UP / DATE

RECRUITER / FIRM/ CITY —— RELATIONSHIP WITH RECRUITER —— FOLLOW-UP / DATE

DATES	PERSON: TITLE, COMPANY, ADDRESS, PHONES	COMMENTS & FOLLOW-UP
PHONE		
VISIT		
LETTER	SOURCE	MENTION YES ☐ MENTION NO ☐
PHONE		
VISIT		
LETTER	SOURCE	MENTION YES ☐ MENTION NO ☐
PHONE		
VISIT		
LETTER	SOURCE	MENTION YES ☐ MENTION NO ☐
PHONE		
VISIT		
LETTER	SOURCE	MENTION YES ☐ MENTION NO ☐

NETWORKING CONTACTS

DATES | PERSON: TITLE, COMPANY, ADDRESS, PHONES | COMMENTS & FOLLOW-UP

PHONE

VISIT

LETTER

SOURCE MENTION YES ☐ MENTION NO ☐

PHONE

VISIT

LETTER

SOURCE MENTION YES ☐ MENTION NO ☐

PHONE

VISIT

LETTER

SOURCE MENTION YES ☐ MENTION NO ☐

PHONE

VISIT

LETTER

SOURCE MENTION YES ☐ MENTION NO ☐

KEY NETWORKING CONTACT

Person/Title: ______________________________

Company: ______________________________

Address: ______________________________
TITLE — STREET ADDRESS — CITY — STATE/ZIP

Phones/Fax: #1 (   ) ____-______ ☐ SWITCHBOARD ☐ PRIVATE #2 (   ) ____-______ ☐ SWITCHBOARD ☐ PRIVATE FAX (   ) ____-______ ☐ GENERAL ☐ PERSONAL/SECURE

Assistant(s): ______________ ______________ FAX (   ) ____-______ ☐ GENERAL ☐ PERSONAL/SECURE

Spouse: __________ **Home Address:** ______________________________
STREET ADDRESS — CITY — STATE/ZIP

Home Phones: #1 (   ) ____-______ ☐ FAMILY PHONE ☐ HOME OFC. #2 (   ) ____-______ ☐ FAMILY PHONE ☐ HOME OFC. FAX (   ) ____-______ ☐ FAMILY ☐ HOME Office

Introduced by: ______________ **Connection:** ______________

CONTACTS: DATE: LETTER/PHONE/MTG.	WHAT ABOUT?	MY FOLLOW-UP	HIS / HER FOLLOW-UP	DATE THANKED
1st				
2nd				
3rd				
4th				
5th				

COMMENTS:

OFFERS OF SEARCH FIRM INTRODUCTIONS:

RECRUITER / FIRM/ CITY — RELATIONSHIP WITH RECRUITER — FOLLOW-UP / DATE

RECRUITER / FIRM/ CITY — RELATIONSHIP WITH RECRUITER — FOLLOW-UP / DATE

NETWORKING CONTACTS

DATES PERSON: TITLE, COMPANY, ADDRESS, PHONES COMMENTS & FOLLOW-UP

PHONE

VISIT

LETTER

SOURCE MENTION YES ☐ MENTION NO ☐

PHONE

VISIT

LETTER

SOURCE MENTION YES ☐ MENTION NO ☐

PHONE

VISIT

LETTER

SOURCE MENTION YES ☐ MENTION NO ☐

PHONE

VISIT

LETTER

SOURCE MENTION YES ☐ MENTION NO ☐

NETWORKING CONTACTS

DATES | PERSON: TITLE, COMPANY, ADDRESS, PHONES | COMMENTS & FOLLOW-UP

PHONE

VISIT

LETTER

SOURCE MENTION **YES** ☐ MENTION **NO** ☐

PHONE

VISIT

LETTER

SOURCE MENTION **YES** ☐ MENTION **NO** ☐

PHONE

VISIT

LETTER

SOURCE MENTION **YES** ☐ MENTION **NO** ☐

PHONE

VISIT

LETTER

SOURCE MENTION **YES** ☐ MENTION **NO** ☐

KEY NETWORKING CONTACT

Person/Title: ______________________________

Company: ______________________________

Address: ______________________________
TITLE STREET ADDRESS CITY STATE/ZIP

Phones/Fax: #1 ( ) ____-______ ☐ SWITCHBOARD ☐ PRIVATE #2 ( ) ____-______ ☐ SWITCHBOARD ☐ PRIVATE FAX ( ) ____-______ ☐ GENERAL ☐ PERSONAL/SECURE

Assistant(s): ______________ ______________ FAX ( ) ____-______ ☐ GENERAL ☐ PERSONAL/SECURE

Spouse: __________ **Home Address:** ______________________________
STREET ADDRESS CITY STATE/ZIP

Home Phones: #1 ( ) ____-______ ☐ FAMILY PHONE ☐ HOME OFC. #2 ( ) ____-______ ☐ FAMILY PHONE ☐ HOME OFC. FAX ( ) ____-______ ☐ FAMILY ☐ HOME Office

Introduced by: ______________ **Connection:** ______________

CONTACTS

DATE: LETTER/PHONE/MTG.	WHAT ABOUT?	MY FOLLOW-UP	HIS / HER FOLLOW-UP	DATE THANKED
1st				
2nd				
3rd				
4th				
5th				

COMMENTS:

OFFERS OF SEARCH FIRM INTRODUCTIONS:

RECRUITER / FIRM/ CITY ——— RELATIONSHIP WITH RECRUITER ——— FOLLOW-UP / DATE

RECRUITER / FIRM/ CITY ——— RELATIONSHIP WITH RECRUITER ——— FOLLOW-UP / DATE

NETWORKING CONTACTS

DATES PERSON: TITLE, COMPANY, ADDRESS, PHONES COMMENTS & FOLLOW-UP

PHONE

VISIT

LETTER

SOURCE MENTION YES ☐ MENTION NO ☐

PHONE

VISIT

LETTER

SOURCE MENTION YES ☐ MENTION NO ☐

PHONE

VISIT

LETTER

SOURCE MENTION YES ☐ MENTION NO ☐

PHONE

VISIT

LETTER

SOURCE MENTION YES ☐ MENTION NO ☐

NETWORKING CONTACTS

DATES PERSON: TITLE, COMPANY, ADDRESS, PHONES COMMENTS & FOLLOW-UP

PHONE

VISIT

LETTER

SOURCE MENTION YES ☐ MENTION NO ☐

PHONE

VISIT

LETTER

SOURCE MENTION YES ☐ MENTION NO ☐

PHONE

VISIT

LETTER

SOURCE MENTION YES ☐ MENTION NO ☐

PHONE

VISIT

LETTER

SOURCE MENTION YES ☐ MENTION NO ☐

KEY NETWORKING CONTACT

Person/Title: ______________________________

Company: ______________________________

Address: ______________________________
TITLE STREET ADDRESS CITY STATE/ZIP

Phones/Fax: #1 (   ) ____-______ ☐ SWITCHBOARD ☐ PRIVATE #2 (   ) ____-______ ☐ SWITCHBOARD ☐ PRIVATE FAX (   ) ____-______ ☐ GENERAL ☐ PERSONAL/SECURE

Assistant(s): ______________ ______________ FAX (   ) ____-______ ☐ GENERAL ☐ PERSONAL/SECURE

Spouse: __________ **Home Address:** ______________________________
STREET ADDRESS CITY STATE/ZIP

Home Phones: #1 (   ) ____-______ ☐ FAMILY PHONE ☐ HOME OFC. #2 (   ) ____-______ ☐ FAMILY PHONE ☐ HOME OFC. FAX (   ) ____-______ ☐ FAMILY ☐ HOME Office

Introduced by: ______________ **Connection:** ______________

NETWORKING

CONTACTS — DATE: LETTER/PHONE/MTG.	WHAT ABOUT?	MY FOLLOW-UP	HIS / HER FOLLOW-UP	DATE THANKED
1st				
2nd				
3rd				
4th				
5th				

COMMENTS:

OFFERS OF SEARCH FIRM INTRODUCTIONS:

RECRUITER / FIRM/ CITY — RELATIONSHIP WITH RECRUITER — FOLLOW-UP / DATE

RECRUITER / FIRM/ CITY — RELATIONSHIP WITH RECRUITER — FOLLOW-UP / DATE

NETWORKING CONTACTS

DATES PERSON: TITLE, COMPANY, ADDRESS, PHONES COMMENTS & FOLLOW-UP

PHONE

VISIT

LETTER

SOURCE MENTION YES ☐ MENTION NO ☐

PHONE

VISIT

LETTER

SOURCE MENTION YES ☐ MENTION NO ☐

PHONE

VISIT

LETTER

SOURCE MENTION YES ☐ MENTION NO ☐

PHONE

VISIT

LETTER

SOURCE MENTION YES ☐ MENTION NO ☐

NETWORKING CONTACTS

DATES | PERSON: TITLE, COMPANY, ADDRESS, PHONES | COMMENTS & FOLLOW-UP

PHONE

VISIT

LETTER

SOURCE MENTION **YES** ☐ MENTION **NO** ☐

PHONE

VISIT

LETTER

SOURCE MENTION **YES** ☐ MENTION **NO** ☐

PHONE

VISIT

LETTER

SOURCE MENTION **YES** ☐ MENTION **NO** ☐

PHONE

VISIT

LETTER

SOURCE MENTION **YES** ☐ MENTION **NO** ☐

 ATTACHE PAGE

KEY NETWORKING CONTACT

Person/Title: ______________________________

Company: ______________________________

Address: ______________________________
TITLE STREET ADDRESS CITY STATE/ZIP

Phones/Fax: #1 (   ) ____-______ ☐ SWITCHBOARD ☐ PRIVATE #2 (   ) ____-______ ☐ SWITCHBOARD ☐ PRIVATE FAX (   ) ____-______ ☐ GENERAL ☐ PERSONAL/SECURE

Assistant(s): ______________ ______________ FAX (   ) ____-______ ☐ GENERAL ☐ PERSONAL/SECURE

Spouse: __________ **Home Address:** ______________________________
STREET ADDRESS CITY STATE/ZIP

Home Phones: #1 (   ) ____-______ ☐ FAMILY PHONE ☐ HOME OFC. #2 (   ) ____-______ ☐ FAMILY PHONE ☐ HOME OFC. FAX (   ) ____-______ ☐ FAMILY ☐ HOME Office

Introduced by: ______________ **Connection:** ______________

CONTACTS

DATE: LETTER/PHONE/MTG.	WHAT ABOUT?	MY FOLLOW-UP	HIS / HER FOLLOW-UP	DATE THANKED
1st				
2nd				
3rd				
4th				
5th				

COMMENTS:

OFFERS OF SEARCH FIRM INTRODUCTIONS:

RECRUITER / FIRM/ CITY—RELATIONSHIP WITH RECRUITER—FOLLOW-UP / DATE

RECRUITER / FIRM/ CITY—RELATIONSHIP WITH RECRUITER—FOLLOW-UP / DATE

DATES PERSON: TITLE, COMPANY, ADDRESS, PHONES COMMENTS & FOLLOW-UP

PHONE

VISIT

LETTER

SOURCE MENTION **YES** ☐ MENTION **NO** ☐

PHONE

VISIT

LETTER

SOURCE MENTION **YES** ☐ MENTION **NO** ☐

PHONE

VISIT

LETTER

SOURCE MENTION **YES** ☐ MENTION **NO** ☐

PHONE

VISIT

LETTER

SOURCE MENTION **YES** ☐ MENTION **NO** ☐

NETWORKING CONTACTS

DATES | PERSON: TITLE, COMPANY, ADDRESS, PHONES | COMMENTS & FOLLOW-UP

PHONE

VISIT

LETTER

SOURCE MENTION YES ☐ MENTION NO ☐

PHONE

VISIT

LETTER

SOURCE MENTION YES ☐ MENTION NO ☐

PHONE

VISIT

LETTER

SOURCE MENTION YES ☐ MENTION NO ☐

PHONE

VISIT

LETTER

SOURCE MENTION YES ☐ MENTION NO ☐

KEY NETWORKING CONTACT

Person/Title: ______________________________

Company: ______________________________

Address: ______________________________
TITLE | STREET ADDRESS | CITY | STATE/ZIP

Phones/Fax: #1 ( ) ____-______ ☐ SWITCHBOARD ☐ PRIVATE #2 ( ) ____-______ ☐ SWITCHBOARD ☐ PRIVATE FAX ( ) ____-______ ☐ GENERAL ☐ PERSONAL/SECURE

Assistant(s): ______________ ______________ FAX ( ) ____-______ ☐ GENERAL ☐ PERSONAL/SECURE

Spouse: __________ **Home Address:** ______________________________
STREET ADDRESS | CITY | STATE/ZIP

Home Phones: #1 ( ) ____-______ ☐ FAMILY PHONE ☐ HOME OFC. #2 ( ) ____-______ ☐ FAMILY PHONE ☐ HOME OFC. FAX ( ) ____-______ ☐ FAMILY ☐ HOME OFFICE

Introduced by: ______________ **Connection:** ______________

NETWORKING

CONTACTS — DATE: LETTER/PHONE/MTG.	WHAT ABOUT?	MY FOLLOW-UP	HIS / HER FOLLOW-UP	DATE THANKED
1st				
2nd				
3rd				
4th				
5th				

COMMENTS:

OFFERS OF SEARCH FIRM INTRODUCTIONS:

RECRUITER / FIRM/ CITY ______ RELATIONSHIP WITH RECRUITER ______ FOLLOW-UP / DATE

RECRUITER / FIRM/ CITY ______ RELATIONSHIP WITH RECRUITER ______ FOLLOW-UP / DATE

NETWORKING CONTACTS

DATES PERSON: TITLE, COMPANY, ADDRESS, PHONES COMMENTS & FOLLOW-UP

PHONE

VISIT

LETTER

SOURCE MENTION **YES** ☐ MENTION **NO** ☐

PHONE

VISIT

LETTER

SOURCE MENTION **YES** ☐ MENTION **NO** ☐

PHONE

VISIT

LETTER

SOURCE MENTION **YES** ☐ MENTION **NO** ☐

PHONE

VISIT

LETTER

SOURCE MENTION **YES** ☐ MENTION **NO** ☐

NETWORKING CONTACTS

DATES | PERSON: TITLE, COMPANY, ADDRESS, PHONES | COMMENTS & FOLLOW-UP

PHONE

VISIT

LETTER

SOURCE MENTION YES ☐ MENTION NO ☐

PHONE

VISIT

LETTER

SOURCE MENTION YES ☐ MENTION NO ☐

PHONE

VISIT

LETTER

SOURCE MENTION YES ☐ MENTION NO ☐

PHONE

VISIT

LETTER

SOURCE MENTION YES ☐ MENTION NO ☐

KEY NETWORKING CONTACT

Person/Title: ______________________

Company: ______________________

Address: ______________________
TITLE STREET ADDRESS CITY STATE/ZIP

Phones/Fax: #1 ( ) ___-____ ☐ SWITCHBOARD ☐ PRIVATE #2 ( ) ___-____ ☐ SWITCHBOARD ☐ PRIVATE FAX ( ) ___-____ ☐ GENERAL ☐ PERSONAL/SECURE

Assistant(s): __________ __________ FAX ( ) ___-____ ☐ GENERAL ☐ PERSONAL/SECURE

Spouse: __________ **Home Address:** ______________________
STREET ADDRESS CITY STATE/ZIP

Home Phones: #1 ( ) ___-____ ☐ FAMILY PHONE ☐ HOME OFC. #2 ( ) ___-____ ☐ FAMILY PHONE ☐ HOME OFC. FAX ( ) ___-____ ☐ FAMILY ☐ HOME Office

NETWORKING

Introduced by: __________ **Connection:** __________

CONTACTS — DATE: LETTER/PHONE/MTG.	WHAT ABOUT?	MY FOLLOW-UP	HIS / HER FOLLOW-UP	DATE THANKED
1st				
2nd				
3rd				
4th				
5th				

COMMENTS:

OFFERS OF SEARCH FIRM INTRODUCTIONS:

RECRUITER / FIRM/ CITY — RELATIONSHIP WITH RECRUITER — FOLLOW-UP / DATE

RECRUITER / FIRM/ CITY — RELATIONSHIP WITH RECRUITER — FOLLOW-UP / DATE

NETWORKING CONTACTS

DATES PERSON: TITLE, COMPANY, ADDRESS, PHONES COMMENTS & FOLLOW-UP

PHONE

VISIT

LETTER

SOURCE MENTION YES ☐ MENTION NO ☐

PHONE

VISIT

LETTER

SOURCE MENTION YES ☐ MENTION NO ☐

PHONE

VISIT

LETTER

SOURCE MENTION YES ☐ MENTION NO ☐

PHONE

VISIT

LETTER

SOURCE MENTION YES ☐ MENTION NO ☐

NETWORKING CONTACTS

DATES | PERSON: TITLE, COMPANY, ADDRESS, PHONES | COMMENTS & FOLLOW-UP

PHONE

VISIT

LETTER

SOURCE MENTION YES ☐ MENTION NO ☐

PHONE

VISIT

LETTER

SOURCE MENTION YES ☐ MENTION NO ☐

PHONE

VISIT

LETTER

SOURCE MENTION YES ☐ MENTION NO ☐

PHONE

VISIT

LETTER

SOURCE MENTION YES ☐ MENTION NO ☐

KEY NETWORKING CONTACT

Person/Title: ______________________________

Company: ______________________________

Address: ______________________________
TITLE STREET ADDRESS CITY STATE/ZIP

Phones/Fax: #1 ( ) ____-______ ☐ SWITCHBOARD ☐ PRIVATE #2 ( ) ____-______ ☐ SWITCHBOARD ☐ PRIVATE FAX ( ) ____-______ ☐ GENERAL ☐ PERSONAL/SECURE

Assistant(s): ______________ ______________ FAX ( ) ____-______ ☐ GENERAL ☐ PERSONAL/SECURE

Spouse: __________ **Home Address:** ______________________________
STREET ADDRESS CITY STATE/ZIP

Home Phones: #1 ( ) ____-______ ☐ FAMILY PHONE ☐ HOME OFC. #2 ( ) ____-______ ☐ FAMILY PHONE ☐ HOME OFC. FAX ( ) ____-______ ☐ FAMILY ☐ HOME Office

Introduced by: ______________ **Connection:** ______________

NETWORKING

CONTACTS	DATE: LETTER/PHONE/MTG.	WHAT ABOUT?	MY FOLLOW-UP	HIS / HER FOLLOW-UP	DATE THANKED
	1st				
	2nd				
	3rd				
	4th				
	5th				

COMMENTS:

OFFERS OF SEARCH FIRM INTRODUCTIONS:

RECRUITER / FIRM/ CITY ______ RELATIONSHIP WITH RECRUITER ______ FOLLOW-UP / DATE

RECRUITER / FIRM/ CITY ______ RELATIONSHIP WITH RECRUITER ______ FOLLOW-UP / DATE

NETWORKING CONTACTS

DATES | PERSON: TITLE, COMPANY, ADDRESS, PHONES | COMMENTS & FOLLOW-UP

PHONE

VISIT

LETTER

SOURCE MENTION **YES** ☐ MENTION **NO** ☐

PHONE

VISIT

LETTER

SOURCE MENTION **YES** ☐ MENTION **NO** ☐

PHONE

VISIT

LETTER

SOURCE MENTION **YES** ☐ MENTION **NO** ☐

PHONE

VISIT

LETTER

SOURCE MENTION **YES** ☐ MENTION **NO** ☐

NETWORKING CONTACTS

DATES PERSON: TITLE, COMPANY, ADDRESS, PHONES COMMENTS & FOLLOW-UP

PHONE

VISIT

LETTER

SOURCE MENTION **YES** ☐ MENTION **NO** ☐

PHONE

VISIT

LETTER

SOURCE MENTION **YES** ☐ MENTION **NO** ☐

PHONE

VISIT

LETTER

SOURCE MENTION **YES** ☐ MENTION **NO** ☐

PHONE

VISIT

LETTER

SOURCE MENTION **YES** ☐ MENTION **NO** ☐

KEY NETWORKING CONTACT

Person/Title: ______________________________

Company: ______________________________

Address: ______________________________
TITLE STREET ADDRESS CITY STATE/ZIP

Phones/Fax: #1 (   ) ____-______ ☐ SWITCHBOARD ☐ PRIVATE #2 (   ) ____-______ ☐ SWITCHBOARD ☐ PRIVATE FAX (   ) ____-______ ☐ GENERAL ☐ PERSONAL/SECURE

Assistant(s): ______________ ______________ FAX (   ) ____-______ ☐ GENERAL ☐ PERSONAL/SECURE

Spouse: __________ **Home Address:** ______________________________
STREET ADDRESS CITY STATE/ZIP

Home Phones: #1 (   ) ____-______ ☐ FAMILY PHONE ☐ HOME OFC. #2 (   ) ____-______ ☐ FAMILY PHONE ☐ HOME OFC. FAX (   ) ____-______ ☐ FAMILY ☐ HOME Office

NETWORKING

Introduced by: ______________ **Connection:** ______________

CONTACTS	DATE: LETTER/PHONE/MTG.	WHAT ABOUT?	MY FOLLOW-UP	HIS / HER FOLLOW-UP	DATE THANKED
	1st				
	2nd				
	3rd				
	4th				
	5th				

COMMENTS:

OFFERS OF SEARCH FIRM INTRODUCTIONS:

RECRUITER / FIRM/ CITY —— RELATIONSHIP WITH RECRUITER —— FOLLOW-UP / DATE

RECRUITER / FIRM/ CITY —— RELATIONSHIP WITH RECRUITER —— FOLLOW-UP / DATE

NETWORKING CONTACTS

DATES	PERSON: TITLE, COMPANY, ADDRESS, PHONES	COMMENTS & FOLLOW-UP
PHONE		
VISIT		
LETTER	SOURCE	MENTION YES ☐ MENTION NO ☐
PHONE		
VISIT		
LETTER	SOURCE	MENTION YES ☐ MENTION NO ☐
PHONE		
VISIT		
LETTER	SOURCE	MENTION YES ☐ MENTION NO ☐
PHONE		
VISIT		
LETTER	SOURCE	MENTION YES ☐ MENTION NO ☐

NETWORKING CONTACTS

DATES PERSON: TITLE, COMPANY, ADDRESS, PHONES COMMENTS & FOLLOW-UP

PHONE

VISIT

LETTER

SOURCE MENTION **YES** ☐ MENTION **NO** ☐

PHONE

VISIT

LETTER

SOURCE MENTION **YES** ☐ MENTION **NO** ☐

PHONE

VISIT

LETTER

SOURCE MENTION **YES** ☐ MENTION **NO** ☐

PHONE

VISIT

LETTER

SOURCE MENTION **YES** ☐ MENTION **NO** ☐

KEY NETWORKING CONTACT

Person/Title: ______________________

Company: ______________________

Address: ______________________
TITLE STREET ADDRESS CITY STATE/ZIP

Phones/Fax: #1 (   ) ___-_____ ☐ SWITCHBOARD ☐ PRIVATE #2 (   ) ___-_____ ☐ SWITCHBOARD ☐ PRIVATE FAX (   ) ___-_____ ☐ GENERAL ☐ PERSONAL/SECURE

Assistant(s): __________ __________ FAX (   ) ___-_____ ☐ GENERAL ☐ PERSONAL/SECURE

Spouse: __________ **Home Address:** ______________________
STREET ADDRESS CITY STATE/ZIP

Home Phones: #1 (   ) ___-_____ ☐ FAMILY PHONE ☐ HOME OFC. #2 (   ) ___-_____ ☐ FAMILY PHONE ☐ HOME OFC. FAX (   ) ___-_____ ☐ FAMILY ☐ HOME Office

Introduced by: __________ **Connection:** __________

NETWORKING

CONTACTS

DATE: LETTER/PHONE/MTG.	WHAT ABOUT?	MY FOLLOW-UP	HIS / HER FOLLOW-UP	DATE THANKED
1st				
2nd				
3rd				
4th				
5th				

COMMENTS:

OFFERS OF SEARCH FIRM INTRODUCTIONS:

RECRUITER / FIRM/ CITY —— RELATIONSHIP WITH RECRUITER —— FOLLOW-UP / DATE

RECRUITER / FIRM/ CITY —— RELATIONSHIP WITH RECRUITER —— FOLLOW-UP / DATE

NETWORKING CONTACTS

DATES	PERSON: TITLE, COMPANY, ADDRESS, PHONES	COMMENTS & FOLLOW-UP
PHONE		
VISIT		
LETTER	SOURCE	MENTION YES ☐ MENTION NO ☐
PHONE		
VISIT		
LETTER	SOURCE	MENTION YES ☐ MENTION NO ☐
PHONE		
VISIT		
LETTER	SOURCE	MENTION YES ☐ MENTION NO ☐
PHONE		
VISIT		
LETTER	SOURCE	MENTION YES ☐ MENTION NO ☐

DATES PERSON: TITLE, COMPANY, ADDRESS, PHONES COMMENTS & FOLLOW-UP

PHONE

VISIT

LETTER

SOURCE MENTION YES ☐ MENTION NO ☐

PHONE

VISIT

LETTER

SOURCE MENTION YES ☐ MENTION NO ☐

PHONE

VISIT

LETTER

SOURCE MENTION YES ☐ MENTION NO ☐

PHONE

VISIT

LETTER

SOURCE MENTION YES ☐ MENTION NO ☐

KEY NETWORKING CONTACT

Person/Title: ____________________

Company: ____________________

Address: ____________________
TITLE STREET ADDRESS CITY STATE/ZIP

Phones/Fax: #1 ( ) ____-______ ☐ SWITCHBOARD ☐ PRIVATE #2 ( ) ____-______ ☐ SWITCHBOARD ☐ PRIVATE FAX ( ) ____-______ ☐ GENERAL ☐ PERSONAL/SECURE

Assistant(s): ____________ ____________ FAX ( ) ____-______ ☐ GENERAL ☐ PERSONAL/SECURE

Spouse: ________ **Home Address:** ____________________
STREET ADDRESS CITY STATE/ZIP

Home Phones: #1 ( ) ____-______ ☐ FAMILY PHONE ☐ HOME OFC. #2 ( ) ____-______ ☐ FAMILY PHONE ☐ HOME OFC. FAX ( ) ____-______ ☐ FAMILY ☐ HOME Office

NETWORKING

Introduced by: ____________ **Connection:** ____________

CONTACTS	DATE: LETTER/PHONE/MTG.	WHAT ABOUT?	MY FOLLOW-UP	HIS / HER FOLLOW-UP	DATE THANKED
	1st				
	2nd				
	3rd				
	4th				
	5th				

COMMENTS:

OFFERS OF SEARCH FIRM INTRODUCTIONS:

RECRUITER / FIRM/ CITY — RELATIONSHIP WITH RECRUITER — FOLLOW-UP / DATE

RECRUITER / FIRM/ CITY — RELATIONSHIP WITH RECRUITER — FOLLOW-UP / DATE

DATES PERSON: TITLE, COMPANY, ADDRESS, PHONES COMMENTS & FOLLOW-UP

PHONE

VISIT

LETTER

SOURCE MENTION YES ☐ MENTION NO ☐

PHONE

VISIT

LETTER

SOURCE MENTION YES ☐ MENTION NO ☐

PHONE

VISIT

LETTER

SOURCE MENTION YES ☐ MENTION NO ☐

PHONE

VISIT

LETTER

SOURCE MENTION YES ☐ MENTION NO ☐

NETWORKING CONTACTS

DATES PERSON: TITLE, COMPANY, ADDRESS, PHONES COMMENTS & FOLLOW-UP

PHONE

VISIT

LETTER

SOURCE MENTION YES ☐ MENTION NO ☐

PHONE

VISIT

LETTER

SOURCE MENTION YES ☐ MENTION NO ☐

PHONE

VISIT

LETTER

SOURCE MENTION YES ☐ MENTION NO ☐

PHONE

VISIT

LETTER

SOURCE MENTION YES ☐ MENTION NO ☐

KEY NETWORKING CONTACT

Person/Title: ______________________________

Company: ______________________________

Address: ______________________________
TITLE STREET ADDRESS CITY STATE/ZIP

Phones/Fax: #1 (   ) ____-______ ☐ SWITCHBOARD ☐ PRIVATE #2 (   ) ____-______ ☐ SWITCHBOARD ☐ PRIVATE FAX (   ) ____-______ ☐ GENERAL ☐ PERSONAL/SECURE

Assistant(s): ______________ ______________ FAX (   ) ____-______ ☐ GENERAL ☐ PERSONAL/SECURE

Spouse: __________ **Home Address:** ______________________________
STREET ADDRESS CITY STATE/ZIP

Home Phones: #1 (   ) ____-______ ☐ FAMILY PHONE ☐ HOME OFC. #2 (   ) ____-______ ☐ FAMILY PHONE ☐ HOME OFC. FAX (   ) ____-______ ☐ FAMILY ☐ HOME Office

Introduced by: __________________ **Connection:** __________________

NETWORKING

CONTACTS — DATE: LETTER/PHONE/MTG.	WHAT ABOUT?	MY FOLLOW-UP	HIS / HER FOLLOW-UP	DATE THANKED
1st				
2nd				
3rd				
4th				
5th				

COMMENTS:

OFFERS OF SEARCH FIRM INTRODUCTIONS:

RECRUITER / FIRM/ CITY —— RELATIONSHIP WITH RECRUITER —— FOLLOW-UP / DATE

RECRUITER / FIRM/ CITY —— RELATIONSHIP WITH RECRUITER —— FOLLOW-UP / DATE

NETWORKING CONTACTS

DATES | PERSON: TITLE, COMPANY, ADDRESS, PHONES | COMMENTS & FOLLOW-UP

PHONE

VISIT

LETTER

SOURCE MENTION YES ☐ MENTION NO ☐

PHONE

VISIT

LETTER

SOURCE MENTION YES ☐ MENTION NO ☐

PHONE

VISIT

LETTER

SOURCE MENTION YES ☐ MENTION NO ☐

PHONE

VISIT

LETTER

SOURCE MENTION YES ☐ MENTION NO ☐

NETWORKING CONTACTS

DATES PERSON: TITLE, COMPANY, ADDRESS, PHONES COMMENTS & FOLLOW-UP

PHONE

VISIT

LETTER

SOURCE MENTION YES ☐ MENTION NO ☐

PHONE

VISIT

LETTER

SOURCE MENTION YES ☐ MENTION NO ☐

PHONE

VISIT

LETTER

SOURCE MENTION YES ☐ MENTION NO ☐

PHONE

VISIT

LETTER

SOURCE MENTION YES ☐ MENTION NO ☐

KEY NETWORKING CONTACT

Person/Title: ______________________________

Company: ______________________________

Address: ______________________________
TITLE STREET ADDRESS CITY STATE/ZIP

Phones/Fax: #1 (   ) ____-______ ☐ SWITCHBOARD ☐ PRIVATE #2 (   ) ____-______ ☐ SWITCHBOARD ☐ PRIVATE FAX (   ) ____-______ ☐ GENERAL ☐ PERSONAL/SECURE

Assistant(s): ______________ ______________ FAX (   ) ____-______ ☐ GENERAL ☐ PERSONAL/SECURE

Spouse: __________ **Home Address:** ______________________________
STREET ADDRESS CITY STATE/ZIP

Home Phones: #1 (   ) ____-______ ☐ FAMILY PHONE ☐ HOME OFC. #2 (   ) ____-______ ☐ FAMILY PHONE ☐ HOME OFC. FAX (   ) ____-______ ☐ FAMILY ☐ HOME Office

Introduced by: ______________ **Connection:** ______________

CONTACTS	DATE: LETTER/PHONE/MTG.	WHAT ABOUT?	MY FOLLOW-UP	HIS / HER FOLLOW-UP	DATE THANKED
	1st				
	2nd				
	3rd				
	4th				
	5th				

COMMENTS:

OFFERS OF SEARCH FIRM INTRODUCTIONS:

RECRUITER / FIRM/ CITY —— RELATIONSHIP WITH RECRUITER —— FOLLOW-UP / DATE

RECRUITER / FIRM/ CITY —— RELATIONSHIP WITH RECRUITER —— FOLLOW-UP / DATE

DATES PERSON: TITLE, COMPANY, ADDRESS, PHONES COMMENTS & FOLLOW-UP

PHONE

VISIT

LETTER

SOURCE MENTION YES ☐ MENTION NO ☐

PHONE

VISIT

LETTER

SOURCE MENTION YES ☐ MENTION NO ☐

PHONE

VISIT

LETTER

SOURCE MENTION YES ☐ MENTION NO ☐

PHONE

VISIT

LETTER

SOURCE MENTION YES ☐ MENTION NO ☐

NETWORKING CONTACTS

DATES PERSON: TITLE, COMPANY, ADDRESS, PHONES COMMENTS & FOLLOW-UP

PHONE

VISIT

LETTER

SOURCE MENTION **YES** ☐ MENTION **NO** ☐

PHONE

VISIT

LETTER

SOURCE MENTION **YES** ☐ MENTION **NO** ☐

PHONE

VISIT

LETTER

SOURCE MENTION **YES** ☐ MENTION **NO** ☐

PHONE

VISIT

LETTER

SOURCE MENTION **YES** ☐ MENTION **NO** ☐

KEY NETWORKING CONTACT

Person/Title: ______________________

Company: ______________________

Address: ______________________
TITLE STREET ADDRESS CITY STATE/ZIP

Phones/Fax: #1 ( ) ___-_____ ☐ SWITCHBOARD ☐ PRIVATE #2 ( ) ___-_____ ☐ SWITCHBOARD ☐ PRIVATE FAX ( ) ___-_____ ☐ GENERAL ☐ PERSONAL/SECURE

Assistant(s): ____________ ____________ FAX ( ) ___-_____ ☐ GENERAL ☐ PERSONAL/SECURE

Spouse: ________ **Home Address:** ______________________
STREET ADDRESS CITY STATE/ZIP

Home Phones: #1 ( ) ___-_____ ☐ FAMILY PHONE ☐ HOME OFC. #2 ( ) ___-_____ ☐ FAMILY PHONE ☐ HOME OFC. FAX ( ) ___-_____ ☐ FAMILY ☐ HOME Office

Introduced by: ____________ **Connection:** ____________

NETWORKING

CONTACTS — DATE: LETTER/PHONE/MTG.	WHAT ABOUT?	MY FOLLOW-UP	HIS / HER FOLLOW-UP	DATE THANKED
1st				
2nd				
3rd				
4th				
5th				

COMMENTS:

OFFERS OF SEARCH FIRM INTRODUCTIONS:

RECRUITER / FIRM/ CITY — RELATIONSHIP WITH RECRUITER — FOLLOW-UP / DATE

RECRUITER / FIRM/ CITY — RELATIONSHIP WITH RECRUITER — FOLLOW-UP / DATE

NETWORKING CONTACTS

DATES PERSON: TITLE, COMPANY, ADDRESS, PHONES COMMENTS & FOLLOW-UP

PHONE

VISIT

LETTER

SOURCE MENTION **YES** ☐ MENTION **NO** ☐

PHONE

VISIT

LETTER

SOURCE MENTION **YES** ☐ MENTION **NO** ☐

PHONE

VISIT

LETTER

SOURCE MENTION **YES** ☐ MENTION **NO** ☐

PHONE

VISIT

LETTER

SOURCE MENTION **YES** ☐ MENTION **NO** ☐

DATES PERSON: TITLE, COMPANY, ADDRESS, PHONES COMMENTS & FOLLOW-UP

PHONE

VISIT

LETTER

SOURCE MENTION YES ☐ MENTION NO ☐

PHONE

VISIT

LETTER

SOURCE MENTION YES ☐ MENTION NO ☐

PHONE

VISIT

LETTER

SOURCE MENTION YES ☐ MENTION NO ☐

PHONE

VISIT

LETTER

SOURCE MENTION YES ☐ MENTION NO ☐

KEY NETWORKING CONTACT

Person/Title: ____________________

Company: ____________________

Address: ____________________
TITLE STREET ADDRESS CITY STATE/ZIP

Phones/Fax: #1 ( ) ____-______ ☐ SWITCHBOARD ☐ PRIVATE #2 ( ) ____-______ ☐ SWITCHBOARD ☐ PRIVATE FAX ( ) ____-______ ☐ GENERAL ☐ PERSONAL/SECURE

Assistant(s): ______________ ______________ FAX ( ) ____-______ ☐ GENERAL ☐ PERSONAL/SECURE

Spouse: __________ **Home Address:** ____________________
STREET ADDRESS CITY STATE/ZIP

Home Phones: #1 ( ) ____-______ ☐ FAMILY PHONE ☐ HOME OFC. #2 ( ) ____-______ ☐ FAMILY PHONE ☐ HOME OFC. FAX ( ) ____-______ ☐ FAMILY ☐ HOME Office

NETWORKING

Introduced by: ______________ **Connection:** ______________

CONTACTS	DATE: LETTER/PHONE/MTG.	WHAT ABOUT?	MY FOLLOW-UP	HIS / HER FOLLOW-UP	DATE THANKED
	1st				
	2nd				
	3rd				
	4th				
	5th				

COMMENTS:

OFFERS OF SEARCH FIRM INTRODUCTIONS:

RECRUITER / FIRM/ CITY — RELATIONSHIP WITH RECRUITER — FOLLOW-UP / DATE

RECRUITER / FIRM/ CITY — RELATIONSHIP WITH RECRUITER — FOLLOW-UP / DATE

DATES	PERSON: TITLE, COMPANY, ADDRESS, PHONES	COMMENTS & FOLLOW-UP
PHONE		
VISIT		
LETTER	SOURCE	MENTION YES ☐ MENTION NO ☐
PHONE		
VISIT		
LETTER	SOURCE	MENTION YES ☐ MENTION NO ☐
PHONE		
VISIT		
LETTER	SOURCE	MENTION YES ☐ MENTION NO ☐
PHONE		
VISIT		
LETTER	SOURCE	MENTION YES ☐ MENTION NO ☐

NETWORKING CONTACTS

DATES PERSON: TITLE, COMPANY, ADDRESS, PHONES COMMENTS & FOLLOW-UP

PHONE

VISIT

LETTER

SOURCE MENTION **YES** ☐ MENTION **NO** ☐

PHONE

VISIT

LETTER

SOURCE MENTION **YES** ☐ MENTION **NO** ☐

PHONE

VISIT

LETTER

SOURCE MENTION **YES** ☐ MENTION **NO** ☐

PHONE

VISIT

LETTER

SOURCE MENTION **YES** ☐ MENTION **NO** ☐

KEY NETWORKING CONTACT

Person/Title: ______________________________

Company: ______________________________

Address: ______________________________
TITLE STREET ADDRESS CITY STATE/ZIP

Phones/Fax: #1 (   ) ___-_____ ☐ SWITCHBOARD ☐ PRIVATE #2 (   ) ___-_____ ☐ SWITCHBOARD ☐ PRIVATE FAX (   ) ___-_____ ☐ GENERAL ☐ PERSONAL/SECURE

Assistant(s): ______________ ______________ FAX (   ) ___-_____ ☐ GENERAL ☐ PERSONAL/SECURE

Spouse: __________ **Home Address:** ______________________________
STREET ADDRESS CITY STATE/ZIP

Home Phones: #1 (   ) ___-_____ ☐ FAMILY PHONE ☐ HOME OFC. #2 (   ) ___-_____ ☐ FAMILY PHONE ☐ HOME OFC. FAX (   ) ___-_____ ☐ FAMILY ☐ HOME Office

Introduced by: ______________ **Connection:** ______________

NETWORKING

CONTACTS: DATE: LETTER/PHONE/MTG.	WHAT ABOUT?	MY FOLLOW-UP	HIS / HER FOLLOW-UP	DATE THANKED
1st				
2nd				
3rd				
4th				
5th				

COMMENTS:

OFFERS OF SEARCH FIRM INTRODUCTIONS:

RECRUITER / FIRM/ CITY ———— RELATIONSHIP WITH RECRUITER ———— FOLLOW-UP / DATE

RECRUITER / FIRM/ CITY ———— RELATIONSHIP WITH RECRUITER ———— FOLLOW-UP / DATE

NETWORKING CONTACTS

DATES PERSON: TITLE, COMPANY, ADDRESS, PHONES COMMENTS & FOLLOW-UP

PHONE

VISIT

LETTER

SOURCE MENTION **YES** ☐ MENTION **NO** ☐

PHONE

VISIT

LETTER

SOURCE MENTION **YES** ☐ MENTION **NO** ☐

PHONE

VISIT

LETTER

SOURCE MENTION **YES** ☐ MENTION **NO** ☐

PHONE

VISIT

LETTER

SOURCE MENTION **YES** ☐ MENTION **NO** ☐

NETWORKING CONTACTS

DATES | PERSON: TITLE, COMPANY, ADDRESS, PHONES | COMMENTS & FOLLOW-UP

PHONE

VISIT

LETTER

SOURCE MENTION YES ☐ MENTION NO ☐

PHONE

VISIT

LETTER

SOURCE MENTION YES ☐ MENTION NO ☐

PHONE

VISIT

LETTER

SOURCE MENTION YES ☐ MENTION NO ☐

PHONE

VISIT

LETTER

SOURCE MENTION YES ☐ MENTION NO ☐

KEY NETWORKING CONTACT

Person/Title: ______________________________

Company: ______________________________

Address: ______________________________
TITLE STREET ADDRESS CITY STATE/ZIP

Phones/Fax: #1 (   ) ____-______ ☐ SWITCHBOARD ☐ PRIVATE #2 (   ) ____-______ ☐ SWITCHBOARD ☐ PRIVATE FAX (   ) ____-______ ☐ GENERAL ☐ PERSONAL/SECURE

Assistant(s): ______________ ______________ FAX (   ) ____-______ ☐ GENERAL ☐ PERSONAL/SECURE

Spouse: __________ **Home Address:** ______________________________
STREET ADDRESS CITY STATE/ZIP

Home Phones: #1 (   ) ____-______ ☐ FAMILY PHONE ☐ HOME OFC. #2 (   ) ____-______ ☐ FAMILY PHONE ☐ HOME OFC. FAX (   ) ____-______ ☐ FAMILY ☐ HOME Office

NETWORKING

Introduced by: ______________ **Connection:** ______________

CONTACTS Date: Letter/Phone/Mtg.	What About?	My Follow-Up	His / Her Follow-Up	Date Thanked
1st				
2nd				
3rd				
4th				
5th				

COMMENTS:

OFFERS OF SEARCH FIRM INTRODUCTIONS:

RECRUITER / FIRM/ CITY—————RELATIONSHIP WITH RECRUITER—————FOLLOW-UP / DATE

RECRUITER / FIRM/ CITY—————RELATIONSHIP WITH RECRUITER—————FOLLOW-UP / DATE

DATES	PERSON: TITLE, COMPANY, ADDRESS, PHONES	COMMENTS & FOLLOW-UP
PHONE VISIT LETTER	SOURCE	MENTION YES ☐ MENTION NO ☐
PHONE VISIT LETTER	SOURCE	MENTION YES ☐ MENTION NO ☐
PHONE VISIT LETTER	SOURCE	MENTION YES ☐ MENTION NO ☐
PHONE VISIT LETTER	SOURCE	MENTION YES ☐ MENTION NO ☐

NETWORKING

NETWORKING CONTACTS

DATES PERSON: TITLE, COMPANY, ADDRESS, PHONES COMMENTS & FOLLOW-UP

PHONE

VISIT

LETTER

SOURCE MENTION YES ☐ MENTION NO ☐

PHONE

VISIT

LETTER

SOURCE MENTION YES ☐ MENTION NO ☐

PHONE

VISIT

LETTER

SOURCE MENTION YES ☐ MENTION NO ☐

PHONE

VISIT

LETTER

SOURCE MENTION YES ☐ MENTION NO ☐

KEY NETWORKING CONTACT

Person/Title: ______________________

Company: ______________________

Address: ______________________
TITLE · STREET ADDRESS · CITY · STATE/ZIP

Phones/Fax: #1 (   ) ____-______ ☐ SWITCHBOARD ☐ PRIVATE #2 (   ) ____-______ ☐ SWITCHBOARD ☐ PRIVATE FAX (   ) ____-______ ☐ GENERAL ☐ PERSONAL/SECURE

Assistant(s): ____________ ____________ FAX (   ) ____-______ ☐ GENERAL ☐ PERSONAL/SECURE

Spouse: ________ **Home Address:** ______________________
STREET ADDRESS · CITY · STATE/ZIP

Home Phones: #1 (   ) ____-______ ☐ FAMILY PHONE ☐ HOME OFC. #2 (   ) ____-______ ☐ FAMILY PHONE ☐ HOME OFC. FAX (   ) ____-______ ☐ FAMILY ☐ HOME Office

Introduced by: ____________ **Connection:** ____________

CONTACTS	DATE: LETTER/PHONE/MTG.	WHAT ABOUT?	MY FOLLOW-UP	HIS / HER FOLLOW-UP	DATE THANKED
	1st				
	2nd				
	3rd				
	4th				
	5th				

COMMENTS:

OFFERS OF SEARCH FIRM INTRODUCTIONS:

RECRUITER / FIRM/ CITY ———— RELATIONSHIP WITH RECRUITER ———— FOLLOW-UP / DATE

RECRUITER / FIRM/ CITY ———— RELATIONSHIP WITH RECRUITER ———— FOLLOW-UP / DATE

NETWORKING CONTACTS

DATES PERSON: TITLE, COMPANY, ADDRESS, PHONES COMMENTS & FOLLOW-UP

PHONE

VISIT

LETTER

SOURCE MENTION **YES** ☐ MENTION **NO** ☐

PHONE

VISIT

LETTER

SOURCE MENTION **YES** ☐ MENTION **NO** ☐

PHONE

VISIT

LETTER

SOURCE MENTION **YES** ☐ MENTION **NO** ☐

PHONE

VISIT

LETTER

SOURCE MENTION **YES** ☐ MENTION **NO** ☐

NETWORKING CONTACTS

DATES | PERSON: TITLE, COMPANY, ADDRESS, PHONES | COMMENTS & FOLLOW-UP

PHONE

VISIT

LETTER

SOURCE MENTION YES ☐ MENTION NO ☐

PHONE

VISIT

LETTER

SOURCE MENTION YES ☐ MENTION NO ☐

PHONE

VISIT

LETTER

SOURCE MENTION YES ☐ MENTION NO ☐

PHONE

VISIT

LETTER

SOURCE MENTION YES ☐ MENTION NO ☐

KEY NETWORKING CONTACT

Person/Title: ____________________

Company: ____________________

Address: ____________________
TITLE STREET ADDRESS CITY STATE/ZIP

Phones/Fax: #1 (   ) ___-____ ☐ SWITCHBOARD ☐ PRIVATE #2 (   ) ___-____ ☐ SWITCHBOARD ☐ PRIVATE FAX (   ) ___-____ ☐ GENERAL ☐ PERSONAL/SECURE

Assistant(s): ____________ ____________ FAX (   ) ___-____ ☐ GENERAL ☐ PERSONAL/SECURE

Spouse: ________ **Home Address:** ____________________
STREET ADDRESS CITY STATE/ZIP

Home Phones: #1 (   ) ___-____ ☐ FAMILY PHONE ☐ HOME OFC. #2 (   ) ___-____ ☐ FAMILY PHONE ☐ HOME OFC. FAX (   ) ___-____ ☐ FAMILY ☐ HOME Office

NETWORKING

Introduced by: ____________ **Connection:** ____________

CONTACTS

DATE: LETTER/PHONE/MTG.	WHAT ABOUT?	MY FOLLOW-UP	HIS / HER FOLLOW-UP	DATE THANKED
1st				
2nd				
3rd				
4th				
5th				

COMMENTS:

OFFERS OF SEARCH FIRM INTRODUCTIONS:

RECRUITER / FIRM/ CITY — RELATIONSHIP WITH RECRUITER — FOLLOW-UP / DATE

RECRUITER / FIRM/ CITY — RELATIONSHIP WITH RECRUITER — FOLLOW-UP / DATE

DATES	PERSON: TITLE, COMPANY, ADDRESS, PHONES	COMMENTS & FOLLOW-UP
PHONE		
VISIT		
LETTER		
	SOURCE	MENTION YES ☐ MENTION NO ☐
PHONE		
VISIT		
LETTER		
	SOURCE	MENTION YES ☐ MENTION NO ☐
PHONE		
VISIT		
LETTER		
	SOURCE	MENTION YES ☐ MENTION NO ☐
PHONE		
VISIT		
LETTER		
	SOURCE	MENTION YES ☐ MENTION NO ☐

NETWORKING CONTACTS

DATES PERSON: TITLE, COMPANY, ADDRESS, PHONES COMMENTS & FOLLOW-UP

PHONE

VISIT

LETTER

SOURCE MENTION YES ☐ MENTION NO ☐

PHONE

VISIT

LETTER

SOURCE MENTION YES ☐ MENTION NO ☐

PHONE

VISIT

LETTER

SOURCE MENTION YES ☐ MENTION NO ☐

PHONE

VISIT

LETTER

SOURCE MENTION YES ☐ MENTION NO ☐

Person/Title: ______

Company: ______

Address: ______
TITLE STREET ADDRESS CITY STATE/ZIP

Phones/Fax: #1 (   ) ___-_____ ☐ SWITCHBOARD ☐ PRIVATE #2 (   ) ___-_____ ☐ SWITCHBOARD ☐ PRIVATE FAX (   ) ___-_____ ☐ GENERAL ☐ PERSONAL/SECURE

Assistant(s): ______ ______ FAX (   ) ___-_____ ☐ GENERAL ☐ PERSONAL/SECURE

Spouse: ______ **Home Address:** ______
STREET ADDRESS CITY STATE/ZIP

Home Phones: #1 (   ) ___-_____ ☐ FAMILY PHONE ☐ HOME OFC. #2 (   ) ___-_____ ☐ FAMILY PHONE ☐ HOME OFC. FAX (   ) ___-_____ ☐ FAMILY ☐ HOME Office

Introduced by: ______ **Connection:** ______

CONTACTS — DATE: LETTER/PHONE/MTG.	WHAT ABOUT?	MY FOLLOW-UP	HIS / HER FOLLOW-UP	DATE THANKED
1st				
2nd				
3rd				
4th				
5th				

COMMENTS:

OFFERS OF SEARCH FIRM INTRODUCTIONS:

RECRUITER / FIRM/ CITY ______ RELATIONSHIP WITH RECRUITER ______ FOLLOW-UP / DATE

RECRUITER / FIRM/ CITY ______ RELATIONSHIP WITH RECRUITER ______ FOLLOW-UP / DATE

NETWORKING CONTACTS

DATES PERSON: TITLE, COMPANY, ADDRESS, PHONES COMMENTS & FOLLOW-UP

PHONE

VISIT

LETTER

SOURCE MENTION YES ☐ MENTION NO ☐

PHONE

VISIT

LETTER

SOURCE MENTION YES ☐ MENTION NO ☐

PHONE

VISIT

LETTER

SOURCE MENTION YES ☐ MENTION NO ☐

PHONE

VISIT

LETTER

SOURCE MENTION YES ☐ MENTION NO ☐

DATES PERSON: TITLE, COMPANY, ADDRESS, PHONES COMMENTS & FOLLOW-UP

PHONE

VISIT

LETTER

SOURCE MENTION YES ☐ MENTION NO ☐

PHONE

VISIT

LETTER

SOURCE MENTION YES ☐ MENTION NO ☐

PHONE

VISIT

LETTER

SOURCE MENTION YES ☐ MENTION NO ☐

PHONE

VISIT

LETTER

SOURCE MENTION YES ☐ MENTION NO ☐

KEY NETWORKING CONTACT

Person/Title: ______________________________

Company: ______________________________

Address: ______________________________
TITLE STREET ADDRESS CITY STATE/ZIP

Phones/Fax: #1 (   ) ____-______ ☐ SWITCHBOARD ☐ PRIVATE #2 (   ) ____-______ ☐ SWITCHBOARD ☐ PRIVATE FAX (   ) ____-______ ☐ GENERAL ☐ PERSONAL/SECURE

Assistant(s): ______________ ______________ FAX (   ) ____-______ ☐ GENERAL ☐ PERSONAL/SECURE

Spouse: __________ **Home Address:** ______________________________
STREET ADDRESS CITY STATE/ZIP

Home Phones: #1 (   ) ____-______ ☐ FAMILY PHONE ☐ HOME OFC. #2 (   ) ____-______ ☐ FAMILY PHONE ☐ HOME OFC. FAX (   ) ____-______ ☐ FAMILY ☐ HOME Office

Introduced by: ______________ **Connection:** ______________

CONTACTS	DATE: LETTER/PHONE/MTG.	WHAT ABOUT?	MY FOLLOW-UP	HIS / HER FOLLOW-UP	DATE THANKED
	1st				
	2nd				
	3rd				
	4th				
	5th				

COMMENTS:

OFFERS OF SEARCH FIRM INTRODUCTIONS:

RECRUITER / FIRM/ CITY——RELATIONSHIP WITH RECRUITER——FOLLOW-UP / DATE

RECRUITER / FIRM/ CITY——RELATIONSHIP WITH RECRUITER——FOLLOW-UP / DATE

NETWORKING CONTACTS

DATES | PERSON: TITLE, COMPANY, ADDRESS, PHONES | COMMENTS & FOLLOW-UP

PHONE

VISIT

LETTER

SOURCE — MENTION YES ☐ MENTION NO ☐

PHONE

VISIT

LETTER

SOURCE — MENTION YES ☐ MENTION NO ☐

PHONE

VISIT

LETTER

SOURCE — MENTION YES ☐ MENTION NO ☐

PHONE

VISIT

LETTER

SOURCE — MENTION YES ☐ MENTION NO ☐

NETWORKING CONTACTS

DATES | PERSON: TITLE, COMPANY, ADDRESS, PHONES | COMMENTS & FOLLOW-UP

PHONE

VISIT

LETTER

SOURCE MENTION YES ☐ MENTION NO ☐

PHONE

VISIT

LETTER

SOURCE MENTION YES ☐ MENTION NO ☐

PHONE

VISIT

LETTER

SOURCE MENTION YES ☐ MENTION NO ☐

PHONE

VISIT

LETTER

SOURCE MENTION YES ☐ MENTION NO ☐

KEY NETWORKING CONTACT

Person/Title: ______________________________

Company: ______________________________

Address: ______________________________
TITLE STREET ADDRESS CITY STATE/ZIP

Phones/Fax: #1 ( ) ____-______ ☐ SWITCHBOARD ☐ PRIVATE #2 ( ) ____-______ ☐ SWITCHBOARD ☐ PRIVATE FAX ( ) ____-______ ☐ GENERAL ☐ PERSONAL/SECURE

Assistant(s): ______________ ______________ FAX ( ) ____-______ ☐ GENERAL ☐ PERSONAL/SECURE

Spouse: __________ **Home Address:** ______________________________
STREET ADDRESS CITY STATE/ZIP

Home Phones: #1 ( ) ____-______ ☐ FAMILY PHONE ☐ HOME OFC. #2 ( ) ____-______ ☐ FAMILY PHONE ☐ HOME OFC. FAX ( ) ____-______ ☐ FAMILY ☐ HOME Office

Introduced by: ______________ **Connection:** ______________

CONTACTS — DATE: LETTER/PHONE/MTG.	WHAT ABOUT?	MY FOLLOW-UP	HIS / HER FOLLOW-UP	DATE THANKED
1st				
2nd				
3rd				
4th				
5th				

COMMENTS:

OFFERS OF SEARCH FIRM INTRODUCTIONS:

RECRUITER / FIRM/ CITY —— RELATIONSHIP WITH RECRUITER —— FOLLOW-UP / DATE

RECRUITER / FIRM/ CITY —— RELATIONSHIP WITH RECRUITER —— FOLLOW-UP / DATE

NETWORKING CONTACTS

DATES | PERSON: TITLE, COMPANY, ADDRESS, PHONES | COMMENTS & FOLLOW-UP

PHONE

VISIT

LETTER

SOURCE MENTION **YES** ☐ MENTION **NO** ☐

PHONE

VISIT

LETTER

SOURCE MENTION **YES** ☐ MENTION **NO** ☐

PHONE

VISIT

LETTER

SOURCE MENTION **YES** ☐ MENTION **NO** ☐

PHONE

VISIT

LETTER

SOURCE MENTION **YES** ☐ MENTION **NO** ☐

DATES PERSON: TITLE, COMPANY, ADDRESS, PHONES COMMENTS & FOLLOW-UP

PHONE

VISIT

LETTER

SOURCE MENTION **YES** ☐ MENTION **NO** ☐

PHONE

VISIT

LETTER

SOURCE MENTION **YES** ☐ MENTION **NO** ☐

PHONE

VISIT

LETTER

SOURCE MENTION **YES** ☐ MENTION **NO** ☐

PHONE

VISIT

LETTER

SOURCE MENTION **YES** ☐ MENTION **NO** ☐

KEY NETWORKING CONTACT

Person/Title: ______________________________

Company: ______________________________

Address: ______________________________
TITLE STREET ADDRESS CITY STATE/ZIP

Phones/Fax: #1 ( ) ____-______ ☐ SWITCHBOARD ☐ PRIVATE #2 ( ) ____-______ ☐ SWITCHBOARD ☐ PRIVATE FAX ( ) ____-______ ☐ GENERAL ☐ PERSONAL/SECURE

Assistant(s): ______________ ______________ FAX ( ) ____-______ ☐ GENERAL ☐ PERSONAL/SECURE

Spouse: __________ **Home Address:** ______________________________
STREET ADDRESS CITY STATE/ZIP

Home Phones: #1 ( ) ____-______ ☐ FAMILY PHONE ☐ HOME OFC. #2 ( ) ____-______ ☐ FAMILY PHONE ☐ HOME OFC. FAX ( ) ____-______ ☐ FAMILY ☐ HOME Office

NETWORKING

Introduced by: ______________ **Connection:** ______________

CONTACTS — DATE: LETTER/PHONE/MTG.	WHAT ABOUT?	MY FOLLOW-UP	HIS / HER FOLLOW-UP	DATE THANKED
1st				
2nd				
3rd				
4th				
5th				

COMMENTS:

OFFERS OF SEARCH FIRM INTRODUCTIONS:

RECRUITER / FIRM/ CITY —— RELATIONSHIP WITH RECRUITER —— FOLLOW-UP / DATE

RECRUITER / FIRM/ CITY —— RELATIONSHIP WITH RECRUITER —— FOLLOW-UP / DATE

NETWORKING CONTACTS

DATES	PERSON: TITLE, COMPANY, ADDRESS, PHONES	COMMENTS & FOLLOW-UP
PHONE VISIT LETTER	SOURCE	MENTION YES ☐ MENTION NO ☐
PHONE VISIT LETTER	SOURCE	MENTION YES ☐ MENTION NO ☐
PHONE VISIT LETTER	SOURCE	MENTION YES ☐ MENTION NO ☐
PHONE VISIT LETTER	SOURCE	MENTION YES ☐ MENTION NO ☐

NETWORKING CONTACTS

DATES PERSON: TITLE, COMPANY, ADDRESS, PHONES COMMENTS & FOLLOW-UP

PHONE

VISIT

LETTER

SOURCE MENTION YES ☐ MENTION NO ☐

PHONE

VISIT

LETTER

SOURCE MENTION YES ☐ MENTION NO ☐

PHONE

VISIT

LETTER

SOURCE MENTION YES ☐ MENTION NO ☐

PHONE

VISIT

LETTER

SOURCE MENTION YES ☐ MENTION NO ☐

KEY NETWORKING CONTACT

Person/Title: ______________________________

Company: ______________________________

Address: ______________________________
TITLE STREET ADDRESS CITY STATE/ZIP

Phones/Fax: #1 ( ) ____-______ ☐ SWITCHBOARD ☐ PRIVATE #2 ( ) ____-______ ☐ SWITCHBOARD ☐ PRIVATE FAX ( ) ____-______ ☐ GENERAL ☐ PERSONAL/SECURE

Assistant(s): ______________ ______________ FAX ( ) ____-______ ☐ GENERAL ☐ PERSONAL/SECURE

Spouse: __________ **Home Address:** ______________________________
STREET ADDRESS CITY STATE/ZIP

Home Phones: #1 ( ) ____-______ ☐ FAMILY PHONE ☐ HOME OFC. #2 ( ) ____-______ ☐ FAMILY PHONE ☐ HOME OFC. FAX ( ) ____-______ ☐ FAMILY ☐ HOME Office

Introduced by: ______________ **Connection:** ______________

CONTACTS	DATE: LETTER/PHONE/MTG.	WHAT ABOUT?	MY FOLLOW-UP	HIS / HER FOLLOW-UP	DATE THANKED
	1st				
	2nd				
	3rd				
	4th				
	5th				

COMMENTS:

OFFERS OF SEARCH FIRM INTRODUCTIONS:

RECRUITER / FIRM/ CITY — RELATIONSHIP WITH RECRUITER — FOLLOW-UP / DATE

RECRUITER / FIRM/ CITY — RELATIONSHIP WITH RECRUITER — FOLLOW-UP / DATE

NETWORKING CONTACTS

DATES | PERSON: TITLE, COMPANY, ADDRESS, PHONES | COMMENTS & FOLLOW-UP

PHONE

VISIT

LETTER

SOURCE MENTION YES ☐ MENTION NO ☐

PHONE

VISIT

LETTER

SOURCE MENTION YES ☐ MENTION NO ☐

PHONE

VISIT

LETTER

SOURCE MENTION YES ☐ MENTION NO ☐

PHONE

VISIT

LETTER

SOURCE MENTION YES ☐ MENTION NO ☐

NETWORKING CONTACTS

DATES PERSON: TITLE, COMPANY, ADDRESS, PHONES COMMENTS & FOLLOW-UP

PHONE

VISIT

LETTER

SOURCE MENTION **YES** ☐ MENTION **NO** ☐

PHONE

VISIT

LETTER

SOURCE MENTION **YES** ☐ MENTION **NO** ☐

PHONE

VISIT

LETTER

SOURCE MENTION **YES** ☐ MENTION **NO** ☐

PHONE

VISIT

LETTER

SOURCE MENTION **YES** ☐ MENTION **NO** ☐

ATTACHE PAGE

KEY NETWORKING CONTACT

Person/Title: ______________________________

Company: ______________________________

Address: ______________________________
TITLE STREET ADDRESS CITY STATE/ZIP

Phones/Fax: #1 (   ) ____-______ ☐ SWITCHBOARD ☐ PRIVATE #2 (   ) ____-______ ☐ SWITCHBOARD ☐ PRIVATE FAX (   ) ____-______ ☐ GENERAL ☐ PERSONAL/SECURE

Assistant(s): ______________ ______________ FAX (   ) ____-______ ☐ GENERAL ☐ PERSONAL/SECURE

Spouse: __________ **Home Address:** ______________________________
STREET ADDRESS CITY STATE/ZIP

Home Phones: #1 (   ) ____-______ ☐ FAMILY PHONE ☐ HOME OFC. #2 (   ) ____-______ ☐ FAMILY PHONE ☐ HOME OFC. FAX (   ) ____-______ ☐ FAMILY ☐ HOME Office

Introduced by: ______________ **Connection:** ______________

CONTACTS DATE: LETTER/PHONE/MTG.	WHAT ABOUT?	MY FOLLOW-UP	HIS / HER FOLLOW-UP	DATE THANKED
1st				
2nd				
3rd				
4th				
5th				

COMMENTS:

OFFERS OF SEARCH FIRM INTRODUCTIONS:

RECRUITER / FIRM/ CITY — RELATIONSHIP WITH RECRUITER — FOLLOW-UP / DATE

RECRUITER / FIRM/ CITY — RELATIONSHIP WITH RECRUITER — FOLLOW-UP / DATE

NETWORKING CONTACTS

DATES | PERSON: TITLE, COMPANY, ADDRESS, PHONES | COMMENTS & FOLLOW-UP

PHONE

VISIT

LETTER

SOURCE MENTION **YES** ☐ MENTION **NO** ☐

PHONE

VISIT

LETTER

SOURCE MENTION **YES** ☐ MENTION **NO** ☐

PHONE

VISIT

LETTER

SOURCE MENTION **YES** ☐ MENTION **NO** ☐

PHONE

VISIT

LETTER

SOURCE MENTION **YES** ☐ MENTION **NO** ☐

NETWORKING CONTACTS

DATES | PERSON: TITLE, COMPANY, ADDRESS, PHONES | COMMENTS & FOLLOW-UP

PHONE

VISIT

LETTER

SOURCE MENTION YES ☐ MENTION NO ☐

PHONE

VISIT

LETTER

SOURCE MENTION YES ☐ MENTION NO ☐

PHONE

VISIT

LETTER

SOURCE MENTION YES ☐ MENTION NO ☐

PHONE

VISIT

LETTER

SOURCE MENTION YES ☐ MENTION NO ☐

KEY NETWORKING CONTACT

Person/Title: ______________________________

Company: ______________________________

Address: ______________________________
TITLE STREET ADDRESS CITY STATE/ZIP

Phones/Fax: #1 (   ) ____-______ ☐ SWITCHBOARD ☐ PRIVATE #2 (   ) ____-______ ☐ SWITCHBOARD ☐ PRIVATE FAX (   ) ____-______ ☐ GENERAL ☐ PERSONAL/SECURE

Assistant(s): ______________ ______________ FAX (   ) ____-______ ☐ GENERAL ☐ PERSONAL/SECURE

Spouse: __________ **Home Address:** ______________________________
STREET ADDRESS CITY STATE/ZIP

Home Phones: #1 (   ) ____-______ ☐ FAMILY PHONE ☐ HOME OFC. #2 (   ) ____-______ ☐ FAMILY PHONE ☐ HOME OFC. FAX (   ) ____-______ ☐ FAMILY ☐ HOME Office

Introduced by: ______________ **Connection:** ______________

CONTACTS	DATE: LETTER/PHONE/MTG.	WHAT ABOUT?	MY FOLLOW-UP	HIS / HER FOLLOW-UP	DATE THANKED
	1st				
	2nd				
	3rd				
	4th				
	5th				

COMMENTS:

OFFERS OF SEARCH FIRM INTRODUCTIONS:

RECRUITER / FIRM/ CITY ———— RELATIONSHIP WITH RECRUITER ———— FOLLOW-UP / DATE

RECRUITER / FIRM/ CITY ———— RELATIONSHIP WITH RECRUITER ———— FOLLOW-UP / DATE

NETWORKING CONTACTS

DATES PERSON: TITLE, COMPANY, ADDRESS, PHONES COMMENTS & FOLLOW-UP

PHONE

VISIT

LETTER

SOURCE MENTION YES ☐ MENTION NO ☐

PHONE

VISIT

LETTER

SOURCE MENTION YES ☐ MENTION NO ☐

PHONE

VISIT

LETTER

SOURCE MENTION YES ☐ MENTION NO ☐

PHONE

VISIT

LETTER

SOURCE MENTION YES ☐ MENTION NO ☐

DATES PERSON: TITLE, COMPANY, ADDRESS, PHONES COMMENTS & FOLLOW-UP

PHONE

VISIT

LETTER

SOURCE MENTION **YES** ☐ MENTION **NO** ☐

PHONE

VISIT

LETTER

SOURCE MENTION **YES** ☐ MENTION **NO** ☐

PHONE

VISIT

LETTER

SOURCE MENTION **YES** ☐ MENTION **NO** ☐

PHONE

VISIT

LETTER

SOURCE MENTION **YES** ☐ MENTION **NO** ☐

KEY NETWORKING CONTACT

Person/Title: ______________________________

Company: ______________________________

Address: ______________________________
TITLE   STREET ADDRESS   CITY   STATE/ZIP

Phones/Fax: #1 (   ) ____-______ ☐ SWITCHBOARD ☐ PRIVATE   #2 (   ) ____-______ ☐ SWITCHBOARD ☐ PRIVATE   FAX (   ) ____-______ ☐ GENERAL ☐ PERSONAL/SECURE

Assistant(s): ______________ ______________   FAX (   ) ____-______ ☐ GENERAL ☐ PERSONAL/SECURE

Spouse: __________ **Home Address:** ______________________________
STREET ADDRESS   CITY   STATE/ZIP

Home Phones: #1 (   ) ____-______ ☐ FAMILY PHONE ☐ HOME OFC.   #2 (   ) ____-______ ☐ FAMILY PHONE ☐ HOME OFC.   FAX (   ) ____-______ ☐ FAMILY ☐ HOME Office

NETWORKING

Introduced by: ________________ **Connection:** ________________

CONTACTS	DATE: LETTER/PHONE/MTG.	WHAT ABOUT?	MY FOLLOW-UP	HIS / HER FOLLOW-UP	DATE THANKED
	1st				
	2nd				
	3rd				
	4th				
	5th				

COMMENTS:

OFFERS OF SEARCH FIRM INTRODUCTIONS:

RECRUITER / FIRM/ CITY ———— RELATIONSHIP WITH RECRUITER ———— FOLLOW-UP / DATE

RECRUITER / FIRM/ CITY ———— RELATIONSHIP WITH RECRUITER ———— FOLLOW-UP / DATE

DATES PERSON: TITLE, COMPANY, ADDRESS, PHONES COMMENTS & FOLLOW-UP

PHONE

VISIT

LETTER

SOURCE MENTION **YES** ☐ MENTION **NO** ☐

PHONE

VISIT

LETTER

SOURCE MENTION **YES** ☐ MENTION **NO** ☐

PHONE

VISIT

LETTER

SOURCE MENTION **YES** ☐ MENTION **NO** ☐

PHONE

VISIT

LETTER

SOURCE MENTION **YES** ☐ MENTION **NO** ☐

NETWORKING CONTACTS

DATES PERSON: TITLE, COMPANY, ADDRESS, PHONES COMMENTS & FOLLOW-UP

PHONE

VISIT

LETTER

SOURCE MENTION **YES** ☐ MENTION **NO** ☐

PHONE

VISIT

LETTER

SOURCE MENTION **YES** ☐ MENTION **NO** ☐

PHONE

VISIT

LETTER

SOURCE MENTION **YES** ☐ MENTION **NO** ☐

PHONE

VISIT

LETTER

SOURCE MENTION **YES** ☐ MENTION **NO** ☐

KEY NETWORKING CONTACT

Person/Title: ______________________________

Company: ______________________________

Address: ______________________________
TITLE STREET ADDRESS CITY STATE/ZIP

Phones/Fax: #1 (   ) ____-______ ☐ SWITCHBOARD ☐ PRIVATE #2 (   ) ____-______ ☐ SWITCHBOARD ☐ PRIVATE FAX (   ) ____-______ ☐ GENERAL ☐ PERSONAL/SECURE

Assistant(s): ______________ ______________ FAX (   ) ____-______ ☐ GENERAL ☐ PERSONAL/SECURE

Spouse: __________ **Home Address:** ______________________________
STREET ADDRESS CITY STATE/ZIP

Home Phones: #1 (   ) ____-______ ☐ FAMILY PHONE ☐ HOME OFC. #2 (   ) ____-______ ☐ FAMILY PHONE ☐ HOME OFC. FAX (   ) ____-______ ☐ FAMILY ☐ HOME Office

Introduced by: ______________ **Connection:** ______________

NETWORKING

CONTACTS — DATE: LETTER/PHONE/MTG.	WHAT ABOUT?	MY FOLLOW-UP	HIS / HER FOLLOW-UP	DATE THANKED
1st				
2nd				
3rd				
4th				
5th				

COMMENTS:

OFFERS OF SEARCH FIRM INTRODUCTIONS:

RECRUITER / FIRM/ CITY ―――― RELATIONSHIP WITH RECRUITER ―――― FOLLOW-UP / DATE

RECRUITER / FIRM/ CITY ―――― RELATIONSHIP WITH RECRUITER ―――― FOLLOW-UP / DATE

NETWORKING CONTACTS

DATES PERSON: TITLE, COMPANY, ADDRESS, PHONES COMMENTS & FOLLOW-UP

PHONE

VISIT

LETTER

SOURCE MENTION YES ☐ MENTION NO ☐

PHONE

VISIT

LETTER

SOURCE MENTION YES ☐ MENTION NO ☐

PHONE

VISIT

LETTER

SOURCE MENTION YES ☐ MENTION NO ☐

PHONE

VISIT

LETTER

SOURCE MENTION YES ☐ MENTION NO ☐

DATES PERSON: TITLE, COMPANY, ADDRESS, PHONES COMMENTS & FOLLOW-UP

PHONE

VISIT

LETTER

SOURCE MENTION YES ☐ MENTION NO ☐

PHONE

VISIT

LETTER

SOURCE MENTION YES ☐ MENTION NO ☐

PHONE

VISIT

LETTER

SOURCE MENTION YES ☐ MENTION NO ☐

PHONE

VISIT

LETTER

SOURCE MENTION YES ☐ MENTION NO ☐

KEY NETWORKING CONTACT

Person/Title: ______________________________

Company: ______________________________

Address: ______________________________
Title | Street Address | City | State/Zip

Phones/Fax: #1 ( ) ____-______ ☐ Switchboard ☐ Private #2 ( ) ____-______ ☐ Switchboard ☐ Private FAX ( ) ____-______ ☐ General ☐ Personal/Secure

Assistant(s): ______________ ______________ FAX ( ) ____-______ ☐ General ☐ Personal/Secure

Spouse: __________ **Home Address:** ______________________________
Street Address | City | State/Zip

Home Phones: #1 ( ) ____-______ ☐ Family Phone ☐ Home Ofc. #2 ( ) ____-______ ☐ Family Phone ☐ Home Ofc. FAX ( ) ____-______ ☐ Family ☐ Home Office

NETWORKING

Introduced by: ______________ **Connection:** ______________

CONTACTS

Date: Letter/Phone/Mtg.	What About?	My Follow-Up	His / Her Follow-Up	Date Thanked
1st				
2nd				
3rd				
4th				
5th				

COMMENTS:

Offers of search firm introductions:

Recruiter / Firm/ City —— Relationship with Recruiter —— Follow-Up / Date

Recruiter / Firm/ City —— Relationship with Recruiter —— Follow-Up / Date

NETWORKING CONTACTS

DATES | PERSON: TITLE, COMPANY, ADDRESS, PHONES | COMMENTS & FOLLOW-UP

PHONE

VISIT

LETTER

SOURCE MENTION **YES** ☐ MENTION **NO** ☐

PHONE

VISIT

LETTER

SOURCE MENTION **YES** ☐ MENTION **NO** ☐

PHONE

VISIT

LETTER

SOURCE MENTION **YES** ☐ MENTION **NO** ☐

PHONE

VISIT

LETTER

SOURCE MENTION **YES** ☐ MENTION **NO** ☐

NETWORKING CONTACTS

DATES PERSON: TITLE, COMPANY, ADDRESS, PHONES COMMENTS & FOLLOW-UP

PHONE

VISIT

LETTER

SOURCE MENTION **YES** ☐ MENTION **NO** ☐

PHONE

VISIT

LETTER

SOURCE MENTION **YES** ☐ MENTION **NO** ☐

PHONE

VISIT

LETTER

SOURCE MENTION **YES** ☐ MENTION **NO** ☐

PHONE

VISIT

LETTER

SOURCE MENTION **YES** ☐ MENTION **NO** ☐

KEY NETWORKING CONTACT

Person/Title: ______________________________

Company: ______________________________

Address: ______________________________
TITLE STREET ADDRESS CITY STATE/ZIP

Phones/Fax: #1 ( ) ____-______ ☐ SWITCHBOARD ☐ PRIVATE #2 ( ) ____-______ ☐ SWITCHBOARD ☐ PRIVATE FAX ( ) ____-______ ☐ GENERAL ☐ PERSONAL/SECURE

Assistant(s): ______________ ______________ FAX ( ) ____-______ ☐ GENERAL ☐ PERSONAL/SECURE

Spouse: __________ **Home Address:** ______________________________
STREET ADDRESS CITY STATE/ZIP

Home Phones: #1 ( ) ____-______ ☐ FAMILY PHONE ☐ HOME OFC. #2 ( ) ____-______ ☐ FAMILY PHONE ☐ HOME OFC. FAX ( ) ____-______ ☐ FAMILY ☐ HOME Office

Introduced by: ______________ **Connection:** ______________

CONTACTS

DATE: LETTER/PHONE/MTG.	WHAT ABOUT?	MY FOLLOW-UP	HIS / HER FOLLOW-UP	DATE THANKED
1st				
2nd				
3rd				
4th				
5th				

COMMENTS:

OFFERS OF SEARCH FIRM INTRODUCTIONS:

RECRUITER / FIRM/ CITY ______ RELATIONSHIP WITH RECRUITER ______ FOLLOW-UP / DATE

RECRUITER / FIRM/ CITY ______ RELATIONSHIP WITH RECRUITER ______ FOLLOW-UP / DATE

NETWORKING CONTACTS

DATES | PERSON: TITLE, COMPANY, ADDRESS, PHONES | COMMENTS & FOLLOW-UP

PHONE

VISIT

LETTER

SOURCE MENTION YES ☐ MENTION NO ☐

PHONE

VISIT

LETTER

SOURCE MENTION YES ☐ MENTION NO ☐

PHONE

VISIT

LETTER

SOURCE MENTION YES ☐ MENTION NO ☐

PHONE

VISIT

LETTER

SOURCE MENTION YES ☐ MENTION NO ☐

NETWORKING CONTACTS

DATES | PERSON: TITLE, COMPANY, ADDRESS, PHONES | COMMENTS & FOLLOW-UP

PHONE

VISIT

LETTER

SOURCE MENTION YES ☐ MENTION NO ☐

PHONE

VISIT

LETTER

SOURCE MENTION YES ☐ MENTION NO ☐

PHONE

VISIT

LETTER

SOURCE MENTION YES ☐ MENTION NO ☐

PHONE

VISIT

LETTER

SOURCE MENTION YES ☐ MENTION NO ☐

KEY NETWORKING CONTACT

Person/Title: ______________________________

Company: ______________________________

Address: ______________________________
TITLE STREET ADDRESS CITY STATE/ZIP

Phones/Fax: #1 (   ) ____-______ ☐ SWITCHBOARD ☐ PRIVATE #2 (   ) ____-______ ☐ SWITCHBOARD ☐ PRIVATE FAX (   ) ____-______ ☐ GENERAL ☐ PERSONAL/SECURE

Assistant(s): ______________ ______________ FAX (   ) ____-______ ☐ GENERAL ☐ PERSONAL/SECURE

Spouse: __________ **Home Address:** ______________________________
STREET ADDRESS CITY STATE/ZIP

Home Phones: #1 (   ) ____-______ ☐ FAMILY PHONE ☐ HOME OFC. #2 (   ) ____-______ ☐ FAMILY PHONE ☐ HOME OFC. FAX (   ) ____-______ ☐ FAMILY ☐ HOME Office

Introduced by: ______________ **Connection:** ______________

CONTACTS — DATE: LETTER/PHONE/MTG.	WHAT ABOUT?	MY FOLLOW-UP	HIS / HER FOLLOW-UP	DATE THANKED
1st				
2nd				
3rd				
4th				
5th				

COMMENTS:

OFFERS OF SEARCH FIRM INTRODUCTIONS:

RECRUITER / FIRM/ CITY — RELATIONSHIP WITH RECRUITER — FOLLOW-UP / DATE

RECRUITER / FIRM/ CITY — RELATIONSHIP WITH RECRUITER — FOLLOW-UP / DATE

NETWORKING CONTACTS

DATES | PERSON: TITLE, COMPANY, ADDRESS, PHONES | COMMENTS & FOLLOW-UP

PHONE

VISIT

LETTER

SOURCE MENTION YES ☐ MENTION NO ☐

PHONE

VISIT

LETTER

SOURCE MENTION YES ☐ MENTION NO ☐

PHONE

VISIT

LETTER

SOURCE MENTION YES ☐ MENTION NO ☐

PHONE

VISIT

LETTER

SOURCE MENTION YES ☐ MENTION NO ☐

NETWORKING CONTACTS

DATES PERSON: TITLE, COMPANY, ADDRESS, PHONES COMMENTS & FOLLOW-UP

PHONE

VISIT

LETTER

SOURCE MENTION **YES** ☐ MENTION **NO** ☐

PHONE

VISIT

LETTER

SOURCE MENTION **YES** ☐ MENTION **NO** ☐

PHONE

VISIT

LETTER

SOURCE MENTION **YES** ☐ MENTION **NO** ☐

PHONE

VISIT

LETTER

SOURCE MENTION **YES** ☐ MENTION **NO** ☐

KEY NETWORKING CONTACT

Person/Title: ______________________________

Company: ______________________________

Address: ______________________________
TITLE STREET ADDRESS CITY STATE/ZIP

Phones/Fax: #1 (   ) ____-______ ☐ SWITCHBOARD ☐ PRIVATE #2 (   ) ____-______ ☐ SWITCHBOARD ☐ PRIVATE FAX (   ) ____-______ ☐ GENERAL ☐ PERSONAL/SECURE

Assistant(s): ______________ ______________ FAX (   ) ____-______ ☐ GENERAL ☐ PERSONAL/SECURE

Spouse: __________ **Home Address:** ______________________________
STREET ADDRESS CITY STATE/ZIP

Home Phones: #1 (   ) ____-______ ☐ FAMILY PHONE ☐ HOME OFC. #2 (   ) ____-______ ☐ FAMILY PHONE ☐ HOME OFC. FAX (   ) ____-______ ☐ FAMILY ☐ HOME Office

Introduced by: ______________ **Connection:** ______________

NETWORKING

CONTACTS	DATE: LETTER/PHONE/MTG.	WHAT ABOUT?	MY FOLLOW-UP	HIS / HER FOLLOW-UP	DATE THANKED
	1st				
	2nd				
	3rd				
	4th				
	5th				

COMMENTS:

OFFERS OF SEARCH FIRM INTRODUCTIONS:

RECRUITER / FIRM/ CITY —— RELATIONSHIP WITH RECRUITER —— FOLLOW-UP / DATE

RECRUITER / FIRM/ CITY —— RELATIONSHIP WITH RECRUITER —— FOLLOW-UP / DATE

NETWORKING CONTACTS

DATES | PERSON: TITLE, COMPANY, ADDRESS, PHONES | COMMENTS & FOLLOW-UP

PHONE

VISIT

LETTER

SOURCE MENTION YES ☐ MENTION NO ☐

PHONE

VISIT

LETTER

SOURCE MENTION YES ☐ MENTION NO ☐

PHONE

VISIT

LETTER

SOURCE MENTION YES ☐ MENTION NO ☐

PHONE

VISIT

LETTER

SOURCE MENTION YES ☐ MENTION NO ☐

NETWORKING CONTACTS

DATES | PERSON: TITLE, COMPANY, ADDRESS, PHONES | COMMENTS & FOLLOW-UP

PHONE

VISIT

LETTER

SOURCE MENTION **YES** ☐ MENTION **NO** ☐

PHONE

VISIT

LETTER

SOURCE MENTION **YES** ☐ MENTION **NO** ☐

PHONE

VISIT

LETTER

SOURCE MENTION **YES** ☐ MENTION **NO** ☐

PHONE

VISIT

LETTER

SOURCE MENTION **YES** ☐ MENTION **NO** ☐

KEY NETWORKING CONTACT

Person/Title: ______________________________

Company: ______________________________

Address: ______________________________
TITLE / STREET ADDRESS / CITY / STATE/ZIP

Phones/Fax: #1 (   ) ___-____ ☐ SWITCHBOARD ☐ PRIVATE #2 (   ) ___-____ ☐ SWITCHBOARD ☐ PRIVATE FAX (   ) ___-____ ☐ GENERAL ☐ PERSONAL/SECURE

Assistant(s): ______________ ______________ FAX (   ) ___-____ ☐ GENERAL ☐ PERSONAL/SECURE

Spouse: ______________ **Home Address:** ______________________________
STREET ADDRESS / CITY / STATE/ZIP

Home Phones: #1 (   ) ___-____ ☐ FAMILY PHONE ☐ HOME OFC. #2 (   ) ___-____ ☐ FAMILY PHONE ☐ HOME OFC. FAX (   ) ___-____ ☐ FAMILY ☐ HOME Office

Introduced by: ______________ **Connection:** ______________

CONTACTS — DATE: LETTER/PHONE/MTG.	WHAT ABOUT?	MY FOLLOW-UP	HIS / HER FOLLOW-UP	DATE THANKED
1st				
2nd				
3rd				
4th				
5th				

COMMENTS:

OFFERS OF SEARCH FIRM INTRODUCTIONS:

RECRUITER / FIRM/ CITY ______ RELATIONSHIP WITH RECRUITER ______ FOLLOW-UP / DATE

RECRUITER / FIRM/ CITY ______ RELATIONSHIP WITH RECRUITER ______ FOLLOW-UP / DATE

DATES PERSON: TITLE, COMPANY, ADDRESS, PHONES COMMENTS & FOLLOW-UP

PHONE

VISIT

LETTER

SOURCE MENTION YES ☐ MENTION NO ☐

PHONE

VISIT

LETTER

SOURCE MENTION YES ☐ MENTION NO ☐

PHONE

VISIT

LETTER

SOURCE MENTION YES ☐ MENTION NO ☐

PHONE

VISIT

LETTER

SOURCE MENTION YES ☐ MENTION NO ☐

NETWORKING CONTACTS

DATES PERSON: TITLE, COMPANY, ADDRESS, PHONES COMMENTS & FOLLOW-UP

PHONE

VISIT

LETTER

SOURCE MENTION **YES** ☐ MENTION **NO** ☐

PHONE

VISIT

LETTER

SOURCE MENTION **YES** ☐ MENTION **NO** ☐

PHONE

VISIT

LETTER

SOURCE MENTION **YES** ☐ MENTION **NO** ☐

PHONE

VISIT

LETTER

SOURCE MENTION **YES** ☐ MENTION **NO** ☐

KEY NETWORKING CONTACT

Person/Title: ______________________________

Company: ______________________________

Address: ______________________________
TITLE STREET ADDRESS CITY STATE/ZIP

Phones/Fax: #1 ( ) ____-______ ☐ SWITCHBOARD ☐ PRIVATE #2 ( ) ____-______ ☐ SWITCHBOARD ☐ PRIVATE FAX ( ) ____-______ ☐ GENERAL ☐ PERSONAL/SECURE

Assistant(s): ______________ ______________ FAX ( ) ____-______ ☐ GENERAL ☐ PERSONAL/SECURE

Spouse: __________ **Home Address:** ______________________________
STREET ADDRESS CITY STATE/ZIP

Home Phones: #1 ( ) ____-______ ☐ FAMILY PHONE ☐ HOME OFC. #2 ( ) ____-______ ☐ FAMILY PHONE ☐ HOME OFC. FAX ( ) ____-______ ☐ FAMILY ☐ HOME Office

Introduced by: ______________ **Connection:** ______________

NETWORKING

CONTACTS — DATE: LETTER/PHONE/MTG.	WHAT ABOUT?	MY FOLLOW-UP	HIS / HER FOLLOW-UP	DATE THANKED
1st				
2nd				
3rd				
4th				
5th				

COMMENTS:

OFFERS OF SEARCH FIRM INTRODUCTIONS:

RECRUITER / FIRM/ CITY —— RELATIONSHIP WITH RECRUITER —— FOLLOW-UP / DATE

RECRUITER / FIRM/ CITY —— RELATIONSHIP WITH RECRUITER —— FOLLOW-UP / DATE

NETWORKING CONTACTS

DATES PERSON: TITLE, COMPANY, ADDRESS, PHONES COMMENTS & FOLLOW-UP

PHONE

VISIT

LETTER

SOURCE MENTION YES ☐ MENTION NO ☐

PHONE

VISIT

LETTER

SOURCE MENTION YES ☐ MENTION NO ☐

PHONE

VISIT

LETTER

SOURCE MENTION YES ☐ MENTION NO ☐

PHONE

VISIT

LETTER

SOURCE MENTION YES ☐ MENTION NO ☐

NETWORKING CONTACTS

DATES	PERSON: TITLE, COMPANY, ADDRESS, PHONES	COMMENTS & FOLLOW-UP
PHONE		
VISIT		
LETTER		
	SOURCE	MENTION YES ☐ MENTION NO ☐
PHONE		
VISIT		
LETTER		
	SOURCE	MENTION YES ☐ MENTION NO ☐
PHONE		
VISIT		
LETTER		
	SOURCE	MENTION YES ☐ MENTION NO ☐
PHONE		
VISIT		
LETTER		
	SOURCE	MENTION YES ☐ MENTION NO ☐

KEY NETWORKING CONTACT

Person/Title: ______________________________

Company: ______________________________

Address: ______________________________
TITLE STREET ADDRESS CITY STATE/ZIP

Phones/Fax: #1 (   ) ____-______ ☐ SWITCHBOARD ☐ PRIVATE #2 (   ) ____-______ ☐ SWITCHBOARD ☐ PRIVATE FAX (   ) ____-______ ☐ GENERAL ☐ PERSONAL/SECURE

Assistant(s): ______________ ______________ FAX (   ) ____-______ ☐ GENERAL ☐ PERSONAL/SECURE

Spouse: __________ **Home Address:** ______________________________
STREET ADDRESS CITY STATE/ZIP

Home Phones: #1 (   ) ____-______ ☐ FAMILY PHONE ☐ HOME OFC. #2 (   ) ____-______ ☐ FAMILY PHONE ☐ HOME OFC. FAX (   ) ____-______ ☐ FAMILY ☐ HOME Office

Introduced by: ______________ **Connection:** ______________

CONTACTS	DATE: LETTER/PHONE/MTG.	WHAT ABOUT?	MY FOLLOW-UP	HIS / HER FOLLOW-UP	DATE THANKED
	1st				
	2nd				
	3rd				
	4th				
	5th				

COMMENTS:

OFFERS OF SEARCH FIRM INTRODUCTIONS:

RECRUITER / FIRM/ CITY—————RELATIONSHIP WITH RECRUITER—————FOLLOW-UP / DATE

RECRUITER / FIRM/ CITY—————RELATIONSHIP WITH RECRUITER—————FOLLOW-UP / DATE

NETWORKING CONTACTS

DATES | PERSON: TITLE, COMPANY, ADDRESS, PHONES | COMMENTS & FOLLOW-UP

PHONE

VISIT

LETTER

SOURCE MENTION YES ☐ MENTION NO ☐

PHONE

VISIT

LETTER

SOURCE MENTION YES ☐ MENTION NO ☐

PHONE

VISIT

LETTER

SOURCE MENTION YES ☐ MENTION NO ☐

PHONE

VISIT

LETTER

SOURCE MENTION YES ☐ MENTION NO ☐

NETWORKING CONTACTS

DATES | PERSON: TITLE, COMPANY, ADDRESS, PHONES | COMMENTS & FOLLOW-UP

PHONE

VISIT

LETTER

SOURCE MENTION YES ☐ MENTION NO ☐

PHONE

VISIT

LETTER

SOURCE MENTION YES ☐ MENTION NO ☐

PHONE

VISIT

LETTER

SOURCE MENTION YES ☐ MENTION NO ☐

PHONE

VISIT

LETTER

SOURCE MENTION YES ☐ MENTION NO ☐

Person/Title: ______________________________

Company: ______________________________

Address: ______________________________
TITLE STREET ADDRESS CITY STATE/ZIP

Phones/Fax: #1 ( ) ____-______ ☐ SWITCHBOARD ☐ PRIVATE #2 ( ) ____-______ ☐ SWITCHBOARD ☐ PRIVATE FAX ( ) ____-______ ☐ GENERAL ☐ PERSONAL/SECURE

Assistant(s): ______________ ______________ FAX ( ) ____-______ ☐ GENERAL ☐ PERSONAL/SECURE

Spouse: __________ **Home Address:** ______________________________
STREET ADDRESS CITY STATE/ZIP

Home Phones: #1 ( ) ____-______ ☐ FAMILY PHONE ☐ HOME OFC. #2 ( ) ____-______ ☐ FAMILY PHONE ☐ HOME OFC. FAX ( ) ____-______ ☐ FAMILY ☐ HOME Office

Introduced by: ______________ **Connection:** ______________

NETWORKING

CONTACTS Date: Letter/Phone/Mtg.	What About?	My Follow-Up	His / Her Follow-Up	Date Thanked
1st				
2nd				
3rd				
4th				
5th				

COMMENTS:

OFFERS OF SEARCH FIRM INTRODUCTIONS:

RECRUITER / FIRM/ CITY —— RELATIONSHIP WITH RECRUITER —— FOLLOW-UP / DATE

RECRUITER / FIRM/ CITY —— RELATIONSHIP WITH RECRUITER —— FOLLOW-UP / DATE

NETWORKING CONTACTS

DATES PERSON: TITLE, COMPANY, ADDRESS, PHONES COMMENTS & FOLLOW-UP

PHONE

VISIT

LETTER

SOURCE MENTION YES ☐ MENTION NO ☐

PHONE

VISIT

LETTER

SOURCE MENTION YES ☐ MENTION NO ☐

PHONE

VISIT

LETTER

SOURCE MENTION YES ☐ MENTION NO ☐

PHONE

VISIT

LETTER

SOURCE MENTION YES ☐ MENTION NO ☐

NETWORKING CONTACTS

DATES	PERSON: TITLE, COMPANY, ADDRESS, PHONES	COMMENTS & FOLLOW-UP
PHONE		
VISIT		
LETTER	SOURCE	MENTION YES ☐ MENTION NO ☐
PHONE		
VISIT		
LETTER	SOURCE	MENTION YES ☐ MENTION NO ☐
PHONE		
VISIT		
LETTER	SOURCE	MENTION YES ☐ MENTION NO ☐
PHONE		
VISIT		
LETTER	SOURCE	MENTION YES ☐ MENTION NO ☐

KEY NETWORKING CONTACT

Person/Title: ______________________________

Company: ______________________________

Address: ______________________________
TITLE STREET ADDRESS CITY STATE/ZIP

Phones/Fax: #1 ( ) ____-______ ☐ SWITCHBOARD ☐ PRIVATE #2 ( ) ____-______ ☐ SWITCHBOARD ☐ PRIVATE FAX ( ) ____-______ ☐ GENERAL ☐ PERSONAL/SECURE

Assistant(s): ______________ ______________ FAX ( ) ____-______ ☐ GENERAL ☐ PERSONAL/SECURE

Spouse: __________ **Home Address:** ______________________________
STREET ADDRESS CITY STATE/ZIP

Home Phones: #1 ( ) ____-______ ☐ FAMILY PHONE ☐ HOME OFC. #2 ( ) ____-______ ☐ FAMILY PHONE ☐ HOME OFC. FAX ( ) ____-______ ☐ FAMILY ☐ HOME Office

NETWORKING

Introduced by: ______________ **Connection:** ______________

CONTACTS: DATE: LETTER/PHONE/MTG.	WHAT ABOUT?	MY FOLLOW-UP	HIS / HER FOLLOW-UP	DATE THANKED
1st				
2nd				
3rd				
4th				
5th				

COMMENTS:

OFFERS OF SEARCH FIRM INTRODUCTIONS:

RECRUITER / FIRM/ CITY —— RELATIONSHIP WITH RECRUITER —— FOLLOW-UP / DATE

RECRUITER / FIRM/ CITY —— RELATIONSHIP WITH RECRUITER —— FOLLOW-UP / DATE

DATES	PERSON: TITLE, COMPANY, ADDRESS, PHONES	COMMENTS & FOLLOW-UP
PHONE		
VISIT		
LETTER	SOURCE	MENTION YES ☐ MENTION NO ☐
PHONE		
VISIT		
LETTER	SOURCE	MENTION YES ☐ MENTION NO ☐
PHONE		
VISIT		
LETTER	SOURCE	MENTION YES ☐ MENTION NO ☐
PHONE		
VISIT		
LETTER	SOURCE	MENTION YES ☐ MENTION NO ☐

NETWORKING CONTACTS

DATES | PERSON: TITLE, COMPANY, ADDRESS, PHONES | COMMENTS & FOLLOW-UP

PHONE

VISIT

LETTER

SOURCE MENTION YES ☐ MENTION NO ☐

PHONE

VISIT

LETTER

SOURCE MENTION YES ☐ MENTION NO ☐

PHONE

VISIT

LETTER

SOURCE MENTION YES ☐ MENTION NO ☐

PHONE

VISIT

LETTER

SOURCE MENTION YES ☐ MENTION NO ☐

KEY NETWORKING CONTACT

Person/Title: ______________________

Company: ______________________

Address: ______________________
TITLE STREET ADDRESS CITY STATE/ZIP

Phones/Fax: #1 (   ) ____-______ ☐ SWITCHBOARD ☐ PRIVATE #2 (   ) ____-______ ☐ SWITCHBOARD ☐ PRIVATE FAX (   ) ____-______ ☐ GENERAL ☐ PERSONAL/SECURE

Assistant(s): ____________ ____________ FAX (   ) ____-______ ☐ GENERAL ☐ PERSONAL/SECURE

Spouse: ____________ **Home Address:** ______________________
STREET ADDRESS CITY STATE/ZIP

Home Phones: #1 (   ) ____-______ ☐ FAMILY PHONE ☐ HOME OFC. #2 (   ) ____-______ ☐ FAMILY PHONE ☐ HOME OFC. FAX (   ) ____-______ ☐ FAMILY ☐ HOME Office

Introduced by: ____________ **Connection:** ____________

NETWORKING

CONTACTS	DATE: LETTER/PHONE/MTG.	WHAT ABOUT?	MY FOLLOW-UP	HIS / HER FOLLOW-UP	DATE THANKED
	1st				
	2nd				
	3rd				
	4th				
	5th				

COMMENTS:

OFFERS OF SEARCH FIRM INTRODUCTIONS:

RECRUITER / FIRM/ CITY ———— RELATIONSHIP WITH RECRUITER ———— FOLLOW-UP / DATE

RECRUITER / FIRM/ CITY ———— RELATIONSHIP WITH RECRUITER ———— FOLLOW-UP / DATE

NETWORKING CONTACTS

DATES PERSON: TITLE, COMPANY, ADDRESS, PHONES COMMENTS & FOLLOW-UP

PHONE

VISIT

LETTER

SOURCE MENTION YES ☐ MENTION NO ☐

PHONE

VISIT

LETTER

SOURCE MENTION YES ☐ MENTION NO ☐

PHONE

VISIT

LETTER

SOURCE MENTION YES ☐ MENTION NO ☐

PHONE

VISIT

LETTER

SOURCE MENTION YES ☐ MENTION NO ☐

NETWORKING CONTACTS

DATES | PERSON: TITLE, COMPANY, ADDRESS, PHONES | COMMENTS & FOLLOW-UP

PHONE

VISIT

LETTER

SOURCE | MENTION YES ☐ | MENTION NO ☐

PHONE

VISIT

LETTER

SOURCE | MENTION YES ☐ | MENTION NO ☐

PHONE

VISIT

LETTER

SOURCE | MENTION YES ☐ | MENTION NO ☐

PHONE

VISIT

LETTER

SOURCE | MENTION YES ☐ | MENTION NO ☐

KEY NETWORKING CONTACT

Person/Title: ______________________________

Company: ______________________________

Address: ______________________________
TITLE STREET ADDRESS CITY STATE/ZIP

Phones/Fax: #1 (   ) ____-______ ☐ SWITCHBOARD ☐ PRIVATE #2 (   ) ____-______ ☐ SWITCHBOARD ☐ PRIVATE FAX (   ) ____-______ ☐ GENERAL ☐ PERSONAL/SECURE

Assistant(s): ______________ ______________ FAX (   ) ____-______ ☐ GENERAL ☐ PERSONAL/SECURE

Spouse: __________ **Home Address:** ______________________________
STREET ADDRESS CITY STATE/ZIP

Home Phones: #1 (   ) ____-______ ☐ FAMILY PHONE ☐ HOME OFC. #2 (   ) ____-______ ☐ FAMILY PHONE ☐ HOME OFC. FAX (   ) ____-______ ☐ FAMILY ☐ HOME Office

NETWORKING

Introduced by: ______________ **Connection:** ______________

CONTACTS — DATE: LETTER/PHONE/MTG.	WHAT ABOUT?	MY FOLLOW-UP	HIS / HER FOLLOW-UP	DATE THANKED
1st				
2nd				
3rd				
4th				
5th				

COMMENTS:

OFFERS OF SEARCH FIRM INTRODUCTIONS:

RECRUITER / FIRM/ CITY ——— RELATIONSHIP WITH RECRUITER ——— FOLLOW-UP / DATE

RECRUITER / FIRM/ CITY ——— RELATIONSHIP WITH RECRUITER ——— FOLLOW-UP / DATE

DATES PERSON: TITLE, COMPANY, ADDRESS, PHONES COMMENTS & FOLLOW-UP

PHONE

VISIT

LETTER

SOURCE MENTION **YES** ☐ MENTION **NO** ☐

PHONE

VISIT

LETTER

SOURCE MENTION **YES** ☐ MENTION **NO** ☐

PHONE

VISIT

LETTER

SOURCE MENTION **YES** ☐ MENTION **NO** ☐

PHONE

VISIT

LETTER

SOURCE MENTION **YES** ☐ MENTION **NO** ☐

NETWORKING CONTACTS

DATES | PERSON: TITLE, COMPANY, ADDRESS, PHONES | COMMENTS & FOLLOW-UP

PHONE

VISIT

LETTER

SOURCE MENTION **YES** ☐ MENTION **NO** ☐

PHONE

VISIT

LETTER

SOURCE MENTION **YES** ☐ MENTION **NO** ☐

PHONE

VISIT

LETTER

SOURCE MENTION **YES** ☐ MENTION **NO** ☐

PHONE

VISIT

LETTER

SOURCE MENTION **YES** ☐ MENTION **NO** ☐

Person/Title: ____________________

Company: ____________________

Address: ____________________
TITLE STREET ADDRESS CITY STATE/ZIP

Phones/Fax: #1 (   ) ___-_____ ☐ SWITCHBOARD ☐ PRIVATE #2 (   ) ___-_____ ☐ SWITCHBOARD ☐ PRIVATE FAX (   ) ___-_____ ☐ GENERAL ☐ PERSONAL/SECURE

Assistant(s): __________ __________ FAX (   ) ___-_____ ☐ GENERAL ☐ PERSONAL/SECURE

Spouse: __________ **Home Address:** ____________________
STREET ADDRESS CITY STATE/ZIP

Home Phones: #1 (   ) ___-_____ ☐ FAMILY PHONE ☐ HOME OFC. #2 (   ) ___-_____ ☐ FAMILY PHONE ☐ HOME OFC. FAX (   ) ___-_____ ☐ FAMILY ☐ HOME Office

Introduced by: __________ **Connection:** __________

CONTACTS

DATE: LETTER/PHONE/MTG.	WHAT ABOUT?	MY FOLLOW-UP	HIS / HER FOLLOW-UP	DATE THANKED
1st				
2nd				
3rd				
4th				
5th				

COMMENTS:

OFFERS OF SEARCH FIRM INTRODUCTIONS:

RECRUITER / FIRM/ CITY — RELATIONSHIP WITH RECRUITER — FOLLOW-UP / DATE

RECRUITER / FIRM/ CITY — RELATIONSHIP WITH RECRUITER — FOLLOW-UP / DATE

NETWORKING CONTACTS

DATES PERSON: TITLE, COMPANY, ADDRESS, PHONES COMMENTS & FOLLOW-UP

PHONE

VISIT

LETTER

SOURCE MENTION YES ☐ MENTION NO ☐

PHONE

VISIT

LETTER

SOURCE MENTION YES ☐ MENTION NO ☐

PHONE

VISIT

LETTER

SOURCE MENTION YES ☐ MENTION NO ☐

PHONE

VISIT

LETTER

SOURCE MENTION YES ☐ MENTION NO ☐

DATES	PERSON: TITLE, COMPANY, ADDRESS, PHONES	COMMENTS & FOLLOW-UP
PHONE		
VISIT		
LETTER	SOURCE	MENTION **YES** ☐ MENTION **NO** ☐
PHONE		
VISIT		
LETTER	SOURCE	MENTION **YES** ☐ MENTION **NO** ☐
PHONE		
VISIT		
LETTER	SOURCE	MENTION **YES** ☐ MENTION **NO** ☐
PHONE		
VISIT		
LETTER	SOURCE	MENTION **YES** ☐ MENTION **NO** ☐

NETWORKING

KEY NETWORKING CONTACT

Person/Title: ______________________

Company: ______________________

Address: ______________________
TITLE STREET ADDRESS CITY STATE/ZIP

Phones/Fax: #1 ( ) ____-______ ☐ SWITCHBOARD ☐ PRIVATE #2 ( ) ____-______ ☐ SWITCHBOARD ☐ PRIVATE FAX ( ) ____-______ ☐ GENERAL ☐ PERSONAL/SECURE

Assistant(s): ____________ ____________ FAX ( ) ____-______ ☐ GENERAL ☐ PERSONAL/SECURE

Spouse: ________ **Home Address:** ______________________
STREET ADDRESS CITY STATE/ZIP

Home Phones: #1 ( ) ____-______ ☐ FAMILY PHONE ☐ HOME OFC. #2 ( ) ____-______ ☐ FAMILY PHONE ☐ HOME OFC. FAX ( ) ____-______ ☐ FAMILY ☐ HOME Office

NETWORKING

Introduced by: ______________ **Connection:** ______________

CONTACTS — DATE: LETTER/PHONE/MTG.	WHAT ABOUT?	MY FOLLOW-UP	HIS / HER FOLLOW-UP	DATE THANKED
1st				
2nd				
3rd				
4th				
5th				

COMMENTS:

OFFERS OF SEARCH FIRM INTRODUCTIONS:

RECRUITER / FIRM/ CITY —— RELATIONSHIP WITH RECRUITER —— FOLLOW-UP / DATE

RECRUITER / FIRM/ CITY —— RELATIONSHIP WITH RECRUITER —— FOLLOW-UP / DATE

NETWORKING CONTACTS

DATES PERSON: TITLE, COMPANY, ADDRESS, PHONES COMMENTS & FOLLOW-UP

PHONE

VISIT

LETTER

SOURCE MENTION YES ☐ MENTION NO ☐

PHONE

VISIT

LETTER

SOURCE MENTION YES ☐ MENTION NO ☐

PHONE

VISIT

LETTER

SOURCE MENTION YES ☐ MENTION NO ☐

PHONE

VISIT

LETTER

SOURCE MENTION YES ☐ MENTION NO ☐

NETWORKING CONTACTS

DATES	PERSON: TITLE, COMPANY, ADDRESS, PHONES	COMMENTS & FOLLOW-UP
PHONE		
VISIT		
LETTER	SOURCE	MENTION YES ☐ MENTION NO ☐
PHONE		
VISIT		
LETTER	SOURCE	MENTION YES ☐ MENTION NO ☐
PHONE		
VISIT		
LETTER	SOURCE	MENTION YES ☐ MENTION NO ☐
PHONE		
VISIT		
LETTER	SOURCE	MENTION YES ☐ MENTION NO ☐

KEY NETWORKING CONTACT

Person/Title: ______________________________

Company: ______________________________

Address: ______________________________
TITLE STREET ADDRESS CITY STATE/ZIP

Phones/Fax: #1 ( ) ____-______ ☐ SWITCHBOARD ☐ PRIVATE #2 ( ) ____-______ ☐ SWITCHBOARD ☐ PRIVATE FAX ( ) ____-______ ☐ GENERAL ☐ PERSONAL/SECURE

Assistant(s): ______________ ______________ FAX ( ) ____-______ ☐ GENERAL ☐ PERSONAL/SECURE

Spouse: __________ **Home Address:** ______________________________
STREET ADDRESS CITY STATE/ZIP

Home Phones: #1 ( ) ____-______ ☐ FAMILY PHONE ☐ HOME OFC. #2 ( ) ____-______ ☐ FAMILY PHONE ☐ HOME OFC. FAX ( ) ____-______ ☐ FAMILY ☐ HOME Office

Introduced by: ______________ **Connection:** ______________

CONTACTS — DATE: LETTER/PHONE/MTG.	WHAT ABOUT?	MY FOLLOW-UP	HIS / HER FOLLOW-UP	DATE THANKED
1st				
2nd				
3rd				
4th				
5th				

NETWORKING

COMMENTS:

OFFERS OF SEARCH FIRM INTRODUCTIONS:

RECRUITER / FIRM/ CITY —— RELATIONSHIP WITH RECRUITER —— FOLLOW-UP / DATE

RECRUITER / FIRM/ CITY —— RELATIONSHIP WITH RECRUITER —— FOLLOW-UP / DATE

NETWORKING CONTACTS

DATES PERSON: TITLE, COMPANY, ADDRESS, PHONES COMMENTS & FOLLOW-UP

PHONE

VISIT

LETTER

SOURCE MENTION **YES** ☐ MENTION **NO** ☐

PHONE

VISIT

LETTER

SOURCE MENTION **YES** ☐ MENTION **NO** ☐

PHONE

VISIT

LETTER

SOURCE MENTION **YES** ☐ MENTION **NO** ☐

PHONE

VISIT

LETTER

SOURCE MENTION **YES** ☐ MENTION **NO** ☐

DATES PERSON: TITLE, COMPANY, ADDRESS, PHONES COMMENTS & FOLLOW-UP

PHONE

VISIT

LETTER

SOURCE MENTION YES ☐ MENTION NO ☐

PHONE

VISIT

LETTER

SOURCE MENTION YES ☐ MENTION NO ☐

PHONE

VISIT

LETTER

SOURCE MENTION YES ☐ MENTION NO ☐

PHONE

VISIT

LETTER

SOURCE MENTION YES ☐ MENTION NO ☐

KEY NETWORKING CONTACT

Person/Title: ______________________________

Company: ______________________________

Address: ______________________________
TITLE STREET ADDRESS CITY STATE/ZIP

Phones/Fax: #1 ( ) ____-______ ☐ SWITCHBOARD ☐ PRIVATE #2 ( ) ____-______ ☐ SWITCHBOARD ☐ PRIVATE FAX ( ) ____-______ ☐ GENERAL ☐ PERSONAL/SECURE

Assistant(s): ______________ ______________ FAX ( ) ____-______ ☐ GENERAL ☐ PERSONAL/SECURE

Spouse: __________ **Home Address:** ______________________________
STREET ADDRESS CITY STATE/ZIP

Home Phones: #1 ( ) ____-______ ☐ FAMILY PHONE ☐ HOME OFC. #2 ( ) ____-______ ☐ FAMILY PHONE ☐ HOME OFC. FAX ( ) ____-______ ☐ FAMILY ☐ HOME Office

Introduced by: ______________ **Connection:** ______________

CONTACTS

DATE: LETTER/PHONE/MTG.	WHAT ABOUT?	MY FOLLOW-UP	HIS / HER FOLLOW-UP	DATE THANKED
1st				
2nd				
3rd				
4th				
5th				

COMMENTS:

OFFERS OF SEARCH FIRM INTRODUCTIONS:

RECRUITER / FIRM/ CITY—— RELATIONSHIP WITH RECRUITER—— FOLLOW-UP / DATE

RECRUITER / FIRM/ CITY—— RELATIONSHIP WITH RECRUITER—— FOLLOW-UP / DATE

NETWORKING CONTACTS

DATES	PERSON: TITLE, COMPANY, ADDRESS, PHONES	COMMENTS & FOLLOW-UP
PHONE		
VISIT		
LETTER	SOURCE	MENTION YES ☐ MENTION NO ☐
PHONE		
VISIT		
LETTER	SOURCE	MENTION YES ☐ MENTION NO ☐
PHONE		
VISIT		
LETTER	SOURCE	MENTION YES ☐ MENTION NO ☐
PHONE		
VISIT		
LETTER	SOURCE	MENTION YES ☐ MENTION NO ☐

NETWORKING CONTACTS

DATES	PERSON: TITLE, COMPANY, ADDRESS, PHONES	COMMENTS & FOLLOW-UP
PHONE		
VISIT		
LETTER		
	SOURCE	MENTION YES ☐ MENTION NO ☐
PHONE		
VISIT		
LETTER		
	SOURCE	MENTION YES ☐ MENTION NO ☐
PHONE		
VISIT		
LETTER		
	SOURCE	MENTION YES ☐ MENTION NO ☐
PHONE		
VISIT		
LETTER		
	SOURCE	MENTION YES ☐ MENTION NO ☐

KEY NETWORKING CONTACT

Person/Title: ________________________________

Company: ________________________________

Address: ________________________________
TITLE STREET ADDRESS CITY STATE/ZIP

Phones/Fax: #1 ( ) ____-______ ☐ SWITCHBOARD ☐ PRIVATE #2 ( ) ____-______ ☐ SWITCHBOARD ☐ PRIVATE FAX ( ) ____-______ ☐ GENERAL ☐ PERSONAL/SECURE

Assistant(s): ______________ ______________ FAX ( ) ____-______ ☐ GENERAL ☐ PERSONAL/SECURE

Spouse: __________ **Home Address:** ________________________________
STREET ADDRESS CITY STATE/ZIP

Home Phones: #1 ( ) ____-______ ☐ FAMILY PHONE ☐ HOME OFC. #2 ( ) ____-______ ☐ FAMILY PHONE ☐ HOME OFC. FAX ( ) ____-______ ☐ FAMILY ☐ HOME Office

Introduced by: ______________ **Connection:** ______________

CONTACTS	DATE: LETTER/PHONE/MTG.	WHAT ABOUT?	MY FOLLOW-UP	HIS / HER FOLLOW-UP	DATE THANKED
	1st				
	2nd				
	3rd				
	4th				
	5th				

COMMENTS:

OFFERS OF SEARCH FIRM INTRODUCTIONS:

RECRUITER / FIRM/ CITY——RELATIONSHIP WITH RECRUITER——FOLLOW-UP / DATE

RECRUITER / FIRM/ CITY——RELATIONSHIP WITH RECRUITER——FOLLOW-UP / DATE

NETWORKING CONTACTS

NETWORKING

DATES | PERSON: TITLE, COMPANY, ADDRESS, PHONES | COMMENTS & FOLLOW-UP

PHONE

VISIT

LETTER

SOURCE — MENTION YES ☐ MENTION NO ☐

PHONE

VISIT

LETTER

SOURCE — MENTION YES ☐ MENTION NO ☐

PHONE

VISIT

LETTER

SOURCE — MENTION YES ☐ MENTION NO ☐

PHONE

VISIT

LETTER

SOURCE — MENTION YES ☐ MENTION NO ☐

NETWORKING CONTACTS

DATES	PERSON: TITLE, COMPANY, ADDRESS, PHONES	COMMENTS & FOLLOW-UP
PHONE VISIT LETTER	SOURCE	MENTION YES ☐ MENTION NO ☐
PHONE VISIT LETTER	SOURCE	MENTION YES ☐ MENTION NO ☐
PHONE VISIT LETTER	SOURCE	MENTION YES ☐ MENTION NO ☐
PHONE VISIT LETTER	SOURCE	MENTION YES ☐ MENTION NO ☐

KEY NETWORKING CONTACT

Person/Title: ______________________

Company: ______________________

Address: ______________________
TITLE STREET ADDRESS CITY STATE/ZIP

Phones/Fax: #1 (   ) ____-______ ☐ SWITCHBOARD ☐ PRIVATE #2 (   ) ____-______ ☐ SWITCHBOARD ☐ PRIVATE FAX (   ) ____-______ ☐ GENERAL ☐ PERSONAL/SECURE

Assistant(s): ____________ ____________ FAX (   ) ____-______ ☐ GENERAL ☐ PERSONAL/SECURE

Spouse: ____________ **Home Address:** ______________________
STREET ADDRESS CITY STATE/ZIP

Home Phones: #1 (   ) ____-______ ☐ FAMILY PHONE ☐ HOME OFC. #2 (   ) ____-______ ☐ FAMILY PHONE ☐ HOME OFC. FAX (   ) ____-______ ☐ FAMILY ☐ HOME Office

NETWORKING

Introduced by: ____________ **Connection:** ____________

CONTACTS — DATE: LETTER/PHONE/MTG.	WHAT ABOUT?	MY FOLLOW-UP	HIS / HER FOLLOW-UP	DATE THANKED
1st				
2nd				
3rd				
4th				
5th				

COMMENTS:

OFFERS OF SEARCH FIRM INTRODUCTIONS:

RECRUITER / FIRM/ CITY —— RELATIONSHIP WITH RECRUITER —— FOLLOW-UP / DATE

RECRUITER / FIRM/ CITY —— RELATIONSHIP WITH RECRUITER —— FOLLOW-UP / DATE

NETWORKING CONTACTS

DATES	PERSON: TITLE, COMPANY, ADDRESS, PHONES	COMMENTS & FOLLOW-UP
PHONE VISIT LETTER		
	SOURCE	MENTION YES ☐ MENTION NO ☐
PHONE VISIT LETTER		
	SOURCE	MENTION YES ☐ MENTION NO ☐
PHONE VISIT LETTER		
	SOURCE	MENTION YES ☐ MENTION NO ☐
PHONE VISIT LETTER		
	SOURCE	MENTION YES ☐ MENTION NO ☐

NETWORKING CONTACTS

DATES | PERSON: TITLE, COMPANY, ADDRESS, PHONES | COMMENTS & FOLLOW-UP

PHONE

VISIT

LETTER

SOURCE MENTION YES ☐ MENTION NO ☐

PHONE

VISIT

LETTER

SOURCE MENTION YES ☐ MENTION NO ☐

PHONE

VISIT

LETTER

SOURCE MENTION YES ☐ MENTION NO ☐

PHONE

VISIT

LETTER

SOURCE MENTION YES ☐ MENTION NO ☐

KEY NETWORKING CONTACT

Person/Title: ____________________

Company: ____________________

Address: ____________________
TITLE STREET ADDRESS CITY STATE/ZIP

Phones/Fax: #1 (   ) ____-______ ☐ SWITCHBOARD ☐ PRIVATE #2 (   ) ____-______ ☐ SWITCHBOARD ☐ PRIVATE FAX (   ) ____-______ ☐ GENERAL ☐ PERSONAL/SECURE

Assistant(s): ____________ ____________ FAX (   ) ____-______ ☐ GENERAL ☐ PERSONAL/SECURE

Spouse: ________ **Home Address:** ____________________
STREET ADDRESS CITY STATE/ZIP

Home Phones: #1 (   ) ____-______ ☐ FAMILY PHONE ☐ HOME OFC. #2 (   ) ____-______ ☐ FAMILY PHONE ☐ HOME OFC. FAX (   ) ____-______ ☐ FAMILY ☐ HOME Office

Introduced by: ____________ **Connection:** ____________

NETWORKING

CONTACTS DATE: LETTER/PHONE/MTG.	WHAT ABOUT?	MY FOLLOW-UP	HIS / HER FOLLOW-UP	DATE THANKED
1st				
2nd				
3rd				
4th				
5th				

COMMENTS:

OFFERS OF SEARCH FIRM INTRODUCTIONS:

RECRUITER / FIRM/ CITY——RELATIONSHIP WITH RECRUITER——FOLLOW-UP / DATE

RECRUITER / FIRM/ CITY——RELATIONSHIP WITH RECRUITER——FOLLOW-UP / DATE

NETWORKING CONTACTS

DATES PERSON: TITLE, COMPANY, ADDRESS, PHONES COMMENTS & FOLLOW-UP

PHONE

VISIT

LETTER

SOURCE MENTION **YES** ☐ MENTION **NO** ☐

PHONE

VISIT

LETTER

SOURCE MENTION **YES** ☐ MENTION **NO** ☐

PHONE

VISIT

LETTER

SOURCE MENTION **YES** ☐ MENTION **NO** ☐

PHONE

VISIT

LETTER

SOURCE MENTION **YES** ☐ MENTION **NO** ☐

DATES PERSON: TITLE, COMPANY, ADDRESS, PHONES COMMENTS & FOLLOW-UP

PHONE

VISIT

LETTER

SOURCE MENTION **YES** ☐ MENTION **NO** ☐

PHONE

VISIT

LETTER

SOURCE MENTION **YES** ☐ MENTION **NO** ☐

PHONE

VISIT

LETTER

SOURCE MENTION **YES** ☐ MENTION **NO** ☐

PHONE

VISIT

LETTER

SOURCE MENTION **YES** ☐ MENTION **NO** ☐

KEY NETWORKING CONTACT

Person/Title: ______________________________

Company: ______________________________

Address: ______________________________
TITLE   STREET ADDRESS   CITY   STATE/ZIP

Phones/Fax: #1 (   ) ____-______ ☐ SWITCHBOARD ☐ PRIVATE #2 (   ) ____-______ ☐ SWITCHBOARD ☐ PRIVATE FAX (   ) ____-______ ☐ GENERAL ☐ PERSONAL/SECURE

Assistant(s): ______________ ______________ FAX (   ) ____-______ ☐ GENERAL ☐ PERSONAL/SECURE

Spouse: __________ **Home Address:** ______________________________
STREET ADDRESS   CITY   STATE/ZIP

Home Phones: #1 (   ) ____-______ ☐ FAMILY PHONE ☐ HOME OFC. #2 (   ) ____-______ ☐ FAMILY PHONE ☐ HOME OFC. FAX (   ) ____-______ ☐ FAMILY ☐ HOME Office

Introduced by: ______________ **Connection:** ______________

CONTACTS	DATE: LETTER/PHONE/MTG.	WHAT ABOUT?	MY FOLLOW-UP	HIS / HER FOLLOW-UP	DATE THANKED
	1st				
	2nd				
	3rd				
	4th				
	5th				

COMMENTS:

OFFERS OF SEARCH FIRM INTRODUCTIONS:

RECRUITER / FIRM/ CITY —— RELATIONSHIP WITH RECRUITER —— FOLLOW-UP / DATE

RECRUITER / FIRM/ CITY —— RELATIONSHIP WITH RECRUITER —— FOLLOW-UP / DATE

NETWORKING CONTACTS

DATES | PERSON: TITLE, COMPANY, ADDRESS, PHONES | COMMENTS & FOLLOW-UP

PHONE

VISIT

LETTER

SOURCE MENTION **YES** ☐ MENTION **NO** ☐

PHONE

VISIT

LETTER

SOURCE MENTION **YES** ☐ MENTION **NO** ☐

PHONE

VISIT

LETTER

SOURCE MENTION **YES** ☐ MENTION **NO** ☐

PHONE

VISIT

LETTER

SOURCE MENTION **YES** ☐ MENTION **NO** ☐

NETWORKING CONTACTS

DATES | PERSON: TITLE, COMPANY, ADDRESS, PHONES | COMMENTS & FOLLOW-UP

PHONE

VISIT

LETTER

SOURCE MENTION **YES** ☐ MENTION **NO** ☐

PHONE

VISIT

LETTER

SOURCE MENTION **YES** ☐ MENTION **NO** ☐

PHONE

VISIT

LETTER

SOURCE MENTION **YES** ☐ MENTION **NO** ☐

PHONE

VISIT

LETTER

SOURCE MENTION **YES** ☐ MENTION **NO** ☐

KEY NETWORKING CONTACT

Person/Title: ______________________________

Company: ______________________________

Address: ______________________________
TITLE STREET ADDRESS CITY STATE/ZIP

Phones/Fax: #1 (   ) ____-______ ☐ SWITCHBOARD ☐ PRIVATE #2 (   ) ____-______ ☐ SWITCHBOARD ☐ PRIVATE FAX (   ) ____-______ ☐ GENERAL ☐ PERSONAL/SECURE

Assistant(s): ______________ ______________ FAX (   ) ____-______ ☐ GENERAL ☐ PERSONAL/SECURE

Spouse: __________ **Home Address:** ______________________________
STREET ADDRESS CITY STATE/ZIP

Home Phones: #1 (   ) ____-______ ☐ FAMILY PHONE ☐ HOME OFC. #2 (   ) ____-______ ☐ FAMILY PHONE ☐ HOME OFC. FAX (   ) ____-______ ☐ FAMILY ☐ HOME Office

Introduced by: ______________ **Connection:** ______________

NETWORKING

CONTACTS	DATE: LETTER/PHONE/MTG.	WHAT ABOUT?	MY FOLLOW-UP	HIS / HER FOLLOW-UP	DATE THANKED
	1st				
	2nd				
	3rd				
	4th				
	5th				

COMMENTS:

OFFERS OF SEARCH FIRM INTRODUCTIONS:

RECRUITER / FIRM/ CITY—————RELATIONSHIP WITH RECRUITER—————FOLLOW-UP / DATE

RECRUITER / FIRM/ CITY—————RELATIONSHIP WITH RECRUITER—————FOLLOW-UP / DATE

THE INTERVIEW DE-BRIEFER

TURN THE PAGE FOR A POWERFUL TOOL. DE-BRIEF WITH ONE OF THESE 4-PAGE QUESTIONNAIRES JUST AS SOON AS YOU'RE ALONE AFTER EACH JOB INTERVIEW...WHETHER YOU'VE MET A RECRUITER OR AN EMPLOYER DECISION-MAKER.

MUCH INFORMATION IS IMPARTED DURING AN INTERVIEW THAT THE SPEAKER WILL NOT REMEMBER PROVIDING DAYS, OR EVEN HOURS, LATER. BY PROMPTLY USING THIS COMPREHENSIVE 4-PAGE QUESTIONNAIRE TO PROBE YOUR MEMORY, YOU CAN PRESERVE FOR FUTURE STUDY VIRTUALLY EVERYTHING YOU FIND OUT FROM EVERYONE YOU MEET.

IN EACH SUBSEQUENT INTERVIEW YOU'LL BE SAYING FAR MORE OF WHAT THE EMPLOYER WANTS TO HEAR THAN ANY OF THE OTHER CANDIDATES PARTICIPATING IN THE PROCESS. UNLESS THEY'RE DOING EXACTLY WHAT YOU'RE DOING, THEY CAN'T POSSIBLY ACHIEVE YOUR IMPRESSIVE KNOWLEDGE OF THE EMPLOYER'S BUSINESS, MARKETPLACE, PROBLEMS, OPPORTUNITIES, STRATEGIES, AND THE CIRCUMSTANCES, OBJECTIVES AND INTENTIONS SURROUNDING THE POSITION TO BE FILLED.

BEYOND YOUR OBVIOUS EDGE IN COMPETING FOR THE POSITION, YOU'LL ALSO BE FIGURING OUT ITS POLITICAL CONTEXT, AS YOU TALK TO THE EMPLOYER'S MANAGEMENT TEAM. THEREFORE, THESE DE-BRIEFERS MAY EVEN WARN YOU AWAY FROM A BAD SITUATION YOU'D NEVER HAVE IDENTIFIED OTHERWISE.

PLEASE BE SURE TO READ WORKBOOK CHAPTER 5 (BEGINNING ON 181) AND USE ITS TOOLS. YOUR INTERVIEWS WILL GO FAR BETTER IF YOU DO.

NOTE: This comprehensive 4-page questionnaire debriefs you after *employment interviews*, not casual networking visits. It prompts you to jot down everything you find out, and helps prepare you for future selling, inquiring, negotiating, and decision-making. If you soak up everything you learn from everyone you talk to within the company (and perhaps close outside observers and former insiders as well), you can accumulate tremendous knowledge in a situation where "Knowledge is power!" (**Fill out afterward; don't reveal at interview.**)

Company: ______

Person Seen: ______

Exact Title (query secretary by phone): ______

Date of Meeting: ______ **Thank You Sent:** ______

Time: ______

Place: ______

Address & Phone:

OFFICE	HOME
______	______
______	______
______	______
______	______
( ) ______ Switchboard	( ) ______ Home Office
( ) ______ Private	( ) ______ Home Fax
( ) ______ Fax	( ) ______ Family Phone
( ) ______ Fax (Secure)	( ) ______ Vacation Home
( ) ______ Secy./Asst.	( ) ______ Home Office

Assistant(s) / **Secretary**(ies): ______ ______ ______

Spouse (if met or mentioned): ______ **Children** (if met): ______

Introduced by: ______ (of what company?) ______

Introducer's Relationship: ______

Interviewer Reports to: ______

Interviewer's Subordinates: ______

______

______

Interviewer's Identifying Appearance: ______

______

Interviewer's Manner / Rapport / Possible Subjective Agenda: ______

______

______

______

______

INTERVIEW

INTERVIEW DE-BRIEFER

Seemed to Like about Me / Sold on:

Seemed *Not* to Like / Doubted:

Hobbies / Interests / Family / Personal Concerns and Social Causes (Don't voluntarily enter hazardous territory, but don't forget anything you happen to learn):

About the Job:

Company or Business Unit (Name / Description / Location / Annual Sales / No. of Employees / Product Lines / Market Shares, etc.):

Title:

Position reports to:

Subordinates reporting to this position:

	Title	# Subordinates	Doing What	$ Volume / Product Lines
1				
2				
3				
4				
5				
6				
7				
8				
9				
10				
11				
12				

Position being re-filled? Newly created? ________________

What happened to the incumbent? ________________

Are there inside candidates?________ **Their positions/names:**________________

What abilities and experience are lacking among insiders that cause outsiders to be considered? ___

What are the #1 and #2 make-or-break skills or talents on which success in the job depends? ______

What are the #1 and #2 make-or-break achievements the person is expected to accomplish? _______

On what timetable? ________________

With what resources? ________________

What is the likely scenario for advancement? ________________

What are the company's overall long-range and near-term strategies? ________________

What are the long-range and near-term strategies for the particular division, business unit, department or function?________________

Is this the kind of place I'd like to work?________ **Positive indications:**________________

Negative Indications:________________

Are their business ethics and human values consistent with mine?_________ **Specific matches and mismatches:** ________________

What is the corporate culture?________________

Will I enjoy it? Fit in? ________________

INTERVIEW

INTERVIEW DE-BRIEFER

Any discussion or clues with respect to money for this job? For other jobs in the company (a clue for later bargaining)? **Base? Bonus? Stock options, grants, etc? Perks and benefits** (don't inquire until job is landed and other particulars are nailed down)?

Will there be an Employment Contract? A *multi-year* contract? An 18-month (or other) **termination arrangement** (see Chapter 16 of *Rites*)? **Or will an Offer Letter incorporate basic understandings** (don't go ahead without it)?

What particulars that should be in a Contract or Offer Letter were covered in this meeting, i.e., responsibility, reporting relationship, location, title, compensation, employment security? What key items haven't been covered?

Anything else I learned at this meeting?

NOTE: THIS COMPREHENSIVE 4-PAGE QUESTIONNAIRE DEBRIEFS YOU AFTER *EMPLOYMENT INTERVIEWS*, NOT CASUAL NETWORKING VISITS. IT PROMPTS YOU TO JOT DOWN EVERYTHING YOU FIND OUT, AND HELPS PREPARE YOU FOR FUTURE SELLING, INQUIRING, NEGOTIATING, AND DECISION-MAKING. IF YOU SOAK UP EVERYTHING YOU LEARN FROM EVERYONE YOU TALK TO WITHIN THE COMPANY (AND PERHAPS CLOSE OUTSIDE OBSERVERS AND FORMER INSIDERS AS WELL), YOU CAN ACCUMULATE TREMENDOUS KNOWLEDGE IN A SITUATION WHERE "KNOWLEDGE IS POWER!" (FILL OUT AFTERWARD; DON'T REVEAL AT INTERVIEW.)

Company: ______________________

Person Seen: ______________________

Exact Title (query secretary by phone): ______________________

Date of Meeting: ______________ **Thank You Sent:** ______________

Time: ______________________

Place: ______________________

Address & Phone:

OFFICE	HOME
______________	______________
______________	______________
______________	______________
______________	______________
( )__________ Switchboard	( )__________ Home Office
( )__________ Private	( )__________ Home Fax
( )__________ Fax	( )__________ Family Phone
( )__________ Fax (Secure)	( )__________ Vacation Home
( )__________ Secy./Asst.	( )__________ Home Office

Assistant(s) / **Secretary**(ies): __________ __________ __________

Spouse (if met or mentioned): __________ **Children** (if met): __________

Introduced by: __________ (of what company?) __________

Introducer's Relationship: ______________________

Interviewer Reports to: ______________________

Interviewer's Subordinates: ______________________

____

____

Interviewer's Identifying Appearance: ______________________

____

Interviewer's Manner / Rapport / Possible Subjective Agenda: ______________________

____

____

____

____

INTERVIEW

INTERVIEW DE-BRIEFER

(Continued, page 2 of 4)

Seemed to Like about Me / Sold on: ______

Seemed *Not* to Like / Doubted: ______

Hobbies / Interests / Family / Personal Concerns and Social Causes (Don't voluntarily enter hazardous territory, but don't forget anything you happen to learn)**:** ______

About the Job:

Company or Business Unit (Name / Description / Location / Annual Sales / No. of Employees / Product Lines / Market Shares, etc.)**:** ______

Title: ______

Position reports to: ______

Subordinates reporting to this position:

	Title	# Subordinates	Doing What	$ Volume / Product Lines
1.				
2.				
3.				
4.				
5.				
6.				
7.				
8.				
9.				
10.				
11.				
12.				

Position being re-filled? Newly created? ______

What happened to the incumbent? ______

Are there inside candidates?______ **Their positions/names:**______

What abilities and experience are lacking among insiders that cause outsiders to be considered? ______

What are the #1 and #2 make-or-break skills or talents on which success in the job depends? ______

What are the #1 and #2 make-or-break achievements the person is expected to accomplish? ______

On what timetable? ______

With what resources? ______

What is the likely scenario for advancement? ______

What are the company's overall long-range and near-term strategies? ______

What are the long-range and near-term strategies for the particular division, business unit, department or function?______

Is this the kind of place I'd like to work?______ **Positive indications:**______

Negative Indications:______

Are their business ethics and human values consistent with mine?______ **Specific matches and mismatches:** ______

What is the corporate culture?______

Will I enjoy it? Fit in? ______

INTERVIEW DE-BRIEFER

Any discussion or clues with respect to money for this job? For other jobs in the company (a clue for later bargaining)**? Base? Bonus? Stock options, grants, etc? Perks and benefits** (don't inquire until job is landed and other particulars are nailed down)**?**

Will there be an Employment Contract? A *multi-year* contract? An 18-month (or other) **termination arrangement** (see Chapter 16 of *Rites*)**? Or will an Offer Letter incorporate basic understandings** (don't go ahead without it)**?**

What particulars that should be in a Contract or Offer Letter were covered in this meeting, i.e., responsibility, reporting relationship, location, title, compensation, employment security? What key items haven't been covered?

Anything else I learned at this meeting?

NOTE: This comprehensive 4-page questionnaire debriefs you after *employment interviews*, not casual networking visits. It prompts you to jot down everything you find out, and helps prepare you for future selling, inquiring, negotiating, and decision-making. If you soak up everything you learn from everyone you talk to within the company (and perhaps close outside observers and former insiders as well), you can accumulate tremendous knowledge in a situation where "Knowledge is power!" (**Fill out afterward; don't reveal at interview.**)

Company: ____________________

Person Seen: ____________________

Exact Title (query secretary by phone): ____________________

Date of Meeting: ____________________ **Thank You Sent:** ____________________

Time: ____________________

Place: ____________________

Address & Phone:

OFFICE		HOME	
____________________		____________________	
____________________		____________________	
____________________		____________________	
____________________		____________________	
( ) ____________	Switchboard	( ) ____________	Home Office
( ) ____________	Private	( ) ____________	Home Fax
( ) ____________	Fax	( ) ____________	Family Phone
( ) ____________	Fax (Secure)	( ) ____________	Vacation Home
( ) ____________	Secy./Asst.	( ) ____________	Home Office

Assistant(s) / **Secretary**(ies): ____________ ____________ ____________

Spouse (if met or mentioned): ____________ **Children** (if met): ____________

Introduced by: ____________ (of what company?) ____________

Introducer's Relationship: ____________________

Interviewer Reports to: ____________________

Interviewer's Subordinates: ____________________

____

____

Interviewer's Identifying Appearance: ____________________

____

Interviewer's Manner / Rapport / Possible Subjective Agenda: ____________________

____

____

____

INTERVIEW DE-BRIEFER

Seemed to Like about Me / Sold on: ______

Seemed *Not* to Like / Doubted: ______

Hobbies / Interests / Family / Personal Concerns and Social Causes (Don't voluntarily enter hazardous territory, but don't forget anything you happen to learn)**:** ______

About the Job:

Company or Business Unit (Name / Description / Location / Annual Sales / No. of Employees / Product Lines / Market Shares, etc.)**:** ______

Title: ______

Position reports to: ______

Subordinates reporting to this position:

	Title	# Subordinates	Doing What	$ Volume / Product Lines
1				
2				
3				
4				
5				
6				
7				
8				
9				
10				
11				
12				

INTERVIEW

Position being re-filled? Newly created? ____________________

What happened to the incumbent? ____________________

Are there inside candidates?__________ **Their positions/names:**____________________

What abilities and experience are lacking among insiders that cause outsiders to be considered? ___

What are the #1 and #2 make-or-break skills or talents on which success in the job depends? ______

What are the #1 and #2 make-or-break achievements the person is expected to accomplish? _______

On what timetable? ____________________

With what resources? ____________________

What is the likely scenario for advancement? ____________________

What are the company's overall long-range and near-term strategies? ____________________

What are the long-range and near-term strategies for the particular division, business unit, department or function?____________________

Is this the kind of place I'd like to work?_________ **Positive indications:**____________________

Negative Indications:____________________

Are their business ethics and human values consistent with mine?__________ **Specific matches and mismatches:** ____________________

What is the corporate culture?____________________

Will I enjoy it? Fit in? ____________________

INTERVIEW DE-BRIEFER

Any discussion or clues with respect to money for this job? For other jobs in the company (a clue for later bargaining)? **Base? Bonus? Stock options, grants, etc? Perks and benefits** (don't inquire until job is landed and other particulars are nailed down)?

Will there be an Employment Contract? A *multi-year* contract? An 18-month (or other) **termination arrangement** (see Chapter 16 of *Rites*)? **Or will an Offer Letter incorporate basic understandings** (don't go ahead without it)?

What particulars that should be in a Contract or Offer Letter were covered in this meeting, i.e., responsibility, reporting relationship, location, title, compensation, employment security? What key items haven't been covered?

Anything else I learned at this meeting?

INTERVIEW

NOTE: This comprehensive 4-page questionnaire debriefs you after *employment interviews*, not casual networking visits. It prompts you to jot down everything you find out, and helps prepare you for future selling, inquiring, negotiating, and decision-making. If you soak up everything you learn from everyone you talk to within the company (and perhaps close outside observers and former insiders as well), you can accumulate tremendous knowledge in a situation where "Knowledge is power!" (**Fill out afterward; don't reveal at interview.**)

Company: ______

Person Seen: ______

Exact Title (query secretary by phone): ______

Date of Meeting: ______ **Thank You Sent:** ______

Time: ______

Place: ______

Address & Phone:

OFFICE	HOME
______	______
______	______
______	______
______	______
( ) ______ Switchboard	( ) ______ Home Office
( ) ______ Private	( ) ______ Home Fax
( ) ______ Fax	( ) ______ Family Phone
( ) ______ Fax (Secure)	( ) ______ Vacation Home
( ) ______ Secy./Asst.	( ) ______ Home Office

Assistant(s) / **Secretary**(ies): ______ ______ ______

Spouse (if met or mentioned): ______ **Children** (if met): ______

Introduced by: ______ (of what company?) ______

Introducer's Relationship: ______

Interviewer Reports to: ______

Interviewer's Subordinates: ______

______

______

Interviewer's Identifying Appearance: ______

______

Interviewer's Manner / Rapport / Possible Subjective Agenda: ______

______

______

______

______

INTERVIEW DE-BRIEFER

(Continued, page 2 of 4)

Seemed to Like about Me / Sold on: ______

Seemed *Not* to Like / Doubted: ______

Hobbies / Interests / Family / Personal Concerns and Social Causes (Don't voluntarily enter hazardous territory, but don't forget anything you happen to learn)**:** ______

About the Job:

Company or Business Unit (Name / Description / Location / Annual Sales / No. of Employees / Product Lines / Market Shares, etc.)**:** ______

Title: ______

Position reports to: ______

Subordinates reporting to this position:

	Title	# Subordinates	Doing What	$ Volume / Product Lines
1				
2				
3				
4				
5				
6				
7				
8				
9				
10				
11				
12				

Position being re-filled? Newly created? ______

What happened to the incumbent? ______

Are there inside candidates?______ **Their positions/names:**______

What abilities and experience are lacking among insiders that cause outsiders to be considered? ______

What are the #1 and #2 make-or-break skills or talents on which success in the job depends? ______

What are the #1 and #2 make-or-break achievements the person is expected to accomplish? ______

On what timetable? ______

With what resources? ______

What is the likely scenario for advancement? ______

What are the company's overall long-range and near-term strategies? ______

What are the long-range and near-term strategies for the particular division, business unit, department or function?______

Is this the kind of place I'd like to work?______ **Positive indications:**______

Negative Indications:______

Are their business ethics and human values consistent with mine?______ **Specific matches and mismatches:** ______

What is the corporate culture?______

Will I enjoy it? Fit in? ______

INTERVIEW DE-BRIEFER

Any discussion or clues with respect to money for this job? For other jobs in the company (a clue for later bargaining)**? Base? Bonus? Stock options, grants, etc? Perks and benefits** (don't inquire until job is landed and other particulars are nailed down)**?**

Will there be an Employment Contract? A *multi-year* contract? An 18-month (or other) **termination arrangement** (see Chapter 16 of *Rites*)**? Or will an Offer Letter incorporate basic understandings** (don't go ahead without it)**?**

What particulars that should be in a Contract or Offer Letter were covered in this meeting, i.e., responsibility, reporting relationship, location, title, compensation, employment security? What key items haven't been covered?

Anything else I learned at this meeting?

INTERVIEW DE-BRIEFER

NOTE: This comprehensive 4-page questionnaire debriefs you after *employment interviews*, not casual networking visits. It prompts you to jot down everything you find out, and helps prepare you for future selling, inquiring, negotiating, and decision-making. If you soak up everything you learn from everyone you talk to within the company (and perhaps close outside observers and former insiders as well), you can accumulate tremendous knowledge in a situation where "Knowledge is power!" (**Fill out afterward; don't reveal at interview.**)

Company: ______________________________

Person Seen: ______________________________

Exact Title (query secretary by phone): ______________________________

Date of Meeting: ____________________ **Thank You Sent:** ____________

Time: ______________________________

Place: ______________________________

Address & Phone: **OFFICE** **HOME**

OFFICE		HOME	
______________		______________	
______________		______________	
______________		______________	
______________		______________	
( )__________	Switchboard	( )__________	Home Office
( )__________	Private	( )__________	Home Fax
( )__________	Fax	( )__________	Family Phone
( )__________	Fax (Secure)	( )__________	Vacation Home
( )__________	Secy./Asst.	( )__________	Home Office

Assistant(s) / **Secretary**(ies):____________ ____________ ____________

Spouse (if met or mentioned):____________ **Children** (if met): ____________

Introduced by:____________________(of what company?) ____________

Introducer's Relationship:______________________________

Interviewer Reports to: ______________________________

Interviewer's Subordinates: ______________________________

____

____

Interviewer's Identifying Appearance: ______________________________

____

Interviewer's Manner / Rapport / Possible Subjective Agenda: ____________

____

____

____

____

INTERVIEW

INTERVIEW DE-BRIEFER

(CONTINUED, PAGE 2 OF 4)

Seemed to Like about Me / Sold on: ______

Seemed *Not* to Like / Doubted: ______

Hobbies / Interests / Family / Personal Concerns and Social Causes (Don't voluntarily enter hazardous territory, but don't forget anything you happen to learn)**:** ______

About the Job:

Company or Business Unit (Name / Description / Location / Annual Sales / No. of Employees / Product Lines / Market Shares, etc.)**:** ______

Title: ______

Position reports to: ______

Subordinates reporting to this position:

	Title	# Subordinates	Doing What	$ Volume / Product Lines
1				
2				
3				
4				
5				
6				
7				
8				
9				
10				
11				
12				

INTERVIEW

(CONTINUED, PAGE 3 OF 4)

Position being re-filled? Newly created? ____________________

What happened to the incumbent? ____________________

Are there inside candidates?__________ **Their positions/names:**____________________

What abilities and experience are lacking among insiders that cause outsiders to be considered? ___

What are the #1 and #2 make-or-break skills or talents on which success in the job depends? ______

What are the #1 and #2 make-or-break achievements the person is expected to accomplish? _______

On what timetable? ____________________

With what resources? ____________________

What is the likely scenario for advancement? ____________________

What are the company's overall long-range and near-term strategies? ____________________

What are the long-range and near-term strategies for the particular division, business unit, department or function?____________________

Is this the kind of place I'd like to work?_________ **Positive indications:**____________________

Negative Indications:____________________

Are their business ethics and human values consistent with mine?__________ **Specific matches and mismatches:** ____________________

What is the corporate culture?____________________

Will I enjoy it? Fit in? ____________________

INTERVIEW DE-BRIEFER

Any discussion or clues with respect to money for this job? For other jobs in the company (a clue for later bargaining)**? Base? Bonus? Stock options, grants, etc? Perks and benefits** (don't inquire until job is landed and other particulars are nailed down)**?**

Will there be an Employment Contract? A *multi-year* contract? An 18-month (or other) **termination arrangement** (see Chapter 16 of *Rites*)**? Or will an Offer Letter incorporate basic understandings** (don't go ahead without it)**?**

What particulars that should be in a Contract or Offer Letter were covered in this meeting, i.e., responsibility, reporting relationship, location, title, compensation, employment security? What key items haven't been covered?

Anything else I learned at this meeting?

NOTE: THIS COMPREHENSIVE 4-PAGE QUESTIONNAIRE DEBRIEFS YOU AFTER *EMPLOYMENT INTERVIEWS*, NOT CASUAL NETWORKING VISITS. IT PROMPTS YOU TO JOT DOWN EVERYTHING YOU FIND OUT, AND HELPS PREPARE YOU FOR FUTURE SELLING, INQUIRING, NEGOTIATING, AND DECISION-MAKING. IF YOU SOAK UP EVERYTHING YOU LEARN FROM EVERYONE YOU TALK TO WITHIN THE COMPANY (AND PERHAPS CLOSE OUTSIDE OBSERVERS AND FORMER INSIDERS AS WELL), YOU CAN ACCUMULATE TREMENDOUS KNOWLEDGE IN A SITUATION WHERE "KNOWLEDGE IS POWER!" (**FILL OUT AFTERWARD; DON'T REVEAL AT INTERVIEW.**)

Company: ______________________________

Person Seen: ______________________________

Exact Title (query secretary by phone)**:** ______________________________

Date of Meeting: ______________________ **Thank You Sent:** ______________

Time: ______________________________

Place: ______________________________

Address & Phone: **OFFICE** **HOME**

OFFICE		HOME	
______________________		______________________	
______________________		______________________	
______________________		______________________	
______________________		______________________	
( )______________	Switchboard	( )______________	Home Office
( )______________	Private	( )______________	Home Fax
( )______________	Fax	( )______________	Family Phone
( )______________	Fax (Secure)	( )______________	Vacation Home
( )______________	Secy./Asst.	( )______________	Home Office

Assistant(s) / **Secretary**(ies)**:** ______________ ______________ ______________

Spouse (if met or mentioned)**:** ______________ **Children** (if met)**:** ______________

Introduced by: ______________________ (of what company?) ______________

Introducer's Relationship: ______________________________

Interviewer Reports to: ______________________________

Interviewer's Subordinates: ______________________________

____

____

Interviewer's Identifying Appearance: ______________________________

____

Interviewer's Manner / Rapport / Possible Subjective Agenda: ______________________________

____

____

____

____

INTERVIEW

INTERVIEW DE-BRIEFER

(CONTINUED, PAGE 2 OF 4)

Seemed to Like about Me / Sold on: ____________________

Seemed *Not* to Like / Doubted: ____________________

Hobbies / Interests / Family / Personal Concerns and Social Causes (Don't voluntarily enter hazardous territory, but don't forget anything you happen to learn)**:** ____________________

About the Job:

Company or Business Unit (Name / Description / Location / Annual Sales / No. of Employees / Product Lines / Market Shares, etc.)**:** ____________________

Title: ____________________

Position reports to: ____________________

Subordinates reporting to this position:

	Title	# Subordinates	Doing What	$ Volume / Product Lines
1				
2				
3				
4				
5				
6				
7				
8				
9				
10				
11				
12				

Position being re-filled? Newly created? ______

What happened to the incumbent? ______

Are there inside candidates?______ **Their positions/names:**______

What abilities and experience are lacking among insiders that cause outsiders to be considered? ______

What are the #1 and #2 make-or-break skills or talents on which success in the job depends? ______

What are the #1 and #2 make-or-break achievements the person is expected to accomplish? ______

On what timetable? ______

With what resources? ______

What is the likely scenario for advancement? ______

What are the company's overall long-range and near-term strategies? ______

What are the long-range and near-term strategies for the particular division, business unit, department or function?______

Is this the kind of place I'd like to work?______ **Positive indications:**______

Negative Indications:______

Are their business ethics and human values consistent with mine?______ **Specific matches and mismatches:** ______

What is the corporate culture?______

Will I enjoy it? Fit in? ______

INTERVIEW DE-BRIEFER

Any discussion or clues with respect to money for this job? For other jobs in the company (a clue for later bargaining)? **Base? Bonus? Stock options, grants, etc? Perks and benefits** (don't inquire until job is landed and other particulars are nailed down)?

Will there be an Employment Contract? A *multi-year* contract? An 18-month (or other) **termination arrangement** (see Chapter 16 of *Rites*)? **Or will an Offer Letter incorporate basic understandings** (don't go ahead without it)?

What particulars that should be in a Contract or Offer Letter were covered in this meeting, i.e., responsibility, reporting relationship, location, title, compensation, employment security? What key items haven't been covered?

Anything else I learned at this meeting?

NOTE: This comprehensive 4-page questionnaire debriefs you after *employment interviews*, not casual networking visits. It prompts you to jot down everything you find out, and helps prepare you for future selling, inquiring, negotiating, and decision-making. If you soak up everything you learn from everyone you talk to within the company (and perhaps close outside observers and former insiders as well), you can accumulate tremendous knowledge in a situation where "Knowledge is power!" (**Fill out afterward; don't reveal at interview.**)

Company: ____________________

Person Seen: ____________________

Exact Title (query secretary by phone): ____________________

Date of Meeting: ____________________ **Thank You Sent:** ____________________

Time: ____________________

Place: ____________________

Address & Phone: **OFFICE** **HOME**

OFFICE	HOME
____________	____________
____________	____________
____________	____________
____________	____________
( )________ Switchboard	( )________ Home Office
( )________ Private	( )________ Home Fax
( )________ Fax	( )________ Family Phone
( )________ Fax (Secure)	( )________ Vacation Home
( )________ Secy./Asst.	( )________ Home Office

Assistant(s) / **Secretary**(ies): ____________ ____________ ____________

Spouse (if met or mentioned): ____________ **Children** (if met): ____________

Introduced by: ____________ (of what company?) ____________

Introducer's Relationship: ____________________

Interviewer Reports to: ____________________

Interviewer's Subordinates: ____________________

____

____

Interviewer's Identifying Appearance: ____________________

____

Interviewer's Manner / Rapport / Possible Subjective Agenda: ____________________

____

____

____

____

INTERVIEW

INTERVIEW DE-BRIEFER

Seemed to Like about Me / Sold on: ______

Seemed *Not* to Like / Doubted: ______

Hobbies / Interests / Family / Personal Concerns and Social Causes (Don't voluntarily enter hazardous territory, but don't forget anything you happen to learn): ______

About the Job:

Company or Business Unit (Name / Description / Location / Annual Sales / No. of Employees / Product Lines / Market Shares, etc.): ______

Title: ______

Position reports to: ______

Subordinates reporting to this position:

	Title	# Subordinates	Doing What	$ Volume / Product Lines
1				
2				
3				
4				
5				
6				
7				
8				
9				
10				
11				
12				

Position being re-filled? Newly created? ______

What happened to the incumbent? ______

Are there inside candidates?______ **Their positions/names:**______

What abilities and experience are lacking among insiders that cause outsiders to be considered? ______

What are the #1 and #2 make-or-break skills or talents on which success in the job depends? ______

What are the #1 and #2 make-or-break achievements the person is expected to accomplish? ______

On what timetable? ______

With what resources? ______

What is the likely scenario for advancement? ______

What are the company's overall long-range and near-term strategies? ______

What are the long-range and near-term strategies for the particular division, business unit, department or function?______

Is this the kind of place I'd like to work?______ **Positive indications:**______

Negative Indications:______

Are their business ethics and human values consistent with mine?______ **Specific matches and mismatches:** ______

What is the corporate culture?______

Will I enjoy it? Fit in? ______

INTERVIEW DE-BRIEFER

Any discussion or clues with respect to money for this job? For other jobs in the company (a clue for later bargaining)? **Base? Bonus? Stock options, grants, etc? Perks and benefits** (don't inquire until job is landed and other particulars are nailed down)?

Will there be an Employment Contract? A *multi-year* contract? An 18-month (or other) **termination arrangement** (see Chapter 16 of *Rites*)? **Or will an Offer Letter incorporate basic understandings** (don't go ahead without it)?

What particulars that should be in a Contract or Offer Letter were covered in this meeting, i.e., responsibility, reporting relationship, location, title, compensation, employment security? What key items haven't been covered?

Anything else I learned at this meeting?

INTERVIEW

INTERVIEW DE-BRIEFER

NOTE: THIS COMPREHENSIVE 4-PAGE QUESTIONNAIRE DEBRIEFS YOU AFTER *EMPLOYMENT INTERVIEWS*, NOT CASUAL NETWORKING VISITS. IT PROMPTS YOU TO JOT DOWN EVERYTHING YOU FIND OUT, AND HELPS PREPARE YOU FOR FUTURE SELLING, INQUIRING, NEGOTIATING, AND DECISION-MAKING. IF YOU SOAK UP EVERYTHING YOU LEARN FROM EVERYONE YOU TALK TO WITHIN THE COMPANY (AND PERHAPS CLOSE OUTSIDE OBSERVERS AND FORMER INSIDERS AS WELL), YOU CAN ACCUMULATE TREMENDOUS KNOWLEDGE IN A SITUATION WHERE "KNOWLEDGE IS POWER!" (**FILL OUT AFTERWARD; DON'T REVEAL AT INTERVIEW.**)

Company: ______________________________

Person Seen: ______________________________

Exact Title (query secretary by phone): ______________________________

Date of Meeting: ____________________ **Thank You Sent:** ____________

Time: ______________________________

Place: ______________________________

Address & Phone: **OFFICE** **HOME**

OFFICE	HOME
____________________	____________________
____________________	____________________
____________________	____________________
____________________	____________________
( )__________ Switchboard	( )__________ Home Office
( )__________ Private	( )__________ Home Fax
( )__________ Fax	( )__________ Family Phone
( )__________ Fax (Secure)	( )__________ Vacation Home
( )__________ Secy./Asst.	( )__________ Home Office

Assistant(s) / **Secretary**(ies): __________ __________ __________

Spouse (if met or mentioned): __________ **Children** (if met): __________

Introduced by: __________ (of what company?) __________

Introducer's Relationship: ______________________________

Interviewer Reports to: ______________________________

Interviewer's Subordinates: ______________________________

____

____

Interviewer's Identifying Appearance: ______________________________

____

Interviewer's Manner / Rapport / Possible Subjective Agenda: ______________________________

____

____

____

____

INTERVIEW

INTERVIEW DE-BRIEFER

Seemed to Like about Me / Sold on: ______

Seemed *Not* to Like / Doubted: ______

Hobbies / Interests / Family / Personal Concerns and Social Causes (Don't voluntarily enter hazardous territory, but don't forget anything you happen to learn)**:** ______

About the Job:

Company or Business Unit (Name / Description / Location / Annual Sales / No. of Employees / Product Lines / Market Shares, etc.)**:** ______

Title: ______

Position reports to: ______

Subordinates reporting to this position:

	Title	# Subordinates	Doing What	$ Volume / Product Lines
1				
2				
3				
4				
5				
6				
7				
8				
9				
10				
11				
12				

Position being re-filled? Newly created? ______

What happened to the incumbent? ______

Are there inside candidates?______ **Their positions/names:**______

What abilities and experience are lacking among insiders that cause outsiders to be considered? ______

What are the #1 and #2 make-or-break skills or talents on which success in the job depends? ______

What are the #1 and #2 make-or-break achievements the person is expected to accomplish? ______

On what timetable? ______

With what resources? ______

What is the likely scenario for advancement? ______

What are the company's overall long-range and near-term strategies? ______

What are the long-range and near-term strategies for the particular division, business unit, department or function?______

Is this the kind of place I'd like to work?______ **Positive indications:**______

Negative Indications:______

Are their business ethics and human values consistent with mine?______ **Specific matches and mismatches:** ______

What is the corporate culture?______

Will I enjoy it? Fit in? ______

INTERVIEW DE-BRIEFER

Any discussion or clues with respect to money for this job? For other jobs in the company (a clue for later bargaining)? **Base? Bonus? Stock options, grants, etc? Perks and benefits** (don't inquire until job is landed and other particulars are nailed down)?

Will there be an Employment Contract? A *multi-year* contract? An 18-month (or other) **termination arrangement** (see Chapter 16 of *Rites*)? **Or will an Offer Letter incorporate basic understandings** (don't go ahead without it)?

What particulars that should be in a Contract or Offer Letter were covered in this meeting, i.e., responsibility, reporting relationship, location, title, compensation, employment security? What key items haven't been covered?

Anything else I learned at this meeting?

INTERVIEW DE-BRIEFER

NOTE: This comprehensive 4-page questionnaire debriefs you after *employment interviews*, not casual networking visits. It prompts you to jot down everything you find out, and helps prepare you for future selling, inquiring, negotiating, and decision-making. If you soak up everything you learn from everyone you talk to within the company (and perhaps close outside observers and former insiders as well), you can accumulate tremendous knowledge in a situation where "Knowledge is power!" (**Fill out afterward; don't reveal at interview.**)

Company: ______________________________

Person Seen: ______________________________

Exact Title (query secretary by phone): ______________________________

Date of Meeting:______________________ **Thank You Sent:** ____________

Time: ______________________________

Place: ______________________________

Address & Phone: **OFFICE** **HOME**

OFFICE		HOME	
( )____________	Switchboard	( )____________	Home Office
( )____________	Private	( )____________	Home Fax
( )____________	Fax	( )____________	Family Phone
( )____________	Fax (Secure)	( )____________	Vacation Home
( )____________	Secy./Asst.	( )____________	Home Office

Assistant(s) / **Secretary**(ies):____________ ____________ ____________

Spouse (if met or mentioned):____________ **Children** (if met): ____________

Introduced by:____________(of what company?) ____________

Introducer's Relationship:______________________________

Interviewer Reports to: ______________________________

Interviewer's Subordinates: ______________________________

Interviewer's Identifying Appearance: ______________________________

Interviewer's Manner / Rapport / Possible Subjective Agenda: ______________________________

INTERVIEW

INTERVIEW DE-BRIEFER

(CONTINUED, PAGE 2 OF 4)

Seemed to Like about Me / Sold on: ______________________________

____

____

Seemed *Not* to Like / Doubted: ______________________________

____

____

Hobbies / Interests / Family / Personal Concerns and Social Causes (Don't voluntarily enter hazardous territory, but don't forget anything you happen to learn)**:** ______________________________

____

____

About the Job:

Company or Business Unit (Name / Description / Location / Annual Sales / No. of Employees / Product Lines / Market Shares, etc.)**:** ______________________________

____

____

____

____

____

____

____

____

____

____

Title: ______________________________

____

Position reports to: ______________________________

____

Subordinates reporting to this position:

	Title	# Subordinates	Doing What	$ Volume / Product Lines
1				
2				
3				
4				
5				
6				
7				
8				
9				
10				
11				
12				

Position being re-filled? Newly created? ______________________

What happened to the incumbent? ______________________

Are there inside candidates?__________ **Their positions/names:**______________________

What abilities and experience are lacking among insiders that cause outsiders to be considered? ___

What are the #1 and #2 make-or-break skills or talents on which success in the job depends? ______

What are the #1 and #2 make-or-break achievements the person is expected to accomplish? _______

On what timetable? ______________________

With what resources? ______________________

What is the likely scenario for advancement? ______________________

What are the company's overall long-range and near-term strategies? ______________________

What are the long-range and near-term strategies for the particular division, business unit, department or function?______________________

Is this the kind of place I'd like to work?_________ **Positive indications:**______________________

Negative Indications:______________________

Are their business ethics and human values consistent with mine?__________ **Specific matches and mismatches:** ______________________

What is the corporate culture?______________________

Will I enjoy it? Fit in? ______________________

INTERVIEW DE-BRIEFER

Any discussion or clues with respect to money for this job? For other jobs in the company (a clue for later bargaining)**? Base? Bonus? Stock options, grants, etc? Perks and benefits** (don't inquire until job is landed and other particulars are nailed down)**?**

Will there be an Employment Contract? A *multi-year* contract? An 18-month (or other) **termination arrangement** (see Chapter 16 of *Rites*)**? Or will an Offer Letter incorporate basic understandings** (don't go ahead without it)**?**

What particulars that should be in a Contract or Offer Letter were covered in this meeting, i.e., responsibility, reporting relationship, location, title, compensation, employment security? What key items haven't been covered?

Anything else I learned at this meeting?

INTERVIEW DE-BRIEFER

NOTE: THIS COMPREHENSIVE 4-PAGE QUESTIONNAIRE DEBRIEFS YOU AFTER *EMPLOYMENT INTERVIEWS*, NOT CASUAL NETWORKING VISITS. IT PROMPTS YOU TO JOT DOWN EVERYTHING YOU FIND OUT, AND HELPS PREPARE YOU FOR FUTURE SELLING, INQUIRING, NEGOTIATING, AND DECISION-MAKING. IF YOU SOAK UP EVERYTHING YOU LEARN FROM EVERYONE YOU TALK TO WITHIN THE COMPANY (AND PERHAPS CLOSE OUTSIDE OBSERVERS AND FORMER INSIDERS AS WELL), YOU CAN ACCUMULATE TREMENDOUS KNOWLEDGE IN A SITUATION WHERE "KNOWLEDGE IS POWER!" (**FILL OUT AFTERWARD; DON'T REVEAL AT INTERVIEW.**)

Company: ______________________________

Person Seen: ______________________________

Exact Title (query secretary by phone): ______________________________

Date of Meeting: ______________________ **Thank You Sent:** ______________

Time: ______________________________

Place: ______________________________

Address & Phone: **OFFICE** **HOME**

OFFICE	HOME
______________________	______________________
______________________	______________________
______________________	______________________
______________________	______________________
( ) ____________ Switchboard	( ) ____________ Home Office
( ) ____________ Private	( ) ____________ Home Fax
( ) ____________ Fax	( ) ____________ Family Phone
( ) ____________ Fax (Secure)	( ) ____________ Vacation Home
( ) ____________ Secy./Asst.	( ) ____________ Home Office

Assistant(s) / **Secretary**(ies): ______________ ______________ ______________

Spouse (if met or mentioned): ______________ **Children** (if met): ______________

Introduced by: ______________________ (of what company?) ______________

Introducer's Relationship: ______________________________

Interviewer Reports to: ______________________________

Interviewer's Subordinates: ______________________________

____

____

Interviewer's Identifying Appearance: ______________________________

____

Interviewer's Manner / Rapport / Possible Subjective Agenda: ______________________________

____

____

____

____

INTERVIEW

INTERVIEW DE-BRIEFER

(CONTINUED, PAGE 2 OF 4)

Seemed to Like about Me / Sold on: ______

Seemed *Not* to Like / Doubted: ______

Hobbies / Interests / Family / Personal Concerns and Social Causes (Don't voluntarily enter hazardous territory, but don't forget anything you happen to learn)**:** ______

About the Job:

Company or Business Unit (Name / Description / Location / Annual Sales / No. of Employees / Product Lines / Market Shares, etc.)**:** ______

Title: ______

Position reports to: ______

Subordinates reporting to this position:

	Title	# Subordinates	Doing What	$ Volume / Product Lines
1				
2				
3				
4				
5				
6				
7				
8				
9				
10				
11				
12				

INTERVIEW DE-BRIEFER

(CONTINUED, PAGE 3 OF 4)

Position being re-filled? Newly created? ______

What happened to the incumbent? ______

Are there inside candidates?______ **Their positions/names:**______

What abilities and experience are lacking among insiders that cause outsiders to be considered? ______

What are the #1 and #2 make-or-break skills or talents on which success in the job depends? ______

What are the #1 and #2 make-or-break achievements the person is expected to accomplish? ______

On what timetable? ______

With what resources? ______

What is the likely scenario for advancement? ______

What are the company's overall long-range and near-term strategies? ______

What are the long-range and near-term strategies for the particular division, business unit, department or function?______

Is this the kind of place I'd like to work?______ **Positive indications:**______

Negative Indications:______

Are their business ethics and human values consistent with mine?______ **Specific matches and mismatches:** ______

What is the corporate culture?______

Will I enjoy it? Fit in? ______

INTERVIEW DE-BRIEFER

Any discussion or clues with respect to money for this job? For other jobs in the company (a clue for later bargaining)**? Base? Bonus? Stock options, grants, etc? Perks and benefits** (don't inquire until job is landed and other particulars are nailed down)**?**

Will there be an Employment Contract? A *multi-year* contract? An 18-month (or other) **termination arrangement** (see Chapter 16 of *Rites*)**? Or will an Offer Letter incorporate basic understandings** (don't go ahead without it)**?**

What particulars that should be in a Contract or Offer Letter were covered in this meeting, i.e., responsibility, reporting relationship, location, title, compensation, employment security? What key items haven't been covered?

Anything else I learned at this meeting?

NOTE: THIS COMPREHENSIVE 4-PAGE QUESTIONNAIRE DEBRIEFS YOU AFTER *EMPLOYMENT INTERVIEWS*, NOT CASUAL NETWORKING VISITS. IT PROMPTS YOU TO JOT DOWN EVERYTHING YOU FIND OUT, AND HELPS PREPARE YOU FOR FUTURE SELLING, INQUIRING, NEGOTIATING, AND DECISION-MAKING. IF YOU SOAK UP EVERYTHING YOU LEARN FROM EVERYONE YOU TALK TO WITHIN THE COMPANY (AND PERHAPS CLOSE OUTSIDE OBSERVERS AND FORMER INSIDERS AS WELL), YOU CAN ACCUMULATE TREMENDOUS KNOWLEDGE IN A SITUATION WHERE "KNOWLEDGE IS POWER!" (FILL OUT AFTERWARD; DON'T REVEAL AT INTERVIEW.)

Company: ____________________

Person Seen: ____________________

Exact Title (query secretary by phone): ____________________

Date of Meeting: ____________________ **Thank You Sent:** ____________________

Time: ____________________

Place: ____________________

Address & Phone: **OFFICE** **HOME**

OFFICE	HOME
____________________	____________________
____________________	____________________
____________________	____________________
____________________	____________________
( ) __________ Switchboard	( ) __________ Home Office
( ) __________ Private	( ) __________ Home Fax
( ) __________ Fax	( ) __________ Family Phone
( ) __________ Fax (Secure)	( ) __________ Vacation Home
( ) __________ Secy./Asst.	( ) __________ Home Office

Assistant(s) / **Secretary**(ies): __________ __________ __________

Spouse (if met or mentioned): __________ **Children** (if met): __________

Introduced by: __________ (of what company?) __________

Introducer's Relationship: ____________________

Interviewer Reports to: ____________________

Interviewer's Subordinates: ____________________

____

____

Interviewer's Identifying Appearance: ____________________

____

Interviewer's Manner / Rapport / Possible Subjective Agenda: ____________________

____

____

____

____

INTERVIEW DE-BRIEFER

Seemed to Like about Me / Sold on:

Seemed *Not* to Like / Doubted:

Hobbies / Interests / Family / Personal Concerns and Social Causes (Don't voluntarily enter hazardous territory, but don't forget anything you happen to learn):

About the Job:

Company or Business Unit (Name / Description / Location / Annual Sales / No. of Employees / Product Lines / Market Shares, etc.):

Title:

Position reports to:

Subordinates reporting to this position:

	Title	# Subordinates	Doing What	$ Volume / Product Lines
1				
2				
3				
4				
5				
6				
7				
8				
9				
10				
11				
12				

Position being re-filled? Newly created? ____________________

What happened to the incumbent? ____________________

Are there inside candidates?__________ **Their positions/names:**____________________

____

What abilities and experience are lacking among insiders that cause outsiders to be considered? ___

____

____

What are the #1 and #2 make-or-break skills or talents on which success in the job depends? ______

____

____

What are the #1 and #2 make-or-break achievements the person is expected to accomplish? _______

____

____

____

On what timetable? ____________________

With what resources? ____________________

____

What is the likely scenario for advancement? ____________________

____

What are the company's overall long-range and near-term strategies? ____________________

____

____

____

What are the long-range and near-term strategies for the particular division, business unit, department or function?____________________

____

____

____

Is this the kind of place I'd like to work?__________ **Positive indications:**____________________

____

____

Negative Indications:____________________

____

Are their business ethics and human values consistent with mine?__________ **Specific matches and mismatches:** ____________________

____

What is the corporate culture?____________________

____

Will I enjoy it? Fit in? ____________________

____

INTERVIEW DE-BRIEFER

Any discussion or clues with respect to money for this job? For other jobs in the company (a clue for later bargaining)? **Base? Bonus? Stock options, grants, etc? Perks and benefits** (don't inquire until job is landed and other particulars are nailed down)?____________________

Will there be an Employment Contract? A *multi-year* contract? An 18-month (or other) **termination arrangement** (see Chapter 16 of *Rites*)? **Or will an Offer Letter incorporate basic understandings** (don't go ahead without it)?____________________

What particulars that should be in a Contract or Offer Letter were covered in this meeting, i.e., responsibility, reporting relationship, location, title, compensation, employment security? What key items haven't been covered?____________________

Anything else I learned at this meeting?____________________

INTERVIEW

INTERVIEW DE-BRIEFER

NOTE: This comprehensive 4-page questionnaire debriefs you after *employment interviews*, not casual networking visits. It prompts you to jot down everything you find out, and helps prepare you for future selling, inquiring, negotiating, and decision-making. If you soak up everything you learn from everyone you talk to within the company (and perhaps close outside observers and former insiders as well), you can accumulate tremendous knowledge in a situation where "Knowledge is power!" (**Fill out afterward; don't reveal at interview.**)

Company: ____________________

Person Seen: ____________________

Exact Title (query secretary by phone): ____________________

Date of Meeting: ____________________ **Thank You Sent:** ____________________

Time: ____________________

Place: ____________________

Address & Phone: **OFFICE** **HOME**

OFFICE		HOME	
____________________		____________________	
____________________		____________________	
____________________		____________________	
____________________		____________________	
( )__________	Switchboard	( )__________	Home Office
( )__________	Private	( )__________	Home Fax
( )__________	Fax	( )__________	Family Phone
( )__________	Fax (Secure)	( )__________	Vacation Home
( )__________	Secy./Asst.	( )__________	Home Office

Assistant(s) / **Secretary**(ies): __________ __________ __________

Spouse (if met or mentioned): __________ **Children** (if met): __________

Introduced by: __________ (of what company?) __________

Introducer's Relationship: ____________________

Interviewer Reports to: ____________________

Interviewer's Subordinates: ____________________

____

____

Interviewer's Identifying Appearance: ____________________

____

Interviewer's Manner / Rapport / Possible Subjective Agenda: ____________________

____

____

____

____

INTERVIEW

INTERVIEW DE-BRIEFER

Seemed to Like about Me / Sold on: ____________________

Seemed *Not* to Like / Doubted: ____________________

Hobbies / Interests / Family / Personal Concerns and Social Causes (Don't voluntarily enter hazardous territory, but don't forget anything you happen to learn)**:** ____________________

About the Job:

Company or Business Unit (Name / Description / Location / Annual Sales / No. of Employees / Product Lines / Market Shares, etc.)**:** ____________________

Title: ____________________

Position reports to: ____________________

Subordinates reporting to this position:

	Title	# Subordinates	Doing What	$ Volume / Product Lines
1				
2				
3				
4				
5				
6				
7				
8				
9				
10				
11				
12				

INTERVIEW

INTERVIEW DE-BRIEFER

(CONTINUED, PAGE 3 OF 4)

Position being re-filled? Newly created? ____________________

What happened to the incumbent? ____________________

Are there inside candidates?__________ **Their positions/names:**____________________

____

What abilities and experience are lacking among insiders that cause outsiders to be considered? ___

____

____

What are the #1 and #2 make-or-break skills or talents on which success in the job depends? ______

____

____

What are the #1 and #2 make-or-break achievements the person is expected to accomplish? _______

____

____

____

On what timetable? ____________________

With what resources? ____________________

____

What is the likely scenario for advancement? ____________________

____

What are the company's overall long-range and near-term strategies? ____________________

____

____

____

What are the long-range and near-term strategies for the particular division, business unit, department or function?____________________

____

____

____

Is this the kind of place I'd like to work?__________ **Positive indications:**____________________

____

____

Negative Indications:____________________

____

Are their business ethics and human values consistent with mine?__________ **Specific matches and mismatches:** ____________________

____

What is the corporate culture?____________________

____

Will I enjoy it? Fit in? ____________________

____

INTERVIEW DE-BRIEFER

Any discussion or clues with respect to money for this job? For other jobs in the company (a clue for later bargaining)? **Base? Bonus? Stock options, grants, etc? Perks and benefits** (don't inquire until job is landed and other particulars are nailed down)?

Will there be an Employment Contract? A *multi-year* contract? An 18-month (or other) **termination arrangement** (see Chapter 16 of *Rites*)? **Or will an Offer Letter incorporate basic understandings** (don't go ahead without it)?

What particulars that should be in a Contract or Offer Letter were covered in this meeting, i.e., responsibility, reporting relationship, location, title, compensation, employment security? What key items haven't been covered?

Anything else I learned at this meeting?

INTERVIEW DE-BRIEFER

NOTE: THIS COMPREHENSIVE 4-PAGE QUESTIONNAIRE DEBRIEFS YOU AFTER *EMPLOYMENT INTERVIEWS*, NOT CASUAL NETWORKING VISITS. IT PROMPTS YOU TO JOT DOWN EVERYTHING YOU FIND OUT, AND HELPS PREPARE YOU FOR FUTURE SELLING, INQUIRING, NEGOTIATING, AND DECISION-MAKING. IF YOU SOAK UP EVERYTHING YOU LEARN FROM EVERYONE YOU TALK TO WITHIN THE COMPANY (AND PERHAPS CLOSE OUTSIDE OBSERVERS AND FORMER INSIDERS AS WELL), YOU CAN ACCUMULATE TREMENDOUS KNOWLEDGE IN A SITUATION WHERE "KNOWLEDGE IS POWER!" (**FILL OUT AFTERWARD; DON'T REVEAL AT INTERVIEW.**)

Company: ______________________

Person Seen: ______________________

Exact Title (query secretary by phone): ______________________

Date of Meeting: ______________ **Thank You Sent:** ______________

Time: ______________________

Place: ______________________

Address & Phone: **OFFICE** **HOME**

OFFICE	HOME
( ) ________ Switchboard	( ) ________ Home Office
( ) ________ Private	( ) ________ Home Fax
( ) ________ Fax	( ) ________ Family Phone
( ) ________ Fax (Secure)	( ) ________ Vacation Home
( ) ________ Secy./Asst.	( ) ________ Home Office

Assistant(s) / **Secretary**(ies): ________ ________ ________

Spouse (if met or mentioned): ________ **Children** (if met): ________

Introduced by: ________ (of what company?) ________

Introducer's Relationship: ______________________

Interviewer Reports to: ______________________

Interviewer's Subordinates: ______________________

Interviewer's Identifying Appearance: ______________________

Interviewer's Manner / Rapport / Possible Subjective Agenda: ______________________

INTERVIEW

INTERVIEW DE-BRIEFER

Seemed to Like about Me / Sold on: ______________________________

Seemed *Not* to Like / Doubted: ______________________________

Hobbies / Interests / Family / Personal Concerns and Social Causes (Don't voluntarily enter hazardous territory, but don't forget anything you happen to learn)**:** ______________________________

About the Job:

Company or Business Unit (Name / Description / Location / Annual Sales / No. of Employees / Product Lines / Market Shares, etc.)**:** ______________________________

Title: ______________________________

Position reports to: ______________________________

Subordinates reporting to this position:

	Title	# Subordinates	Doing What	$ Volume / Product Lines
1				
2				
3				
4				
5				
6				
7				
8				
9				
10				
11				
12				

INTERVIEW DE-BRIEFER

(CONTINUED, PAGE 3 OF 4)

Position being re-filled? Newly created? ______________________________

What happened to the incumbent? ______________________________

Are there inside candidates?__________ **Their positions/names:**______________________________

What abilities and experience are lacking among insiders that cause outsiders to be considered? ___

What are the #1 and #2 make-or-break skills or talents on which success in the job depends? ______

What are the #1 and #2 make-or-break achievements the person is expected to accomplish? _______

On what timetable? ______________________________

With what resources? ______________________________

What is the likely scenario for advancement? ______________________________

What are the company's overall long-range and near-term strategies? ______________________________

What are the long-range and near-term strategies for the particular division, business unit, department or function?______________________________

Is this the kind of place I'd like to work?__________ **Positive indications:**______________________________

Negative Indications:______________________________

Are their business ethics and human values consistent with mine?__________ **Specific matches and mismatches:** ______________________________

What is the corporate culture?______________________________

Will I enjoy it? Fit in? ______________________________

INTERVIEW DE-BRIEFER

Any discussion or clues with respect to money for this job? For other jobs in the company (a clue for later bargaining)? **Base? Bonus? Stock options, grants, etc? Perks and benefits** (don't inquire until job is landed and other particulars are nailed down)?

Will there be an Employment Contract? A *multi-year* contract? An 18-month (or other) **termination arrangement** (see Chapter 16 of *Rites*)? **Or will an Offer Letter incorporate basic understandings** (don't go ahead without it)?

What particulars that should be in a Contract or Offer Letter were covered in this meeting, i.e., responsibility, reporting relationship, location, title, compensation, employment security? What key items haven't been covered?

Anything else I learned at this meeting?

NOTE: This comprehensive 4-page questionnaire debriefs you after *employment interviews*, not casual networking visits. It prompts you to jot down everything you find out, and helps prepare you for future selling, inquiring, negotiating, and decision-making. If you soak up everything you learn from everyone you talk to within the company (and perhaps close outside observers and former insiders as well), you can accumulate tremendous knowledge in a situation where "Knowledge is power!" (**Fill out afterward; don't reveal at interview.**)

Company: ______

Person Seen: ______

Exact Title (query secretary by phone): ______

Date of Meeting: ______ **Thank You Sent:** ______

Time: ______

Place: ______

Address & Phone: **OFFICE** **HOME**

OFFICE	HOME
______	______
______	______
______	______
______	______
( )______ Switchboard	( )______ Home Office
( )______ Private	( )______ Home Fax
( )______ Fax	( )______ Family Phone
( )______ Fax (Secure)	( )______ Vacation Home
( )______ Secy./Asst.	( )______ Home Office

Assistant(s) / **Secretary**(ies): ______ ______ ______

Spouse (if met or mentioned): ______ **Children** (if met): ______

Introduced by: ______ (of what company?) ______

Introducer's Relationship: ______

Interviewer Reports to: ______

Interviewer's Subordinates: ______

______

______

Interviewer's Identifying Appearance: ______

______

Interviewer's Manner / Rapport / Possible Subjective Agenda: ______

______

______

______

______

INTERVIEW

INTERVIEW DE-BRIEFER

Seemed to Like about Me / Sold on: ______

Seemed *Not* to Like / Doubted: ______

Hobbies / Interests / Family / Personal Concerns and Social Causes (Don't voluntarily enter hazardous territory, but don't forget anything you happen to learn)**:** ______

About the Job:

Company or Business Unit (Name / Description / Location / Annual Sales / No. of Employees / Product Lines / Market Shares, etc.)**:** ______

Title: ______

Position reports to: ______

Subordinates reporting to this position:

	Title	# Subordinates	Doing What	$ Volume / Product Lines
1				
2				
3				
4				
5				
6				
7				
8				
9				
10				
11				
12				

Position being re-filled? Newly created? ____________________

What happened to the incumbent? ____________________

Are there inside candidates?________ **Their positions/names:**____________________

____

What abilities and experience are lacking among insiders that cause outsiders to be considered? ___

____

____

What are the #1 and #2 make-or-break skills or talents on which success in the job depends? ______

____

____

What are the #1 and #2 make-or-break achievements the person is expected to accomplish? _______

____

____

____

On what timetable? ____________________

With what resources? ____________________

____

What is the likely scenario for advancement? ____________________

____

What are the company's overall long-range and near-term strategies? ____________________

____

____

____

What are the long-range and near-term strategies for the particular division, business unit, department or function?____________________

____

____

____

Is this the kind of place I'd like to work?________ **Positive indications:**____________________

____

____

Negative Indications:____________________

____

Are their business ethics and human values consistent with mine?_________ **Specific matches and mismatches:** ____________________

____

What is the corporate culture?____________________

____

Will I enjoy it? Fit in? ____________________

____

INTERVIEW DE-BRIEFER

Any discussion or clues with respect to money for this job? For other jobs in the company (a clue for later bargaining)**? Base? Bonus? Stock options, grants, etc? Perks and benefits** (don't inquire until job is landed and other particulars are nailed down)?

Will there be an Employment Contract? A *multi-year* contract? An 18-month (or other) **termination arrangement** (see Chapter 16 of *Rites*)**? Or will an Offer Letter incorporate basic understandings** (don't go ahead without it)?

What particulars that should be in a Contract or Offer Letter were covered in this meeting, i.e., responsibility, reporting relationship, location, title, compensation, employment security? What key items haven't been covered?

Anything else I learned at this meeting?

NOTE: This comprehensive 4-page questionnaire debriefs you after *employment interviews*, not casual networking visits. It prompts you to jot down everything you find out, and helps prepare you for future selling, inquiring, negotiating, and decision-making. If you soak up everything you learn from everyone you talk to within the company (and perhaps close outside observers and former insiders as well), you can accumulate tremendous knowledge in a situation where "Knowledge is power!" (**Fill out afterward; don't reveal at interview.**)

Company: ______

Person Seen: ______

Exact Title (query secretary by phone): ______

Date of Meeting: ______ **Thank You Sent:** ______

Time: ______

Place: ______

Address & Phone: **OFFICE** **HOME**

OFFICE		HOME	
______		______	
______		______	
______		______	
______		______	
( )______	Switchboard	( )______	Home Office
( )______	Private	( )______	Home Fax
( )______	Fax	( )______	Family Phone
( )______	Fax (Secure)	( )______	Vacation Home
( )______	Secy./Asst.	( )______	Home Office

Assistant(s) / **Secretary**(ies): ______ ______ ______

Spouse (if met or mentioned): ______ **Children** (if met): ______

Introduced by: ______ (of what company?) ______

Introducer's Relationship: ______

Interviewer Reports to: ______

Interviewer's Subordinates: ______

______

______

Interviewer's Identifying Appearance: ______

______

Interviewer's Manner / Rapport / Possible Subjective Agenda: ______

______

______

______

______

INTERVIEW

INTERVIEW DE-BRIEFER

Seemed to Like about Me / Sold on: ______________________

Seemed *Not* to Like / Doubted: ______________________

Hobbies / Interests / Family / Personal Concerns and Social Causes (Don't voluntarily enter hazardous territory, but don't forget anything you happen to learn)**:** ______________________

About the Job:

Company or Business Unit (Name / Description / Location / Annual Sales / No. of Employees / Product Lines / Market Shares, etc.)**:** ______________________

Title: ______________________

Position reports to: ______________________

Subordinates reporting to this position:

	Title	# Subordinates	Doing What	$ Volume / Product Lines
1				
2				
3				
4				
5				
6				
7				
8				
9				
10				
11				
12				

INTERVIEW

INTERVIEW DE-BRIEFER

(CONTINUED, PAGE 3 OF 4)

Position being re-filled? Newly created? ______

What happened to the incumbent? ______

Are there inside candidates?______ **Their positions/names:**______

What abilities and experience are lacking among insiders that cause outsiders to be considered? ______

What are the #1 and #2 make-or-break skills or talents on which success in the job depends? ______

What are the #1 and #2 make-or-break achievements the person is expected to accomplish? ______

On what timetable? ______

With what resources? ______

What is the likely scenario for advancement? ______

What are the company's overall long-range and near-term strategies? ______

What are the long-range and near-term strategies for the particular division, business unit, department or function?______

Is this the kind of place I'd like to work?______ **Positive indications:**______

Negative Indications:______

Are their business ethics and human values consistent with mine?______ **Specific matches and mismatches:** ______

What is the corporate culture?______

Will I enjoy it? Fit in? ______

INTERVIEW DE-BRIEFER

Any discussion or clues with respect to money for this job? For other jobs in the company (a clue for later bargaining)? **Base? Bonus? Stock options, grants, etc? Perks and benefits** (don't inquire until job is landed and other particulars are nailed down)?

Will there be an Employment Contract? A *multi-year* contract? An 18-month (or other) **termination arrangement** (see Chapter 16 of *Rites*)? **Or will an Offer Letter incorporate basic understandings** (don't go ahead without it)?

What particulars that should be in a Contract or Offer Letter were covered in this meeting, i.e., responsibility, reporting relationship, location, title, compensation, employment security? What key items haven't been covered?

Anything else I learned at this meeting?

NOTE: This comprehensive 4-page questionnaire debriefs you after *employment interviews*, not casual networking visits. It prompts you to jot down everything you find out, and helps prepare you for future selling, inquiring, negotiating, and decision-making. If you soak up everything you learn from everyone you talk to within the company (and perhaps close outside observers and former insiders as well), you can accumulate tremendous knowledge in a situation where "Knowledge is power!" (**Fill out afterward; don't reveal at interview.**)

Company: ______________________

Person Seen: ______________________

Exact Title (query secretary by phone): ______________________

Date of Meeting: ______________________ **Thank You Sent:** ______________________

Time: ______________________

Place: ______________________

Address & Phone:

OFFICE	HOME
______________________	______________________
______________________	______________________
______________________	______________________
______________________	______________________
( ) __________ Switchboard	( ) __________ Home Office
( ) __________ Private	( ) __________ Home Fax
( ) __________ Fax	( ) __________ Family Phone
( ) __________ Fax (Secure)	( ) __________ Vacation Home
( ) __________ Secy./Asst.	( ) __________ Home Office

Assistant(s) / **Secretary**(ies): ______________ ______________ ______________

Spouse (if met or mentioned): ______________ **Children** (if met): ______________

Introduced by: ______________ (of what company?) ______________

Introducer's Relationship: ______________________

Interviewer Reports to: ______________________

Interviewer's Subordinates: ______________________

____

____

Interviewer's Identifying Appearance: ______________________

____

Interviewer's Manner / Rapport / Possible Subjective Agenda: ______________________

____

____

____

____

INTERVIEW

INTERVIEW DE-BRIEFER

Seemed to Like about Me / Sold on: ______________________________

Seemed *Not* to Like / Doubted: ______________________________

Hobbies / Interests / Family / Personal Concerns and Social Causes (Don't voluntarily enter hazardous territory, but don't forget anything you happen to learn): ______________________________

About the Job:

Company or Business Unit (Name / Description / Location / Annual Sales / No. of Employees / Product Lines / Market Shares, etc.): ______________________________

Title: ______________________________

Position reports to: ______________________________

Subordinates reporting to this position:

	Title	# Subordinates	Doing What	$ Volume / Product Lines
1				
2				
3				
4				
5				
6				
7				
8				
9				
10				
11				
12				

Position being re-filled? Newly created? ______

What happened to the incumbent? ______

Are there inside candidates? ______ **Their positions/names:** ______

What abilities and experience are lacking among insiders that cause outsiders to be considered? ______

What are the #1 and #2 make-or-break skills or talents on which success in the job depends? ______

What are the #1 and #2 make-or-break achievements the person is expected to accomplish? ______

On what timetable? ______

With what resources? ______

What is the likely scenario for advancement? ______

What are the company's overall long-range and near-term strategies? ______

What are the long-range and near-term strategies for the particular division, business unit, department or function? ______

Is this the kind of place I'd like to work? ______ **Positive indications:** ______

Negative Indications: ______

Are their business ethics and human values consistent with mine? ______ **Specific matches and mismatches:** ______

What is the corporate culture? ______

Will I enjoy it? Fit in? ______

INTERVIEW DE-BRIEFER

Any discussion or clues with respect to money for this job? For other jobs in the company (a clue for later bargaining)? **Base? Bonus? Stock options, grants, etc? Perks and benefits** (don't inquire until job is landed and other particulars are nailed down)?

Will there be an Employment Contract? A *multi-year* contract? An 18-month (or other) **termination arrangement** (see Chapter 16 of *Rites*)? **Or will an Offer Letter incorporate basic understandings** (don't go ahead without it)?

What particulars that should be in a Contract or Offer Letter were covered in this meeting, i.e., responsibility, reporting relationship, location, title, compensation, employment security? What key items haven't been covered?

Anything else I learned at this meeting?

NOTE: This comprehensive 4-page questionnaire debriefs you after *employment interviews*, not casual networking visits. It prompts you to jot down everything you find out, and helps prepare you for future selling, inquiring, negotiating, and decision-making. If you soak up everything you learn from everyone you talk to within the company (and perhaps close outside observers and former insiders as well), you can accumulate tremendous knowledge in a situation where "Knowledge is power!" (**Fill out afterward; don't reveal at interview.**)

Company: ____________________

Person Seen: ____________________

Exact Title (query secretary by phone): ____________________

Date of Meeting: ____________________ **Thank You Sent:** ____________________

Time: ____________________

Place: ____________________

Address & Phone:

OFFICE	HOME
____________________	____________________
____________________	____________________
____________________	____________________
____________________	____________________
( )__________ Switchboard	( )__________ Home Office
( )__________ Private	( )__________ Home Fax
( )__________ Fax	( )__________ Family Phone
( )__________ Fax (Secure)	( )__________ Vacation Home
( )__________ Secy./Asst.	( )__________ Home Office

Assistant(s) / **Secretary**(ies): __________ __________ __________

Spouse (if met or mentioned): __________ **Children** (if met): __________

Introduced by: __________ (of what company?) __________

Introducer's Relationship: ____________________

Interviewer Reports to: ____________________

Interviewer's Subordinates: ____________________

____

____

Interviewer's Identifying Appearance: ____________________

____

Interviewer's Manner / Rapport / Possible Subjective Agenda: ____________________

____

____

____

INTERVIEW DE-BRIEFER

Seemed to Like about Me / Sold on: ______

Seemed *Not* to Like / Doubted: ______

Hobbies / Interests / Family / Personal Concerns and Social Causes (Don't voluntarily enter hazardous territory, but don't forget anything you happen to learn)**:** ______

About the Job:

Company or Business Unit (Name / Description / Location / Annual Sales / No. of Employees / Product Lines / Market Shares, etc.)**:** ______

Title: ______

Position reports to: ______

Subordinates reporting to this position:

	Title	# Subordinates	Doing What	$ Volume / Product Lines
1				
2				
3				
4				
5				
6				
7				
8				
9				
10				
11				
12				

INTERVIEW DE-BRIEFER

(CONTINUED, PAGE 3 OF 4)

Position being re-filled? Newly created? ______

What happened to the incumbent? ______

Are there inside candidates?______ **Their positions/names:**______

What abilities and experience are lacking among insiders that cause outsiders to be considered? ______

What are the #1 and #2 make-or-break skills or talents on which success in the job depends? ______

What are the #1 and #2 make-or-break achievements the person is expected to accomplish? ______

On what timetable? ______

With what resources? ______

What is the likely scenario for advancement? ______

What are the company's overall long-range and near-term strategies? ______

What are the long-range and near-term strategies for the particular division, business unit, department or function?______

Is this the kind of place I'd like to work?______ **Positive indications:**______

Negative Indications:______

Are their business ethics and human values consistent with mine?______ **Specific matches and mismatches:** ______

What is the corporate culture?______

Will I enjoy it? Fit in? ______

INTERVIEW DE-BRIEFER

Any discussion or clues with respect to money for this job? For other jobs in the company (a clue for later bargaining)? **Base? Bonus? Stock options, grants, etc? Perks and benefits** (don't inquire until job is landed and other particulars are nailed down)?

Will there be an Employment Contract? A *multi-year* contract? An 18-month (or other) **termination arrangement** (see Chapter 16 of *Rites*)? **Or will an Offer Letter incorporate basic understandings** (don't go ahead without it)?

What particulars that should be in a Contract or Offer Letter were covered in this meeting, i.e., responsibility, reporting relationship, location, title, compensation, employment security? What key items haven't been covered?

Anything else I learned at this meeting?

INTERVIEW

NOTE: This comprehensive 4-page questionnaire debriefs you after *employment interviews*, not casual networking visits. It prompts you to jot down everything you find out, and helps prepare you for future selling, inquiring, negotiating, and decision-making. If you soak up everything you learn from everyone you talk to within the company (and perhaps close outside observers and former insiders as well), you can accumulate tremendous knowledge in a situation where "Knowledge is power!" (Fill out afterward; don't reveal at interview.)

Company: ______________________________

Person Seen: ______________________________

Exact Title (query secretary by phone): ______________________________

Date of Meeting: ____________________ **Thank You Sent:** ____________

Time: ______________________________

Place: ______________________________

Address & Phone: **OFFICE** **HOME**

OFFICE		HOME	
____________		____________	
____________		____________	
____________		____________	
____________		____________	
( ) ____________	Switchboard	( ) ____________	Home Office
( ) ____________	Private	( ) ____________	Home Fax
( ) ____________	Fax	( ) ____________	Family Phone
( ) ____________	Fax (Secure)	( ) ____________	Vacation Home
( ) ____________	Secy./Asst.	( ) ____________	Home Office

Assistant(s) / **Secretary**(ies): ____________ ____________ ____________

Spouse (if met or mentioned): ____________ **Children** (if met): ____________

Introduced by: ____________ (of what company?) ____________

Introducer's Relationship: ______________________________

Interviewer Reports to: ______________________________

Interviewer's Subordinates: ______________________________

____

____

Interviewer's Identifying Appearance: ______________________________

____

Interviewer's Manner / Rapport / Possible Subjective Agenda: ______________________________

____

____

____

____

INTERVIEW

INTERVIEW DE-BRIEFER

Seemed to Like about Me / Sold on: ______

Seemed *Not* to Like / Doubted: ______

Hobbies / Interests / Family / Personal Concerns and Social Causes (Don't voluntarily enter hazardous territory, but don't forget anything you happen to learn)**:** ______

About the Job:

Company or Business Unit (Name / Description / Location / Annual Sales / No. of Employees / Product Lines / Market Shares, etc.)**:** ______

Title: ______

Position reports to: ______

Subordinates reporting to this position:

	Title	# Subordinates	Doing What	$ Volume / Product Lines
1				
2				
3				
4				
5				
6				
7				
8				
9				
10				
11				
12				

Position being re-filled? Newly created? ______

What happened to the incumbent? ______

Are there inside candidates?______ **Their positions/names:**______

What abilities and experience are lacking among insiders that cause outsiders to be considered? ______

What are the #1 and #2 make-or-break skills or talents on which success in the job depends? ______

What are the #1 and #2 make-or-break achievements the person is expected to accomplish? ______

On what timetable? ______

With what resources? ______

What is the likely scenario for advancement? ______

What are the company's overall long-range and near-term strategies? ______

What are the long-range and near-term strategies for the particular division, business unit, department or function?______

Is this the kind of place I'd like to work?______ **Positive indications:**______

Negative Indications:______

Are their business ethics and human values consistent with mine?______ **Specific matches and mismatches:** ______

What is the corporate culture?______

Will I enjoy it? Fit in? ______

INTERVIEW DE-BRIEFER

Any discussion or clues with respect to money for this job? For other jobs in the company (a clue for later bargaining)? **Base? Bonus? Stock options, grants, etc? Perks and benefits** (don't inquire until job is landed and other particulars are nailed down)?

Will there be an Employment Contract? A *multi-year* contract? An 18-month (or other) **termination arrangement** (see Chapter 16 of *Rites*)? **Or will an Offer Letter incorporate basic understandings** (don't go ahead without it)?

What particulars that should be in a Contract or Offer Letter were covered in this meeting, i.e., responsibility, reporting relationship, location, title, compensation, employment security? What key items haven't been covered?

Anything else I learned at this meeting?

INTERVIEW DE-BRIEFER

NOTE: This comprehensive 4-page questionnaire debriefs you after *employment interviews*, not casual networking visits. It prompts you to jot down everything you find out, and helps prepare you for future selling, inquiring, negotiating, and decision-making. If you soak up everything you learn from everyone you talk to within the company (and perhaps close outside observers and former insiders as well), you can accumulate tremendous knowledge in a situation where "Knowledge is power!" (**Fill out afterward; don't reveal at interview.**)

Company: ____________________

Person Seen: ____________________

Exact Title (query secretary by phone): ____________________

Date of Meeting: ____________________ **Thank You Sent:** ____________________

Time: ____________________

Place: ____________________

Address & Phone:

OFFICE		HOME	
____________________		____________________	
____________________		____________________	
____________________		____________________	
____________________		____________________	
( ) ____________	Switchboard	( ) ____________	Home Office
( ) ____________	Private	( ) ____________	Home Fax
( ) ____________	Fax	( ) ____________	Family Phone
( ) ____________	Fax (Secure)	( ) ____________	Vacation Home
( ) ____________	Secy./Asst.	( ) ____________	Home Office

Assistant(s) / **Secretary**(ies): ____________ ____________ ____________

Spouse (if met or mentioned): ____________ **Children** (if met): ____________

Introduced by: ____________ (of what company?) ____________

Introducer's Relationship: ____________________

Interviewer Reports to: ____________________

Interviewer's Subordinates: ____________________

____

____

Interviewer's Identifying Appearance: ____________________

____

Interviewer's Manner / Rapport / Possible Subjective Agenda: ____________________

____

____

____

____

INTERVIEW DE-BRIEFER

(Continued, page 2 of 4)

Seemed to Like about Me / Sold on: ______

Seemed *Not* to Like / Doubted: ______

Hobbies / Interests / Family / Personal Concerns and Social Causes (Don't voluntarily enter hazardous territory, but don't forget anything you happen to learn)**:** ______

About the Job:

Company or Business Unit (Name / Description / Location / Annual Sales / No. of Employees / Product Lines / Market Shares, etc.)**:** ______

Title: ______

Position reports to: ______

Subordinates reporting to this position:

	Title	# Subordinates	Doing What	$ Volume / Product Lines
1				
2				
3				
4				
5				
6				
7				
8				
9				
10				
11				
12				

Position being re-filled? Newly created? ______________________________

What happened to the incumbent? ______________________________

Are there inside candidates?_________ **Their positions/names:**______________________________

What abilities and experience are lacking among insiders that cause outsiders to be considered? ___

What are the #1 and #2 make-or-break skills or talents on which success in the job depends? ______

What are the #1 and #2 make-or-break achievements the person is expected to accomplish? _______

On what timetable? ______________________________

With what resources? ______________________________

What is the likely scenario for advancement? ______________________________

What are the company's overall long-range and near-term strategies? ______________________________

What are the long-range and near-term strategies for the particular division, business unit, department or function?______________________________

Is this the kind of place I'd like to work?_________ **Positive indications:**______________________________

Negative Indications:______________________________

Are their business ethics and human values consistent with mine?_________ **Specific matches and mismatches:** ______________________________

What is the corporate culture?______________________________

Will I enjoy it? Fit in? ______________________________

INTERVIEW

INTERVIEW DE-BRIEFER

Any discussion or clues with respect to money for this job? For other jobs in the company (a clue for later bargaining)? **Base? Bonus? Stock options, grants, etc? Perks and benefits** (don't inquire until job is landed and other particulars are nailed down)?

Will there be an Employment Contract? A *multi-year* contract? An 18-month (or other) **termination arrangement** (see Chapter 16 of *Rites*)? **Or will an Offer Letter incorporate basic understandings** (don't go ahead without it)?

What particulars that should be in a Contract or Offer Letter were covered in this meeting, i.e., responsibility, reporting relationship, location, title, compensation, employment security? What key items haven't been covered?

Anything else I learned at this meeting?

INTERVIEW DE-BRIEFER

NOTE: This comprehensive 4-page questionnaire debriefs you after *employment interviews*, not casual networking visits. It prompts you to jot down everything you find out, and helps prepare you for future selling, inquiring, negotiating, and decision-making. If you soak up everything you learn from everyone you talk to within the company (and perhaps close outside observers and former insiders as well), you can accumulate tremendous knowledge in a situation where "Knowledge is power!" (**Fill out afterward; don't reveal at interview.**)

Company: ______________________

Person Seen: ______________________

Exact Title (query secretary by phone): ______________________

Date of Meeting: ______________________ **Thank You Sent:** ____________

Time: ______________________

Place: ______________________

Address & Phone: **OFFICE** **HOME**

OFFICE		HOME	
( ) ______	Switchboard	( ) ______	Home Office
( ) ______	Private	( ) ______	Home Fax
( ) ______	Fax	( ) ______	Family Phone
( ) ______	Fax (Secure)	( ) ______	Vacation Home
( ) ______	Secy./Asst.	( ) ______	Home Office

Assistant(s) / **Secretary**(ies): ____________ ____________ ____________

Spouse (if met or mentioned): ____________ **Children** (if met): ____________

Introduced by: ____________ (of what company?) ____________

Introducer's Relationship: ______________________

Interviewer Reports to: ______________________

Interviewer's Subordinates: ______________________

Interviewer's Identifying Appearance: ______________________

Interviewer's Manner / Rapport / Possible Subjective Agenda: ______________________

INTERVIEW

INTERVIEW DE-BRIEFER

Seemed to Like about Me / Sold on: ______

Seemed *Not* to Like / Doubted: ______

Hobbies / Interests / Family / Personal Concerns and Social Causes (Don't voluntarily enter hazardous territory, but don't forget anything you happen to learn)**:** ______

About the Job:

Company or Business Unit (Name / Description / Location / Annual Sales / No. of Employees / Product Lines / Market Shares, etc.)**:** ______

Title: ______

Position reports to: ______

Subordinates reporting to this position:

	Title	# Subordinates	Doing What	$ Volume / Product Lines
1				
2				
3				
4				
5				
6				
7				
8				
9				
10				
11				
12				

INTERVIEW DE-BRIEFER

(CONTINUED, PAGE 3 OF 4)

Position being re-filled? Newly created? ______________________________

What happened to the incumbent? ______________________________

Are there inside candidates?________ **Their positions/names:**______________________________

____

What abilities and experience are lacking among insiders that cause outsiders to be considered? ___

____

____

What are the #1 and #2 make-or-break skills or talents on which success in the job depends? ______

____

____

What are the #1 and #2 make-or-break achievements the person is expected to accomplish? _______

____

____

____

On what timetable? ______________________________

With what resources? ______________________________

____

What is the likely scenario for advancement? ______________________________

____

What are the company's overall long-range and near-term strategies? ______________________________

____

____

____

What are the long-range and near-term strategies for the particular division, business unit, department or function?______________________________

____

____

____

Is this the kind of place I'd like to work?________ **Positive indications:**______________________________

____

____

Negative Indications:______________________________

____

Are their business ethics and human values consistent with mine?_________ **Specific matches and mismatches:** ______________________________

____

What is the corporate culture?______________________________

____

Will I enjoy it? Fit in? ______________________________

____

INTERVIEW DE-BRIEFER

Any discussion or clues with respect to money for this job? For other jobs in the company (a clue for later bargaining)? **Base? Bonus? Stock options, grants, etc? Perks and benefits** (don't inquire until job is landed and other particulars are nailed down)?

Will there be an Employment Contract? A *multi-year* contract? An 18-month (or other) **termination arrangement** (see Chapter 16 of *Rites*)? **Or will an Offer Letter incorporate basic understandings** (don't go ahead without it)?

What particulars that should be in a Contract or Offer Letter were covered in this meeting, i.e., responsibility, reporting relationship, location, title, compensation, employment security? What key items haven't been covered?

Anything else I learned at this meeting?

INTERVIEW

INTERVIEW DE-BRIEFER

NOTE: This comprehensive 4-page questionnaire debriefs you after *employment interviews*, not casual networking visits. It prompts you to jot down everything you find out, and helps prepare you for future selling, inquiring, negotiating, and decision-making. If you soak up everything you learn from everyone you talk to within the company (and perhaps close outside observers and former insiders as well), you can accumulate tremendous knowledge in a situation where "Knowledge is power!" (**Fill out afterward; don't reveal at interview.**)

Company: ____________________

Person Seen: ____________________

Exact Title (query secretary by phone): ____________________

Date of Meeting: ____________________ **Thank You Sent:** ____________________

Time: ____________________

Place: ____________________

Address & Phone:

OFFICE	HOME
____________________	____________________
____________________	____________________
____________________	____________________
____________________	____________________
( )__________ Switchboard	( )__________ Home Office
( )__________ Private	( )__________ Home Fax
( )__________ Fax	( )__________ Family Phone
( )__________ Fax (Secure)	( )__________ Vacation Home
( )__________ Secy./Asst.	( )__________ Home Office

Assistant(s) / **Secretary**(ies): __________ __________ __________

Spouse (if met or mentioned): __________ **Children** (if met): __________

Introduced by: __________ (of what company?) __________

Introducer's Relationship: ____________________

Interviewer Reports to: ____________________

Interviewer's Subordinates: ____________________

____

____

Interviewer's Identifying Appearance: ____________________

____

Interviewer's Manner / Rapport / Possible Subjective Agenda: ____________________

____

____

____

____

INTERVIEW

INTERVIEW DE-BRIEFER

Seemed to Like about Me / Sold on: ______________________________

Seemed *Not* to Like / Doubted: ______________________________

Hobbies / Interests / Family / Personal Concerns and Social Causes (Don't voluntarily enter hazardous territory, but don't forget anything you happen to learn)**:** ______________________________

About the Job:

Company or Business Unit (Name / Description / Location / Annual Sales / No. of Employees / Product Lines / Market Shares, etc.)**:** ______________________________

Title: ______________________________

Position reports to: ______________________________

Subordinates reporting to this position:

	Title	# Subordinates	Doing What	$ Volume / Product Lines
1				
2				
3				
4				
5				
6				
7				
8				
9				
10				
11				
12				

Position being re-filled? Newly created? ____________________

What happened to the incumbent? ____________________

Are there inside candidates?__________ **Their positions/names:**____________________

What abilities and experience are lacking among insiders that cause outsiders to be considered? ____

What are the #1 and #2 make-or-break skills or talents on which success in the job depends? ____

What are the #1 and #2 make-or-break achievements the person is expected to accomplish? ____

On what timetable? ____________________

With what resources? ____________________

What is the likely scenario for advancement? ____________________

What are the company's overall long-range and near-term strategies? ____________________

What are the long-range and near-term strategies for the particular division, business unit, department or function?____________________

Is this the kind of place I'd like to work?__________ **Positive indications:**____________________

Negative Indications:____________________

Are their business ethics and human values consistent with mine?__________ **Specific matches and mismatches:** ____________________

What is the corporate culture?____________________

Will I enjoy it? Fit in? ____________________

INTERVIEW DE-BRIEFER

Any discussion or clues with respect to money for this job? For other jobs in the company (a clue for later bargaining)? **Base? Bonus? Stock options, grants, etc? Perks and benefits** (don't inquire until job is landed and other particulars are nailed down)?

Will there be an Employment Contract? A *multi-year* contract? An 18-month (or other) **termination arrangement** (see Chapter 16 of *Rites*)? **Or will an Offer Letter incorporate basic understandings** (don't go ahead without it)?

What particulars that should be in a Contract or Offer Letter were covered in this meeting, i.e., responsibility, reporting relationship, location, title, compensation, employment security? What key items haven't been covered?

Anything else I learned at this meeting?

Tax / Expense Tools

Please turn the page for an ample supply of monthly expense sheets. You certainly don't want to forget any job-changing costs that may be deductible when tax time rolls around.

Please read Chapter 6 of the Workbook (page 237) before using these forms. Here, too, there's a more-than-ample supply. Again we're carrying an umbrella to assure sunshine. Having plenty is insurance against needing a lot and running short.

TAX / EXPENSES

Month of _______________________(Start)

Date	Mileage	Car Rental Gas / Tolls	Taxis	Air Fares Railroad	Phone	Hotel	Meals Entertain	Equipment Software	Printing Secretarial	Postage Overnight	Daily Totals
1											
2											
3											
4											
5											
6											
7											
8											
9											
10											
11											
12											
13											
14											
15											
16											
Category Totals											

Month of ______________________(Finish)

Date	Mileage	Car Rental Gas / Tolls	Taxis	Air Fares Railroad	Phone	Hotel	Meals Entertain	Equipment Software	Printing Secretarial	Postage Overnight		Daily Totals
17												
18												
19												
20												
21												
22												
23												
24												
25												
26												
27												
28												
29												
30												
31												
Category Totals												
Entire Month												Month's Total

EXPENSES

TAX / EXPENSES

Month of ________________________(Start)

Date	Mileage	Car Rental Gas / Tolls	Taxis	Air Fares Railroad	Phone	Hotel	Meals Entertain	Equipment Software	Printing Secretarial	Postage Overnight	Daily Totals
1											
2											
3											
4											
5											
6											
7											
8											
9											
10											
11											
12											
13											
14											
15											
16											
Category Totals											

Month of ________________________(Finish)

Date	Mileage	Car Rental Gas / Tolls	Taxis	Air Fares Railroad	Phone	Hotel	Meals Entertain	Equipment Software	Printing Secretarial	Postage Overnight	Daily Totals
17											
18											
19											
20											
21											
22											
23											
24											
25											
26											
27											
28											
29											
30											
31											
Category Totals											
Entire Month											Month's Total

EXPENSES

TAX / EXPENSES

Month of ________________________(Start)

Date	Mileage	Car Rental Gas / Tolls	Taxis	Air Fares Railroad	Phone	Hotel	Meals Entertain	Equipment Software	Printing Secretarial	Postage Overnight	Daily Totals
1											
2											
3											
4											
5											
6											
7											
8											
9											
10											
11											
12											
13											
14											
15											
16											
Category Totals											

Month of ____________________(Finish)

Date	Mileage	Car Rental Gas / Tolls	Taxis	Air Fares Railroad	Phone	Hotel	Meals Entertain	Equipment Software	Printing Secretarial	Postage Overnight	Daily Totals
17											
18											
19											
20											
21											
22											
23											
24											
25											
26											
27											
28											
29											
30											
31											
Category Totals											
Entire Month											Month's Total

TAX / EXPENSES

Month of ______________________(Start)

Date	Mileage	Car Rental Gas / Tolls	Taxis	Air Fares Railroad	Phone	Hotel	Meals Entertain	Equipment Software	Printing Secretarial	Postage Overnight	Daily Totals
1											
2											
3											
4											
5											
6											
7											
8											
9											
10											
11											
12											
13											
14											
15											
16											
Category Totals											

Month of ____________________(Finish)

Date	Mileage	Car Rental Gas / Tolls	Taxis	Air Fares Railroad	Phone	Hotel	Meals Entertain	Equipment Software	Printing Secretarial	Postage Overnight	Daily Totals
17											
18											
19											
20											
21											
22											
23											
24											
25											
26											
27											
28											
29											
30											
31											
Category Totals											
Entire Month											Month's Total

EXPENSES

TAX / EXPENSES

Month of ________________________(Start)

Date	Mileage	Car Rental Gas / Tolls	Taxis	Air Fares Railroad	Phone	Hotel	Meals Entertain	Equipment Software	Printing Secretarial	Postage Overnight	Daily Totals
1											
2											
3											
4											
5											
6											
7											
8											
9											
10											
11											
12											
13											
14											
15											
16											
Category Totals											

EXPENSES

Month of ______________________(Finish)

Date	Mileage	Car Rental Gas / Tolls	Taxis	Air Fares Railroad	Phone	Hotel	Meals Entertain	Equipment Software	Printing Secretarial	Postage Overnight	Daily Totals
17											
18											
19											
20											
21											
22											
23											
24											
25											
26											
27											
28											
29											
30											
31											
Category Totals											
Entire Month											Month's Total

TAX / EXPENSES

Month of ______________________(Start)

Date	Mileage	Car Rental Gas / Tolls	Taxis	Air Fares Railroad	Phone	Hotel	Meals Entertain	Equipment Software	Printing Secretarial	Postage Overnight	Daily Totals
1											
2											
3											
4											
5											
6											
7											
8											
9											
10											
11											
12											
13											
14											
15											
16											
Category Totals											

Month of ______________________(Finish)

Date	Mileage	Car Rental Gas / Tolls	Taxis	Air Fares Railroad	Phone	Hotel	Meals Entertain	Equipment Software	Printing Secretarial	Postage Overnight	Daily Totals
17											
18											
19											
20											
21											
22											
23											
24											
25											
26											
27											
28											
29											
30											
31											
Category Totals											
Entire Month											Month's Total

EXPENSES

TAX / EXPENSES

Month of ______________________(Start)

Date	Mileage	Car Rental Gas / Tolls	Taxis	Air Fares Railroad	Phone	Hotel	Meals Entertain	Equipment Software	Printing Secretarial	Postage Overnight	Daily Totals
1											
2											
3											
4											
5											
6											
7											
8											
9											
10											
11											
12											
13											
14											
15											
16											
Category Totals											

Month of ______________________ (Finish)

Date	Mileage	Car Rental Gas / Tolls	Taxis	Air Fares Railroad	Phone	Hotel	Meals Entertain	Equipment Software	Printing Secretarial	Postage Overnight	Daily Totals
17											
18											
19											
20											
21											
22											
23											
24											
25											
26											
27											
28											
29											
30											
31											
Category Totals											
Entire Month											Month's Total

EXPENSES

TAX / EXPENSES

Month of ______________________(Start)

Date	Mileage	Car Rental Gas / Tolls	Taxis	Air Fares Railroad	Phone	Hotel	Meals Entertain	Equipment Software	Printing Secretarial	Postage Overnight		Daily Totals
1												
2												
3												
4												
5												
6												
7												
8												
9												
10												
11												
12												
13												
14												
15												
16												
Category Totals												

TAX / EXPENSES

Month of ______________________(Finish)

Date	Mileage	Car Rental Gas / Tolls	Taxis	Air Fares Railroad	Phone	Hotel	Meals Entertain	Equipment Software	Printing Secretarial	Postage Overnight	Daily Totals
17											
18											
19											
20											
21											
22											
23											
24											
25											
26											
27											
28											
29											
30											
31											
Category Totals											
Entire Month											Month's Total

EXPENSES

TAX / EXPENSES

Month of ______________________(Start)

Date	Mileage	Car Rental Gas / Tolls	Taxis	Air Fares Railroad	Phone	Hotel	Meals Entertain	Equipment Software	Printing Secretarial	Postage Overnight	Daily Totals
1											
2											
3											
4											
5											
6											
7											
8											
9											
10											
11											
12											
13											
14											
15											
16											
Category Totals											

Month of ______________________(Finish)

Date	Mileage	Car Rental Gas / Tolls	Taxis	Air Fares Railroad	Phone	Hotel	Meals Entertain	Equipment Software	Printing Secretarial	Postage Overnight	Daily Totals
17											
18											
19											
20											
21											
22											
23											
24											
25											
26											
27											
28											
29											
30											
31											
Category Totals											
Entire Month											Month's Total

EXPENSES

TAX / EXPENSES

Month of ________________________(Start)

Date	Mileage	Car Rental Gas / Tolls	Taxis	Air Fares Railroad	Phone	Hotel	Meals Entertain	Equipment Software	Printing Secretarial	Postage Overnight	Daily Totals
1											
2											
3											
4											
5											
6											
7											
8											
9											
10											
11											
12											
13											
14											
15											
16											
Category Totals											

EXPENSES

Month of ______________________(Finish)

Date	Mileage	Car Rental Gas / Tolls	Taxis	Air Fares Railroad	Phone	Hotel	Meals Entertain	Equipment Software	Printing Secretarial	Postage Overnight	Daily Totals
17											
18											
19											
20											
21											
22											
23											
24											
25											
26											
27											
28											
29											
30											
31											
Category Totals											
Entire Month											Month's Total

EXPENSES

TAX / EXPENSES

Month of ______________________(Start)

Date		Mileage	Car Rental Gas / Tolls	Taxis	Air Fares Railroad	Phone	Hotel	Meals Entertain	Equipment Software	Printing Secretarial	Postage Overnight		Daily Totals
1													
2													
3													
4													
5													
6													
7													
8													
9													
10													
11													
12													
13													
14													
15													
16													
Category Totals													

EXPENSES

Month of ______________________(Finish)

Date	Mileage	Car Rental Gas / Tolls	Taxis	Air Fares Railroad	Phone	Hotel	Meals Entertain	Equipment Software	Printing Secretarial	Postage Overnight	Daily Totals
17											
18											
19											
20											
21											
22											
23											
24											
25											
26											
27											
28											
29											
30											
31											
Category Totals											
Entire Month											Month's Total

EXPENSES

TAX / EXPENSES

Month of ______________________(Start)

Date	Mileage	Car Rental Gas / Tolls	Taxis	Air Fares Railroad	Phone	Hotel	Meals Entertain	Equipment Software	Printing Secretarial	Postage Overnight	Daily Totals
1											
2											
3											
4											
5											
6											
7											
8											
9											
10											
11											
12											
13											
14											
15											
16											
Category Totals											

Month of ______________________(Finish)

Date	Mileage	Car Rental Gas / Tolls	Taxis	Air Fares Railroad	Phone	Hotel	Meals Entertain	Equipment Software	Printing Secretarial	Postage Overnight	Daily Totals
17											
18											
19											
20											
21											
22											
23											
24											
25											
26											
27											
28											
29											
30											
31											
Category Totals											
Entire Month											Month's Total

EXPENSES

TAX / EXPENSES

Month of ______________________(Start)

Date	Mileage	Car Rental Gas / Tolls	Taxis	Air Fares Railroad	Phone	Hotel	Meals Entertain	Equipment Software	Printing Secretarial	Postage Overnight	Daily Totals
1											
2											
3											
4											
5											
6											
7											
8											
9											
10											
11											
12											
13											
14											
15											
16											
Category Totals											

EXPENSES

Month of ______________________(Finish)

Date	Mileage	Car Rental Gas / Tolls	Taxis	Air Fares Railroad	Phone	Hotel	Meals Entertain	Equipment Software	Printing Secretarial	Postage Overnight	Daily Totals
17											
18											
19											
20											
21											
22											
23											
24											
25											
26											
27											
28											
29											
30											
31											
Category Totals											
Entire Month											Month's Total

TAX / EXPENSES

Month of ______________________(Start)

Date	Mileage	Car Rental Gas / Tolls	Taxis	Air Fares Railroad	Phone	Hotel	Meals Entertain	Equipment Software	Printing Secretarial	Postage Overnight	Daily Totals
1											
2											
3											
4											
5											
6											
7											
8											
9											
10											
11											
12											
13											
14											
15											
16											
Category Totals											

Month of ____________________(Finish)

Date	Mileage	Car Rental Gas / Tolls	Taxis	Air Fares Railroad	Phone	Hotel	Meals Entertain	Equipment Software	Printing Secretarial	Postage Overnight	Daily Totals
17											
18											
19											
20											
21											
22											
23											
24											
25											
26											
27											
28											
29											
30											
31											
Category Totals											
Entire Month											Month's Total

EXPENSES

The RITES OF PASSAGE Program

...the ultimate resources for executive-level career development

Rites of Passage at $100,000 to $1 Million+

...the insider's guide to executive job-changing

Ever since it first appeared over a decade ago, *RITES OF PASSAGE* has been America's and the world's #1 bestselling and most used and respected book of job-changing and career advice for executives. Now comprehensively revised, updated and expanded, *RITES* covers every avenue of job-hunting and career development at the executive level, including cautious use of the Internet. You've seen *RITES* in *Business Week, The Wall Street Journal, The New York Times, USA Today, Working Woman* and virtually every other major newspaper and business publication in the U.S. and, increasingly, around the world as well. "If you're not using *RITES*, you're at a severe disadvantage, because you're probably competing with other executives who are," says John Drake, founder of Drake Beam Morin. "Very few people have John Lucht's knowledge of executive job-hunting and recruiting. None can match his uniquely practical way of sharing that know-how."

HARDCOVER, 640 pages, $29.95. Viceroy Press, ISBN No. 0-942785-30-4.

Executive Job-Changing *Workbook*

Here are unique tools to develop your thoughts and speed your work. Proceed confidently step-by-step under the personal guidance of John Lucht. By means of pen-and-paper fill-ins, he helps you figure out how best to present yourself...what to emphasize and de-emphasize, and what to write, say, and do to surmount the most daunting obstacles of an executive-level job search...planning your campaign, writing your resume and cover letter, networking, and interviewing. The challenging need to present yourself effectively on-paper and in interviews is greatly eased by the *WORKBOOK'S* templates and techniques. There's also a carefully selected list of outstanding retainer-compensated executive search firms.

PAPERBACK, 576 pages, $29.95. Viceroy Press, ISBN No. 0-942785-22-3.

Insights for the Journey...Navigating to Thrive, Enjoy, and Prosper in Senior Management

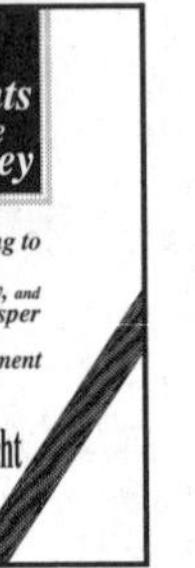

Here is John Lucht's latest and most intimately personal sharing of his many years of experience in consulting to—and coaching of—senior executives. Experts are extravagant in their praise of this unique new guide to achieving success, enjoyment, recognition, and financial rewards by excelling in a senior executive career. Yvonne Jackson, Chief Human Resources Officer of Compaq says, "*INSIGHTS FOR THE JOURNEY* is, by far the best book I've ever read on senior executive leadership, performance, and strategy. Here are truths you've never seen before, plus the basics we all should live my...now together in one book *INSIGHTS* can elevate your performance while lowering stress and tension." Gerard Roche, Senior Chairman of Heidrick and Struggles says, "Profound and important...yet fun to read. Once won't be enough!"

HARDCOVER, 104 pages, $19.95. Viceroy Press, ISBN No. 0-942785-31-2.

To Purchase: **Most local and online bookstores carry all 3 books.**
If you prefer to order by phone, call **1 800 JANUARY**.

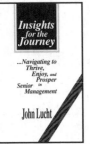

To Make the WORKBOOK Portable!

For your convenience the WORKBOOK is in two parts.

The front is "at home" activity. But the ATTACHE PAGES can be a lot more helpful if you can slip them inconspicuously into your attache. Then in your first private moments after a networking appointment and after every job interview, you can jot notes while they're fresh-in-mind. You can also refresh your memory immediately prior to any meeting. And you'll always have all the names, addresses, phone numbers, and current status of everyone involved in your search at your fingertips, no matter where you are.

To achieve this goal, we've used America's highest-quality producer of large size paperbacks, and have had them bind in 2 sheets of cardboard (this is one) between the front and back sections. Their adhesive is extremely strong and resilient. Hence, (1) if you're careful you've got a good chance—though no guarantee—of winding up with *two* books...a bit corner-frayed, perhaps, but still together solidly enough to carry. But (2) unless you aggressively stretch, flex, and bend the parts over against themselves as shown here, you'll have a hard time severing them.

Caution!

1. Separate the Workbook on the ***other*** side of this cardboard (the severed parts will have plain unprinted back covers).

2. Flex/bend repeatedly until you've really broken and stretched the spine at the point between the cardboards. See illustration.

3. Use a tough kitchen or garden ***shears***, not granny's antique sewing scissors or your long sleek bond-clipping ones.

4. Work on a table (preferably protected by a couple fat newspapers), ***not*** on your lap.

5. Cut only with a tough shears, ***not*** with any kind of knife, razor blade or any other keen-unshielded instrument.

6. Cut with the book opened downward (the glossy outside covers will face upward toward you as in the illustration). This will result in a far easier and much neater cut than if you work with the book opened to face you in the usual way.

EXECUTIVE JOB-CHANGING WORKBOOK

EXECUTIVE JOB-CHANGING WORKBOOK

JOHN LUCHT

THE VICEROY PRESS
NEW YORK

DISTRIBUTED BY HENRY HOLT AND COMPANY, INC.
NEW YORK

For additional coordinated help from author John Lucht, go to...

RiteSite.com

...America's #1 on-line service site for executive career development.

 Manufactured in the United States of America. Distributed to the trade in the USA by Henry Holt and Company, Inc., 115 West 18th Street, New York, NY 10011.

Designers: John Charles, Erik Jensen
Editors: Amanda Hawker, Pam Deutmeyer, Jean Sanders
Drawings: Erik Jensen

“Few have John Lucht’s knowledge of executive job-hunting and recruiting.

None can match his uniquely practical way of sharing that know-how.

In the EXECUTIVE JOB-CHANGING WORKBOOK he deals with the world as it really is. Platitudes and generalities are out. Pragmatic individually tailored step-by-step direction is in.

The EXECUTIVE JOB-CHANGING WORKBOOK puts truly professional assistance at every executive’s fingertips.

And anyone who adds the vast wealth of inside information that is *RITES OF PASSAGE AT $100,000 TO $1 MILLION+* will be armed with the strongest and most comprehensive total program available in print.”

John Drake*

*Founder and CEO of Drake Beam Morin Inc. and, after retiring from DBM, also of Drake Inglesi Milardo Inc., both outstanding human resources consulting organizations.

To Help With Your Search...

CONTENTS

(FROM THE FRONT)

Plus 288 Attache Pages to Manage Your Search!

(FROM THE BACK)

To Help With Your Search...

How the Workbook Works

RITES OF PASSAGE AT $100,000 TO $1MILLION+ *covers* ***what to do.***

The EXECUTIVE JOB-CHANGING WORKBOOK ***helps you do it*** *...with sophisticated tools to speed your progress.*

The Quickest Route to Your Ideal Job

Is your goal job-satisfaction?

At the right compensation?

As fast as possible?

The ideal executive-level job is never easy to find...and especially not these days. This WORKBOOK is your tool kit of advanced techniques and shortcuts to help you with everything you've got to accomplish:

- a clear knowledge of *what you're selling* that *employers want and need*
- self-understanding of what *you really want* in your next job
  ("Be careful what you seek; you might find it!")
- a *powerfully persuasive resume*
  (and a compelling *cover letter* for any mailings you may do)
- *referrals by the leading executive search firms*
- maximum help from your current *personal contacts* and from new ones made through *networking*
- help with your *research* and *tax / record-keeping.*

Not Tied to *RITES*

Unlike any workbook you may have used in college, this one is ***not*** going to send you back and forth to its accompanying textbook. *RITES OF PASSAGE AT $100,000 TO $1 MILLION+* is the text, and this *WORKBOOK* supplements it. So please do read *RITES*. Without it, you're missing a lot of useful information you won't find anywhere else.*

But this *WORKBOOK* is a complete system of speed-up and short-cut tools for your executive job search. It will be useful, whether you take advantage of *RITES* or not.

Action, Not Words

This is mainly an action book...not a word book. You'll be writing and doing, not just reading and then copying. And everything you do will be uniquely tailored to your own career and accomplishments...solving *your* problems and maximizing *your* opportunities. You won't be asked to adapt examples from other people's paperwork. Today's difficult marketplace no longer responds to "cookie cutter" methods.

The "Front Pages"

The WORKBOOK is a comprehensive tool kit. There's an aid for every part of your executive job search. In the front pages, you prepare your campaign. You examine what you've done so far in your career. And what you want to do. And which of your accomplishments will most intrigue and persuade the types of employers you'd prefer to work for. How have you succeeded? What have you found most enjoyable and rewarding? What would you like to do *more*...and *less*?

Next you'll map your strategy and develop your paperwork, keeping in mind the objectives you've defined. Tools for all of these steps are in the "Front Pages"...the ones you're reading right now.

The "Attache Pages"

The back half of the WORKBOOK is an entirely separate set of pages on which to keep track of all the people you're contacting, the recruiters you're approaching, and the interviews you're having...as well as the money you're spending which will be deductible when tax time rolls around. These pages begin inside the back cover, which becomes that section's front cover, and you can separate it by just snipping the binding with a scissors. I call those your "ATTACHE PAGES." They're based in large part on the sophisticated networking methods of the executive recruiting profession. You'll be glad they're portable, so you can conveniently have them with you wherever you go.

---

*Also, please be sure you're reading the latest fully revised edition of *RITES OF PASSAGE*. Earlier copies found in most homes and libraries do not include *RITES'* current comprehensive coverage of the Internet and its executive job-changing issues.

Please

At the outset, this one suggestion:

Proceed straight through the entire* WORKBOOK, *doing the reading, thinking, and writing step-by-step in sequence.

You can't possibly get all the help that awaits you here, unless you fully participate in each section. In ways that intentionally are not always shown or stated, each part lays a foundation for everything else that comes later.

To Help With Your

Campaign Strategy

Executive job-changing boils down to 2 essentials and 5 considerations.

Deal realistically with each of them, and you will mount your strongest possible search.

The Two Essentials

To be hired, you absolutely must offer employers these two essentials:

1. ***Something* THEY *need and want***
   (and not your needs and desires), and
2. ***Proof that you can be* RELIED ON *to deliver it***
   (and more surely relied on than anyone competing with you for the job).

The only reason you'll be hired is to fulfill the employer's needs and desires. Yours are irrelevant...at least until after the employer is convinced that you're the #1 answer to his or her needs, and must be courted with every inducement that might sway you.

Mishandling The Essentials

Sadly, the vast majority of job-seekers make the same serious mistakes. Most of the time they're busily communicating what *they want*, rather than what *employers want that they can deliver*. And their *proof* is equally off-base. They state their "skills," as reasons they can be relied on to get results. What they don't realize is that others won't accept their "skill" evaluations, because their judgment (1) may not be accurate and (2) is self-interestedly biased.

The only convincing proof of how well any job-changer will perform when handed a new opportunity is how well they've performed in the past. And that is communicated, not in flattering self-assessments, but in specifically described prior accomplishments.

Your Communication Strategy

Resolve right now as we begin working together, that you will always try to tell an employer or recruiter briefly but specifically what you have succeeded in doing. Trust her or him to be smart enough to infer what skills were involved.

Remember that all your generalizations are self-serving, and therefore suspect. On the other hand, when you straightforwardly present facts and let the observer draw his or her own conclusions (which, in the end, she or he will always do anyway), the generalization *will* be trusted. Why? Because the conclusions are *not* yours. They are not biased. They *can* be trusted. Indeed, if you're adroit and lucky you may even provoke in him or her some thrill-of-discovery and pride-of-authorship.

The Five Key Considerations

Now let's look at the five most important issues you must resolve as you map your campaign strategy. We'll give more attention to these items and their implications elsewhere in this WORKBOOK. But here they are in their clearest, most fundamental form. Never lose sight of them:

1. *Your "Highest And Best Use"*

Think of the real estate axiom. Land should be used for a building and/or an activity that provide the best return.

What do you do especially well that (1) employers need most and pay most for and that (2) your accomplishments (and not self-assessment) prove you can do?

2. *Your Most Impressive Achievements*

What have you actually done that demonstrates you'll perform the job you want to be hired for? What achievements show you were outstanding in earlier and lesser positions?

3. *Your Most Enthusiastic And Prominent Supporters*

Who are the outstanding people in your field who (1) know from firsthand experience that you are outstanding and (2) are willing to put their credibility behind you?

4. *The Likeliest And Strongest Reasons* **Not** *To Hire You*

Why are you most likely to be turned down? What's likely to be held against you? Correctly or incorrectly, fairly or unfairly. Only by identifying your vulnerability can you defend and launch a counteroffensive.

Bear in mind that often the best defense against a seeming lack of depth in a certain area is to boldly cite specific achievements in that sector (do you have any?). Your implicitly staking it out as a strength won't magically make you a world-beater. But you can probably cause your resume-reader or interviewer to think, "Well, he or she even has some experience in the area where I wouldn't have expected any. I guess I should continue."

Before We Go On

Please notice that considerations 1, 2, and 4 are all entirely or mainly oriented to what the *employer* wants...not what you want. That's still true as we proceed to point 5. However, there's more to life than just getting and holding a job. *You've got to **plan** for your self-satisfaction.* If you don't, who will? Therefore, the fifth consideration:

5. *What Do You Really* Want *To Do*?

Face it. If you want work you'll enjoy (and your career will flourish when you find it) you'd better carefully consider what positions, industries, and companies would be best for you...and target your search toward them.

You've undoubtedly seen sayings like these:

"Be careful what you seek. You might find it!"

OR

"Be careful what you wish for. You might get it!"

No question about it. There's truth in those aphorisms. And never more so than at the outset of a job change...a potential turning point in your career.

We'll keep your desire for job satisfaction in mind throughout this WORKBOOK. But now we'll get down to business, by examining each of the five essentials:

Think About:

1. *Your "Highest And Best Use"*

Here we have the classic real estate concept everyone understands. Different things can be done with a parcel of raw land. And some "uses" will yield more profit than others. If the location and fertility are right, the same acreage may be used for growing cabbages, for an auto salvage yard, or for a luxurious suburban office park. The question is, "Which use is 'highest and best?'" Which will yield the highest return?

The concept is simple. But coming to grips with it when seeking employment is trickier than you might think. Not because you won't see at a glance which among several possible jobs is likely to be highest paying and/or most enjoyable. In that sense, everyone always reaches instantly for the "highest and best." Even a child reaches for the biggest cookie.

The problem is to keep constantly in mind *who the "user" is.* And the answer, of course, is *the employer.* If you can always do that...while writing your resume and correspondence and while interviewing and networking...you'll be way ahead of almost everyone you compete with for virtually every job you seek. There's a TOOL coming up that will solve this problem for you once and for all. But before we go ahead to anything else, please do this:

Write down (1) the title and (2) a brief description of your current or latest job:

TITLE ______________________________

JOB DESCRIPTION ______________________________

____

____

____

____

____

____

____

____

____

What did you say your title was? Did you say President? Product Manager? Vice President - Technology? Region Manager? Director - Training and Development? EVP? Branch Manager? CEO? Medical Director?

Or did you use a generic description? Head of systems development? Chief of environmental compliance? Head tax accountant? In charge of various support functions, including real estate, risk management, security, and maintenance? Co-founder and head of operations?

The "Who . . ." Test

Whether you describe yourself by title or generically, here's a way to make sure that, in mapping your campaign strategy and in carrying it out, you will always speak and write in terms of your "highest and best use" to the *employer*...of what he or she needs and wants that you deliver, rather than what you desire that comes from getting the job and doing it well. Just fill in the blanks in this sentence:

"I'm a ____(fill in your title or functional description)____ **who**

____(fill in what you do that the employer needs and wants)____."

Now let's look at a good and a bad handling of those blanks. Most important, of course, is the one that follows the "who." First, read this very appealing characterization. A great many employers would find it attractive...and especially so, when accompanied by several impressive examples:

"I'm a General Manager **who**

turns around problem businesses, makes them profitable, and puts them on a growth track."

Here, on the other hand, is a very bad and yet surprisingly prevalent way of handling the "who" statement:

"I'm a very profit-oriented General Manager with superb leadership skills and a superior track record **who**

seeks to use all my many skills and abilities and my 14 years of successful experience in the widget industry to the benefit of a forward-looking growth-oriented manufacturing company."

Of course, people who proceed that way never put their words in a "Who . . ." sentence. If they did, the weakness of their approach would be obvious. But what I've shown *is* what they say. And now you see what the "Who . . ." Test does. It states the proposed "use" in terms of the employer's needs, not the job-seeker's. Look at the second person's statement again. When you strip away all the self-praising and employer-flattering adjectives, it boils down to this:

"I'm a boastful General Manager, who seeks to be employed."

Not much of a turn-on for an employer, is it? What can this person be *used* for? We don't know. He or she hasn't said.

You have multiple potential "Uses." Choose the "Highest and Best" one.

Very soon, I'll ask you to devise several "I'm a ______ who _______" statements. Each will say what "use" can be made of you by a potential employer. And unless you're far more narrowly specialized than the rest of us, you can be "used" to accomplish several results. Moreover, just as you may have different "uses," you may also have different titles or generic descriptions that match your "uses."

For example, the General Manager who chose to market as his or her "use" the turning around of troubled businesses, may also be an excellent administrator...a Group Executive capable of monitoring and supervising a portfolio of companies. And a superb one-on-one salesperson. And an outstanding leader of a sales force! What then is his or her "*highest and best* use?" That may differ, depending on the most urgent needs of various potential employers...and of the total marketplace.

Ordinarily turning around money-losing businesses and making them thrive, or guiding an array of companies would be the most-needed and highly paid "use" of such a person. But maybe he or she should be an independent broker of businesses. Knowing how to turn around companies, our friend can spin plausible scenarios that make even the "doggiest" business seem attractive, and can line up competing buyers willing to pay top dollar. The fee on just one of those deals may exceed several years' pay for any of the person's other "uses." Voila! His or her "Highest and Best Use!"

A "Use" without *Proof* is no "Use" at all.

This is the EXECUTIVE JOB-CHANGING WORKBOOK. You don't have to be a "big shot" to be using it. In fact you can *almost* be a beginner. But I do assume you've had at least one or two previous jobs. You're not without *any* experience.

So, for any "use" you're likely to claim, every employer will expect to see *examples of your actually delivering it.* You can't get by without them. If the only proof you offer is a list of self-proclaimed "skills" or "strengths" or—God forgive the pretentious jargon—"skill-sets" or "competencies," plus a list of formerly large "responsibilities," then the sophisticated employer won't even give you a second glance.

Which is a long way of saying that, as you frame your "Who . . ." statements and as you finally select the "use" you propose to an employer, you absolutely *must* state achievements that prove you can be *relied on* to deliver the result you're claiming.

Unfair!

Time out.

Your "I'm a ______ who _______" statements can wait another minute while I answer a question that comes screaming into the minds of a great many folks at this point:

> *"Isn't it unfair—and even impractical—to demand as a pre-condition of hiring me to do something* now *that I must have done the same thing earlier? And that I must state specific examples as proof! Isn't that too much to ask?*
>
> *"If everyone made that demand, how could anyone's career ever progress? How would we ever get new Managers? New General Managers? New CEOs? How could business, and indeed the world, ever move ahead?"*

The answer, as you've probably already guessed, is that the examples you must give of having delivered the same "use" previously needn't involve doing *exactly* the same thing. The prior accomplishments you point out as "proof" can be very persuasive if they're merely *similar* to what the hiring employer wants to "use" you for. They should be analogous. They needn't be identical.

Also, different employers are willing to take differing degrees of risk in giving you a chance to do what you haven't quite done before. A current or former boss or co-worker who knows you well may see little risk in handing you a job far above your latest one. After all, he or she has observed firsthand your prodigious skills and abilities that should be more than adequate to the challenge.

But not a stranger! Notice the difference. Your current or former colleague has actually *seen* you do what your examples are needed to *tell* others about, and is relying on "skills" and "abilities" *he or she* has defined and ascribed to you. That situation bears no similarity to the one where *you* approach a stranger and *you* define and ascribe your own skills and abilities, asking him or her to rely on you. Then you'd better prove your assertions with examples.

It's *not* unfair that you can't get by on hot air!

Loosen up and get creative.

One comment about the TOOLS before you pick up your pen or pencil and start using the first one. They're designed to stimulate your creativity and prompt you to think about yourself, your objectives, and the whole job-changing process in ways that might not otherwise occur to you. They are *not* designed to be some kind of a test or—even worse—a chore to complete in a certain time or a certain way.

The more you find yourself freely and almost casually scribbling random thoughts into the blanks throughout this WORKBOOK, the more helpful it will be. Cross out. Put down the same thought six times in six ways. Start out six times to write something different and wind up again and again with the same words. That's okay!

If ever there was a time and place where "Neatness Does NOT Count!" it's here and now. So loosen up. It's not white-knuckle time. It's spelunking time...exploration time. It's *"I never thought about myself...my career...my accomplishments...my wants and needs...employers' wants and needs...the job-changing process...and on and on...quite that way before"* time. Hopefully these pages will become a journey of self-discovery and self-appreciation that ends with new skills and enthusiasm for self-marketing. That's what I've tried to prepare for you and what I hope is already underway.

Now let's really dig into Consideration #1, your "Highest and Best Use." It's the single most important concept in mapping your Campaign Strategy. And from what we've already discussed, you can see the importance of presenting and regarding yourself in terms of being useful to meet a need or desire that the employer has, and not merely your own objectives and preferences.

What is it that you have shown by past accomplishments an employer can reliably expect to use you for? Surely you've proven you can fulfill more than one need. And just as surely, you can characterize yourself more than one way. Note the example in the middle of page 9. Review your career, your various jobs, and your greatest successes in each. Is there a pattern? Or several strong patterns? Try to be objective. Step outside yourself. If you were an employer, what use would you make of you? What would you hire you to do?

Here are 15 "I'm a _________ who______________" statements. Force yourself to fill in all of them. Try at first to make each title and generic description of yourself as different from the others as possible. Do the same with the "uses" to which you can be put. As you proceed, give thought to which uses are "highest and best" in terms of meeting employer needs that are both prevalent and not easy or inexpensive to get filled. If, with examples of past achievements, you can show yourself meeting such a need, you've probably found your "highest and best use"...the one employers will be most interested in and pleased to give you the most pay, recognition, and job-satisfaction for meeting:

I'M A__________________________________WHO__________________________

____

I'M A__________________________________WHO__________________________

____

I'M A__________ WHO __________

I'M A__________ WHO __________

I'M A__________ WHO __________

I'M A__________ WHO __________

I'M A__________ WHO __________

I'M A__________ WHO __________

I'M A__________ WHO __________

I'M A__________ WHO __________

I'M A__________ WHO __________

I'M A__________ WHO __________

I'M A__________ WHO __________

I'M A__________ WHO __________

I'M A__________ WHO __________

Think About:

2. *Your Most Impressive Achievements*

Here we are at the second major consideration. What have you done up to now that is really impressive? What can be used to convince an employer that, if hired, you can be relied on to deliver the results you're being paid to accomplish?

Take plenty of time now, at this early stage of your campaign strategy, to think about all your achievements during your entire lifetime. Of course, for job-hunting you'll want to stress recent achievements over ancient ones, because you'll want to appear to be at the height of your powers...not having already peaked and started to decline.

But for now, consider everything you've ever done! Many of the items you'll list below should *never* get into your resume or your job-hunting conversation (too early, personal, not job/work-related, etc.), but dredge them out of memory and write them down anyway. Even if you never refer to them again, they may show you strengths and satisfactions you don't normally associate with work...and perhaps ought to.

Above all, think of and list achievements that support Consideration #1, your "Highest and Best Use." Those are the ones you're most likely to feature in your resume and cover letter and to bring up during interviews and networking.

Use these slots to jot down achievements just as they happen to come to mind. Don't worry about having them in any particular order...whether biggest-to-smallest or in a reverse chronology as they'd appear in a resume. Now you're just brainstorming. Later you can cull, edit, and polish.

ACHIEVEMENT ____

____

ACHIEVEMENT ____

____

ACHIEVEMENT ____

____

ACHIEVEMENT ____

____

ACHIEVEMENT ____________________

____

ACHIEVEMENT ____________________

____

ACHIEVEMENT ____________________

____

ACHIEVEMENT ____________________

____

ACHIEVEMENT ____________________

____

ACHIEVEMENT ____________________

____

ACHIEVEMENT ____________________

____

ACHIEVEMENT ____________________

____

ACHIEVEMENT ____________________

____

ACHIEVEMENT ____________________

____

ACHIEVEMENT ____________________

____

ACHIEVEMENT ____________________

____

ACHIEVEMENT ____________________

____

ACHIEVEMENT ____________________

____

ACHIEVEMENT ____________________

____

ACHIEVEMENT ____________________

____

ACHIEVEMENT ____________________

____

ACHIEVEMENT ____________________

____

ACHIEVEMENT ____________________

____

ACHIEVEMENT ____________________

____

ACHIEVEMENT ____________________

____

ACHIEVEMENT ____________________

____

ACHIEVEMENT ____________________

____

ACHIEVEMENT ____________________

____

ACHIEVEMENT ____________________

____

ACHIEVEMENT ____________________

____

Think About:

3. *Your Most Enthusiastic And Prominent Supporters*

No job campaign can succeed without help.

And probably your strongest and best help—certainly your *earliest*—will come from your current personal contacts. Those folks already know and respect you. Forget (but only for the moment) networking among strangers. That comes later. But right now...as you map campaign strategy at the outset of your search...you really must take inventory of the contacts you already have. And you must also establish priorities as to who you'll get in touch with first and what if anything you'll ask them to do.

Why?

Because getting in touch with people is time-consuming. And time spent with some is likely to be more productive than equal time spent with others, as I explain in the chapter on how to deal with your personal contacts in *RITES OF PASSAGE:*

Who to contact earlier...and spend more time with...
is a trade-off between two issues:

1. **Relevance: how likely to control, or at least know of, appropriate jobs, and**
2. **Knowledgeable Enthusiasm: how likely to react favorably to your availability.**

Obviously, if you know her well, the CEO of the company in your industry you'd most like to work for should be your #1 priority. She controls at least one job you'd want...maybe several. But if you merely shook hands at a convention four years ago, and she's unlikely to remember, then you'd better get a new introduction. Or write her a letter, as you would any other important stranger.

On the other hand, a first-class former subordinate who's always considered you a genius, and who now runs a small but respected supply, distribution, or service company in your industry, might also be a high-priority contact. There's no spot for you in his organization. But he knows what's happening in your field; he's enthusiastic about you and eager to help; and he's intelligent and discreet...not an oaf who might smudge your image while trying to polish it. His eyes and ears could be very beneficial.

Above all, beware of the perverse natural tendency we all have, to get in touch with the people we know best and are most comfortable with, rather than the ones who can do us the most good. Remember:

You can make a relevant contact more enthusiastic,
but you can't make an enthusiastic one more relevant.

That's why I included in the Personal Contacts chapter of *RITES* the following hierarchy for ranking the twin trade-offs. Fortunately, now that we have this WORKBOOK to share, I can make that process a lot easier, as you'll see when you turn the page. But first let's look at the trade-offs as they appear in *Rites:*

Relevance

1. Control of Jobs. These top-priority people have hire/fire power, or at least influence, over a job you'd want. Think of CEOs, outside Directors, and heads of functions such as Human Resources, Finance, Marketing, Manufacturing, R&D, etc.

2. Vantage Point. Lower-priority, but still valuable, these contacts are extra eyes and ears. Consider middle managers in companies that interest you, and other people in your field...suppliers, customers, and consultants.

3. Neither Control nor Vantage Point. Lowest in relevance are the people outside your field altogether. Some may be widely connected, and you may be greatly helped by an off-the-wall suggestion. There's no harm in an occasional try for serendipity. But give it lower priority.

And now the opposite trade-off. How well and how favorably does the contact know your achievements, and how well does he or she like you personally?

Knowledgeable Enthusiasm

1. Co-Workers. First-priority goes to your former supervisors, subordinates, and peers. No need to convince. Just update them on your latest exploits, and they're automatically enthusiastic. On the other hand, if you suspect their opinion from the past is negative, don't bother. Nothing you say now will overcome what they believe they saw with their own eyes.

2. Closely Dealt-with Outsiders. Suppliers, customers, consultants, and others you've dealt with also have enthusiasm...or lack of it...based on prior direct experience. Moreover, they've probably heard about you from your superiors and subordinates. They can't be quite as sure as if they'd seen you from inside your company, but they're capable of justified enthusiasm. If it exists, take advantage.

3. By-Reputation-Only Contacts. You've met these people and know them slightly. And, although they've never done business with you, they've surely heard others speak about you. Consider trade press editors, trade association executives, competitors you've met at industry functions, suppliers who've solicited you and customers you've solicited where no business ensued, etc. There's a little more going for you than with a stranger, but not much.

4. Non-Business Connections. These are the very same people listed as Number 3 under "Relevance." You may know them very well indeed, but they're not part of your business milieu. Hence, they're "long shots" as job-advancement contacts. Do play them. But not first.

Scoring Your Contacts

The purpose of these lists is to encourage you to think about all your possible contacts and emphasize the ones most likely to be helpful, rather than the ones you'd most enjoy getting in touch with. Also, you can use the lists in a combine-the-numbers process, if you temper it with judgment. The lowest combined number, 2, is obviously best, as Matt Marketczar demonstrated *Rites of Passage.* The highest, 7, is least likely to be helpful. And the numbers in between provide roughly comparative rankings.

So much for the reasons why. Now relax and take plenty of time to think about and write down the names of folks you already know, who might conceivably be of some assistance to your job-changing efforts. Again, "Loosen up and get creative." The best approach at this early stage, when you're still mapping your overall campaign strategy, is to list and think about the very best possible way to use absolutely every resource you have. And, no doubt about it, the people you already know are (quite literally) "head-and-shoulders" over every other resource you have.

We're at Consideration #3, Your Most Enthusiastic and Prominent Supporters. Jot down the names of everyone you know, including all of your business contacts from close to distant and all of your reasonably strong social and civic contacts from school days to now. Rate them downward from 1 to 3 on potential relevance to your employment scene and downward from 1 to 4 on knowledgeable enthusiasm with respect to your performance.

Obviously the highest priority anyone can earn on this system is a #2. But don't hesitate to breach the formula and give a #2—or even a #1—to the exceptionally prominent and well-connected nonbusiness contact who thinks extremely highly of you and is very eager to help.

Bear in mind that in dire employment circumstances, as in others, "a friend in need is a friend indeed." For example, I've seen a CEO lose three jobs in five years and still get several outstanding offers of a fourth by conducting a "sponsored" direct mail campaign (see RITES *for details) using the letterhead and warm endorsement letter of one of America's most prominent CEOs who'd been his boss a decade earlier!*

	Relevance #1 down to #3	Knowledgeable Enthusiasm #1 down to #4	Priority #2 down to #7
PERSON____			
PERSON____			
PERSON____			
PERSON____			
PERSON____			
PERSON____			
PERSON____			
PERSON____			
PERSON____			

	Relevance #1 down to #3	Knowledgeable Enthusiasm #1 down to #4	Priority #2 down to #7
PERSON			
PERSON			
PERSON			
PERSON			
PERSON			
PERSON			
PERSON			
PERSON			
PERSON			
PERSON			
PERSON			
PERSON			
PERSON			
PERSON			
PERSON			
PERSON			
PERSON			
PERSON			
PERSON			
PERSON			
PERSON			
PERSON			
PERSON			

	Relevance #1 down to #3	Knowledgeable Enthusiasm #1 down to #4	Priority #2 down to #7
PERSON			
PERSON			
PERSON			
PERSON			
PERSON			
PERSON			
PERSON			
PERSON			
PERSON			
PERSON			
PERSON			
PERSON			
PERSON			
PERSON			
PERSON			
PERSON			
PERSON			
PERSON			
PERSON			
PERSON			
PERSON			
PERSON			
PERSON			

	Relevance #1 down to #3	Knowledgeable Enthusiasm #1 down to #4	Priority #2 down to #7
PERSON			
PERSON			
PERSON			
PERSON			
PERSON			
PERSON			
PERSON			
PERSON			
PERSON			
PERSON			
PERSON			

I hope you've been able to fill several of these pages with names. Indeed, I'd be delighted if you've had to grab additional paper to deal with even more names than you've had room for.

Regardless of how many people you've come up with, you've at least given organized thought to all the people you already know who may be able to provide reconnaissance, suggestions and possibly introductions, as you launch into an all-out job-changing effort. And you've considered which of these folks *are most likely to be helpful*, so that you can go about contacting them in a time-efficient priority order.

Either now or later on, skim the cream off this list and write the names you've decided are comparably high priority into the INDEX to the "ATTACHE PAGES" at the back of this WORKBOOK. Don't copy all of the names. Only the most promising. That way you'll start your networking with the people most likely to lead you to other people of similarly high relevance to your search. Who knows? You may reach your goal without ever "coming back to the well" (these 5 pages).

On the other hand, whenever your networking activities bog down for want of additional contacts to make, you can immediately come back here for more "starting-point" names. They'll be waiting, already sorted so you can handle them most efficiently.

Think About:

4. *The Likeliest And Strongest Reasons* Not *To Hire You*

Here's another very important factor in mapping campaign strategy that most executive job-changers tend to overlook. They're so totally involved in thoughts of why they ***should*** be hired, that they don't pay any attention to why they ***may not*** be. One major reason is that employers and executive recruiters hardly ever tell them the actual basis for rejection. It may be illegal. And often, of course, the decision-maker simply prefers someone else...and doesn't fully analyze why.

But negatives and "turn-offs" always exist. So I want you to think right now of the most likely reasons an employer may reject you. This can be painful stuff, and you may not like my bringing it up. But I'm on your side. Together let's try to identify possible problems. Then, in your resume- and letter-writing and in networking and interviewing, you may be able to inject a vaccine.

The trick is to identify the viruses. Recognition is critical, so we'll double-check.

Here are slots for your guesses as to the ***worst areas of negativity you're likely to face****. Please fill them in right now, while your thinking is still unaffected by mine. You'll see important personal issues that I can't possibly think of. So write your thoughts first. Then look at my list of prevalent negatives...and potential antidotes. Afterward there'll be more blanks, for a synthesis of your thoughts and mine.*

POTENTIAL NEGATIVE ____

____

____

____

____

POTENTIAL NEGATIVE ____

____

____

____

____

POTENTIAL NEGATIVE ____

____

____

____

____

POTENTIAL NEGATIVE ____

____

____

____

____

POTENTIAL NEGATIVE ____

____

____

____

____

POTENTIAL NEGATIVE ____

____

____

____

____

Potential Negatives to Eliminate

RITES OF PASSAGE AT $100,000 TO $1 MILLION+ has hundreds of pages of help to put you ahead of other candidates for every job you seek. We can't repeat those here. Instead, now that you've thought of your own reasons why decision-makers may *not* hire you, I'm going to list some further negative possibilities based on my 31 years of executive search experience. Between us, we should surely be able to identify almost everything that decision-makers may hold against you...all the while, of course, hiding behind their smokescreen of vague words like "overqualified."

A Mixed Bag

As you study this list of potential issues *and remedies*, you'll see two different types of problems. Some have to do with real or unfairly perceived shortcomings in you. Others are very real faults in the decision-maker, which you shouldn't have to worry about at all. But this is the real world. Take a look at those enemies too. Forewarned, you can plot your strategy to engage and defeat them...even though they never come out from behind the bushes.

1. Too Many Jobs Recently. This is the #1 potential killer...on your resume and in interviews. But it can be defended against. Merely explain. Did you follow the same person to more than one job? Or rejoin a former boss? *They wanted you because they knew how good you are!* Make that fact clear in your resume and in interviews, and the apparent negative will become a plus. Were you redundant after a merger? Three mergers in a row? Did a new higher-up bring in his or her own people? Don't be defensive...or a whiner. Be subtle. But don't just stand there with a black eye!

2. Reference Problems—Deserved or Not. Worried what might be said? Recognize that corporations *hate* to speak up these days for fear of law suits: (1) defamation (libel and slander), (2) unlawful discharge (age, gender, minority, and other discrimination), (3) "sexual harassment" and (4) "failure to inform" (if they *don't* tell an inquiring potential employer about bad behavior, they can be sued when something similar happens). So most companies try only to give employment dates...and they refer all queries to Personnel. But you *do* want inquirers to get reassurance. So combine "My-life's-an-open-book" and "There's-safety-in-numbers" as your strategy. Give a fairly long list of references...maybe upwards of a dozen. Include your bosses (the list looks fishy without them) *and others in the company who'll be more favorable.* When called, your "negative" references may not call back or may hide behind policy...while favorable ones will be reachable and complimentary. Another strategy is to negotiate with your former bosses a written "reference statement" as to just what they *will* say. Even after you do, you can still drown them in a sea of other references you're less concerned about.

3. Out of a BIG Company. Medium-sized—and especially smaller and entrepreneurial—companies often reject folks from behemoths like GM, GE, IBM, AT&T, etc., figuring that those folks usually deal only with small parts of giant problems and seldom have personal responsibility for anything major. Also, they're accustomed to vast staff support and even waste. Fair or unfair, that's what *lots* of people think. But don't let them apply those notions to you! Point out the waste and inefficiency you couldn't abide and/or helped end. Be "one of us"...not "one of them."

4. Out of the Military, the Government, or any Non-Profit. This is just another strain of the same flu that afflicts folks who are leaving a "BIG Company." Only more virulent, because it's multiple: Not only do you face (1) "They're so big nobody really has to work very hard or accomplish very much," you also face (2) "What they do is nothing like what we do," (3) "Their culture is nothing like ours," (BIG Company folks get some of this too) and (4) "They've never had to make a profit!" Your strategy? Same as for the "BIG Company" people. In addition, purge your speech and writing (resume) of words that are specific to your field. Say "300 people," not "Squadron" or "Company," and "got an unusually large raise," rather than "went from a GS-15 to an ES-2."

5. Out of an Unsuccessful Company. (Which these days may also be BIG.) A strong offense is the best defense. Emphasize how very successful *your* parts of the operation were. Show you saw and understood the mistakes and tried to help. But stop short of saying or writing anything that implies, "I was powerless to stop them." (You *are* persuasive, aren't you?) Also, reveal a bit of loyalty along with your 20/20 hindsight.

6. Tagged with a Turkey. So you've spent the last few years working on a notably unsuccessful project. If you weren't the #1 person in charge, you can stress the ways your part succeeded (met schedules, costs, and/or exceeded the norms for your types of activities in other more successful companies and projects). Even if you *were* in charge, you can still claim some of the same. Another strategy is to focus your search in somewhat different fields...particularly ones where you've had earlier successes. People there (1) will be less aware of your recent stumble and (2) will consider it far less interesting than your earlier successes on their turf.

7. Racial or Ethnic Minority. If they discriminate, then don't go to them. However, sometimes your particular decision-maker will still be biased, even after the overall organization has been straightened out. In which case, you may have a special opportunity. Dress, act, and talk "Main-stream Establishment" during your entire job-changing process. Avoid having some bigot block your entry. But investigate the culture *independently and carefully* before saying, "Yes, I'll join." This single issue can be so important to your long-range success that perhaps one of your earliest strategies should be to network among others of your background to identify a large number of congenial corporations. Then you can point your networking toward getting acquainted in those companies.

8. Severely Overweight. Man or woman, you've got a serious job-hunting handicap. No one will mention it. Everyone will consider it. Whether there's a medical basis or not doesn't matter. Apart from losing weight, there are only two strategies...neither easy: (1) Make an overwhelmingly compelling resume, loaded with succinctly worded far-beyond-the-ordinary accomplishments. And (2) Plan to work several times as hard as the average person and get several times as many interviews. You'll lose out on an unfair proportion. But there *are* objective employers in this world. Sift through lots of others to find them.

9. Too Experienced (read OLD). Twenty years ago when headhunters were instructed by their clients to conduct age-and gender-discriminatory searches (not illegal then), early- to mid-30s was considered ideal; today early- to mid-50s is just as appealing for high-level jobs. Unfortunately, in some companies "older" *is* less appealing at lower levels. As with overweight, your best strategy is simply to search harder and get more interviews; your statistical odds improve accordingly. Also consider using a "sponsored" direct mail campaign (see the sample letter mentioning age on page 161). Your "sponsor" can speak of your age gracefully, whereas you cannot. (True, too, of obesity and other prejudicial matters.) Be sure to read all of *RITES OF PASSAGE AT $100,000 TO $1 MILLION+*, going straight through front-to-back in sequence. Take advantage of every technique. Pay special attention to the material on consulting, which can often be a good strategy for an older person.

10. Lack of a College or Advanced Degree. If, by mid-career, you've scored impressive achievements despite less education than you'd prefer, "Congratulations!" You've arrived. Today you're far more likely to be hired for your accomplishments than for your schooling. And that probably will still be true, even if you go back and get more education. So your #1 strategy on this, too, should be a compelling resume, which you load with succinctly worded examples of impressive achievements and then circulate to lots of employers who need what you do. The smart ones will wisely choose proven performance over credential potential. And ***please***, don't listen to any mini-minded recruiter who points to the empty square on your bingo card and shouts, "Ah Ha!" Take time to study *RITES OF PASSAGE* before you bother to pick up any college text at this late date. Far too many self-doubting folks wind up writing an academic thesis, when similar effort on a stronger resume would have done them lots more good a whole lot faster.

11. Foreign Accent. If it's slight and charming, NO problem! But if even a few people find you somewhat hard to understand until they get to know you, you're in deep trouble as a job-hunter. The first few sentences of your interview could kill you, even if talk continues for an hour. Chances are, what follows will proceed merely from (1) courtesy and/or (2) curiosity to know your credentials, so a recruiter can be asked to find someone comparable but easier to communicate with. This is a harsh message, but one you need to hear. Please see a speech therapist. They're listed in the Yellow Pages. Many don't cost too much. And most do near-miracles in a hurry. So make the most worthwhile career investment of your lifetime. The best complementary and/or alternate strategy is to focus on international and/or foreign-owned companies. Their ears are sharper and their minds are more open...at least on this issue.

12. Hair "Replacement" on a Man. Glued on or knotted on, "replacements" *are* obvious. And unless you're lucky enough to find a potential boss who also has one, yours *will* be detected and *will* be held against you. If it looks silly—and despite the TV ads nearly all do almost every time you leave the house—you'll be faulted both for personal insecurity and for bad judgment. Ironic, isn't it, that you're stuck with an insecurity label, even though it takes more guts to wear a "piece" than not to. Your campaign strategy? Simple. Go naked on top...at least until your employment contract is signed.

13. Fear of a Too-Strong Subordinate. Now we're totally into the area of things that can be fundamentally wrong with some *decision-makers*—and not you at all—which you, nonetheless, may be prone to bump up against and should map a strategy to cope with. Do you have a strong personality and presence? Have you been a widely well-known player? Are you almost *too* promotable into the decision-maker's job? If so, what should be your strategy? First of all, do *not* dilute your resume. Let it be fully as strong and successful as you are. But *do* take a very strategic approach to interviews: (1) Be absolutely your warmest and most unthreatening self. And (2) Bend your knee to all your *former bosses.* Speak glowingly of their brilliance and kindness...and of your deep personal friendships with them which endure, even to this moment. Obviously you haven't bitten others. You must be a Doberman that loves children.

14. Fear of a Life Outside the Office...Maybe Even a Family! This employer fault has always unfairly plagued women, and now dogs everyone suspected of nurturing anything but the corporation. You may not like this advice one bit. But in the spirit of what we're doing together, I must provide it, regardless. Let your resume and interviews be reassuring on all the issues that can't legally be probed. Show you *don't* have a household (if true), and subtly show *fail-safe systems* if you do: "I was stranded for two days in Denver; fortunately, when that happens the kids go next door for dinner and stay 'til I'm home. I pay $80 a month for that, whether I need it or not."

15. Fear You Can't Be Managed. If you've grown up in a family business, or if you're an entrepreneur and have been doing *your* way what the corporation wants done *its* way, then the corporate corporals will worry that you won't be listening when they explain how the business world works. Probably true! This prejudice is very tough to overcome. Your best strategies: Soft pedal in the resume how infallibly secure your position may have been. And in interviews, try to ask lots of questions. Perhaps even feign some "Gee whiz!" at the answers. The opposite could be deadly in your case.

16. Fear of Insufficient Fear. If you've got a trust fund, or have made a bundle on an LBO, or stand to inherit a fortune, or have a spouse earning megabucks, you've probably got a potential fear deficiency. After all, how scared can you get? At least until you're hired, try not to let them realize that you need them a lot less than they need you.

Now it's time to take advantage of our combined thoughts and develop strategies with respect to all the negative reactions you're likely to encounter. Notice that this time there's space to fill-in not only the potential negative itself, but also your strategy either to head it off, or to deal with it if and when it arises. Please repeat the problems you put on your original list...and add any of the potential "turn-offs" I brought up that may apply to your job-campaign:

POTENTIAL NEGATIVE ____

____

STRATEGY FOR HANDLING ____

____

____

____

POTENTIAL NEGATIVE ____

____

STRATEGY FOR HANDLING ____

____

____

____

POTENTIAL NEGATIVE ____

____

STRATEGY FOR HANDLING ____

____

____

____

POTENTIAL NEGATIVE ____

____

STRATEGY FOR HANDLING ____

____

____

____

POTENTIAL NEGATIVE ____________________

STRATEGY FOR HANDLING ____________________

POTENTIAL NEGATIVE ____________________

STRATEGY FOR HANDLING ____________________

POTENTIAL NEGATIVE ____________________

STRATEGY FOR HANDLING ____________________

POTENTIAL NEGATIVE ____________________

STRATEGY FOR HANDLING ____________________

POTENTIAL NEGATIVE ____________________

STRATEGY FOR HANDLING ____________________

Think About:

5. *What Do You Really* Want *To Do*?

Up to now I've been stressing that—in looking for a job—the point is always what the *employer* wants that you provide, and not what *you* want that the employer's job can provide.

Absolutely true.

But that does *not* mean you shouldn't seek and obtain the greatest possible satisfaction and compensation from your career. Of course you should! Indeed, we looked at these sayings before, and they're worth repeating:

"Be careful what you seek. You might find it!"

AND

"Be careful what you wish for. You might get it!"

Here in Section 5 we'll polish your "seeking" and "wishing." With skill and maybe a bit of luck, your "getting" will improve accordingly.

Notice the shift of gears. So far, we've been selling...figuring out what the customer wants, and trying to package and present it as persuasively as possible. *After* this section, we'll go back to selling...and continue all the way to the end of this WORKBOOK. Indeed, we hope, all the way to your ideal job.

For the present, however, we're on the *buying* side of the equation. *Bartering* would be a better word, because employment is a process of *exchanging* one thing for another. You give up days, weeks and years in return for a package called "employment." And it's not just money. If it were, you'd merely be selling. But it's more. Beyond the money for a certain standard of living for yourself and your family, it's also the pleasure you get during the time you put in, the pride you take in the products or services you work on, the prestige of the organization and your status in it, the number and calibre of people you deal with, and the memories, satisfactions (or lack of them), and financial security you wind up with when you retire.

Now that's pretty heavy stuff.

And most people don't give it proper attention. Indeed, most folks *can't* give it attention. They're too busy working! If there's anything at all that's good about currently not having a job—or being in a concerted effort to get a different one—it's the chance to make the next job something you really *want* to do, rather than just something circumstances have imposed on you.

Enjoyment in Your Employment

Robert Frost wrote *The Road Less Traveled* as he gave up his secure job teaching school in a small town in New Hampshire and went to England to study and write poetry.* He wanted to spend his time on what he loved, and therefore decided to try to earn his living with it. How outrageously self-indulgent...and even stupid! Even in 1916 everyone knew you couldn't make a living as a poet. "The rest," as they say, "is history."

Here are Frost's words as he took a personal risk that—at least in monetary terms—had no reasonable chance of paying off as it ultimately did:

I shall be telling this with a sigh
Somewhere ages and ages hence:
Two roads diverged in a wood, and I—
I took the one less traveled by,
And that has made all the difference.

Today you're at a crossroad. Either you don't have a job, or are seeking an improvement on your current one. But what? More of the same? Or something different?

And how different? Can you afford a move as radical and gutsy as Robert Frost's? School teaching normally pays better than writing poetry. But it doesn't support an expensive lifestyle. Have you reached levels of earning *and spending* where your next job had better be fairly similar to your latest one or you can't make ends meet?

That's most people's situation as they read *Rites of Passage at $100,000 to $1 Million+* and use this Workbook. Yours too?

Which makes me a little hesitant to urge anything drastic. However, I do ask you to really spend time with the exercises in this section. They may be the only minutes during your weeks or months of job-changing that you'll ask, "Is there something more enjoyable for me than what I've been doing? And if I can't afford a radical change, is there a modest shift that could yield more pleasure *and* enough money.

Maybe there is.

Probing and Stretching

That's why the tools in this section (1) probe your interests and (2) stretch what—up to now—you've considered doing. What are some jobs that could pay you what you need and yet actually deal to some extent with subject matter that really turns you on?

People *do* enter by the side door. For example, several lawyers have become top executives in the record and publishing industries. They loved the subject matter and decided to do their legal work in those fields. Having had an ear or eye for what the public wants, some eventually became CEOs—and even founders—of major companies.

*Of course, he returned and was the quintessential American poet.

Maybe you're now a Partner in an accounting firm or a corporate Controller or CFO. But your real passion is music...even though your closest brush with it—beyond collecting CDs—was playing third chair bassoon in the high school orchestra. Does your local symphony need a CFO? Or the opera? Or a national foundation for the arts? Do your "artsy" or intellectual interests extend beyond music? Maybe there's an intriguing and—to you at least—fulfilling position as financial and administrative head of a college or university. Or do you love professional sports? Travel? History? Architecture? Horse racing? Oceanography? Would you like to be doing something—even in a tangential way—toward alleviating the world's hunger? Or helping the homeless?

Let's hope that never again in your lifetime will you conduct an all-out search for employment. So why not make the most of this one?

Which brings us to the two categories of tools in this section: (1) ***"Think-of-Your-Interests-and-Enjoyments"*** and (2) ***"Think-of-Jobs-You-Could-Do."*** Grab these tools and use them wholeheartedly. They will substantially expand the range of jobs you can envision yourself filling and enjoying. And, as your number of thought-about jobs increases, so do your statistical odds of getting interviews and offers by pursuing that larger number of possibilities!

1. Your Interests and Enjoyments

1. ***Consider*** *all the activities and events you've ever enjoyed. Don't struggle; just work with casual top-of-mind thoughts.* ***Fill in*** *the following 21* "ENJOYMENTS" *with things to do and some major events that you have enjoyed. Don't worry that they're not sorted in any way. "Reading the newspaper; fishing; sewing; travel; playing football; trip to Rome; restoring/trading antique cars; planning Jennifer's wedding; floating the Eurobond issue" would all be perfectly OK for this purpose.*

2. ***When you're finished****, go back over the list and* ***fill in*** *at least two jobs at approximately the level of status and compensation you require, which would be somehow involved in the activity or event you've listed.*

Unless you're willing to take a pay cut and utterly change your lifestyle, Flight Attendant *would* not *be a reasonable* "ASSOCIATED JOB THOUGHT" *to go with your* "Trip to Rome" *entry. However,* New England Marketing Manager, American Airlines *might (don't worry whether AA has such a position; this is merely a mind-stretching exercise). So might* Regional (or Corporate) Controller, American Express Travel Services, *if you're a finance and not a marketing person. You get the idea. These people don't necessarily take any more trips than you do...although there's a good chance they may...but getting into their industries at their levels might make your next 22 years on this planet more interesting and enjoyable than continuing to work in the widget business.*

ENJOYMENT ______________________________

ASSOCIATED JOB THOUGHTS ______________________________

____

____

ENJOYMENT ______________________________

ASSOCIATED JOB THOUGHTS ______________________________

____

____

ENJOYMENT ______________________________

ASSOCIATED JOB THOUGHTS ______________________________

____

____

ENJOYMENT ______________________________

ASSOCIATED JOB THOUGHTS ______________________________

____

____

ENJOYMENT ______________________________

ASSOCIATED JOB THOUGHTS ______________________________

____

____

ENJOYMENT ______________________________

ASSOCIATED JOB THOUGHTS ______________________________

____

____

ENJOYMENT ______________________________

ASSOCIATED JOB THOUGHTS ______________________________

____

____

ENJOYMENT ____________________

ASSOCIATED JOB THOUGHTS ____________________

ENJOYMENT ____________________

ASSOCIATED JOB THOUGHTS ____________________

ENJOYMENT ____________________

ASSOCIATED JOB THOUGHTS ____________________

ENJOYMENT ____________________

ASSOCIATED JOB THOUGHTS ____________________

ENJOYMENT ____________________

ASSOCIATED JOB THOUGHTS ____________________

ENJOYMENT ____________________

ASSOCIATED JOB THOUGHTS ____________________

ENJOYMENT ____________________

ASSOCIATED JOB THOUGHTS ____________________

ENJOYMENT ____________________

ASSOCIATED JOB THOUGHTS ____________________

ENJOYMENT ____________________

ASSOCIATED JOB THOUGHTS ____________________

ENJOYMENT ____________________

ASSOCIATED JOB THOUGHTS ____________________

ENJOYMENT ____________________

ASSOCIATED JOB THOUGHTS ____________________

ENJOYMENT ____________________

ASSOCIATED JOB THOUGHTS ____________________

ENJOYMENT ____________________

ASSOCIATED JOB THOUGHTS ____________________

ENJOYMENT ____________________

ASSOCIATED JOB THOUGHTS ____________________

2. Jobs You Could Do

If you notice overlap in the career possibilities these tools help you think about, or if you find yourself describing similar jobs several times over, don't be dismayed. Just "go with the flow." The whole idea is to probe and stretch your thinking. Naturally, in probing you're likely to find the same thing more than once. And in stretching, you may repeatedly reach similar limits. Some of those "repeats" may point out and reinforce a valid insight. Others may just mean you're not being as "loose" and creative as you're capable of being. So what? Fresh thoughts *will* arise. And they're what you're working to accomplish.

Now jot down titles and brief descriptions of the ***greatest jobs you can imagine****. Make each one a job you'd love (even if you can't quite see yourself getting it at this stage in life) in terms of all the rewards and satisfactions it might bring: intellectual challenge, interest and pride in the product/service/industry involved, right amount of dealing with people, the type of people you'd like and respect, location and ambience, preferred amount of travel, demanding or nonstressful involvement, prestige/status, near- and long-term compensation, self-image and (bottom line) self-fulfillment:*

IDEAL JOB ______________________________

DESCRIPTION ______________________________

____

IDEAL JOB ______________________________

DESCRIPTION ______________________________

____

IDEAL JOB ______________________________

DESCRIPTION ______________________________

____

IDEAL JOB ______________________________

DESCRIPTION ______________________________

____

IDEAL JOB ______________________________

DESCRIPTION ______________________________

____

IDEAL JOB ______________________________

DESCRIPTION ______________________________

____

IDEAL JOB ______________________________

DESCRIPTION ______________________________

____

IDEAL JOB ______________________________

DESCRIPTION ______________________________

____

IDEAL JOB ______________________________

DESCRIPTION ______________________________

____

IDEAL JOB ______________________________

DESCRIPTION ______________________________

____

IDEAL JOB ______________________________

DESCRIPTION ______________________________

____

IDEAL JOB ______________________________

DESCRIPTION ______________________________

____

Okay. Now let's get practical. We're coming down to the wire. Please go back over the two lists of possible jobs you've just created...the ones related to your "ENJOYMENT" *and the* "IDEAL"*ones...and pick out just* ***5 jobs that really appeal to you and you feel you have a realistic chance of getting and performing well.*** *Don't hesitate to be optimistic. Stretch. But make this a list you can work toward as your job search proceeds. And this time, as you describe the jobs, jot down any extra specifics that occur to you...names of companies that might have such jobs, or people you might talk to about them. No need to fill in anything extra, but if a thought occurs to you, put it down.*

REALISTIC JOB POSSIBILITY______________________________

OBSERVATIONS ______________________________

____

____

REALISTIC JOB POSSIBILITY______________________________

OBSERVATIONS ______________________________

____

____

REALISTIC JOB POSSIBILITY______________________________

OBSERVATIONS ______________________________

____

____

REALISTIC JOB POSSIBILITY______________________________

OBSERVATIONS ______________________________

____

____

REALISTIC JOB POSSIBILITY______________________________

OBSERVATIONS ______________________________

____

____

We're finished "probing"...having framed your basic list of target jobs to stalk. Now please give very serious thought to this final and most interesting "stretch." Staying in the realm of jobs you could do and have some realistic chance of getting, **list 5 jobs that are each as different from the other 4 as they can possibly be.** *As benchmarks use one or two from the opposite page. Go back over your previous ideas. Think up* **new** *possibilities. Even include one or two you don't like terribly much. Stretch the boundaries. Lay claim to as much potential job-finding territory as possible. With this list and the opposite one, you'll approach the marketplace with your eyes wide open to all possibilities.*

BOUNDARY-STRETCHING JOB POSSIBILITY ______________________________

OBSERVATIONS ______________________________

____

____

BOUNDARY-STRETCHING JOB POSSIBILITY ______________________________

OBSERVATIONS ______________________________

____

____

BOUNDARY-STRETCHING JOB POSSIBILITY ______________________________

OBSERVATIONS ______________________________

____

____

BOUNDARY-STRETCHING JOB POSSIBILITY ______________________________

OBSERVATIONS ______________________________

____

____

BOUNDARY-STRETCHING JOB POSSIBILITY ______________________________

OBSERVATIONS ______________________________

____

____

To Help With Your

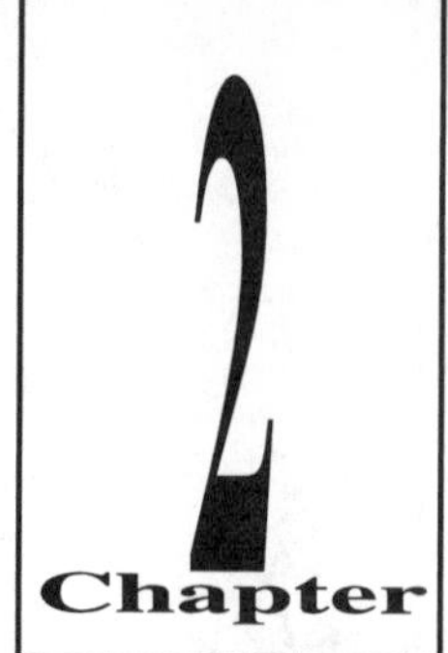

Resume

Nothing is more important to your success in changing jobs than the document that defines who you are and describes what you've accomplished.

It's your personal sales representative...able to be where you can't be and sell when you're not there.

A Radical Idea?

Does it strike you as odd to think of your resume as a personal sales representative?

In looking for another or a better job, *are* you selling? Isn't it enough merely to make your existence known?

Face it. When you enter the job market, you *do* enter a selling situation. And it's extremely competitive. Almost never will you be the only candidate. And almost never will all the others be clearly less likely to fulfill the employer's needs.

People Are *Not* All the Same. What if They Were?

People don't come off an assembly line like a Ford® or a Mercedes.® Or like cans of Maxwell House.® Do you want blue or grey? Regular or decaffeinated? The factories do turn out choices. But the greatness of modern manufacturing is that, except for intentional variety, every unit is identical to every other one.

If only people were like that!

Then hiring a senior executive would be as simple as ordering a car. And recruiting a junior manager would be as easy as phoning for a pizza. Every CFO with 14 years of appropriate experience would be just like every other. It wouldn't matter which the executive searcher "found" or the employer hired.

Performance would be uniform. And with executives as identical as SONY® CD-players, selection could be based on discount pricing. "Find me the CFO with at least 14 years in our industry who'll come here for the least money," the CEO would tell the search consultant.

For Standardized Executives, a Standard Resume

If executives were a factory product and interchangeable, then each resume would be just a spec sheet...merely stating name, address, phone numbers, current and past employers, titles, dates, responsibilities, and in the briefest possible way perhaps a list of identifying achievements. It surely wouldn't be longer than one page. And it wouldn't be hard to write!

"But," you say, "personalities would still be different. "I'd still want to tell them that I'm intelligent, creative, profit-oriented, cheerful, optimistic, loaded with leadership, good at selecting and motivating people, adept at team-building, and so on."

And I'd remind you that those are the kind of self-flattering comments that don't help you in a resume. They can't be believed because the reader (1) can't be sure you're an accurate judge and (2) realizes your self-praise is likely to be biased.

Besides, for the moment, you and I are in fantasy land. We're where executives with comparable education and experience in comparable fields are all alike. They all produce fine performances. And since they do, they must have the necessary traits.

Communicating in the Real World

Back to reality.

Executives are not factory-made. Their performances are not even remotely uniform. Sadly, what they'll be able to accomplish in the future is only a guess. And our only basis for guessing favorably—and hiring one person instead of others—is what he or she has accomplished in the past.

Self-flattering adjectives are no help. And neither is a mere data sheet containing nothing more than education, times, titles, employers, and responsibilities.

Everyone who has been around 12 years has "twelve years experience." And anyone who has been anywhere has been "responsible for" something.

The question is, during X years with Y responsibilities, what did he or she *accomplish*? And how does it compare with what others accomplished under similar circumstances? If it's not notably better, then we'd be just as well off hiring one of the others. In fact we'd be *better* off, because several of "them" have told us about very impressive things they have accomplished for previous employers...and are therefore likely to accomplish for us.

"Product; Meet Your Sales Representative"

So you see, in a sense you are a product. The performance you'll deliver, if hired, is like the music the CD player will put out. You have to be sold in a competitive marketplace, and your prior accomplishments are the only proof of your attributes. They are the closest things to the "performance specs" you'd insist on if you were buying a sports car or a computer. Not nearly as reliable...but at least an indication.

Since you're a product, wouldn't it be nice if you could find a sales rep who'd memorize your competitive sales pitch and "take it on the road."

In fact, of course, that's what a resume is often asked to do.

Maybe you'll mail or e-mail your resume to an employer or to an executive recruiter. Probably you'll supply a few copies to one of your close personal contacts, or to someone you've newly met through networking...and they'll send or hand your resume to others. Imagine for a moment that you're already a finalist candidate on a job you'd love. At this point, your potential boss probably hands a copy of your resume to his or her boss...or a CEO hands it to his or her Board...in order to get final approval to hire you.

In each instance your resume must give a compelling sales pitch for you. It must be where you can't be and sell when you're not there.

The *Rites of Passage* Way of Looking at Resumes

The concept that a resume must sell the executive it's representing is at the heart of *Rites'* resume advice, which has been widely endorsed as a welcome departure from the noncompetitive sameness of most resumes. For example, in a full page review complimenting many other aspects of *Rites* as well, here's what *Financial World* said about the *Rites* approach to resumes:

> "The side effect of this advice may well be that corporate executives will start seeing lots of resumes and cover letters looking like Lucht's examples. If so, it will be a small price to pay for the improvements cloned approaches will embody."

Exactly what has happened! That was 325,000 copies ago. Today, *Rites* is by far the most widely followed guide to executive job-changing, and thousands of people are presenting their past performances very persuasively. Not only has their job-hunting become more aggressive and effective, it now has a competitive advantage over the efforts of other unemployed executives who are still relying on traditionally bland and cliché-based resumes.

However, a great many outstanding executives do not find it easy to write a resume that is custom-tailored to their own personal accomplishments. They are able executives, but not necessarily adept resume writers.

So let's work together. First we'll review what *RITES* has to say about resumes, and then we'll get busy with tools to help you achieve the objectives *RITES* lays out.

As an upwardly-mobile executive, you need a really good personal sales representative...one that can be where you can't be, and sell when you're not there.

You need a resume.

And it should be as persuasive as you can possibly make it. Indeed, it should be compelling enough to take on the hardest selling challenge of all: to make "cold calls" on complete strangers...and get results.

That's what a resume has to do as the core of a direct mail campaign. It arrives uninvited and unexpected. And usually it's assisted by nothing more than a brief covering letter. If it can convince someone who's never before met or heard about you to call you up or to write you a letter, then surely it can do everything else you could ask a resume to do.

You can trust such a resume to be your spokesperson whenever you can't be present. Whether you leave it behind after a successful interview, or send it ahead hoping to get an appointment, it will give every recipient the same persuasive, ungarbled message you'd convey in person. Effective all by itself, your resume will also be an indispensable aid to anybody who wants to "sell" you to someone else...from the recruiter telling his client about you, to your potential boss telling her boss, to the CEO telling his Board.

Before we start creating your optimum "Sales Representative" resume, let's consider why it's worth a substantial effort and dispose of any excuses for not putting that much work into it.

It'$ your most valuable credential.

How long did you spend in undergraduate college...four years? And maybe in grad school after that...two to five years? And besides the time...the money? And for what?

Alphabet soup. Credentials! Stuff on paper that you hoped...and to some extent you've found...could enhance your earning power and career achievement, in addition to culturally enriching your life.

Suppose it takes you a week working full-time, or a month of nights and weekends, to compile a succinct but compellingly information-packed statement of what you've accomplished for employers since college...the only things a potential employer really cares about and pays you "$100,000 to $1 million+" for. The resume you wind up with is the most valuable credential you can have today. Again it's symbols on paper. But this time, far more negotiable at the bank.

Persuaded? Some people still come up with reasons not to make a first-class resume. Here they are ...with my answers:

"I don't need a resume because it's classier not to have one."

Well, at least it's less work.

"I don't need a resume because I'm basing my campaign on getting the prestigious retainer recruiting firms to come after me. They'll create my resume."

If you succeed in turning the headhunters' heads, that will be true. At least so it will seem to their clients. Even if you hand one of those top recruiters an excellent resume, his or her assistant will re-type it so that it will appear consistent with the papers presented on other candidates.

But suppose the job's a really terrific opportunity for you...and five other people. Do you want to rest your case on what the recruiter will write from memory after an hour or so of conversation? If you hand her a highly persuasive resume, she won't make it worse to match the rest. And if she has to write it, chances are she can't make it good enough to match the best.

"Fortunately, I don't have to bother writing my own resume; the people who fired me have paid for outplacement services."

Some things are more important to you and to your future than they are to anyone else. The document that positions you in the employment world is one of them.

PLEASE DO NOT BE MISLED. THE WORKBOOK HELPS YOU CREATE A RESUME AND COVER LETTER STRONG ENOUGH FOR DIRECT MAIL...AND HENCE IDEAL FOR ANY OTHER USE.

IT DOES NOT, HOWEVER, COVER HOW TO CONDUCT A DIRECT MAIL CAMPAIGN. NOR DOES IT WARN YOU AGAINST WASTING MONEY AND EFFORT ON DIRECT MAIL WHEN IT IS VERY LIKELY TO PROVE FUTILE IN YOUR CASE.

THAT INFORMATION COMPRISES CHAPTERS 11 AND 13 OF *RITES OF PASSAGE AT $100,000 TO $1 MILLION+.*

(MUCH OF CHAPTER 12 IS PRESENTED HERE AS A FOUNDATION FOR THE EXAMPLES, TOOLS AND GUIDES TO COME.)

Okay, the usual objections and excuses are out of the way. Now let's talk about your ultimate credential, the true "Sales Representative" resume... strong enough for use in direct mail, and therefore best for every other use, too.

Direct mail selling is the hardest test persuasive writing can be put to. By mailing to large numbers of potential purchasers, it's possible to blanket so many that you'll surely hit a few who have a need at the exact moment your envelope arrives. But grabbing attention, engaging interest, and convincing strongly enough to stimulate action...that's still a lot to ask of mere words on paper. You'd better send something powerful. And the core of the package is the resume.

The only reason that a resume delivered by the Postal Service or by e-mail prods any recipient into action is that it's an effective sales rep. It's *a persuasive piece of writing* that communicates enticingly and fully enough to convince the reader that the person behind the resume might be the solution to the reader's problem.

That's what your resume is: your "Sales Representative" on paper, who'll speak for you when you can't be there. And that's true regardless of whether your resume:

1. *arrives "cold"* in the mail, or by accident, or
2. *is hand delivered*...by you yourself, or by someone who's met you and wants another person to know you as fully and favorably as he or she does.

Indeed, as we shall see, a resume effective enough to perform in this situation will also be effective when:

3. *you offer it as an orientation aid at an interview.*

...And now for the shocker. What's the number-one principle of direct mail copywriting?

In almost every industry, there's a bedrock principle discovered years ago...and reconfirmed again and again through the experience of everyone in the field...until it becomes the rule that all know and follow. In real estate, for example, it's:

"Location is everything."

Or, stated another way...

"The three principles of real estate are:
(1) Location, (2) location, and (3) location."

In direct mail copywriting, as in real estate, success or failure is proven in dollars and cents. Before any company sends a mailing to 5 million or 15 million households, several different versions are tested, ranging from short to long copy, and trying new gimmicks, such as envelopes that look like bank statements, bills, personal notes, etc. Objective: to see which variation pulls most orders per thousand dollars of cost.

Some of the new gimmicks test well and are used. Others are forgotten. But, like real estate, direct mail copywriting has one bedrock principle that everyone respects...proven during fifty years of testing and reconfirmed by test after test today:

"Long copy sells."

Proof of this honored axiom is delivered to your home every day. If shortness worked, brevity would be in your mailbox. And all the companies now using long-copy direct mail could achieve multi-million dollar savings in paper, printing, and postage...everything that makes a fat letter or brochure more expensive than a thin one. Those companies aren't stupid. They test. They don't spend more money unless the results *more* than justify the extra cost.

However, this proven axiom should, as advertising guru David Ogilvy pointed out, be more accurately stated:

"Factual copy sells."

Famous for his "long-copy" ads, Mr. Ogilvy is also a crusader for very clear and ***succinct*** writing. He conveys each fact with arresting clarity and *brevity*, and then piles up a wealth of these impressive facts to prove that his client's product is superior to competitive brands. Master of the concise well-turned phrase, Ogilvy sums up the principle this way: "*The more you **tell**, the more you **sell**.*"

Incidentally, the experts I've talked to tell me that the only exceptions to the "long copy sells" rule occur with simple products that every recipient is already thoroughly familiar with before the mailing arrives. In such cases, explanation of the *product* is unnecessary, because only the briefly stated *offer* is new.

For example, you can sell someone a half-price subscription to *Time* or *Fortune* with a postcard or a little self-mailer envelope, whereas it will take several pages of facts and pictures to persuade the same person to sign up for a "four-months-free, cancel-and-pay-nothing" offer on a new publication.

When you get in touch with a prospective employer, you're always an unknown new publication. You're not *Business Week*, *Forbes*, or *The Wall Street Journal*, and don't you forget it!

There are always, of course, a few "celebrity" executives in any field who...at least during their transitory heyday...could get by with brevity instead of a convincing dose of long copy. Remember when just this sort of note from someone like Jack Welch would have produced a flood of inquiries?

> I've pretty much finished what I set out to do here.
>
> If you think I could be helpful to your company, please give me a call.
>
> Sincerely,

Q: What happens when you apply direct mail copywriting to your resume?

A: It goes from 2 pages to 3 or 4 pages... and it contains 3 or 5 times as much of the persuasive information employers are interested in.

"Look, John," I'll bet you're saying, "forgetting for the moment the fact that everyone has always told me resumes should be brief, not long...and maybe conceding that the direct mail people do know about stimulating action through a written sales presentation...still, I can't let you get away with saying that *doubling* the pages from two to four will provide *five times* as much persuasive information."

I knew I'd grab you with that idea.

But think about it for a minute. On two pages you're barely able to list your name, address, office and home phone numbers, college degrees, a couple personal facts, and lay out a reverse-chronological listing of all the companies you've worked for and the progression of titles and responsibilities from college to now...all requisites of a good resume. Certainly that's true if you create a nice clean layout with lots of white space separating all the elements, so that where you've been and what you've done is easy to scan...a point we'll get back to later.

So in two pages, you *are* able to list all the job titles you've held and give a skimpy description of responsibilities for the more recent and important ones. Unfortunately, you haven't got room to say much, if anything, about what you *achieved* when you held those responsibilities. And achievements proving you're special are what a prospective employer is looking for.

Everyone has been given responsibility. Only a special few...you among them, I hope...have given back anything really substantial in the way of achievement.

Let's say that in a nice, open, quick-to-scan layout, with your chronological units floating in a decent amount of white space, you get 400 to 500 words on a page, 800 to 1,000 on two pages...and 75% of them are devoted to covering the mandatory data. That leaves about 200 to 250 words for accomplishments that could make you stand out as interesting...and hopefully special...in the eyes of a potential employer.

Now go from two pages to four. You've got room for 1,600 to 2,000 words...800 to 1,000 more than before. And *every additional word* can be devoted to achievements, because the basics were already covered in the two-page version. Add your original 200 to 250 words on achievements, and the box score looks like this:

	Total Words	Basic Data (Words)	Achievements (Words)	How Many Times As Many Achievement Words?
2 Pages	800-1000	600-750	200-250	1
3 Pages	1200-1500	600-750	600-750	3
4 Pages	1600-2000	600-750	1000-1250	5

But now let's go back to the point about everyone telling you to keep your resume brief. Who told you? And when? And why?

Who and When?

Was it your "Counselor" at the contingency firm that helped you get your first job out of college or graduate school? Was it someone who "worked with" you or "headhunted" you as you moved into middle management with your second or third job?

Face it: in those days you hadn't done anything really significant yet. At that stage no one has. Or if they have, nobody is prepared to believe they have.

From entry level up through middle management you're somewhere from a "GI Joe" to a first lieutenant in the army of industry. What an employer wants to know is where you've been...how fast you're moving up...and how closely your experience matches what she wants done. That information fits neatly on one page...certainly no more than two. Indeed, if you're bright, attractive, and ambitious, it won't matter if your entire early career has been spent working on a string of corporate *flops!* You won't be blamed. You didn't commit the corporation to those misadventures. And you weren't so centrally responsible for implementation that anyone will figure you made a good idea fail.

Today, however, you're in an altogether different situation. You're earning "$100,000 to $1 million+." Now you're at least a "field commander." You legitimately *can* claim some victories. And you can be held responsible for some defeats. *Your resume must deliver more factual information.*

Also consider the "why" behind the advice you're given.

If you're now earning $300,000+, and "*when*" you were told to "keep it brief" was yesterday, and "*who*" told you was a prestigious retainer recruiter...then maybe we should consider "*why*" he said that.

The most obvious reason is that you only have a fleeting moment of your reader's time and attention before he'll give up on your resume as too tedious to figure out, and toss it aside. *This reason I totally agree with.* However, I don't agree that the solution to the problem is to strip away your persuasive factual information.

The other reason could be that the retainer recruiter has orally "pre-sold" you to his client, so your resume doesn't have to be persuasive. My reaction to this reason from your standpoint is "OK...*but.*" The recruiter is introducing several other candidates besides you, and if you have some impressive achievements, you want them clearly known to the employer as she chooses between you and the others.

Your resume must perform two functions. Brevity suits one...and defeats the other.

Your resume absolutely must do two things. Unfortunately, while brevity achieves one, it defeats the other. Therefore, unless you're Lee Iacocca, brevity isn't your answer.

1. Quick Orientation

Your reader will allow your resume only about thirty seconds...no more than a minute...to orient him to who you are, and whether you might be relevant to his needs right now. Certainly that's true if it arrives "cold" in the mail; he'll spend *more* time with it, not less, if he's paid a retainer recruiter over $80,000 to look for it.

Most of the time your resume will reach the reader when he doesn't need you. And you'll have his attention for less than a minute. By then, if you've done a poor orientation job, he'll have dumped you for being too tedious and confusing. And even if you've done a good job, he'll almost always have dumped you for not being needed right now.

2. Thorough Convincing

But in the rare, rare instance when you do happen to hit a reader at the moment she has a need you might fill, and you quickly orient her to that fact, then she's willing to extend her attention span a bit further.

She didn't find you irrelevant. Now she's looking to find you ordinary. But, wait a minute; you've been involved in several things that were impressively successful...another "turn off" bypassed. Okay, but probably these programs were conceived, planned, and strategically implemented by others, and you were merely a supporting player. No, wait another minute; your clear, succinct explanation of the reasons underlying the actions that were taken certainly sounds like you were the strategist, not just the "gofer." Your reader decides:

> "This guy is *interesting*. I'll read to the end. And then I'll go back over this whole thing again. If he still looks okay, maybe I'll even call him up."

As you see, a very brief resume could have performed the quick orientation and helped your reader turn off. Unfortunately, it probably couldn't have turned her on...and on...and on...to the point of picking up the phone and calling you.

Fortunately, a resume written according to the "long copy sells" principle of direct mail copywriting is capable of walking and chewing gum at the same time.

Right away you're probably saying, "I can see, John, where long copy will be great at 'Thorough Convincing,' but won't it interfere with 'Quick Orientation'?"

No. Not if you're careful to make your resume *visually accessible*. Format and layout become extremely important. Just make your resume:

Scannable!

Your reader will glance at 3, 4, 5, or 6 pages if it's instantly evident with just one glance what's on each of those pages. If you arrange your resume right, the recipient will probably glance through *all* of the pages before reading *any* of them. That's everyone's normal impulse as a reader anyway. You probably flipped through this book before you began reading it page-by-page. Fortunately, with resumes in particular, it's easy to help that normal human tendency along.

Don't you just hate topically oriented resumes? Don't you wish everyone did?

I have never yet met anyone who likes to receive a topically oriented resume.

You know the kind...where practically the whole thing is a list of claimed accomplishments, presented entirely out of context of when they happened...who the executive was working for...what his title, responsibilities, reporting relationships, and staff were...and what the size and nature of the businesses were. Finally, if you're lucky...and it's not always there...you find a deliberately sketchy little "Chronology of Employment" buried at the end, from which...if you're not already too turned off...you try to guess when and for whom and from what position of how much authority those previously claimed management miracles were achieved.

You and I are in the overwhelming majority in disliking topically oriented resumes (also sometimes euphemistically referred to as "achievement-oriented"). When on the receiving end, virtually everybody prefers the good, honest, comfortable, easy-to-read old-fashioned kind, where name, address, and business and home phone numbers are at the top, and work history proceeds backwards from current job on the first page to earliest on the last page.

**Everyone's recognition of...and preference for...
the standard-format resume solves your "scannability"
problem, without getting you into the brevity trap.**

If you don't go out of your way to confuse your reader, you've got the scannability problem solved... no matter how long you choose to make your resume.

Everyone in a position to read the resume of anyone in the "$100,000 to $1 Million+" bracket has read hundreds of resumes before. If yours is in standard reverse-chronology format, and each employer/time/position copyblock floats in enough white space to make it clear where one segment ends and the earlier one begins, *your reader will go on automatic pilot*...scanning through any number of pages in just a very few seconds.

One page or four, he quickly sees that you're *not* somebody he can use right now. But if by stroke of lightning you happen to have dropped into his hands at precisely the time he *does* need someone with a background even remotely like yours, he'll read on. Unless, of course, your writing is wordy or boring! But we'll work on avoiding that.

**Not only does the standard reverse-chronology resume
solve the scannability problem; it's also more convincing,
because it's more straightforward.**

Forget about "long copy sells." Assume that two resumes, one reverse-chronological and the other topical, are *the same length...any length.*

The one that deliberately strips away the employment context from the claimed accomplishments not only frustrates the reader's comprehension, *it also raises the presumption that there must have been some very good reason for doing so.* "This woman obviously has something to hide," thinks the reader. "I wonder what it is."

Usually it's too-brief tenure at the latest or two latest jobs...and maybe at lots of jobs along the way. That's what the reader immediately suspects. And readily confirms, if a truthful "chronology" is included anywhere in the resume. And assumes if it's not.

Wanting to de-emphasize their latest job and not put it at the top of a reverse-chronological list is overwhelmingly the reason executives turn to a topically-oriented resume...even though when they're personally hiring, they hate to receive one. That's a mistake. It's better to deal with the problem straightforwardly.

On the next page you see a successful lead-off entry for a reverse-chronological resume. This person has a problem that many executives face at least once...a brief latest job. It's the #1 cause of resume writer's panic. Lots of executives "solve" this problem by shooting themselves in the foot, the thigh, and maybe the heart with a topical resume. But this person has stayed calmly in control:

2002 (9 months)

FLY-BY-NIGHT SCHLOCK ELECTRONICS CORP.

Vice President - Engineering

After seven years of increasing project management responsibility at IBM, I was recruited as Chief Engineering Officer of this fast-growing four-year-old maker of video games and electronic gambling devices ('01 sales, $62.5 million), by the Founder/CEO, who'd been his own chief engineer.

Six months later, I still hadn't received the equity stake which was a primary incentive to join, and still hadn't been allowed to install any of the operating changes I felt could benefit the company. So I proposed and the Chairman agreed that I should redistribute my duties to subordinates and seek a situation where I can assume a more assertive role.

1996 - 2002

ADVANCED DESIGN LABORATORIES, IBM CORP.

Group Director - Laser Engineering Department

As you see, by the third paragraph on the top page of her resume this writer is back to talking about the IBM chronology and the accomplishments she loves to discuss. Above all, she hasn't been forced into a topical resume...a cure far worse than her mild disease.

If you're right, John, that almost everyone prefers to read standard-format resumes, why do people write the other kind? And do the executives who write them also dislike receiving them?

Questions I've always been curious about, too. So I've checked into them with people who've handed me topical resumes during my 31 years as an executive recruiter.

Invariably, once we got down to talking frankly, these people pointed out problems similar to the one we just saw, which made me feel they felt *forced* to give up the standard reverse-chronological format. I can't recall a single person maintaining that he went to the topical format because that's the type he preferred to receive.

Sadly, very strong and highly successful executives tend to become putty in the hands of "counselors" and well-meaning friends who spout common folk lore about resumes and job-hunting. Unemployment does that to people. It bruises the ego and scares away common sense.

Don't ever let that happen to you. Don't do anything in searching for a job that you'd consider not-too-smart or not-very-nice if you were the employer on the receiving end of the tactic being recommended.

Trust your own instincts and feelings. And if a strategy is suggested to you that seems to rely on an assumption that others won't be as smart as you'd be in their place, throw that strategy in the trash along with your topical resume.

The Good Use of Topical Resumes

Topical resumes *do* have a use. There's nothing better when you're just getting out of college and want to explain a wide-ranging mixture of part time jobs to an employment counselor trying to help you land on the first rung of the right ladder at XYZ corporation. Same is true if you've finished raising a family and are re-entering the job market. A topical resume will help you display your 20-years-ago work in business along with a wide variety of more recent volunteer work.

In situations where your experience is not appropriate to anything you want to do, a topical discussion of it on paper and in person—plus throwing yourself on the mercy of the interviewer—is clearly your best shot. But here in the EXECUTIVE JOB-CHANGING WORKBOOK we're assuming that you have substantial pertinent experience in the work you seek. If so, nothing will serve you better than a very clear and unevasive telling of your true story.

And now, maestro...an appropriate drum roll and cymbal crash as we unveil a truly executive-strength resume.

Written according to the "factual copy sells" principle of direct mail copywriting, it's the most powerful statement this individual could make about himself.

It will serve him better in all circumstances than anything less clear and factual...even if he never mails out a single copy.

It comes from Sam Sage, one of the many executives you'll meet when you view an executive search through the eyes of the partner handling the fictionalized assignment at one of the very largest and most prestigious retainer search firms. Sam's in the novella/case study that summarizes the techniques shown in *RITES OF PASSAGE* (see *RITES* Appendix I, pp. 509-575). He's one of the job-hunters who do things creatively and aggressively, while others fail to see opportunities and mishandle the ones they do see. Meanwhile, the search firm pursues its own agenda, which is not apparent to outsiders.

Treat this resume as if you were a CEO and you just got it—unsolicited—in this morning's mail.

View it as if you were its target. If it wouldn't work with you, chances are that it wouldn't work with a CEO either.

NOTE: You will not be asked to copy this resume or anything about it. What you and I are doing together is helping you make your own resume...to fit *your* salable accomplishments, work around *your* problems and get *you* a job. Our approach will NOT be: "Here are lots of samples. Copy from the ones you like best." We'll take an even easier—and I know more productive and enjoyable—approach to creating your paperwork.

1. As you review Sam's resume...begin by doing what everyone always does with a resume. Flip the pages. Scan it for a few seconds.

   What function does Sam perform?

   Who's he done it for?

   How long has he been at it?

2. See if Sam's someone you might need right now. Chances are he's not. You'll see that at a glance.

3. Next...before you actually read the resume...do me a favor. Ask yourself:

   Could a shorter resume have turned you off any faster?

   Would Sam be any further ahead if it had?

4. Having scanned the resume, do me another favor. Change the facts. Pretend that you now have even the slightest...the weakest possible...glimmer of interest in someone even remotely like Sam. For that reason, you're inclined to begin *reading* the resume.

   Are you interested enough to continue from page 1 to page 2?

   From page 2 to 3? All the way to the end?

   Face it. If you're not interested enough to spend the two or three extra minutes it'll take you to finish reading about Sam, you're certainly not interested enough to call him up and kill an hour or two meeting him face-to-face.

5. After you *have* read all the way to the end, ask yourself:

   Could Sam have "sold" you better with a shorter resume?

   Would knowing less about Sam have made you like him more?

   What information could he have withheld in order to *really* turn you on?

   And is that information anything that even the briefest one-page resume *could* conceal?

6. And Bottom Line: If you were putting the marketing and sales future of your company—its triumph over and vulnerability to its competitors—in the hands of a new person from the outside, would you want to know less about that person than you know about Sam?

SAMUEL P. SAGE

219 Waring Drive
Denton, New Jersey 07299
Home: (201) 719-0932 Office: (212) 121-3000
spsage@aota.com

1997 - Present

FARRINGTON LABORATORIES

(Merged into Pan Global Pharmaceuticals Ltd. in June '02)
New York, New York

Vice President - Chief Marketing Officer

Recruited to this privately-owned $1 billion maker of prescription drugs as Vice President - Chief Marketing Officer by Blair Farrington, Founder/Owner/CEO in 1997, when sales were $448 million.

Mr. Farrington doubled what I'd been making in the same position at the much larger (then $1.18 billion) Swiss-owned Medica Suisse USA Ltd. But the primary incentive was this 72 year-old gentleman's plan to take the business public with me as his successor after we'd worked a few years together to increase volume and improve profitability. Instead, the company has been purchased by—and merged into—Pan Global Pharmaceuticals (June '02). With Pan Global's acquiescence, I'm seeking a new challenge...hopefully a Presidency; otherwise Chief Marketing Officer with early transition to general management.

Following (with Mr. Farrington's permission) is a summary of the company's performance since I joined in '97 and 3 years prior:

	Sales ($millions)	% Change	Pre-Tax Net ($millions)	% Change	% ROI
'02	1014.4	+31.5	169.2	+62.4	28.1
'01	771.4	+24.9	104.2	+52.3	24.6
'00	617.6	+36.1	68.4	+43.1	17.2
'99	453.8	+23.2	47.8	+39.8	12.7
'98	368.4	-17.7	34.2	+81.9	9.4
'97	447.6	-2.4	18.8	-16.8	3.6
'96	458.8	+4.5	22.6	+6.6	4.9
'95	439.2	+7.2	21.2	+8.2	5.7
'94	409.8	+6.1	19.6	-1.1	9.1

The product line was reduced from 618 SKUs in '97 to 309 profitable items in '00 (expanded with new products to 384 by '02). The 109-person sales force was reorganized into 11 regions in '98 and expanded to 225 people by '02.

Nine profitable new drugs were introduced via cross-licensing agreements with other manufacturers ('02 sales, $258 million; $62 million pre-tax net), and $23.4 million pre-tax was generated by granting licenses to other companies.

Physicians' top-of-mind brand-name awareness of our three largest-selling drugs was raised from 18% in '97 to 62% in '02 by a massive sampling, detailing, and professional advertising campaign (budget tripled from $18.8 million in '97 to $58.2 million in '02).

As a result of Farrington Labs' excellent growth trend and high profitability, Pan Global paid 30 times estimated '02 earnings in a 50%-cash/50%-stock transaction.

1994 - 1997

MEDICA SUISSE USA LTD.

Marshall Plains, New Jersey

Vice President - Pharmaceutical Marketing

Rejoined this $3.6 billion Zurich-based maker of prescription drugs, veterinary biologicals, and fine chemicals as Director of Pharmaceutical Marketing, reporting to the Managing Director - USA, and heading all marketing and sales for all North American pharmaceutical lines (total '94 sales, $630 million) after a two-year hiatus to aid my family's automobile business in Ohio.

By 1997 sales were nearly double ($1.180 billion) 1994 volume, and ROI had increased from 17% ('94) to 24% ('97). Market share of U.S. prescription tranquilizer market rose from 11.6% in '94 to 19.2% in '97, and veterinary products gained 1.3 share points to 7.2% in '97.

My earlier recommendation (in '92) that the company's consumer pet-health lines be sold to generate cash for acquisition of young growth companies in the higher-margined ethical drug field was implemented while I was away ('93), and I helped identify and purchase in '94 and '95 three small companies...BioTRITON, Radio-Tra-Chem, and Synestial Laboratories...which have all grown and prospered under Medica Suisse ownership. One of these, BioTRITON, was publicly reported as having worldwide sales of $560 million in '01, with the highest ROI of any Medica Suisse business anywhere in the world.

'95 *Vice President - Pharmaceutical Marketing* Promotion in title, no change in duties.

'94 *Director - Pharmaceutical Marketing.* Rejoined Medica Suisse in charge of corporate Marketing, Market Research, Telemarketing, and Sales Promotion departments (totalling 41 people); plus two sales forces...Ethical Drug (135-person) and Veterinary (32-person).

1992 - 1994

SAGE CHRYSLER / TOYOTA, INC.

Kensington, Ohio

Upon my father's sudden death in February '92, I took charge of the family business

($2.8 million sales in '92, $4.4 million in '94), holding it together until my younger brother could finish his MBA at Wharton ('93) and join my mother in the company.

Increased TV advertising, and diversified by building two Taco Bell fast food franchises (since expanded to seven). Profits nearly doubled in two years.

1990 - 1992

MEDICA SUISSE USA LTD.

Marshall Plains, New Jersey

Group Product Director

Invited to join my client from New World Advertising Agency as Group Product Director (with 4 Product Managers and 5 Assistant PMs), in charge of:

(1) Marketing existing U.S. lines...$68 million consumer (Krueger's flea-and-tick collars and home remedies for pets) and $96 million professional ($42 million veterinary and $54 million human prescription drugs); and

(2) Introducing new family of prescription tranquilizers (Dopatreem) for Rx sales in the U.S.

Since introduction of a major new Rx drug is impossible without a large field force (and Medica Suisse had only 22 salespeople carrying both Rx and veterinary lines), I cut off advertising on all lines for 10 months; used the cash flow to build a 100-person field force calling only on MDs; and launched a $20 million sampling and ad campaign for the Dopatreem line.

Result: 14 months after introduction, Dopatreem and Dopatreem X were #2 and #5 tranquilizers in the U.S., with $440 million combined annualized rate of sales. Profit from Rx lines was then temporarily diverted to help rebuild other lines to all-time high share levels.

1986 - 1990

NEW WORLD ADVERTISING AGENCY

New York, New York

Vice President - Account Group Supervisor

Joined as Account Executive on $38 million Whiskers cat food account when the AE on my P&G business moved to New World as Account Supervisor and asked me to join him. Through growth of Whiskers and acquiring new accounts, became VP - Account Group Supervisor in charge of $102 million in billings (4 AEs and 3 Assistant AEs) from Megopolitan Foods ($76 million on Whiskers and Arf! brands) and Medica Suisse ($14 million on consumer items and $12 million on veterinary and Rx human drugs).

As AE in '86, led the task force that "re-staged" Whiskers brand with CLIO-winning "Caesar-the-Cat" TV commercials and portion-control packaging that doubled Whiskers' market share from 5% ('86) to 11.2% ('90). Factory sales rose from $106 million ('86) to $298 million ('90); and advertising rose from $18 million to $52 million. Led successful solicitation of $14 million Arf! dog food account ('87), which billed $24 million in '90 (sales rose from $64 million to $158 million). Personally brought in Krueger's flea-and-tick collars ($8 million in '88) from Medica Suisse, which consolidated all their North American business with us in '89.

'88 *Vice President - Account Group Supervisor.* A 26% 12-month sales increase in Krueger's flea collars, etc. from Medica Suisse enabled us to win their veterinary and prescription drug accounts...the first medical advertising handled by New World. Promoted for building of Megopolitan and Medica Suisse accounts.

'87 *Account Supervisor.* Turnaround on Whiskers enabled us to land $14 million Arf! dog food billings ('87) and Krueger's consumer pet items ('88).

'85 *Account Executive.* Entered on the Whiskers account with assignment to stem share decline (averaging 0.9 point per year since '81).

1983 - 1986

PROMOTE & GAMBOL COMPANY

Cincinnati, Ohio

'85 *Assistant Brand Manager.* Handled $32 million TV & print media and $8 million sales promotion budget on GLOSS-X floor cleaner. Promoted to head successful test marketing and regional expansion of new GLOSS-O floor wax.

'83 *Brand Assistant.* Traditional P&G home office and field sales training assignments; handled TV copy testing for Soft-Ah! paper products.

EDUCATION: BA, University of Michigan, 1980
MBA, Harvard Business School, 1983

PERSONAL: Born June 1, 1958.
Married, 3 children.
6' 1", 185 lbs.

Could Sam have made you like him better by omitting something you just read?

And if so, could even the shortest one-page resume have concealed that *particular* "something"?

You scanned Sam's resume in seconds.

You saw at a glance that he's a *marketing* executive. And a very *high-level* one.

Is there any kind of resume, no matter how brief...or any kind of letter, no matter how vague and misleading...that could have hidden Sam's basic information from you? And could he have benefited from the concealment, even if it were possible?

I don't think so.

If you didn't need what Sam was selling, merely limiting your knowledge couldn't have increased your need.

But if you'd had even the slightest interest in anyone even remotely like Sam, then seeing how very special he is would have made you more...not less...interested.

What did Sam manage to tell us?

Sam told us that he believes he's ready to be a president. Moreover, he clearly implied that he's recently been functioning almost like one. And he demonstrated over and over that he certainly thinks like one.

We saw, too, that Sam's been transplanted several times and has succeeded in each new context...even running the family car dealership. He's versatile. And his sense of loyalty...as extended to his mother and brother...is also admirable. Many people would have tried to sweep this episode under the rug.

What should Sam have hidden?

About the only thing you could imagine Sam wanting to hide is the fact that he's spent the most-recent and highest-level part of his career marketing *drugs*...a fact which, if known, might turn off a CEO looking for someone to market cellular telephone equipment or panty hose.

But Sam can't even *name* his employers without letting his "drug experience" out of the bag. And no CEO...indeed, no reader...is going to be turned on by self-praise in mere "percentage" terms by someone who refuses to reveal whom he's worked for until *after* he's been granted an interview. Straight to the wastebasket with a letter or resume like that!

After reading Sam's resume, you and I suspect that he could market just about anything...phones and stockings included. Nonetheless, no retainer recruiter being paid, say $90,000, to find a "communications" or a "soft goods" person can get by with just offering Sam plus a "he-could-do-it" pitch...even though Sam might make a good "wild card," tucked in among several "on-target" candidates.

On the other hand, if Sam can somehow get the resume we've just read into the hands of the CEO of a telephone equipment or a hosiery company *before* he's paying somebody $90,000 to find exactly what he wants, the CEO may think:

"What the hell? It won't cost anything just to meet this Sam Sage. He's done some very impressive things. And frankly, most of the marketing people in our industry don't impress me at all. Marketing is *marketing!* A smart outsider like Sage might just show us a few tricks we never thought of.. And besides, the Board is mumbling that I need a strong person around here as a potential successor. This guy might quiet them down on that issue."

Common Sense...the Bottom Line on Executive Resumes

Face it. Despite any kooky advice to the contrary, there's no way Sam can "package" himself differently for different employers. So he's being straightforward. And he's right! Just like you and me, others will also admire Sam's achievements...their diversity...and *the thinking behind them.* They too will envision him doing an outstanding job, no matter where he ends up.

No question about it. Sam's taken the best possible approach with his resume. He's told the *truth* openly, voluntarily, and impressively.

David Ogilvy knew what he was talking about when he said:

"The more you *tell*, the more you *sell!*"

Notice that Sam used narrative paragraphs, rather than "bullets" to tell his story.

There are two common approaches to presenting a work history. One is to use paragraphs, with each job written up as a mini-essay. The other is to use "bullets"...sentence fragments preceded by a raised dot. Pioneered by advertising copywriters, the "bullet" format attempts to make every single point seem like a highlight.

Either style is acceptable. But, for several reasons, I strongly prefer paragraphs...very tightly and specifically written. Sentences in paragraphs are easier for the reader to comprehend and believe, because they closely resemble what he or she sees in newspapers, magazines, books, memos, and other informational writing. Bullets, on the other hand, resemble advertising copy...subliminally *not* an aid to believability.

Also, sentences in paragraphs enable you to use transition phrases and conjunctions that *connect* the various statements in ways that serve your purposes better than a series of unrelated exclamations. It helps to be able to say: "In recognition, I was promoted to..." "When my report was accepted by the Board, I was asked to assemble a team..." "After consolidating these three acquisitions..." You get the idea.

Sam also made his resume factual and concrete ...something many people have trouble doing. Here are four tips:

1. Orient your reader with specifics.

For each management-level job, orient your reader to the size, nature, and trend of (1) the larger unit in which you participated and (2) the part of it you were responsible for. What was the size of your operation in people, sales, and profit? What was its mandate? The general business climate around it? The problems and opportunities you identified? The strategies you came up with? And the results you achieved?

2. Use numbers wherever possible.

Focus on quantifiable data. Give dollar figures for sales, profits, ROI, costs, inventories, etc. before and after your programs were implemented. When you use percentages, you'll usually want to give the *base* ...plus any comparative figures on the rest of the industry or another part of your company that will show your numbers are special.

3. Avoid empty words and statements.

Omit the self-praising adjectives that losers wallow in..."major," "significant," "substantial," and "outstanding." Wherever such a word is justified, a number will be far more persuasive. And never make meaningless over-generalized statements like this:

> "Responsible for managing the strategic technical issues impacting the company's on-going core businesses."

What does this person do all day? What's his budget? Who does he report to and who reports to him? Has his employer gained anything from having him around?

4. Create a mosaic.

You've seen those pictures made out of lots of little colored stones. Imagine that each promotion to a new job, each numerical improvement, each specific point of analysis and strategy is a stone. When put together in the right order, these fragments will be connected by your reader into an image of you. Don't assert what the shape of it is. Just lay out enough specific facts...stone by stone...so she'll see for herself the favorable patterns they imply. Let her create her own picture in her own mind.

If you'd like to change industries or career fields, consider making a second version of your resume... but even then, don't switch to topical organization.

Maybe you're in a declining field and you'd like to move into a growth industry. Or you're re-entering the commercial sector after a sojourn in the military, government, or academia. If so, make a special version of your resume that drains off industry-specific buzz-words and explains your exploits in terms everyone can appreciate. But resist the temptation to "go topical" and try to hide "where" while emphasizing "what."

Your reader will never quite be able to believe your claimed achievements unless he has a mental picture of you located at some specific place and time in the real world actually doing them. Withdraw orientation, and he drops belief...and probably attention, too.

Rather than resort to a topical resume, you should:

1. **Write a covering letter** that says what *specific need* your reader may have that you from another field can fill for him in his field. Don't say, "Here I am; guess what I can do for you."

2. **And be realistic.** If you're stumped when you try to write a persuasive covering letter explaining how you can fill a specific need of an employer in an unrelated field, then stop.

Think of someone else in a different field for whom you *do* have a persuasive message. Don't pursue a hopeless mis-match. If *you're* not persuaded, you can be absolutely certain that no one else will be either.

Should you include a "Career Objective"?

Many resumes begin with a statement of what-kind-of-job-I-want labeled "*Career Objective*," or simply "*Objective*."

This is a good idea when you're fresh out of college or grad school and you want to orient the "Counselor" at an employment agency, or the personnel department of a corporation, to what you're looking for. But it's seldom necessary after your career is well underway. By then, what you're prepared to do next should be pretty evident from what you've already done.

If you're retiring from the military or the diplomatic corps, or leaving academia or the priesthood, then maybe your resume should begin with a statement of what you seek in the business world. Otherwise, let your resume be a clear and self-confident statement of where you've been and what you've achieved. Say what you're looking for in your covering letter and through personal contact.

Exception on "Career Objective" if You're Mass-Mailing to Executive Recruiters

Generally when you're handing out your resumes in person or mailing them to potential employers along with a crisp, clear cover letter *and* you're not trying for a sharp departure from what you've done before, a statement of what you are and what you want is not necessary at the top of your resume.

However, if you're mass-mailing to recruiters, it's *not* a bad idea to put some kind of bold statement at the top to double-alert the person handling the mail (often all too-casually) to think of your papers in terms of the title that may be at the top of the spec sheet for one of their searches.

If you do this, do NOT label it "Career Objective." DO NOT LABEL IT AT ALL! By its very placement—after your name and address and before any data on your latest job—the statement is obviously intended to say who you are and what you want. Remember: *You will almost always score minus points for explicitly labeling anything that is obvious on a resume.* Reasons: (1) you imply that you think the reader isn't smart enough to grasp the obvious; (2) the reader realizes you aren't very smart to think that; (3) the reader labels you as just another in the vast crowd of job-seekers thoughtlessly ginning out statements of the obvious; (4) after these negatives the reader is far less interested in reading any further; and (5) you've wasted precious vertical space on your page. Unneeded labels take up three lines (including blanks before and after) for such clinkers as these: "Career Objective," "Resume," "Curriculum Vitae," "Chronology of Employment," "Work History," "Experience," "Achievements," "Some Selected Accomplishments," and on and on.

Creative Use of Avocational Interests in Your Resume

In general, never mention your hobbies and other outside interests.

If you had time to be assistant pastor of your church, chair the United Fund drive, coach a Little League team, do petit point, build an extension on your home, train for and run a marathon, and groom and show poodles in the U.S. and three foreign countries last year, when did you have time to work?

But if you're 58 years old, it might be good to mention your marathon running, and the fact that you're an avid scuba diver and an instructor for Outward Bound. Your stamp collection, of course, will remain in the closet.

And if you're a paraplegic, your competitive sports car driving and skeet shooting might just be a worthwhile inclusion. So might building that wing on your house, if you're only missing one arm or one leg.

If you just have a high school diploma, the fact that you're an amateur writer who's published stories in *Harper's* and *The New Yorker*...or even a trade journal or the business section of your daily newspaper...could help show that you have a mature, cultivated mind others respect. So might your membership on the Mayor's Commission for the Arts, writing computer programs as a hobby, creating mathematical puzzles, and playing duplicate bridge.

And if you're in a racial or ethnic minority and have the stomach for such a gambit, you may feel like listing your memberships in exclusive social and athletic clubs that, until recently, didn't seem to have people with names or faces like yours. Everyone else should maintain a discreet silence on all clubs.

Now, as we finish our summary of resume coverage from *RITES OF PASSAGE AT $100,000 TO $1 MILLION+*, let's look at these last items of purely personal information and how to handle them.

Age

Don't fall into the trendy trap of leaving age off your resume and omitting years from college degrees so it can't be calculated. True, employers can't ask. But voluntarily listing year, month, and day of birth subliminally shouts "forthright and self-confident," whereas concealing age just because the law permits you to do so sends out the opposite "vibes"...and raises a presumption that *you* think you may be over the hill.

Believe it or not, in the late '60s and early '70s employers considered 30 to 35 the ideal age. Now they seem to feel that way regarding mid-to-late-40s, and they have virtually no qualms about dynamic people in their 50s. They still find a young hotshot attractive. But they no longer insist on one. I absolutely refuse to discriminate on the basis of age, and recently had a 60-year-old candidate win out over excellent candidates ten and twenty years younger.

Education

List college degrees, *with years*...highest and latest degree first. Forget about Cum Laude, Class President, Varsity Letters, and college work experience. You've moved on to more recent and bigger achievements.

If you have several years but no sheepskin, say: "Completed three years toward B.A. at Syracuse University." And if you flunked out of several fine schools, say: "Two years of college, intermittently at Carleton, Dartmouth, and the University of Virginia." With no college, you may want to say, "Self-educated during an uninterrupted career," and then bail yourself out under the heading "Other Interests," with some suitably cerebral and cultural avocations.

Marital Status

Say "Married," "Divorced," or "Single," whichever applies and, if you wish, number of children (not names, ages, or with how many and which mates).

Gender

If you're a woman with a name like Lindsay or Leslie, or a man with a name like Carroll or Kelley, use a middle name to be more specific...or just let your reader be surprised when he or she meets you.

Height and Weight

Nice to put in if it's favorable; although women often omit because it seems sexist to raise the subject. Overweight men and women might consider listing an optimistic weight toward which they're dieting, as a way of cushioning the inevitable visual shock with some advance notice.

Religion, Politics, and National Origin

Silence! If the reader has a prejudice, you may stimulate it.

Race

Probably silence. For all minorities but African-American, surnames dispel any impending visual surprise...hardly a major consideration anyway. For the person of color who wants to dispel surprise, mentioning support of any obviously African-American institution...possibly along with one or two non-racially-defined institutions...will do the trick.

Health

Don't mention. It's fine, or you should be writing a will instead of a resume.

Picture

Never, *NEVER, NEVER!* Nobody could possibly be attractive enough to justify the narcissism implied by attaching a picture.

WE'VE NOW COMPLETED OUR EXCERPTS ON RESUMES FROM *RITES.* YOU'VE GOT THE GIST OF ITS 25 PAGES, WHETHER YOU'VE READ THEM OR NOT.

FROM HERE ON WE HAVE THE LUXURY OF (1) GOING INTO GREATER DEPTH, (2) TAKING ADVANTAGE OF WHAT, AS AN EXECUTIVE RECRUITER, I'VE SEEN FOLKS DOING WELL AND NOT SO WELL IN IMPLEMENTING WHAT THEY'VE READ, AND (3) USING TOOLS TO HELP GUIDE YOUR PEN AS YOU PREPARE YOUR OWN PERSONAL "SALES REPRESENTATIVE" RESUME.

I don't want to scare you BUT...

Writing resumes is about the same "degree of difficulty," as they say in competition diving, as writing ***poetry***. The highest!

Why?

Because, when you do it well, you're squeezing a huge amount of meaning into incredibly few words. It's nothing like writing a letter to Mom...or even producing a fine business memo, a short story, or a newspaper article. And who finds even those jobs easy?

But hard work you're used to, or you couldn't have become an executive. And the importance to your future of developing a great resume now is worth any effort it takes. No other investment of your time can possibly pay a higher dividend than creating a "Sales Rep" that will outsell the "Reps" of all the other candidates competing for the jobs you're interested in (and impress all the search firms you'll never hear from if your resume isn't outstanding).

How much work will that take?

Far more than you may expect, even with the best help I can give you. And especially if you choose the sophisticated senior-executive-level "Sam Sage" format, using paragraphs, rather than bullets.

Many folks who are superb executives just can't write as logically and succinctly as "Sam" does. Or *think* they can't. Really they *can.* But they just won't spend the necessary time editing and rewriting to boil down their facts into numbers, charts, and just a few clear words.

Fortunately, it takes more time than talent.

To show you how to do it—and let you know how much time it *does* take—I have permission from the person who wrote the bottom version on the next page to share it with you, along with my revision of it into a briefer and more favorable sales pitch.

Both summaries of one of his years-ago assignments at a "Big 3" auto company (name disguised here) are equally true. However, one is much shorter, more inviting to read, easier to understand, and far more persuasive than the other. And how long did it take me to edit the long statement into the short one?

More than four hours!

Please study both examples very carefully, and we'll get back together when you turn the page. Then I'll have good news for you...if you've really soaked up these two examples.

Two Qualities of Resume-Writing

TRUCK AND BUS OPERATIONS

(Detroit, MI)

'99 - '02 **Director - Product Line Competitiveness**

Acme's uncompetitive costs now receiving so much press are not a new discovery. Over 5 years ago, I was very vocal on the subject, and formed a team that identified major cost-reduction opportunities on the truck product lines. Our methods—disassembly and analysis of competitive vehicles—revealed cost-disadvantages of $700 to $900 (depending on the competitor) due to our up to 30% more parts and 21% more labor, plus the industry's most costly design solutions.

The bottom line: Working closely with Manufacturing, Engineering and Purchasing we revealed cost-reduction opportunities of *$37.8 million at the Michigan Axle plant, $9.6 million at the Detroit assembly plant; also $1,200 per unit cost-lowering targets for future truck designs.*

TRUCK AND BUS OPERATIONS

(Detroit, MI)

'99 - '02 **Director - Product Line Competitiveness**

The uncompetitive cost position of the Acme Company receiving so much press has been known internally for some time. Over five years ago, I was a vocal advocate for change to reduce the cost of our products. My recommendations for action were heard and a staff was formed to develop and facilitate a cost-reduction process. I was assigned the truck product lines. Though my team's accomplishments were significant, the organization has only recently begun to act aggressively on the results of our analyses.

The disassembly and analysis of competitive vehicles was initiated through my team. A system-by-system evaluation revealed a cost-disadvantage of $700 to $900 (depending on the competitor) due to having up to 30% more parts, 21% more direct labor, and most costly design solutions. These findings became part of a target-costing process, which set a goal for the current product of over $1,200 reduction and provided the basis for setting cost goals for future design updates. I also introduced the methodology developed by my team to the Program Team responsible for the next generation truck. It became the basis for developing program targets.

In parallel with the competitive teardown analysis, my team—along with manufacturing—identified potential cost-reductions of $37.8 million at the Michigan Axle plant, and $9.6 million at the Detroit assembly plant. And the team—with engineering and purchasing—developed the specific design and specifications proposals supporting the $1,200 per unit cost reductions through product design.

First Several Items of Good News

You can do it. ***If you could tell the differences*** between the top and bottom versions, then you can produce the same results. All you have to do is write your information as well as you can...*and then start all over again* saying, "Now I've got to remove at least half the words" (partly done by changing long vague words to short clear ones). Invest four hours and you'll get the same improvement I got.

More good news. Proof you can do it is that others no smarter than you and I are do it all the time. The fellow on the prior page did it. Once he saw the changes and knew how long I'd spent on them, he realized he could do exactly the same thing. Today he's a very fine writer...with new skills from wrestling the resume alligator.

How long would it have taken me to complete the entire 3- or 4-page resume to the same level of quality? At least 35 to 70 hours. Same as it took the writer to finish it.

But please read both versions again. Notice that brevity is *not* the only improvement. *The whole story is different!* The long version confirms the prejudice of point 3 on page 24. The short one blows it away. "Spin doctoring" is what the politicians call this technique, which is equally helpful to resume writers. No longer a small cog on a huge slow and slipping wheel, this executive is now a remarkable achiever getting impressive results under difficult circumstances. Not bad for four hours' work!

More Good News

Fortunately, there are an infinite number of very effective ways to write a resume. They range from the "Sam Sage" senior executive style in paragraphs (which you'll admit did wonders for the fellow on the prior page) all the way to simpler yet strong styles relying mainly on bullets. Please read the coming examples very carefully. They're written by real people who are *not* CEOs or VPs with a string of zooming sales and profit numbers. Readers of *Rites of Passage*, they adapted its concepts to their own needs and tastes... and got excellent results. So can you.

And Now Some Unavoidably Bad News

No one cares as much about your current wealth and future employment as you do. And certainly no one who's out to make a fast buck on the distress and frustration of unemployed executives. Only you have the knowledge and self-interest to dig out the wealth of impressive facts needed to make your "sales representative" resume. And only you will care enough to take the time needed to string them together in a succinct and persuasive fashion.

Throwing several thousand bucks to a persuasive stranger seldom solves the problem. After we've looked at these next examples, I'll tell you about my phone call from the proprietor of one of those "let-us-write-your-resume-and-send-it-out" operations.

Dr. Richard A. Sawyer
1202 Dawson Road
Silver Dell, Ohio 44041
Home: (216) 010-2345 Office: (216) 600-2000
richardas@piotel.net

SUMMARY

High level executive with proven expertise in technology and general management, business and product development, technical marketing, computer and operating systems, embedded processors, and power electronics. Effective visionary leader and innovator in technical and manufacturing companies.

BUSINESS EXPERIENCE

2000 - present **J. W. Harley Inc.**
Twinsburg, Ohio

Sixteen million dollar manufacturer supplying computerized condition monitoring equipment, remanufactured pumps, and compressors nationwide to the power utility industry.

General Manager and Director of Technical Development

- Managed a start-up business unit to provide microprocessor based, on-line condition monitoring equipment for the power utility industry. Wrote proposals, conference papers, and an international paper to capture $4.8 million in sales.
- To respond to the needs of a cost driven market, developed a low-cost embedded processor system and real-time display that lowered product cost by 90%. Introduced program management techniques, and implemented methods to reduce the development time (6-9 months vs. 3 years) in commercializing the technology.
- Formed self-directed work teams, empowering employees to handle tasks normally assigned to managers. Initiated cross-training of personnel to teach overlapping tasks and functions. Continuously increased productivity by 25% through expansion of computing capabilities and use of local area networks to tie together multiple workstations and remote plant locations.
- Hired key technical personnel to transfer product development from various outside consultants to an in-house team. Established new production procedures while supporting marketing and sales efforts through forecasting and managing controlled growth of the product line.
- In order to create a niche market for sensor components, established strategic partnerships and alliances with vendors and manufacturers of large power and instrumentation transformers. Explored partnerships with companies doing international business to expand product into global markets.

1993 - 2000 **Westinghouse Naval Systems Division**
Cleveland, Ohio

'97-'00 **General Manager and Director of Technical Development**

- Managed and doubled the sales of a $7.6 million stand alone business group within the

Naval Systems Division directing a staff of 30 professionals. The main product areas included power electronic controllers, high power density motors, and pulse power energy sources.

- Led all phases of the business development cycle, controlling $1.56 million of strategic management capital. Generating five successful proposals for new business resulted in $7.6 million in 2000 sales which was a 36% increase over 1999. One of these programs led to a multi-year $120 million contract.
- Introduced software management tools for program control. This resulted in 20% lower program management costs, and a reduction in proposal preparation costs. Proposal costs were 2% of contract value.

'94-'97 **Manager - Electric Propulsion Systems**

- In response to the Navy's need for a high power density propulsion system for their advanced weapon platforms, managed both in-house programs and outside contracts for developing these power systems. Prepared the proposals and won the competitive procurements totalling $3.2 million. Accelerated one of the programs to exceed the required contract goals two years ahead of schedule.
- Directed a $4.8 million internal research and development program for a multiphase, high-power motor, inverter, and energy source. The multiphase inverter had a power density of 8kW/lb. Built and tested a motor with a power density of 4 hp/lb.
- Helped to maintain an average annual R&D budget of $18 million for the Division by achieving the highest scores for both the 1995 R&D brochure section, and the 1994 off-site presentation.

'93-'94 **Consulting Engineer**

- Worked with marketing and a major customer to respond to their needs for an underwater electric propulsion system. Defined the preliminary subsystem requirements, provided a conceptual layout of a high-power (240kW) electric waterjet propulsion system, and performed analytical system trade-offs.
- Provided preliminary designs for the power electronics, motor, controls, and battery subassemblies. Designed a compact six phase electronic power stage section. Prepared four technical white papers describing the propulsion subsystem which resulted in winning two contracts.

1980-1993 NASA Lewis Research Center

Cleveland, Ohio

'88-'93 **Research Scientist**

- Developed advanced spacecraft power management and distribution systems for space station applications. Chaired meetings between three NASA centers for planning and coordination of the engineering development effort.
- Applied advanced mathematical techniques to model the performance of ac-dc power electronics circuits. Developed new analytical techniques for predicting the operating characteristics of magnetic devices used in high frequency power conditioning circuits. Developed costing models for predicting the platform costs of advanced communication satellites.

'85-'88 Program Manager - Power Electronics Branch

- Directed both contracted and internal research in the areas of low cost standardized control of power systems, modeling and analysis of power processing systems, and high power inverters for communication satellites and experimental satellites.
- Designed and developed a miniature high voltage interaction experiment for examining spacecraft charging of high voltage solar arrays. Designed multiple output high voltage supplies for high efficiency traveling wave tubes used on communication satellites.
- Chaired an international subcommittee for high voltage applications on communication satellites using multiple depressed collector traveling wave tubes.

'80-'85 Aerospace Engineer - Spacecraft Technology Division

- Designed and tested digitally controlled high voltage solar arrays for advanced spacecraft applications, high frequency power conditioning equipment for electric propulsion systems, advanced microvoltmeter measurement equipment, and fiber optic instrumentation systems.
- Developed advanced ultra-high vacuum systems using cryogenic pumping techniques. Applied techniques for measuring surface and bulk resistivity of Kapton, borosilicate glass, and Teflon.
- Ran the environmental test facility which included shock and vibration equipment, high vacuum test chambers, vacuum vibration equipment, screen room facilities, and high voltage equipment for testing prototype and flight spacecraft and subsystem components.

OTHER EXPERIENCE

1992 - 1993 Microprocessor Consultant

Designed, built, coded, and tested a microprocessor-based process control system for bulk parylene deposition equipment that was used by Delco Electronics to coat sensors for their emission control system. The program controlled the process, displayed a real-time graphic of the equipment and its condition, and recorded statistical process control information throughout the coating process.

1987 - 1992 Electrical Contractor, City of Cleveland

Publications - Author of 35 papers covering transformer condition monitoring, system trade studies, advanced power electronics, and electrical systems design.

IR-100 Awards - Winner of 3 IR-100 awards for the Ultralightweight Printed Circuit Rectenna (1993), the Cuk Buck-boost Switching converter (1991), and the Magnetic Material Analyzer Model 1 (1991).

Professional Societies - Member of IEEE, ETA KAPPA NU, PI MU EPSILON

EDUCATION and TRAINING

Leadership Through the Awareness and Development of Personal Impact
FARR Associates 2001-2002
Ph.D., Engineering Science, University of Toledo, 1990
M.S.E.E., University of Toledo, 1985
B.E.E., Cleveland State University, 1980
Security Clearance - Secret

What did you think?

Did this fellow do everything the way I would have?

Absolutely not!

And I'm *delighted* he didn't. It's his resume, not mine. He probably didn't do everything your favorite way either. And that's great too. It's not your resume.

The point is that nothing is more personal than a resume. As the old hamburger commercial goes, you should *"Have it YOUR way!"* By now you know I do NOT endorse tricky resumes and letters designed to evade what the reader will surely think about. He or she isn't any more stupid than you and I, and you'll always run into trouble on that assumption. So I hope I've dissuaded you from a topical resume or a "no-resume letter."

But anywhere within the range of sanity and the serious business purpose of an executive-level resume, you can take your stand and be perfectly right...*for you*. What I find appalling is the vast number of people who'll tell you with absolute certainty that a resume can only be the *one way* it is in their minds...or in folklore...or in the 3-ring binder they received when somebody hired them at a headhunting or an outplacement firm. Recognize now and forever that you are just as smart as "they"...and I...and all the book writers...in applying common sense to *your* resume. Put yourself on the hiring side. If what you have in mind would persuade you, do it. If not, forget it.

What was great?

The ***clarity***. He covered technical matters and we understood. Also, we ***weren't bored***. Why? Because his modified bullets gave enough information to picture him at work. They weren't just a fatiguing stack of one-liners, each requiring us to ponder whether it was amazing or ordinary...only to wind up realizing we had no basis to know.

And above all, the ***scanability***. In a 5-second glance, we got the gist of all three pages. If we'd needed someone even remotely like him, we'd have felt like reading his resume. Very few resumes achieve that, even—and perhaps especially—the crammed-full one- and two-pagers with no "white space" that seem to be swirling on every breeze.

What was *not* so great?

You can guess. Ordinarily I don't like self-flattering adjectives like those in his "Summary." And I see no need to *label* it *or* "Experience." But he used the adjectives so sparingly that (backed up by his three pages) they're okay...a matter of taste. He didn't rest his case on them, which is what I warned you against. What I *did* hunger for is his reason for leaving. But maybe his cover letter—or he—always explains that. His size-of-staff is a mystery (perhaps intentional). And I wish he'd developed something with annual sales of $200 million. But if we had a job for someone like him we'd surely want to meet him...and that's the bottom line. (I *have* met him and he's *terrific!*)

Anne M. Lohmann

12 Hillcrest Place
Cloververvale, Minnesota 55403
(612) 033-1632 E-mail: anneml@sterlingxt.net

Chief Financial Officer

Financial leadership of a growth- and internationally-oriented public company.

Extensive corporate finance experience—both as a CFO with a CPA and as an investment banker—plus lots of international experience and a knack for languages has been very useful to my current employer.

When I joined, we were perilously undercapitalized and operations were barely breaking even. With improved cost controls and a workable capital structure our operating units have improved their market positions. Shareholder approval is now pending on our being acquired by a major privately-owned European company at a very high multiple of our modest but now-growing earnings. As operating head of our very successful international activities (since '02), and CFO (since '01), I've played a key role on a hardworking management team that has turned around a bad situation and rewarded our shareholders.

2001 - Present **Flora-Dormé Farms, Ltd.**
Minneapolis, MN

Publicly-held, $620 million company in up-market food, cooking wines, seasonings, and fragrances.

2001 - Present **Vice President - Finance & Treasurer/C.F.O.**

Reporting to the Chief Executive, I manage all corporate financial functions including treasury, cash management, corporate control, internal audit, SEC reporting, financial planning/budgeting, taxation, acquisition/divestiture analysis, risk management, and investor relations. Also supervise human resources and legal administrative functions. Staff of 12.

- Negotiated $160 million unsecured bank financing in 2001 with 3 new banks that reduced borrowing cost by 50 basis points.
- Negotiated $110 million unsecured bank financing in 2002 at a borrowing rate of more than 1% below prime in spite of reported losses.
- Negotiated $60 million secured revolving credit/term loan in 2003 with a new lender that improved availability by 15% and reduced financial covenants.
- Developed cash flow control and forecasting system to monitor availability of borrowing.
- Negotiated the divestiture of Rosrita Frappe for $18 million and the acquisition of European Dormé trademark rights for strategic purposes.
- Maintained and enhanced relationships with institutional investors during period of stock under-performance; largest institutional investor added to their position.
- Managed share repurchase program and repricing of stock options.

2002 - Present (also) **Vice President - International**

Reporting to the Chief Executive, I hold this position concurrently with being CFO. I'm responsible for all customer relationships outside of the U.S. and the company's international trademark portfolio.

- Managed customer relationships in France, Germany, Italy, The Netherlands, Portugal, United Kingdom, Canada, and Israel, and have developed new businesses in South America.
- Researched European imported gourmet foods market; selected new French distributor and won government approval for first artificially-flavored wine product in France.
- Selected and negotiated the agreements to set up new distributors in Canada and Mexico.

1995 - 2001 Dalton Securities

New York, NY

Vice President - Corporate Finance

Focused on business development in the Midwest.

- Financing experience included underwritings of equity (IPO and secondary), convertible, and high-yield securities as well as private placements of debt and equity, exchange offers, and unrated commercial paper. Instrumental in doing initial business with Chrysler and U.S. Steel.
- Merger and acquisition experience included tender defense advisory, strategic acquisition targeting and consummation as financial advisor and dealer manager of tender offer, leveraged buyouts, exclusive sale assignments, divestitures, and a "highly confident" letter.
- Converted 3 former Sterling Rosenthal clients to Dalton clients.
- Produced $2 million in fee income during first year; assignments included two private placements, an acquisition search assignment, a fairness opinion, and financial advisory.
- Retained by **Flora-Dormé** for financial advisory service in 2000.

1988 - 1995 Sterling Rosenthal & Company

Chicago, IL

Vice President - Investment Banking

Hired as Associate in 1988; promoted to Vice President in 1992.

- During 1994 and 1995, originated and processed 6 equity offerings, two convertibles, two private placements, and Sterling Rosenthal's first debt defeasance.
- Consummated $150 million Eurobond offering for Community-Edison and $1.10 billion O.I.D. debenture and note offering for Amalgamated Stores.
- M&A work involved tender defense, a divestiture, and a contested tender offer.
- Headed Sterling Rosenthal's Chicago office in early '90s; hired two associates.

1987 - 1988 U.S. FoodCo Inc.

Norwalk, CT

Treasury Department

Developed and implemented Industrial Revenue Bond program that financed 10 FoodCo projects. Managed conversion of convertible Eurobond. Analytical work on dividend policy, capital structure, division cash flow forecasting, and rating agency presentations.

1985 - 1987 UNITAS BANK, N.A., World Corporation Group

New York, NY

Account Officer

A very wide variety of lending experience with multinational companies in the U.S. and abroad.

EDUCATION M.B.A., University of Michigan, 1985 (Finance and International Business)
B.A., Syracuse University, 1982. (Graduated with honors in Economics).
CPA, Minnesota, 2001.

LANGUAGES Conversational French; understanding of Spanish, Italian and Russian.

PERSONAL Born September 18, 1959. Married, two adult children.

On This One I Cheated!

On "Dick Sawyer's" resume I didn't change a single word, except his name and address. His resume appears (with his permission, of course) exactly as it came to me in the mail. This chapter shows you authentic material, because I want you to see what fine work real people are doing on their own resumes...a quality level you too can achieve, if you'll only put in as much effort as they did. The resume that follows is from "Mitchell Arnold," an officer leaving the military. It, too, is exactly as he sent it to me, with only these exceptions: (1) he and I changed a few identifying names and (2) I changed a few pronouns (as discussed in the text). Both "Dick" and "Mitch" created their own resumes exactly as you see them, with no professional help.

"Anne Lohmann's" resume also came to me in the mail. The achievements in its "bullets" are also authentic. However, here I've "cheated." The real person's work isn't shown until the line that says "*2001 - Present — Flora-Dormé Farms, Ltd.*" (all names are changed). It then continues all the way to the end. Moreover, in developing those brilliantly succinct "bullets" and headings, the real person was helped by one of America's very best outplacement counselors.

I loved and wanted to show you those elements. But I didn't particularly care for the overall format and the array of bullets and headings that *preceded* what's shown here. So I changed the format throughout and wrote what you see *above* the *"Flora-Dormé"* line...using *some* of the original words and facts, but also writing convenient fiction. And since my paragraphs take less vertical space than the deleted bullets did, I was able to float the remaining material in a sea of white space. The result is a fine example. But it's too slick and synthetic to be compared with the "real" people's resumes that precede and follow it. So consider "Anne" a "Sam Sage with bullets."

The Ideal Use of Bullets

The achievements shown here are especially well-suited to the bullet format. Any CEO (or recruiter) who'd be looking for a CFO would instantly understand both the nature and the "degree-of-difficulty" of the financial transactions shown here. Could there possibly be any confusion or ambiguity in this?

- Negotiated $110 million unsecured bank financing in 2002 at a borrowing rate of more than 1% below prime in spite of reported losses.

Of course not. Which takes nothing away from the outstanding quality of the writing. Many people would never state the same accomplishment with such clarity and simplicity!

Notice, too, that most of the achievements are rather similar. They are all financial and they all relate to well-made deals, well-conducted negotiations, and adroit influencing of the financial community. Bullets are ideal for showing lists of similar facts that don't require "set-up" or explanation.

By using bullets to show us great successes in every facet of an entire genre, "Anne" telegraphs that she'd be an ideal person to meet and consider...if her type of work is mainly what we want our CFO to do.

How is "Anne's" most obvious negative minimized?

Clearly Anne would be our ideal choice for CFO if our main problems are raising cash, doing deals, influencing the financial community and maybe floating an IPO.

Where is she weak?

Probably, in the operational areas. She has not risen through the accounting and control functions, and may pretty much be forced to accept what subordinates tell her on those matters. Apparently realizing this vulnerability (in her resume, if not in fact), she sat for the CPA exam and achieved that credential in 2001, the same year she moved from investment banking, finance, and securities work to being CFO of a company. Her new CPA is a minimal credential at best. But notice how the resume deals with the problem. I don't claim credit for the solution. In fact, I got the lead sentence by copying the exact words (and they are brilliant!) that she and her counselor used as the second bullet in their introductory series.

Showing the Real Person

The point is that "Anne" has shown us who she really is. Despite her recent CPA, she's probably *not* a clean-up-the-mess accounting whiz. Or at least she hasn't claimed to be (although the introductory paragraphs *imply* she *may* be). What she *has* communicated is what she does consummately well and probably enjoys doing most...all the *outwardly facing* functions of a CFO.

Great!

Her resume is honest. Therefore it's going to lead her toward the right job.

Suppose you and I are a CEO and an outside director. Today we're looking for a CFO. We've got plenty of capital. But our costs are soaring out of control, our systems are confused and obsolete, and our public accountants are threatening not to approve our annual statement. You and I are probably not interested in "Anne," and she'd have a tough job convincing us we should be.

But suppose, on the other hand, we've got a very young and still slightly unpolished but fast-learning and fabulously competent Controller, who came to us just two years ago from our public accounting firm. He's just about got all of our income- and cost-tracking, forecasting, budgeting, and planning disciplined to an absolute science, and he won't have the slightest difficulty getting the desired opinion from our CPAs. With some regret, we must pass over him now, and hire someone who'll clearly have what he lacks...and can groom him to be CFO in about 7 to 10 years. "Anne's" our answer!

Mitchell G. Arnold

92 Outer Circle Road
Randolph Air Force Base, Texas 78148
Home: (512) 210-2305
Office: (512) 601-1128/7360
mitchga@rcn.com

OBJECTIVE

Seek responsible leadership position in program/city management, human resources management, or marketing/public relations.

QUALIFICATIONS SUMMARY

25 years of experience managing people, programs, and budgets at various responsibility and organizational levels. Proven success in recruiting, training, motivating, and achieving goals. Last ten years in senior executive positions of both large and small organizations. Extensive computer experience. I've had a rewarding military career, but it's time to move to the civilian sector.

2001- Present **Air Force ROTC, Southwest Region**
San Antonio, TX

Commander (Colonel)

One of five national region commanders. Report directly to the Commanding General who selected me over 100 other candidates. With an immediate staff of 18, I direct 29 senior military leaders, 270 staff, 14,000 students, and a $8.0 million scholarship, travel, and advertising budget at 29 universities and 76 high schools in a nine-state area.

Use network efficiencies and extensive personal travel/involvement to ensure program quality. Evaluate executive leadership, recruiting and retention programs. After traveling through heavily Hispanic south Texas, developed concept for English-Spanish recruiting brochure which the USAF will use throughout the Southwest.

Superiors and outside inspectors consider this region most efficient in the nation. During the 2001-2002 inspection cycle 100% of my personnel/programs passed rigorous mission compliance inspections, and 60% received the highest possible ratings.

1999 - 2001 **University of Texas at Austin**
Austin, TX

Department Chair/Detachment Commander (Colonel)
Air Force ROTC Department

Reported directly to the Central Region (US) Commander. Senior military officer on campus; held professor's title. With staff of nine and a budget of $170,000, recruited, educated, trained, motivated, and screened 150 - 190 officer candidates through a 4-year academic and leadership program. Recruited largest freshman/sophomore classes in two decades.

Using the university infrastructure, I formed an AFROTC alumni association which raised thousands of scholarship dollars. Many other universities emulated the concept. Taught sophomore-level history course. Authored text used by 150 universities entitled *The History of US Involvement in Vietnam.*

In 2001 the program was selected as the best of 32 major university programs in the Central US. Upon my boss's retirement, he selected me as his replacement.

1997 - 1999 US Air Force Flying Organization

Victorville, CA

Commander (Colonel)

Performed hands-on, day-to-day supervision and training of six senior managers who led 500 people in the operations and maintenance divisions of a USAF flying organization. In charge of $60 million in capital assets with a $5.2 million operations and maintenance budget. Unit flew missions throughout the US and in Central America. Other unit personnel were deployed throughout West Germany.

The unit was initially plagued with morale problems, poor facilities, and budget reductions. Through a strong public relations effort and hard work we were able to turn that completely around—people received their due recognition, facilities got upgraded, and we met all organizational goals with a 20% budget cut. In that process, I made numerous decisions involving personnel, administration, financial and resource management, counseling and personal affairs/fiscal responsibility. Also had many civic public relations/speaking engagements.

Using Quality Circles/TQM concepts, I created two employee advisory councils which opened communications channels and resulted in an improved work environment and increased unit and individual productivity. Retention rates hit all time high of 80%.

Our maintenance division was rated number one organizationally in both 1997 and 1998. We cut flying-hours costs 20% through effective parts ordering and preventive maintenance—funded other units with our excess. Superiors recognized me as a mission-minded commander with a people-oriented perspective. Promoted to Colonel in 1998.

1994 - 1997 International Fighter Programs, The Pentagon

Washington, DC

Chief (Lieutenant Colonel)

Reported to the USAF Director of International Programs. I was the project manager for marketing fighter aircraft worldwide for the US government. Primary Department of Defense (DOD)/USAF focal point for foreign countries requesting USAF fighter aircraft, technical performance, and cost data. Priced, planned, and developed disclosure guidance (protecting technology transfer) for worldwide security assistance programs.

Developed and obtained DOD and State Department approval for foreign military sales (releasable) configuration of the General Dynamics F-16 and the Northrop F-20 aircraft. The two competing aircraft manufacturers saved millions of dollars due to the standardization.

I prepared and presented aircraft briefings around the world to the highest level political, military, and civilian leaders. Traveled extensively throughout Europe, Southeast Asia, and the Middle East. Presentations ultimately led to multi-billion dollar F-16 purchases by Turkey, Singapore, Thailand, and Indonesia. Prepared fighter aircraft export policy decision matrices used by the Secretary of State and the Secretary of Defense. Defused potential conflict with Jordan over cost data.

I had more latitude and more responsibility than anyone else of my rank in the business—performance resulted in selection as commander of USAF flying organization.

1990 - 1994 US Air Force, Operations & Training Division

Las Vegas, NV

Chief (Lieutenant Colonel)

Directly reported to the Director of Operations in an organization of 2000 people. Managed all inbound/outbound relocations for about 200 critical personnel.

With staff of 14, I directed current operations (generated flying schedule, and produced ground, simulator, and flying training programs) of this F-16 wing. All programs received excellent ratings from outside inspectors. I wrote the omnibus training document implemented for all F-16 pilots worldwide. Promoted to Lieutenant Colonel in 1992. Track record resulted in being hand-picked for a critical position at the Pentagon.

1987 - 1990 Headquarters Tactical Air Command

Hampton, VA

Programmer / Presentations Officer (Major)

As command briefer, prepared and presented classified briefings to high-level US and foreign political, diplomatic, and military dignitaries.

Conducted operations research and analysis. Project manager/editor for special TAC issue of *Aviation Week and Space Technology.*

Liaison for matters relating to acquisition, integration, logistical support, and operational employment of F-16 during full-scale development phase. Promoted to Major in 1987.

PRIOR

Liaison Officer to South Korean Army and Air Force. Flightline and academic instructor pilot. Fighter pilot. Have flown every jet fighter the Air Force currently deploys and also several test models never put into production.

EDUCATION

Defense Institute of Security Assistance Management (foreign military sales), 1995.
MBA, Management, Golden Gate University, 1989.
BA, Business Administration, Rutgers University, 1976.

PERSONAL

Computer literate. Physically fit non-smoker. Top Secret (codeword) clearances.
Married. Born November 24, 1953.

What did you think?

Did this man write himself up exactly the way I would have?

Of course not. Or the way you would have? Probably not.

But he did a superb job at a very difficult task that utterly stumps many people in all sorts of businesses and not-for-profit organizations.

He took his highly specialized career and made it totally understandable to a couple outsiders...you and me. He also managed to show us through his obviously excellent work and his just as obviously excellent thinking and writing (which he *demonstrated*) that he is an extremely fine person. We came away knowing that, having done many difficult things very well in his area, he could emerge just about anywhere in our area and perform just as well for us.

Now that's an accomplishment!

Also, in retrospect...

Here's something I'll bet you didn't think of at the time...and probably wouldn't now, if I didn't bring it up.

The resume was *extremely easy to read.* Fully as easy as the previous one, despite being in paragraphs, rather than bullets. Many people assume that, because paragraphs are harder to write, they must also be harder to read. That is not true. Or, I should say, not IF you work very hard to make them easy to read, and IF you work equally hard to make them say exactly what is most beneficial to you. Of course, those are big "ifs."

In that regard, please go back to page 69 for proof. Nothing could have been more damaging to the fellow on 69 than to send out his first version (the long one). If he had, no one would have bothered to read it! Which, on second thought might not have been so bad because, in its "original" state, its *message* was also damaging.

So deciding to write your resume in paragraphs is a serious decision, calling for lots of serious extra work. And some people, who are terrific executives but not extremely sensitive and hard-working writers, shouldn't even attempt that style.

Are you one of them?

If so, as you've already seen, there are other very good ways to proceed.

What was *bad* about the "Arnold" resume?

A few things, certainly. But all of them insignificant when weighed against the fine overall impression it made. Remember, resumes are a game of overall impression. They're like a championship fight. You can be losing all the way on points, but if you deliver the KO punch—i.e., overall impression—nothing else matters.

Interruption for a Story:

When *RITES* first appeared, I received a "thank you" note I still treasure from a man who had never enjoyed a title higher than Plant Manager, but had a string of truly remarkable accomplishments. He typed them into a resume on what appeared to be an old Remington or Smith-Corona portable typewriter and mailed them off in the way *RITES* prescribes for a direct mail campaign. He did not buy any elegant personal stationery, engraved or otherwise. He or maybe his spouse merely typed them—return address and all—on the same old typewriter.

The words and syntax also left a bit to be desired. But his accomplishments did not! And they were so honestly and straightforwardly stated, that they rang absolutely true.

WOW! I was impressed.

As I read, I pictured the Plant Manager as a business frontiersman out in the Southwest...a composite of John Wayne, Henry Ford, and Bill Gates.

Also, as I read, I pictured a smooth MBA in a dark suit or dress in a New England boardroom pointing at charts and claiming as the result of sophisticated strategy and planning the dollars rolling in from the many product innovations and global sourcing coups that our hero was spontaneously ginning up in that dusty little town a thousand miles away.

The outcome? You guessed it. One of the people this man mailed to was the foreign entrepreneur/owner of companies making and selling similar products all over the world. He snapped up this fellow to be President of his U.S. operations!

Style is very important. And we'll polish it to a high gloss. But a fundamentally convincing overall impression wins by a knock out!

The "I"s have it!

Which is NOT to say that the Colonel was behind on points. He was winning all the way. In fact, the #1 thing to improve in his resume I fixed before showing it to you.

Our military friend was originally...like most other folks...a little *too* reticent about using the personal pronoun. And no wonder! Not only is it military protocol that you don't go around saying "I"..."I" all day long, there's also plenty of civilian folklore that says, "You must never say 'I' in a resume."

Actually, there's justification for all that nervousness. Your paperwork is examined for clues about your personality. If you seem like an egomaniac and not at all a team-player, who will want to hire you?

On the other hand, there's the matter of common sense...of being practical and modern. And of giving yourself *credit for your accomplishments.* After all, they are your only proof that you deliver a good product. *They are all you have to sell.* So, if you *did* something, it's totally wrong to write that event up in the "passive voice," as if it just *happened*, without asserting that you or anyone else *made* it happen. The only sensible way to talk about what you did is to claim credit for it. Remember...

I is not a four-letter word.

The Colonel was so averse to the use of "I" that I added a few "I s" here and there (my *only* adulterations). On the other hand, what Mitch Arnold did very well...and what I believe in also...is seldom start an entirely new section or paragraph with "I." On page 79, note the paragraphs beginning "One of..." and "Reported..." and on page 80 the ones beginning "Performed..." Reported to..." and "Developed..."

Notice too, how you can also use a descriptive phrase ("participial," if you're a grammarian) to begin a sentence. The phrase modifies "I," but pushes the I *inside* the paragraph. Mr. Arnold did this very skillfully on pages 79 and 80, at the start of his paragraphs that begin with "Using..."

Our is DEFINITELY *not a four-letter word.*

In fact, "our" is extremely useful. When applied to a business or a group you supervise, it claims the unit's achievement as yours—or at least under your leadership, which is probably even better—and it simultaneously demonstrates you're the very sort of collegial team-leader that using "I" might have implied you're not. So do say "our" and "we" a lot.

But be careful. Remember that unless the context makes it absolutely clear that you are or were the *leader* of the team, using "our" or "we" places you merely *on* the team and not in a management role. Frequently I find (in my work as an executive recruiter) that a person who imprecisely uses the "our" or "we" has, in my mind as a reader, made him- or herself merely a supporting player, when he or she was the one person without whose creativity and leadership the achievement would never have happened.

What did you think of the "OBJECTIVE"?

Surprise. I liked it. As I pointed out on page 65, when you're doing something so different as leaving the military, academia, the clergy, etc. you absolutely *must* orient your reader to what you are looking for in his or her organization. It's not enough merely to say, "Here I am. Figure out how you might use me." Most folks with the power and position to hire you are far too busy to play that game.

In Mr. Arnold's case, I didn't even hate "Seek responsible leadership position in..." To any business executive, I'd say, "It's obvious. Get rid of it!"

But for the Colonel, it works. Words that would be hollow for every civilian are meaningful for him. He's saying, "Don't mark me for a low-pay or low-level job just because I've got a monthly Government check and may not have the precise experience you have in mind."

And "Qualifications Summary"?

Those are a couple words I'd usually try to get you to eliminate, as you strive for your own personal style. I'd say, "If you want a summary, just put it there." Needless labels like "Qualifications Summary" are so common on resumes of the people being assembly-lined out of down-sizing corporations, that their mere presence tends to say, "Just another discard; don't bother reading."

But for Mr. Arnold, who is **NOT** coming out of a corporation and may actually benefit from looking a little bit more "corporate," this touch of "mass-production"—especially when his overall paperwork is so refreshingly clear—may not be an entirely bad idea.

Leaving Out the Ordinary

Did you notice that Colonel Arnold says hardly anything about what he was doing from college graduation in '76 until he hits headquarters in '87? He realizes that piling on more early history that we will not consider pertinent to any of our jobs would only make him seem more different from us...and therefore more irrelevant.

Radically condensing early work history is something *you* should also consider... although from a different angle. No matter what your field, during your early years in it you were doing essentially what every beginner does. That is *not* interesting, and it's *not* why we'll hire you. Be sure to give us dates and employers for those early years, so we won't think you're hiding anything. But don't waste your space and our attention span with ordinariness, when you should be stressing the really major things we might want to hire you for.

The Military-to-Civilian Transition

Why did I include a military example? For two reasons.

Above all, for its illustrative value. Thousands of readers of this book will have been working in specialized fields that are shrinking. They're not likely to find the job they need in the same area where 100% of their experience—and thus all of their achievements—are centered. What are they to do? Never work again?

One part of the answer, of course, is to write a resume...and put their successes in general terms that show how formidable those accomplishments were, while still not making them seem so different from what fine managers do in other fields that readers will tag them "irrelevant." The military-to-civilian transition is the classic example of this difficult resume-writing problem. So if you're in the civilian model of the same boat, please pay special attention to the Arnold resume (particularly '97-'99 and '94-'97).

Secondly, there are lots of military people these days who need the information. Often military executives hit the civilian job market when the market is crowded and therefore difficult. Please, when you have the executive job you're seeking and are back on the hiring side, do yourself a favor. Give creative consideration to filling your appropriate positions with exiting military people. They deserve your attention and, appropriately chosen, will deliver exceptional commitment and performance.

A Touch of Warmth and Personality

Please don't go overboard, just because I bring up the subject. Trying to accomplish "personality" in a resume gravely risks obnoxious cuteness. Charm has to enter almost by accident...as it did with Colonel Arnold.

He said so much about himself that was strong, sensible, realistic, self-aware, self-confident and yet by no means self-important or imperious (an unwarranted potential prejudice against departing military people), when he said: "I've had a rewarding military career, but it's time to move to the civilian sector."

I don't know how or when something real and human might tend to creep into your resume, but when it does—and you're about to cross it out for not being rigid and formal enough—give it a second thought. Sleep on it overnight. And maybe leave it in.

What's going on here?

Do you see what we're doing...and why?

We're discussing and thinking about resumes as if they're something very ordinary. Something you—like Dick Sawyer, Anne Lohmann, Mitch Arnold and Sylvia Dorrington, whom you're about to meet—are totally capable of dealing with in a highly intelligent and even inspired way. Resumes must communicate. But, beyond that, they are a matter of creativity and taste. A matter on which many fine people have different views. And one on which your views are just as insightful as anyone else's.

Resumes are a matter totally within the realm of common sense. One where you can say, "How would *I* react to that?" and get the best possible answer.

One More to Look at...Then Yours to Make

As you see, this is *not* one of those pick-one-and-copy-it books. On the contrary, the message is, "See the infinite wealth of possibilities. Pick none...and copy nothing!" I just hope you're feeling more and more empowered to criticize, reject, and launch out creatively on your own. Devise, organize and tell your own story in your own way. It's the only way to wind up with your best "Sales Representative."

Sylvia P. Dorrington
476 Stone Wall Road
Pleasant Hills, Illinois 60057
Phone: (708) 012-2347
Fax: (708) 012-3691
E-mail: sylviapd@inzanet.net

Senior Human Resources Executive

Comprehensive policy and operational leadership...domestic and international.

1986 - Present **PREFERRED CONSUMER BRANDS, INC.**
Chicago, IL

During 16 years with one of the world's largest consumer products companies, I've progressed from Employee Relations Specialist ('86-'87) and Manager-level Employee Relations and Staffing positions ('87-'90) to Director of all Human Resources activities for our 2,000 people at Corporate Headquarters ('90-'93)... to Director and then Vice President heading Human Resources for all of our International Division [18,000 people in 26 countries with $3.2 billion annual sales]('93-'98)...to Vice President - Human Resources for all U.S. activities [now 7,225 people, $3.0 billion annual sales] since 1998.

I've succeeded by fostering innovation to get more and better work from fewer, more highly-motivated people. Also, as an African-American woman, I've often been helpful in managing a diverse U.S. work force and in relating PCBrands to employees—and even customers—from foreign cultures.

Now, having succeeded as #2 in Human Resources responsibility to an outstanding person only a few years beyond my age, I've decided to seek a larger challenge outside of Preferred Consumer.

'98 - Present **Vice President - Human Resources U.S.**

Since June '96, I've headed Human Resources for this now $3.0 billion business...then 9,354 people, now 7,225 [600 in headquarters Product Marketing and Merchandising, Finance, and H.R.; 2,300 in Manufacturing (3 plants in the U.S.), 2,425 in 5 Logistics/Distribution facilities; and 1,900 Sales and Sales Management people]. Here are the dimensions of our organization:

	'98	'99	'00	'01	'02
Employees	9,354	8,898	8,332	7,920	7,225
U.S. Sales	$2.80 billion	$2.86 billion	$2.82 billion	$2.92 billion	$3.00 billion*
U.S. Sales per Employee	$299,340	$321,420	$338,454	$368,686	$415,224*

*Estimated

As head of U.S. Human Resources, I've been in charge of all U.S. HR Strategy, Employee Relations, Compensation, Benefits, Succession Planning, Career Development, Management & Organizational

Development, Organizational Restructuring, and Managing Diversity. I reported to the President - U.S., and was a member of the U.S. Executive Operating Committee.

Work Redesign - Headquarters Marketing We're saving $18 million annually and getting our new products out much faster. Reason: a flatter organization with fewer people working in much closer cooperation:

	Before	After
Product Development Time from Concept to Market:	22 Months	11 Months
HQ Product Marketing Group Headcount:	497 people	340 people
Cost of HQ Product Marketing Group:	$60 million	$42 Million

Streamlining Logistics / Distribution / Manufacturing We're saving $40 million per year by closing one of five logistics / distribution centers. Cut 782 jobs in Minneapolis (while adding 140 in St. Louis and Omaha) at a one-time cost of $46 million. Innovatively humane and smooth transition.

Conversion to Flex / Cost-Contained Benefits We've moved from a company-funded 1950s program to modern flex-benefits. Costs, now shared by employees, are up only 10% this year vs. a 17% industry-average rise. Conversion was entirely electronic, with enrollment by an automated telephone procedure.

Variable Incentive Compensation Program Covering All Employees We'd long had profit-related incentives for Managers. Now every Associate (employee) is covered by a variable plan (4% of compensation) based on company profits.

Managing Diversity I've put in strong programs...a Diversity Leadership Council that includes Senior Officers, workshops for Senior Executives, segments on diversity in "core" training programs for new Supervisors and Managers, and a one-day course on diversity for every associate. Often invited to speak on Diversity, I've addressed the FBI, Salomon Brothers, General Mills, Continental Illinois, United Air Lines, Columbia University, the National Black MBA Association, and many others.

'93 - '98 **Vice President - Human Resources International**
Director - Human Resources International ('93-'94)

As Director and then promoted to Vice President, I headed Human Resources for Preferred Consumer's non-U.S. operations...over 18,000 employees in 26 countries generating $3.2 billion annual sales. Reporting to the President of International stationed in Chicago, I worked approximately 50% of the time in Chicago and 50% overseas, supporting the development and compensation of our 200 key executives worldwide, 26 Country General Managers, 60 expatriates or Third Country Nationals and key U.S.-based international executives, and 18,000 employees outside the U.S. I was a member of the International Executive Council and reported directly to the President - International Operations.

Decentralization and Establishing Foreign Regional Offices We decentralized our Senior Management by establishing Regional Offices abroad: Europe in London; and Asia in Hong Kong. Latin America continued to be headquartered in New York. Besides achieving our decentralization goals, we saved $6 million annually.

International Management Development Two key programs: (1) Our International Team Leadership Program provided training to Country General Managers and their direct reports, and (2) Our International Cadre Program identified and developed 23 of our highest-potential internationalists.

Special Emphasis on Mexico Mexico was our #1 international market, with over $400 million annual sales, and I spent quite a lot of time there. I recruited Mexican nationals as our CFO and as our VP Marketing, and I helped with our eventual transition to a Mexican President.

Understanding Local Cultural Issues Whenever I visited a country I always did an assessment of the demographics and customs of the country and of our workforce. Particularly in Mexico and Brazil, two of our largest markets, I was very active in investigating the role of women managers in women-centered companies. That work led to useful suggestions for dealing with our customers as well as our employees.

'90 - '93 Director - Headquarters Human Resources

Developed and implemented policies and processes for several restructurings, downsizings, decentralizations, and relocations, and supported the growth of several small businesses, while also maintaining employee relations, employment, compensation, and benefits support at 2,000-employee headquarters.

'87 - '90 Manager - Employee Relations and Staffing
for Operations, Legal, Finance and Information Services
'86 - '87 Employee Relations Specialist

Entering as an Executive Recruiter, I moved up rapidly through several Manager-level positions.

1977 to 1986 SEARS, ROEBUCK & COMPANY
Chicago and New York City

Joined Sears in their Evanston store, as a Chicago area Management Trainee. The first 2 of 8 promotions in 9 years were in Evanston...to Assistant Manager ('77) and then Manager ('78) of the Toy Department. Offered a headquarters assignment in New York, I entered as a Buyer's Assistant ('78), then Assistant Buyer ('79-'81) on fabrics, etc. for home sewing. Promoted to Assistant Retail Sales Manager (for the Eastern and Southwestern U.S.) ('82-'84). In mid-'84 I became Personnel Manager (one of 3 serving Sears' 2,300 people in NYC...the Buying Departments, Product Testing Labs, Marketing Research, and Information Services). My duties included the added responsibility of EEO Manager and management of the College Recruiting Program.

Education: Spelman College, B.A., History/Business, 1977
Stanford University Executive Education Program, 1992
Served as Adjunct Professor, Fashion Institute of Technology, 1984-91

Personal: Married
Board of Directors, Northside Center for Child Development
Member, Spelman College Corporate Women's Roundtable

What do you think of Sylvia's Resume?

Obviously she's a superior person with a great career up to now...and a great future. That's what she wanted to tell us, and what we find virtually impossible to doubt. We're *not* on the borderline. There may be others in the resume pile we'll like just as well. But clearly Sylvia is somebody we *must* call up. What more could her resume possibly accomplish?

She gets off to a fast start.

She's really told us everything we need to know by the middle of her first page! The rest just proves it's true. Notice that before she gets into specifics, she gives a sweeping review of her career with "PCBrands." If she had worked for several companies in her career—or in its most recent and important segment—she could have summarized those jobs in a similar fashion. This is often a very useful technique. Consider it for yourself.

Why is she leaving?
Is there anything negative about her being available?

Notice that Sylvia has told us right up front why she has quit her job to seek another one. She's not about to let us think she's been fired when she hasn't.

Other folks are job hunting for other reasons. And these days the reasons are hardly ever an indictment of the people themselves. Never before in recent history has an executive's being out of work been less a reflection on his or her performance. You can be *superb* and out of work...and today every employer knows it.

However, to benefit from today's presumption, you must build a short explanation into the resume, and put it in quite a prominent place as Sylvia has done. Indeed, if she'd worked for multiple employers, she would probably have mentioned the reasons for most of the transitions...either in her description of the job she left, or the one she went to.

Nine Early Years in Eight Lines

Sylvia did a great job of showing us her early years ('77-'86) were just as outstanding as her latest ones. And yet she didn't use much vertical space...only eight lines. Alternatively, she could merely have put companies and titles in a vertical list (although that would have taken *more* space). This way we get a few details that make us feel we know her somewhat as a person...a nice touch in a resume.

A Personal History in a Personal Style

Another interesting touch is the way Sylvia gave several of her achievements a descriptive title. Her choice of items to talk about also tells us a lot about Sylvia. Her genuine interest in people from other cultures ties in with the critical HR need to manage diversity here in the U.S. Something else I like a lot about Sylvia's resume is the fact that she has *loaded it with numbers* and she *doesn't use a single self-flattering adjective*. That's not surprising, considering that her specialty is Human Resources. She's undoubtedly read too many resumes that are weighted the opposite way...and she knows what happens to *them!*

And Now Finally...Back to the Bad News

Just before we looked at the Sawyer resume, I promised to tell you about the phone call I got from the proprietor of the "let-us-write-your-resume-and-send-it-out" business.

He complained that executives were reading *RITES OF PASSAGE* and wanting his writers to produce longer and more personalized resumes than his standard product. But with padding, the resumes get worse, not better and—beyond a certain point—cost more to mail. Didn't I want to recant? He'd pass my words along to his customers and potential customers.

I asked if he'd read the Sam Sage resume. Of course. Did he believe that, if Sam were real rather than fictional, Sam would be more likely to be hired if we knew less about him? "No, of course not." How long did his writers spend, on average, to produce a letter-and-resume? Silence. Surely not more than two or three hours? Silence. Was it possible to hire and adequately compensate anyone for his business who was even remotely capable of writing a Sam Sage resume? "No," he admitted, and therein lay the fundamental problem. He tried to give a "good value" to his customers. And he really *did* send out the number of letters contracted for.

The problem, obviously, was that the material sent out had to be *almost generic*, or he couldn't produce it. Even if he *could* afford someone like me—or you—on his staff, we couldn't produce any faster than I did in helping the fellow on page 69. Even if his "customers" sent us drafts as good as the one on the bottom of 69 (extremely unlikely), it would take you or me or any other deeply committed person at least a week of fulltime work—more likely two—to generate a real Sam Sage resume. We could dump an extra page or two of words into his standard 2- or 3-hour product. In fact our production time on that one would probably go *down* to 1 or 2 hours, because we'd merely edit it less stringently in the first place.

So you see why I feel compelled to hand you the bad news. Plenty of people are willing to take money from you at any time for any reason. But nobody besides you really cares enough about your future—or knows enough about your past—to take on, in a serious way, the hard job of producing a really powerful executive-level resume for you.

There is one utterly superb resume writer I know of, who personally writes wonderful stuff for nonexecutive-level people, and she has helpers who, I presume, also do good work. But, while they can turn out quick, charming, persuasive one-pagers for junior people in a couple hours for maybe $425, they have no desire whatsoever to become embroiled in the kind of stuff you're looking at in any example in this book.

So the bad news is that, for your executive-level resume to be really good, you've got to make it yourself.

A Silver Lining

However, there's more *good* news. The very arduousness of the task prepares you as nothing else can for the interviewing process. You really examine your career and learn to the marrow of your bones the best possible points that can be made in your favor, and the best answers to all possible negatives that can be brought up against you.

Do your own resume to its ultimate perfection, and you will sing like a bird in your interviews. You won't need any further preparation (except, of course, for learning about the company you're talking to).

And Now Down to Work!

If you've seriously considered every page up to this point, you're plenty ready now to write *somebody's* resume.

The trick now is to develop the ideal personal "Sales Representative" to sell YOU.

As a third party helping from the sidelines, the best thing I can do is to guide you toward an examination of your own life's work as if it were someone else's career. Together, we'll look for your outstanding accomplishments that prove you're the best person who can be found and hired—or at least who's currently in view—for the employer to use to get what he or she wants accomplished.

Also, we'll look for potential blemishes and gaps-of-experience (we all have them) that must be identified and dealt with, so that they won't be used against you to tear down the favorable impression your achievements can be used to build up.

To help you do that, here are the:

#1. Blueprint of the Perfect Selling Message

You'll never have perfection.

Not in breadth or depth of experience...nor in stellar achievements to illustrate prior success in everything that could possibly be asked of you.

All we can hope to do is marshal the strongest facts you have in your favor—and disarm the most damaging arguments that can be made against you. Do that as well as possible, and you will have the strongest "Sales Representative" resume you can possibly produce. And it will be *very strong indeed!*

As we set out with that goal in mind, let's consider what the perfect Selling Message would be if it *were* attainable, and use it as a blueprint to build the nearest-thing-to-perfection. It would:

1. Identify your Highest and Best Use (from the employer's point of view).

2. Prove that you'd be the Best Person (among all candidates) an employer can hire for that use. The proof is two-sided...presence of positives and absence of negatives.

Positives: You have outstanding previous performances of:

Identical work, of

Equal or greater degree-of-difficulty, and with respect to

Every aspect of that work, not just some parts of it:

You've done it.

You've done it outstandingly.

Negatives: You've never failed in any previous attempt to perform:

Similar work, or even

Different work, and there are

No prejudices operating against you.

So you're human!

Wouldn't you rather be perfect?

So would I.

Onward!

But the good news is that nobody else is perfect either. Therefore, there will never be anyone perfect competing against you. So polish up your resume. Make it sell you as effectively as possible. You're in a game that anyone can play...and skilled players can *win*.

From here on, tools will challenge you to:

1. Identify the ideal aspects of experience and prior superior performance of the best imaginable candidate for the job you seek, and
2. Bring forward the strongest/closest possible proof that you have them.

By stretching to think what the ideal—the maximum world-beating—items in each category would be, you'll set yourself up to identify them—or their nearest equivalent—among your achievements. And those will be the ones to display in your resume in order to "win the category."

Afterward, we'll examine each separate component of your resume (the entry for each job), and focus on making it as individually strong and as supportive of a winning overall impression as possible.

#2. What is your Highest and Best Use?

Please flip back through all the pages of Chapter 1. Read your "write-ins." One of the main purposes of Chapter 1 was to get you to give some fresh thought to the nature of the job you ought to be seeking.

What job or jobs would you like your resume to help you get? Fill in the title or titles; also a comprehensive job description broad enough to cover all the duties inherent in the title or titles you have selected. Are you going for top-of-pyramid *general management*...CEO, President, COO, Group Executive, General Manager? Are you going after a position at the top of—or another level in—one of the *functions*... Marketing, Sales, Finance, Manufacturing, R&D, Technology/Information, Administration, Purchasing, Law, Advertising, Public Relations, Plant Management, etc.? Identify your own function and pick your rung of the ladder from Specialist or Manager on up to VP - Chief Officer of it.

Referring back to all the thinking you did in Chapter 1 (especially pp. 11-12 and 36-39), now write down the title or titles (no more than 2 or 3) that cover your "Highest and Best Use." What do you want an employer to use you for? Then create a rough job description broad enough to cover all of those duties.

TITLE / TITLES ______________________________

JOB DESCRIPTION ______________________________

____

____

____

____

____

____

____

____

____

____

#3. What would the ideal person with your title and "job description" be expected to accomplish, and which expected accomplishments are most important?

You know what a person doing the job you're seeking is expected to do...and should have demonstrated some success in doing up to now.

You know, too, that nobody has already done everything that might be expected...and certainly not with notable distinction in every category.

So here again, it pays to let your mind sweep over everything that's ideal, before you begin to write. That way, you'll be tuned to your reader's (the employer's) wave length, looking to include in your resume what he or she will be looking to find.

Also, you know that some areas of experience/accomplishment are far more basic and therefore important than others...almost to the point of being essential. Therefore, you'll try to make sure to "cover those bases."

For example, a CEO or General Manager would love to show: growth in sales and earnings of ongoing businesses; increasing ROI; rising market shares; turnarounds of troubled businesses; internal generation of new products and businesses; acquisitions, mergers and divestitures; selecting and developing fine people; success in labor relations; cost-cutting and restructuring; international successes; obtaining capital through debt, equity and possibly an IPO...and on and on. Your function or specialty too has plenty of things it is expected to accomplish.

Please jot down the various types of prior accomplishments likely to be expected of candidates for the position you're seeking. Afterward fill in the right hand column, numbering them from #1 downward, in roughly what you think will be their order of importance to employers.

	Priority No.
EXPECTED ACCOMPLISHMENT ______________________	______
______________________________________	______
EXPECTED ACCOMPLISHMENT ______________________	______
______________________________________	______

	Priority No.
EXPECTED ACCOMPLISHMENT	
EXPECTED ACCOMPLISHMENT	
EXPECTED ACCOMPLISHMENT	
EXPECTED ACCOMPLISHMENT	
EXPECTED ACCOMPLISHMENT	
EXPECTED ACCOMPLISHMENT	
EXPECTED ACCOMPLISHMENT	
EXPECTED ACCOMPLISHMENT	
EXPECTED ACCOMPLISHMENT	
EXPECTED ACCOMPLISHMENT	
EXPECTED ACCOMPLISHMENT	
EXPECTED ACCOMPLISHMENT	

#4. What are the traditional *MEASUREMENTS* of excellent performance in your function?

You've just finished listing what people in the position you're seeking are expected to *accomplish.*

Now please think about all of the traditional *measurements* used in your field.

Obviously there's overlap between #3 and #4, because often what executives must *accomplish* is to *increase or improve* the relevant measurements. Indeed, bonuses often hinge on ups and downs in those measurements.

However there are traditional yardsticks of good performance that go *beyond* the obvious. For example, if you're a marketing person, not just share-of-market, but also number of new customers gained, sales leads generated, old accounts reactivated, increases in average order-size, share of retailer shelf-space, brand awareness levels, advertising recall scores, etc. Or if you're an R&D executive, perhaps number of new compounds tested, patents applied for and granted, favorable rulings by government regulatory agencies, favorable studies placed in professional journals, etc.

You get the idea. Try to think of all the ways good performance can be measured in your field. Jot them down here, so that your mind will be tuned to them as you examine your career and write your resume.

Let your mind run free. Try to think of every potential yardstick you may be able to use to prove you are a fine performer in your field. Here too, you may want to think in terms of "priorities," since some measurements are likely to be stronger and more universal "head-turners" than others.

	Priority No.
MEASUREMENT I CAN USE ______________________	______
______________________	______
MEASUREMENT I CAN USE ______________________	______
______________________	______
MEASUREMENT I CAN USE ______________________	______
______________________	______

	Priority No.
MEASUREMENT I CAN USE ______	
MEASUREMENT I CAN USE ______	
MEASUREMENT I CAN USE ______	
MEASUREMENT I CAN USE ______	
MEASUREMENT I CAN USE ______	
MEASUREMENT I CAN USE ______	
MEASUREMENT I CAN USE ______	
MEASUREMENT I CAN USE ______	
MEASUREMENT I CAN USE ______	
MEASUREMENT I CAN USE ______	
MEASUREMENT I CAN USE ______	
MEASUREMENT I CAN USE ______	

#5. What are some *OTHER PROOFS* you've done very good work?

You've just reviewed the various traditional measurements of superior performance in your field.

Now let's consider other proofs of excellent work that are ***universal.*** When they're conferred on any person in any field, we automatically know that he or she has done a fine job...even if we know nothing whatsoever about the field.

Quite a few such proofs pop automatically into my mind, so I'll provide a list to get your thinking started. Then you can continue the list with others that occur to you. Fortunately, some of your ideas will come to mind because they've actually happened to you. Great! They can go straight into your resume.

Promoted. The #1 best proof of excellence. If this is why your title changed, be sure to say so...and tell which achievements were the main reason.

Expanded. No new title, but they liked your work so well they gave you more...wider geography, broader product line, more subordinates / departments / locations.

Given Money. You got a bonus or a raise from the achievement. Was the cash also beyond guidelines, given during a pay freeze, or simultaneous with layoffs?

Wanted back. Your former boss persuaded you to rejoin him or her...either inside or outside the company. Joyous! But also the reason for many ill-timed departures ...and sometimes to embarrassingly short-term jobs. Put this reason—happy or sad—on your resume. If there are two or three short-timers in a row, lump them in a single-dated overall header-paragraph, as if the *person* were a single employer, and under or inside that explanation list the dates, companies and details of the three black holes he or she sucked you into during "1999-2002."

Put to wider use. You originated a method or wrote a manual that was so successful in your part of the organization that it is now applied elsewhere. Maybe today the whole company is doing certain things your way.

Copied by competitors. Not only did the innovation succeed at your place, it swept the market. Today the whole industry does things your way.

BUT BE CAREFUL! Do *not* state as a personal accomplishment the fact that you had the idea years ago for something that has now swept the field, but the dolts in your company wouldn't let you go ahead with it. Lots of folks bring up such matters, not realizing that they may be indicting themselves for failure-to-persuade. We can't check for phony creativity, but we can surely smell sour grapes on the breath of some of those folks!

Doing BIG DEALS. Really noteworthy breakthroughs are always admired. Mention record-breaking contracts, prestigious accounts nobody else could crack, freezing out bigger competitors with single-supplier deals, etc.

Doing a rising % of total-company business. The product lines you're responsible for or the products of your laboratory were only X% of total-company volume when you took over; now they're 3X%.

Going North as they go South. Maybe you went up only 2%, but if competition simultaneously went down 18%...WOW!

Succeeding when it's not your job. You headed Manufacturing, not Marketing, and yet you saw a potential new use and a customer for it. You made contact... and opened up a whole new sales channel. The stripes of a general management tiger cub are clearly visible under that shop coat.

Capturing and training tigers. Say so, if an impressive group of executives you've hired and trained are now highly placed in your company and around the industry. Just be careful there's no hint that you can't retain bright, strong subordinates.

Winning industry and company awards. You're probably very good if your peers are singing your praises. Be aware, however, that displaying your trophies can hurt, if you got them too long ago. You must seem at your peak, not coasting down the other side of the hill.

Speaking and writing. Your speeches, articles and columns can be accolades... especially if you were invited to do them because of a specific accomplishment that made the company money and got you a promotion. Mention them alongside the accomplishment, not in a caboose at the end of the resume...unless you're an academician or a scientist and that's expected. Realize, however, that too much pontificating when accompanied by lukewarm recent accomplishments and an unemployed status can suggest to a "lean-'n-mean" management that you've become an industry socialite...more ornamental than useful.

Being written about. Your exploits or the fine products or services you've been responsible for may have been featured in industry or general media. If so, an exceedingly brief quote or round-up of quotes may enhance your resume.

There are surely other proofs I didn't think of. Jot down any that occur to you...particularly ones that may be unique to your company or field. Also, while you're thinking along these lines, jot down notable examples of this sort of proof from your own career, so you'll be sure to remember to include them in your resume.

OTHER PROOFS ____________________

OTHER PROOFS ____________________

OTHER PROOFS ____________________

OTHER PROOFS ____________________

OTHER PROOFS ____________________

OTHER PROOFS ____________________

OTHER PROOFS ____________________

OTHER PROOFS ____________________

OTHER PROOFS ____________________

OTHER PROOFS ____________________

OTHER PROOFS ____________________

#6. What are the negatives to be kept in mind and abolished?

Please go back and read again pages 22 through 29. Reconsider the strongest apparent reasons *not* to hire you. Notice I said *apparent* reasons. There are *no real reasons.* But appearances are extremely important in the job-search process...and nowhere more so than in the resume.

Suppose you've had what some might consider too many too-brief recent jobs. Or you've worked for a giant corporation that most smaller and more entrepreneurial companies may feel is so bureaucratic that its managers have little relevance to them. Or your former job was in a specialized and declining industry unlikely to provide a repeat engagement. Or your career evolved in an unusual way that leaves what some might consider a gaping hole in needed experience.

Can you lump some of those recent jobs into a single entry? Did one evolve from another or involve some of the same people? Make those connections explicit! Can you show that *you* did fast-paced and fruitful work within the giant? Did you do universally-needed work in that narrowly-specific field? Can you show closely related achievements that span the "gaping hole"? Study pages 51, 69 and the top of 70 again.

In writing the best possible "Sales Representative" resume you absolutely must consider potential customer objections right along with your strongest selling points. That's what selling is all about!

Jot down the most likely reasons not to hire you for the position you've decided to seek. Right or wrong. Fair or unfair. What are the potential negatives and what achievements and/or other information can be written into your resume to offset or disprove them? (*Bring forward from pp. 28-29. Any new thoughts? Sharpen strategy if possible.*)

POTENTIAL NEGATIVE ______________________________

____

STRATEGY FOR HANDLING ______________________________

____

____

____

POTENTIAL NEGATIVE ______________________________

____

STRATEGY FOR HANDLING______________________________

____

____

____

POTENTIAL NEGATIVE ______________________________

____

STRATEGY FOR HANDLING______________________________

____

____

____

POTENTIAL NEGATIVE ______________________________

____

STRATEGY FOR HANDLING______________________________

____

____

____

POTENTIAL NEGATIVE ______________________________

____

STRATEGY FOR HANDLING______________________________

____

____

____

POTENTIAL NEGATIVE ______________________________

____

STRATEGY FOR HANDLING______________________________

____

____

____

#7. Basic Resume *ARCHITECTURE* and *DESIGN* Tools

I hope you've read this WORKBOOK page-by-page from Chapter 1 right up to here and have picked up the Tools and used them thoroughly. If you haven't, please go back and do that now.

Your knowledge and viewpoint already put you way ahead of most folks you'll be up against in the competitive battle of the resumes. You know how much selling power you can—with intelligence and diligence—load onto blank sheets of paper...something most executive job-hunters never realize. Indeed, they assume the opposite. They tend to believe the popular saying, "Resumes don't matter."

Let's not change their minds. Then when your resume meets theirs—on a recruiter's or an employer's desk—you'll get a phone call. They won't. And their opinion will still be correct.

Infinite Room for Individuality

From here on, your options are wide open. You have a sales message to devise and deliver. And you can succeed in an infinite number of ways. If you write well and can readily see the many differences between the top and bottom of page 69...*and* if you'll keep working until each paragraph has a low word-count and a high gloss...then you may want to use paragraphs. Otherwise you may choose bullets. Or you may use a combination. Ask yourself, "Does this scan easily? If I needed somebody like this, and started reading, would I get bored?" (Hack out words whenever you hit such a point!) "And after I finished reading, would I be so impressed, I'd have to pick up the phone and call?" Keep working until you can say, "Yes!" Then you'll have your "Sales Representative Resume."

Architecture and Design Tools

The next several pages will help you organize your thinking. There will be empty slots for you to scribble in rough ideas you want to communicate (1) in your overall document and (2) in the entry for each of your positions that is substantial and recent enough (a) to be covered and (b) to contribute to your overall impression.

Read again the bottom of page 63 and the top of 64. And then go to work!

I've done everything I can to put you in charge of the process...relieved of the folklore about resumes, and ready to make your own original contribution to the art.

ARCHITECTURE

PAGE 1:

(First Impression)

Your O. Name
328 Your Winding Road
Your City, Your State 10957
Phone: (999) 012-3456
Fax: (999) 012-3459
E-mail: yname@aol.com

Title or Titles of Position(s) You Seek
(If you decide to use this technique)

Summary of Your Highest and Best Use *to an Employer*
(*...as conclusively proven by your work history and this resume and NOT your desires and self-flattering adjectives!*)
(If you decide to use this technique)

THIS IS YOUR MAIN SHOWCASE. If you have a straightforward story, and your best job with your finest employer is your latest, begin with ***no*** (p.55), or with *minimal* preliminary distractions.

If your latest job has been brief try, if possible, to find a way to cover it quickly (p. 51), and start your best material out here where people can see it at a glance and get drawn into it.

If you've had two or more short and unhappy recent jobs, you may want to try some sort of expanded summary describing both your earlier classic successes and your recent entrepreneurial plunges, and including dates that go back to when your stability would not have been doubted.

In no event will you want to display nothing but several very brief jobs on page 1. Nor will you want to frustrate every reader's craving for time orientation with a "Topical" resume, which hides chronology until the very end. Everyone knows why this is done and makes far more damaging assumptions than your true story would permit if promptly and skillfully told.

ARCHITECTURE
Structure
(How Many Pages?)

How many pages you use should depend entirely on the most advantageous telling of your story.

Do you have lots of extraordinary accomplishments and the writing skill to compress them into extremely brief, clear prose (p.69) and/or a non-boring grid of bullets? Then you may do well to plan a 4-page (probably not longer) resume. If you have a few great achievements, they'll shine brighter if you stick to two pages and seem curtailed by space. Extra length is never an advantage; extra facts definitely *can* be. But only if they are what I jokingly call "truly amazing." If you devote much space to things everyone else in your field has also done, you not only cause your reader to dump your resume (and you) as boring, but also as *ordinary.*

So take time now to architecturally plan how much space on which page you'll give what jobs and achievements. Where will "Company X" and "Achievement Y" begin and end? "Thumbnail" layouts here and on the next 3 pages enable you to test dozens of ways easily.

Note: the small rectangles are (top) your address/phone and (bottom) education/personal data.

ARCHITECTURE

Structure

(What's on the Pages?)

ARCHITECTURE

Structure

(What's on the Pages?)

ARCHITECTURE

Structure

(What's on the Pages?)

ARCHITECTURE Help from Entry *DESIGN* Sheets

By now you have a good start on the "architecture" of your resume...how much emphasis in terms of space you'll give to (1) your tenure with each employer, (2) your time in each title, and (3) each major accomplishment illustrating your work, having marked up "Thumb-nails" to achieve the right balancing of space to tell your overall story.

Spotlight on Largest and Latest

You'll strive, of course, to spotlight recent successes, in order to show you're at the peak of your career...not headed down hill. On the other hand, if your latest or an interim job was meaningless, you won't try to fluff it into a coup (see p.51). And in describing each job, you'll want to put it to its very best use in shaping a really powerful selling message. To help in your analysis and writing, here are:

Entry *DESIGN* Sheets

Use one of these double-page worksheets as your thought-organizer and scribble pad to develop your entry on each (1) ***multi-job employer*** and each (2) ***multi-achievement job*** you wish to spotlight. "Beginner" jobs needn't be examined. But for jobs at the core of your sales message—and for recent ones that require the right "spin" in order *not to hurt* you—the design sheets will be extremely helpful. They have slots for:

PAGE ONE: 1. ***Dates and Titles.*** Put down each new title *and* each major increase in responsibility *without* a new title (describe it in about 4 to 7 words and note it and its date along with title changes on your resume). *Don't fail to take credit for any major advancement!* 2. ***Main Message.*** Here you can jot notes on all the main points you want to make about your tenure with this company or in this major job. 3. ***Check-offs*** on the style(s) you're planning for this entry.

PAGE TWO: 4. ***Components of the Entry.*** These range downward from ***Selling Points*** (spotlighted achievements that show you're excellent), through ***Qualifiers*** (proofs you've done the things everyone seeking your position should have done), ***Round-outs*** (to be included if you have extra space), ***Look-ups*** (notes on figures to check and former colleagues to locate as possible references, etc.), ***Potential Negatives*** (problems to think about and solve on this segment) and ***Reason for Joining*** and ***Reason for Leaving*** (*must* be considered and *may* go in if a *"plus"* (former boss wanted you) or an *explanation* (merger, etc).

Entry *DESIGN* Sheet

MULTI-ACHIEVEMENT COMPANY AND/OR SPOTLIGHTED JOB: ____________________

OVERALL DATES AT THE COMPANY OR WITHIN THE JOB: ____________________

IN-PROGRESS DATES	TITLE / NEW TITLE / EXPANDED RESPONSIBILITIES (IN REVERSE CHRONOLOGICAL ORDER)

MAIN MESSAGE OF THIS ENTRY

BEST TOLD IN: ☐ PARAGRAPHS ☐ BULLETS ☐ COMBINATION

Entry *DESIGN* Sheet

COMPONENTS OF THIS ENTRY

SELLING POINTS (SPOTLIGHTED ACHIEVEMENTS THAT SHOW YOU'RE EXCELLENT)

QUALIFIERS (PROOF YOU'VE DONE THE WORK EVERYONE SEEKING THE POSITION SHOULD HAVE DONE)

ROUND-OUTS (COULD BE INCLUDED IF YOU HAVE EXTRA SPACE TO FILL)

LOOK-UPS (REMINDERS OF FIGURES TO CHECK AND POTENTIAL REFERENCES TO LOCATE, ETC.)

POTENTIAL NEGATIVES (PROBLEMS TO THINK ABOUT AND SOLVE ON THIS COMPANY OR POSITION)

REASON FOR JOINING (USE IF/WHEN HELPFUL)

REASON FOR LEAVING (USE IF/WHEN HELPFUL)

Entry *DESIGN* Sheet

MULTI-ACHIEVEMENT COMPANY AND/OR SPOTLIGHTED JOB: ____________________

OVERALL DATES AT THE COMPANY OR WITHIN THE JOB: ____________________

IN-PROGRESS DATES	TITLE / NEW TITLE / EXPANDED RESPONSIBILITIES (IN REVERSE CHRONOLOGICAL ORDER)

MAIN MESSAGE OF THIS ENTRY

BEST TOLD IN: ☐ PARAGRAPHS ☐ BULLETS ☐ COMBINATION

Entry *DESIGN* Sheet

COMPONENTS OF THIS ENTRY

SELLING POINTS (SPOTLIGHTED ACHIEVEMENTS THAT SHOW YOU'RE EXCELLENT)

QUALIFIERS (PROOF YOU'VE DONE THE WORK EVERYONE SEEKING THE POSITION SHOULD HAVE DONE)

ROUND-OUTS (COULD BE INCLUDED IF YOU HAVE EXTRA SPACE TO FILL)

LOOK-UPS (REMINDERS OF FIGURES TO CHECK AND POTENTIAL REFERENCES TO LOCATE, ETC.)

POTENTIAL NEGATIVES (PROBLEMS TO THINK ABOUT AND SOLVE ON THIS COMPANY OR POSITION)

REASON FOR JOINING (USE IF/WHEN HELPFUL)

REASON FOR LEAVING (USE IF/WHEN HELPFUL)

Entry *DESIGN* Sheet

MULTI-ACHIEVEMENT COMPANY AND/OR SPOTLIGHTED JOB: ______________________

OVERALL DATES AT THE COMPANY OR WITHIN THE JOB: ______________________

IN-PROGRESS DATES	TITLE / NEW TITLE / EXPANDED RESPONSIBILITIES (IN REVERSE CHRONOLOGICAL ORDER)

MAIN MESSAGE OF THIS ENTRY

BEST TOLD IN: ☐ PARAGRAPHS ☐ BULLETS ☐ COMBINATION

Entry *Design* Sheet

Components of this Entry

Selling Points (spotlighted achievements that show you're excellent)

Qualifiers (proof you've done the work everyone seeking the position should have done)

Round-Outs (could be included if you have extra space to fill)

Look-Ups (reminders of figures to check and potential references to locate, etc.)

Potential Negatives (problems to think about and solve on this company or position)

Reason for Joining (use if/when helpful)

Reason for Leaving (use if/when helpful)

Entry ***Design*** Sheet

Multi-Achievement Company and/or Spotlighted Job: ____________________

Overall Dates at the Company or within the Job: ____________________

In-Progress Dates	Title / New Title / Expanded responsibilities (in reverse chronological order)

Main Message of this entry

Best told in: ☐ Paragraphs ☐ Bullets ☐ Combination

Entry ***Design*** Sheet

Components of this entry

Selling Points (spotlighted achievements that show you're excellent)

Qualifiers (proof you've done the work everyone seeking the position should have done)

Round-Outs (could be included if you have extra space to fill)

Look-Ups (reminders of figures to check and potential references to locate, etc.)

Potential Negatives (problems to think about and solve on this company or position)

Reason for Joining (use if/when helpful)

Reason for Leaving (use if/when helpful)

Entry *DESIGN* Sheet

MULTI-ACHIEVEMENT COMPANY AND/OR SPOTLIGHTED JOB: ______________________________

OVERALL DATES AT THE COMPANY OR WITHIN THE JOB: ______________________________

IN-PROGRESS DATES	TITLE / NEW TITLE / EXPANDED RESPONSIBILITIES (IN REVERSE CHRONOLOGICAL ORDER)

MAIN MESSAGE OF THIS ENTRY

BEST TOLD IN: ☐ PARAGRAPHS ☐ BULLETS ☐ COMBINATION

Entry *DESIGN* Sheet

COMPONENTS OF THIS ENTRY

SELLING POINTS (SPOTLIGHTED ACHIEVEMENTS THAT SHOW YOU'RE EXCELLENT)

QUALIFIERS (PROOF YOU'VE DONE THE WORK EVERYONE SEEKING THE POSITION SHOULD HAVE DONE)

ROUND-OUTS (COULD BE INCLUDED IF YOU HAVE EXTRA SPACE TO FILL)

LOOK-UPS (REMINDERS OF FIGURES TO CHECK AND POTENTIAL REFERENCES TO LOCATE, ETC.)

POTENTIAL NEGATIVES (PROBLEMS TO THINK ABOUT AND SOLVE ON THIS COMPANY OR POSITION)

REASON FOR JOINING (USE IF/WHEN HELPFUL)

REASON FOR LEAVING (USE IF/WHEN HELPFUL)

Entry *DESIGN* Sheet

MULTI-ACHIEVEMENT COMPANY AND/OR SPOTLIGHTED JOB: ____________________

OVERALL DATES AT THE COMPANY OR WITHIN THE JOB: ____________________

IN-PROGRESS DATES	TITLE / NEW TITLE / EXPANDED RESPONSIBILITIES (IN REVERSE CHRONOLOGICAL ORDER)

MAIN MESSAGE OF THIS ENTRY

BEST TOLD IN: ☐ PARAGRAPHS ☐ BULLETS ☐ COMBINATION

Entry *DESIGN* Sheet

COMPONENTS OF THIS ENTRY

SELLING POINTS (SPOTLIGHTED ACHIEVEMENTS THAT SHOW YOU'RE EXCELLENT)

QUALIFIERS (PROOF YOU'VE DONE THE WORK EVERYONE SEEKING THE POSITION SHOULD HAVE DONE)

ROUND-OUTS (COULD BE INCLUDED IF YOU HAVE EXTRA SPACE TO FILL)

LOOK-UPS (REMINDERS OF FIGURES TO CHECK AND POTENTIAL REFERENCES TO LOCATE, ETC.)

POTENTIAL NEGATIVES (PROBLEMS TO THINK ABOUT AND SOLVE ON THIS COMPANY OR POSITION)

REASON FOR JOINING (USE IF/WHEN HELPFUL)

REASON FOR LEAVING (USE IF/WHEN HELPFUL)

Entry *DESIGN* Sheet

MULTI-ACHIEVEMENT COMPANY AND/OR SPOTLIGHTED JOB: ____________________

OVERALL DATES AT THE COMPANY OR WITHIN THE JOB: ____________________

IN-PROGRESS DATES	TITLE / NEW TITLE / EXPANDED RESPONSIBILITIES (IN REVERSE CHRONOLOGICAL ORDER)

MAIN MESSAGE OF THIS ENTRY

BEST TOLD IN: ☐ PARAGRAPHS ☐ BULLETS ☐ COMBINATION

Entry *DESIGN* Sheet

COMPONENTS OF THIS ENTRY

SELLING POINTS (SPOTLIGHTED ACHIEVEMENTS THAT SHOW YOU'RE EXCELLENT)

QUALIFIERS (PROOF YOU'VE DONE THE WORK EVERYONE SEEKING THE POSITION SHOULD HAVE DONE)

ROUND-OUTS (COULD BE INCLUDED IF YOU HAVE EXTRA SPACE TO FILL)

LOOK-UPS (REMINDERS OF FIGURES TO CHECK AND POTENTIAL REFERENCES TO LOCATE, ETC.)

POTENTIAL NEGATIVES (PROBLEMS TO THINK ABOUT AND SOLVE ON THIS COMPANY OR POSITION)

REASON FOR JOINING (USE IF/WHEN HELPFUL)

REASON FOR LEAVING (USE IF/WHEN HELPFUL)

Entry *DESIGN* Sheet

MULTI-ACHIEVEMENT COMPANY AND/OR SPOTLIGHTED JOB: ______________________________

OVERALL DATES AT THE COMPANY OR WITHIN THE JOB: ______________________________

IN-PROGRESS DATES	TITLE / NEW TITLE / EXPANDED RESPONSIBILITIES (IN REVERSE CHRONOLOGICAL ORDER)

MAIN MESSAGE OF THIS ENTRY

BEST TOLD IN: ☐ PARAGRAPHS ☐ BULLETS ☐ COMBINATION

Entry *DESIGN* Sheet

COMPONENTS OF THIS ENTRY

SELLING POINTS (SPOTLIGHTED ACHIEVEMENTS THAT SHOW YOU'RE EXCELLENT)

QUALIFIERS (PROOF YOU'VE DONE THE WORK EVERYONE SEEKING THE POSITION SHOULD HAVE DONE)

ROUND-OUTS (COULD BE INCLUDED IF YOU HAVE EXTRA SPACE TO FILL)

LOOK-UPS (REMINDERS OF FIGURES TO CHECK AND POTENTIAL REFERENCES TO LOCATE, ETC.)

POTENTIAL NEGATIVES (PROBLEMS TO THINK ABOUT AND SOLVE ON THIS COMPANY OR POSITION)

REASON FOR JOINING (USE IF/WHEN HELPFUL)

REASON FOR LEAVING (USE IF/WHEN HELPFUL)

Entry *DESIGN* Sheet

MULTI-ACHIEVEMENT COMPANY AND/OR SPOTLIGHTED JOB: ______________________

OVERALL DATES AT THE COMPANY OR WITHIN THE JOB: ______________________

IN-PROGRESS DATES	TITLE / NEW TITLE / EXPANDED RESPONSIBILITIES (IN REVERSE CHRONOLOGICAL ORDER)

MAIN MESSAGE OF THIS ENTRY

BEST TOLD IN: ☐ PARAGRAPHS ☐ BULLETS ☐ COMBINATION

Entry *DESIGN* Sheet

COMPONENTS OF THIS ENTRY

SELLING POINTS (SPOTLIGHTED ACHIEVEMENTS THAT SHOW YOU'RE EXCELLENT)

QUALIFIERS (PROOF YOU'VE DONE THE WORK EVERYONE SEEKING THE POSITION SHOULD HAVE DONE)

ROUND-OUTS (COULD BE INCLUDED IF YOU HAVE EXTRA SPACE TO FILL)

LOOK-UPS (REMINDERS OF FIGURES TO CHECK AND POTENTIAL REFERENCES TO LOCATE, ETC.)

POTENTIAL NEGATIVES (PROBLEMS TO THINK ABOUT AND SOLVE ON THIS COMPANY OR POSITION)

REASON FOR JOINING (USE IF/WHEN HELPFUL)

REASON FOR LEAVING (USE IF/WHEN HELPFUL)

Entry *DESIGN* Sheet

MULTI-ACHIEVEMENT COMPANY AND/OR SPOTLIGHTED JOB: ______________________________

OVERALL DATES AT THE COMPANY OR WITHIN THE JOB: ______________________________

IN-PROGRESS DATES	TITLE / NEW TITLE / EXPANDED RESPONSIBILITIES (IN REVERSE CHRONOLOGICAL ORDER)

MAIN MESSAGE OF THIS ENTRY

BEST TOLD IN: ☐ PARAGRAPHS ☐ BULLETS ☐ COMBINATION

Entry *DESIGN* Sheet

COMPONENTS OF THIS ENTRY

SELLING POINTS (SPOTLIGHTED ACHIEVEMENTS THAT SHOW YOU'RE EXCELLENT)

QUALIFIERS (PROOF YOU'VE DONE THE WORK EVERYONE SEEKING THE POSITION SHOULD HAVE DONE)

ROUND-OUTS (COULD BE INCLUDED IF YOU HAVE EXTRA SPACE TO FILL)

LOOK-UPS (REMINDERS OF FIGURES TO CHECK AND POTENTIAL REFERENCES TO LOCATE, ETC.)

POTENTIAL NEGATIVES (PROBLEMS TO THINK ABOUT AND SOLVE ON THIS COMPANY OR POSITION)

REASON FOR JOINING (USE IF/WHEN HELPFUL)

REASON FOR LEAVING (USE IF/WHEN HELPFUL)

Entry ***Design*** Sheet

Multi-Achievement Company and/or Spotlighted Job: ______________________

Overall Dates at the Company or within the Job: ______________________

In-Progress Dates	Title / New Title / Expanded responsibilities (in reverse chronological order)

Main Message of this entry

Best told in: ☐ Paragraphs ☐ Bullets ☐ Combination

Entry *DESIGN* Sheet

COMPONENTS OF THIS ENTRY

SELLING POINTS (SPOTLIGHTED ACHIEVEMENTS THAT SHOW YOU'RE EXCELLENT)

QUALIFIERS (PROOF YOU'VE DONE THE WORK EVERYONE SEEKING THE POSITION SHOULD HAVE DONE)

ROUND-OUTS (COULD BE INCLUDED IF YOU HAVE EXTRA SPACE TO FILL)

LOOK-UPS (REMINDERS OF FIGURES TO CHECK AND POTENTIAL REFERENCES TO LOCATE, ETC.)

POTENTIAL NEGATIVES (PROBLEMS TO THINK ABOUT AND SOLVE ON THIS COMPANY OR POSITION)

REASON FOR JOINING (USE IF/WHEN HELPFUL)

REASON FOR LEAVING (USE IF/WHEN HELPFUL)

A Few Last Thoughts on Resumes

As you've readily figured out by now, this entire WORKBOOK so far has been largely aimed at making sure you have the best possible selling message in mind...and on paper.

Chapter 1 on *Campaign Strategy* prepared you in indispensable ways for this chapter on actually writing your resume. If you happened to plunge in here without first reading and doing everything in Chapter 1, please go back and put yourself through its hoops. Also, please be sure to read all of *RITES OF PASSAGE AT $100,000 TO $1 MILLION+* (get the latest totally revised and expanded edition, not the pre-Internet ones still in most public and outplacement libraries). *RITES* covers what this WORKBOOK does *not* cover.

What Really Matters

Whether you've chosen to make a two- three- or four-page resume, and whether you've used paragraphs, bullets, or a combination is NOT important.

Why?

Because an uninviting-to-read, "This-person-certainly-doesn't-seem-special" resume can be created in any length and any style. So can a superbly inviting, "This-person-seems-outstanding!" resume. And the difference has vastly more to do with knowledge (of your career, NOT resume-writing), concern-for-outcome, and sheer time-and-thought-expended, than it has to do with the presumed skill and experience of the person actually writing and/or advising (and that includes me, *RITES*, and this WORKBOOK!). Please read pages 69-70, 83-85, and 90-104 again. If you personally have spent less than 35 to 70 hours on your resume, it's very unlikely that you've developed your strongest possible selling message.

Delaying a Fast Start?

Does taking the time to do a total-immersion study of your career and distill it into a compelling resume waste time and get your search off to a slow start?

No way!

Chances are, you'll spend *several months* searching for your next executive-level job. Almost everyone always does. And every future day, you'll be handing out, mailing, and leaving behind resumes. To everyone you deal with—and especially to everyone evaluating and discussing you when you're not present—you'll be who the resume says you are. And in selection situations—recruiter and employer—you'll be in stiff competition with other candidates who'll be who their resumes say they are. Can you afford to have anything less than the best possible "sales representative" making your pitch?

Two Last Warnings

Beware of being too fond of your previous brilliant writing. If, years ago you created a superb resume, you're severely tempted merely to tack on what's happened since.

Dumb! And, admit it, *lazy.* When you do that, the pastiche usually becomes too long. It's probably boring...and it may even suggest that the time to hire you was then, not now. Go back to your "Thumb-nail" allocation of space. Chances are it was right. Do make the extra effort to achieve it.

Also, no matter how you've designed your resume, some people will say they don't like it! Realize that if you cater to one of "them" you'll probably soon meet another who'd have preferred something else. Use your common sense...and stick with it. There are too much folklore and too many commercial formulas around to please everyone. And above all, beware of anything you're told by anyone who is absolutely sure of the one true way. When Moses came back, there was nothing on those stones about resumes (except "Don't lie," which is *always* good advice).

Time *Very* Well Spent

How often have I said it? Yet it bears repeating. Every minute you spend at the outset of your search working on your resume is a minute you spend rehearsing and perfecting your networking spiel and your answers to difficult interview questions.

Make that investment. It will pay huge dividends!

To Help With Your

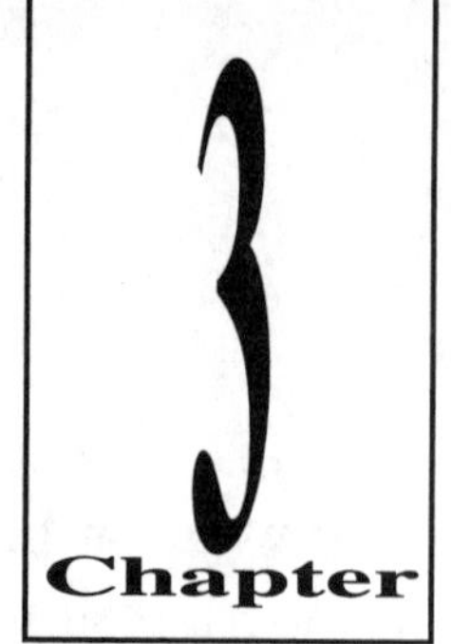

Cover Letter

A persuasive cover letter for your resumé is absolutely essential to an effective search.

It's the perfect summary of your selling message. You'll use it often...even if you never conduct a direct mail campaign!

Your Ideal Story Perfectly Told

Obviously, if you're sending your resume to a stranger, you need a cover letter.

But that same letter will be just as useful when you're getting in touch with an old school chum or a former colleague at work.

Why?

Because it delivers your selling message so clearly and succinctly that you just can't improve on it.

In the advertising business, the essence of an ad campaign is called the "copy platform." It conveys in the purest possible way the product's advantages and what the agency and client have agreed should be emphasized. Clever gimmicks may be added to attract attention or promote memorability. But every such "execution" must convey the "platform's" full message and cannot be at all inconsistent with it.

Your cover letter, when well done, serves the same purpose. It's so clear and persuasive that even a complete stranger instantly understands you and, hopefully, is very favorably impressed.

Therefore, when a dear personal friend or your favorite former boss asks you to send several resumes so he or she can help you by passing them along, you use exactly the same words to describe your circumstances and recent stellar achievements that you'd use to indoctrinate a stranger. You merely personalize a standard cover letter, top-and-bottom, with something more intimate. Or tuck in a warm handwritten note.

They "go together like a horse and carriage."

As Mr. S belted out about "Love and Marriage," the right resume coupled with the right cover letter are one of the truly great combinations. To use other clichés: "The whole is greater than the sum of the parts." There's "*synergy!*"

Why?

Because the cover letter crystallizes and states ever so briefly the overarching message of your candidacy. Done well, it's the appetizer that intrigues and challenges the reader to bite into the resume. It makes strong statements that—standing alone—might be dismissed as unlikely (which is why I hate *and dump* those "teaser letters" making such statements and *not* enclosing a resume). But with the resume right at hand, there's a temptation to dip in and see what, if any, proof you're offering.

Then, if you've enclosed a powerful "sales representative" resume, you've got a very good chance of providing enough factual reassurance to overcome the reader's innate skepticism. And if he or she needs anyone even remotely like you, you may get a phone call.

But there's so much more to be thought and said about cover letters! Let's dip into *Rites of Passage* at this point:

Now let's design a cover letter that will do the best possible job of making whoever receives it want to look at your resume.

To get any attention at all for your resume, your covering letter absolutely must convey two essential messages regarding you as a human being, and you as the potential solution to an immediate business problem:

1. This is a ***fine person***, obviously desirable as an employee.
2. He or she might be ***for me***, possibly the executive I need right now.

If your papers in the reader's hand don't shout "fine person," then there's no point in reading them to see if your background might be what's needed right now.

So first of all we'll make sure your covering letter conveys the right personal impression. Then we'll perfect the story it tells.

Right away and above all, your covering note must...at a glance...label you as a first-class individual, regardless of background.

You must instantly be perceived as an intelligent, well-educated, socially poised, tasteful person... dynamic not passive, self-confident and cordial but not obnoxiously pushy, oriented toward delivering what others are interested in, an effective communicator, basically competent and commonsensical, and maybe even *interesting!*

Now I'm not saying that you, I, or anyone else can instantly prove for sure that we have all those fine characteristics in 300 words or less. But we'd better not give off even the slightest subliminal hint that we *don't* have them. Your reader won't even consider the contribution you could make to the organization, if you don't seem like the right sort of person to bring into it.

There's a double standard. Employers will tolerate employees with less than ideal human characteristics if they're outstanding performers on the job. But they won't go out of their way to bring in anyone who doesn't "feel" right to begin with. And face it...perusing your resume is going out of the way. The easiest reaction is just to throw it in the wastebasket. *Your covering note must not give off any negative "vibes."* And in that regard I submit the following:

Don't seem insensitive, bumbling, and not customer-oriented.

You've already avoided the biggest pitfall in this direction by phoning ahead to make sure you've got your reader's name-spelling, function, and title right. Your letter has come to the right person, and has approached him or her with impeccable courtesy.

AGAIN, PLEASE DO NOT BE MISLED. THE SAME NOTICE YOU SAW ON PAGE 44 APPLIES HERE. THE WORKBOOK HELPS YOU CREATE A RESUME AND COVER LETTER STRONG ENOUGH FOR DIRECT MAIL...AND HENCE FOR ANY OTHER USE.

IT DOES NOT, HOWEVER, COVER HOW TO CONDUCT A DIRECT MAIL CAMPAIGN. NOR DOES IT WARN YOU AGAINST WASTING MONEY AND EFFORT ON DIRECT MAIL WHEN IT IS VERY LIKELY TO PROVE FUTILE IN YOUR CASE. IT ALSO DOES NOT COVER ANY OF THE ASPECTS OF STYLING AND PROCEDURE THAT ARE OPTIONAL OR MATTERS OF TASTE, PHILOSOPHY AND/OR INCREMENTAL COST AS COVERED IN *RITES OF PASSAGE.*

(ABOUT 16 OUT OF 60 PAGES IN *RITES* ON DIRECT MAIL TECHNIQUES AND STYLING ARE INCORPORATED HERE.)

Avoid looking tasteless and cheap.

Recent college graduates can get by with plain typing paper for their covering letter. You can't. Good quality stationery with your name, home address, and phone number, steel-engraved at the top, is ideal. Monarch size (7 1/4" x 10 1/2") looks especially nice clipped to a standard-size (8 1/2" x 11") resume, and if you boil your message down to attention-grabbing brevity, it'll fit on a Monarch page. Paper should be crisp, with rag/cotton fiber, in classic white or a *very* pale tint of grey or ivory. Ink should be black (or possibly grey, navy, or ***deep*** maroon or green).

Unfortunately about eight weeks' lead time is required for true steel engraving. If you're rushed, or short on cash, substitute ordinary printing. *Or use plain but rich paper and a laser printer, applying a letterhead in contrasting type as you print your letters.* Keep the design understated...three or four lines, each no more than 2 1/4 inches long...with your phone number e-mail address smaller but legible on the bottom line.

Unless your covering letter describes unusual circumstances that make it appropriate, never use your current employer's stationery.

Don't appear pretentious.

Veer toward modesty and matter-of-factness in name, address...and stationery. Imagine a letterhead from "Cottsworth O.M. Kensington-Smithers IV," saying he lives at "Nine Chimneys," followed by street number, etc. What fun it would be to throw *his* resume into the waste basket! Moreover, since you're sending a business letter, avoid all gimmicks on the stationery...family crest, house-picture, yachting flags, crossed polo mallets, colored or shaggy borders, etc.

So much for appearances.
Now let's get to the content of your covering letter.

This is your "free sample."
It demonstrates that you're a "fine person"
in terms of thinking and communication skills.

Only after evaluating "how you say it"
will your reader weigh "what you say."

To succeed, your covering letter must be pleasantly businesslike in tone, and conjure up the image of a competent, self-confident executive who's letting a colleague know that he or she is available to help, if there's a need. Somehow, a letter from such a person is never a jarring intrusion, whereas a letter from the typical "job applicant" always is.

The difference is dramatic. So few people are able to write a really good covering letter that, when one arrives, it stands out like a beacon. Its author is immediately given "plus points" for outstanding executive communication skills, and the resume is almost always scanned, in the hope that it offers something the recipient...corporate officer or recruiter...can take advantage of.

Fortunately, creating such an impressive covering letter isn't difficult, if you incorporate the four central attributes that outstanding ones have and poor ones don't. Be sure your covering letter:

1. **is not too long.** Brevity is essential! Get right to the point, and leave out all the useless and obnoxious things that "job applicants" put in their letters.

2. **has a central theme.** Your message must be arrestingly clear...not diffuse and blurred.

3. **offers benefit to the reader,** rather than merely harping on what *you* want.

4. **deals with compensation.**

Later on I'll cover point 1 by giving you a list of stuff to get rid of, so your letter won't be cluttered with the unproductive statements "job applicants" put in theirs. And after that, I'll show you in detail how to handle compensation to your advantage. But first let me cover points 2 and 3 by showing you a covering letter that has a clear central theme (point 2) of benefit to the reader (point 3).

This letter is from Sam Sage, whose resume we've already reviewed.

Sam's an exceptionally competent executive. And from the minute we first glance at his covering letter, we begin to see how very special he is. No nonsense. No wasted words. And no claims that aren't fully backed up by his accompanying resume.

Note:

I happen to like monarch-sized cover letters which, when placed over business-sized resumes, show a margin. Since the pages of this book are business-sized, I've placed the examples at the upper and outside edges, as if they were in use.

What do you think?

Samuel P. Sage
219 Waring Drive
Denton, New Jersey 07299
Home: (201) 719-0932 Office: (212) 121-3000
spsage@aota.com

(Date)

Mr. Sherman J. Summit
Chairman and Chief Executive
Integrated Standard Corporation
4225 Scenic Parkway
Lovelytown, New York 10591

Dear Mr. Summit:

Could I help you as a divisional president...or corporate chief marketing officer?

The $1.1 billion company I've helped build over the past five years as Chief Marketing Officer has more than doubled sales, increased profits nine-fold, and raised ROI from 3.6% in '96 to over 28% in '01.

We've done so well, in fact, that we've just been bought out at 30 times our estimated '02 earnings by a company that's absorbing us into their own operations.

Although I'm far more interested in a fine company and an intriguing challenge than merely in money, you should know that in recent years my total compensation has been in the range of $350,000 to $500,000.

May we talk?

Sincerely,

Sam Sage

Samuel P. Sage

SPS:mj

Sam rang all the bells!

Sam's central theme is sure to dilate the pupils and speed the pulse of any red-blooded CEO...impressive advances, in sales, profit, and ROI.

For many letter-writers those claims would be too bold. They'd be mom-pie-'n-flag *clichés* that the accompanying resume couldn't possibly live up to. But Sam's got the stuff. So he flaunts it.

Notice too, that Sam didn't waste words on anything that's obvious. His resume *is* enclosed...no need to say so. And *of course* Sam would like Mr. Summit to get in touch with him...or Sam may call Mr. S. No need to talk about that either.

Moreover, Sam didn't invoke self-praising adjectives and adverbs. Rather, by making numerical claims, he directed attention to his resume, which is packed with specific facts and figures that *demonstrate* what he can do. Sam also treated compensation in an advantageous way that we'll discuss later.

Above all, the sparseness and directness of Sam's letter tell us a lot about him. He's an exceptionally dynamic, clear-thinking person. On the rare occasions when a letter from someone like Sam comes in, the reader will always glance at the attached resume. Indeed Mr. Summit became quite interested, as you'll see in Appendix I.*

Changing Your Letter for Recruiters

These examples are addressed to employers. For recruiters, merely change your opening question from "Do *you* need...?" to "Does *one of your clients* need...?" or "Are you looking for...?" Replacing just a few words in the first one or two sentences will neatly reposition any letter, without destroying the brevity and directness that are just as attractive to recruiters as they are to employers.

---

*Of *Rites of Passage*. Appendix I is a fictionalized behind-the-scenes case history of an executive-level position being filled through a search conducted by a large retainer search firm, as seen through the eyes of the recruiter.

Matt Ginyus
146 College Point Drive
Skilton, Massachusetts 01128
(413) 112-2465 drmg@aol.com

(Date)

Ms. Gloria P. Global, President
International Interchemicals, Inc.
1202 Industrial Beltline
Wilmington, Delaware 19808

Dear Ms. Global:

Could any of your laboratories...corporate or divisional...be more innovative?

If so, perhaps I can help.

Within the spending limits of a young fast-growing $86 million company, and with only a 26-person laboratory, my staff and I during the past five years have produced 14 commercially exploitable new compounds...6 of which are already on the market, providing 72% of current revenue. During that time I've personally received 8 patents, and my staff has received 46.

Having proven what I can produce for a small company, I'd like to do a lot more for a much larger organization.

An exciting challenge will be the main reason, if and when I move. But you should know that in recent years my total compensation has been in the range of $195,000 to $280,000.

Please keep my inquiry confidential, Mr. Global. The published rumors that we may be acquired have prompted me to think about the world outside DrexelChem. Nevertheless, I don't want to disturb either my staff or the rest of the company just by considering alternatives.

Thank you.

Sincerely,

Matt Ginyus

Matt Ginyus

Karen S. Kash
12 Countinghouse Road
Pittsburgh, Pennsylvania 15213
(412) 999-1814 kkash@tollnext.net

(Date)

Mr. Peter R. Pinnacle
Chairman
Acme Consolidated Corporation
6902 Postal Turnpike
Pittsburgh, Pennsylvania 15224

Dear Mr. Pinnacle:

Could Acme Consolidated...or one of your largest divisions... benefit from a strong chief financial officer?

Having been continually challenged and rapidly promoted at U.S. Heavy Industries...last year I became our youngest CFO since USHI was founded in 1869...I've never before thought about joining any other employer.

But now we're shutting down our steel mills and home office here in Pittsburgh, and headquartering at our insurance company in Hartford. Relocation would be a hardship for my family. So I'm contacting a few outstanding Pittsburgh area companies before committing to a move.

If you have a need, I could do an excellent job for you.

Sincerely,

Karen Kash

Karen Kash

P.S. Money is <u>not</u> my main consideration, but in recent years my total compensation has been in the range of $280,000 to $450,000.

Different Pokes from Different Folks!

Different as they were, all three of the letters you just read would have stimulated the interest of any reader who needed what they offered.

Why?

Because each:

1. was **not too long,** and
2. had a **central theme**
3. of **benefit to the reader.**

Sam Sage presented his outstanding track record as a marketing virtuoso-cum-general-manager. Matt Ginyus amply demonstrated his ability to get results in the laboratory. And Karen Kash showed that she was an outstanding employee, who'd never have been available, if not for exceptional circumstances. Her letter said, "Help yourself to someone else's superstar."

Of course, the very best thing about each of these letters is that only one person in all the world could have written it. Each person came to life through mere words on paper, because those words were clear and specific, and *applied only to him or her.* There were none of the vague generalities that give most such letters a boring fill-in-any-job-applicant similarity.

So before we move on to point 4, **dealing with compensation,** let's list some things you'll make sure to *leave out*, which litter the letters of "job applicants."

OMIT...OMIT...OMIT!

Everything obvious, and all clichés. Letters from "job applicants" always state the obvious, and lean heavily on clichés: "Enclosed please find..." "I would like to take this opportunity to..." "This letter will serve to..." "Here is a copy of my resume for your review and consideration." "If my background and accomplishments are of interest, I would appreciate hearing from you." "Thank you in advance for your interest."

Self-evaluations. Don't bother describing your personality or your performance. You're biased, so we can't take your word for it. And if you enclose or quote something from a psychologist, we'll *know* you're on the defensive. Don't say, "I'm a results-oriented executive with a proven track record," or that you're "intelligent," "analytical," "profit-minded," "honest," "hardworking," "loyal," "reliable," or any of that stuff. "Job applicants" use those words.

Willingness to relocate. "Ho hum," if you're willing to move for a great opportunity. So is everyone else. Don't bring up relocation unless the fact that you won't relocate is the reason a lucky local employer has received your letter. If your employer...or your specific job...is leaving town and you don't want to, you've got a good believable reason for writing your letter. Exploit it. Otherwise say nothing about relocation. And don't give personal hardship details. Just say, "My family and I prefer to stay in Indianapolis." The fact that your spouse's real estate practice brings in twice what you do, or that your mother has a health problem doesn't make you any more attractive as a potential employee.

"Further information and references." Every "job applicant" is "pleased to supply further information and a list of references." But you're smart enough not to say so, and thus you further differentiate your letter from theirs. Besides, your "sales representative" resume...unlike theirs...has "further information" built right in. The next thing your reader will need or want is to see you.

The Mafia approach. Don't end your letter with a warning that you intend to make a follow-up phone call. "Job applicants," salespeople, and Cosa Nostra do that. If your reader is a prospective "buyer," he or she will probably take the next step. The "foot-in-the-door" approach needlessly makes you look pushy, because without the warning you are just as free to call as with it. Indeed, including it may prompt the reader to give orders to block your call.

And now "point 4"...current compensation.
Rightly or wrongly, it's the #1 screening criterion.

Every employer wants to know that "money is right" before "wasting time" on any candidate.

The ideal covering letter gives that assurance ...and rushes the reader right into your resume.

One of the most important factors in establishing the "this-person-might-be-***for-me***" reaction on the part of your reader...and indeed any employer...is your level of compensation.

Yet most executives omit any mention of money...either current or desired. They worry that some employers may be frightened off because the figure is too high, and others may lose interest because it's too low. And any employer who winds up making an offer, they fear, may propose less than he otherwise would, if he knows what they're accustomed to.

What these wary executives don't realize is that by *not* mentioning salary, they've created a situation that's even *more* limiting. Compensation is the *single most important factor* in categorizing people as appropriate or inappropriate for a particular job. For employers...and executive recruiters as well...it provides a quick and easy way to figure out whether a candidate is "the right size." Titles can be misleading, and the importance of a given position can vary considerably from one organization to the next. Salary remains the most reliable index, since it's determined by the marketplace.

So the challenge is to mention compensation in a way that *encourages* consideration. You want every potential employer to look at your money and think:

"Well, that's in the ballpark. He might be ***for me***."

Obviously, if your money is above what the position pays, she'll figure she can't attract or hold you. And if you're earning far less, that's a pretty good indication that you're not yet ready for the responsibility the position entails.

So how do you handle compensation?

Here's a magic sentence that will do the best possible job of getting you considered:

> "Although other factors such as (fill in your own non-financial 'turn-ons') are of primary importance to me, you should know that in recent years, my total compensation has been in the range of ________ to ________."

To appreciate what that disclosure accomplishes, you must first:

Meet the weasels.

In consumer-products marketing, there's a term for wordings that state the truth precisely enough to wiggle through the narrow openings defined by company attorneys and government regulators. They're called "*weasels*," after the squirmy little animals that are almost impossible to catch.

The three key phrases..."weasels"...in your compensation statement are: "*in recent years*," "*total compensation*," and "*in the range of*." Used together, they open the way for you to state, *perfectly truthfully*, a broad range that will make you seem "right ***for me***" in the mind of every reader who controls a position you could possibly be interested in and qualified for.

The "*low-end*" figure will be the least take-home pay you'd consider, assuming the job offers major advantages beyond immediate compensation. After all, the preface to your "three-weasel" sentence said, in effect, "money isn't everything to me." For this bottom figure, use a round number that approximates your tax-return "income-from-employment" for a recent lean year.

For the "*high-end*" figure, start with your top base salary within the past few years. Then add everything else you're getting:

> performance bonuses (use the figures that...combined with base...represent your best year);
>
> the amount of your employer's contribution to FICA;
>
> the value of medical, dental, and life insurance provided by your employer;
>
> money paid by the firm into pension and profit-sharing accounts in your name (whether or not fully vested);
>
> any other tax-deferred compensation, such as annualized incremental value of your stock options, and your employer's matching contribution to thrift and stock-purchase plans;
>
> and the pre-tax value of miscellaneous perks, such as a company car (less your pay-back for personal use), city and country club memberships, the right to use the company condo in Nassau for two weeks vacation per year, and the college scholarship your child receives under a competitive company-wide program.

You can even estimate this year's raise, and include that in the base of your "high-end" figure.

Thus, using the three "weasels," you can truthfully state a wide range. You'll probably end up with numbers that are $40,000 to $80,000 or $150,000 apart...maybe even more. *It's perfectly reasonable for the second figure to be 50% larger than the first:* $160,000 to $240,000 for example, or $420,000 to $580,000.

Let's imagine that you've specified a range of $180,000 to $260,000.

First we'll picture your letter reaching the CEO of a young growth company with great prospects, but with venture capitalists on its Board who don't want Management draining its life blood with high salaries. This CEO looks at your low number, $180,000, and figures she can realistically reach *up* to you. She can't offer more than $150,000 in cash compensation. But you'll have the opportunity to purchase at 50 cents per share 55,000 shares of treasury stock the company expects to take public at about $20 per share within 18 to 24 months; and as an officer, you'll have a company car. She's pretty sure she can grab your attention. So she calls to suggest a get-acquainted lunch.

Now picture the CEO of a large multi-national corporation who must fill a job he thinks is worth about $300,000. He sees your top figure of $260,000...assumes it represents your most recent year...and reaches *down* to you. After all, you're probably expecting an increase of at least 10% or 20% for making a move. Obviously, your next job should be in the neighborhood of $300,000...just what he expects to pay. So he asks his assistant to give you a call.

As you see, your "three-weasel" range of $180,000 to $260,000 has actually triggered a "***for me***" response in the minds of two very differently situated employers. You're being considered for jobs paying anywhere from $150,000 to $300,000 a year. Cash compensation on one job is 100% more than on the other.

Moreover, you haven't given up any negotiating flexibility. You've got a shot at a job that pays even more than the top figure you mentioned. And of course you can always settle for less, depending on the job's advantages that extend beyond immediate in-pocket cash.

Mentioning money...and having it "right" for your reader...encourages her or him to consider your resume. And using a "three-weaseled" range lets you be "right" for every reader whose job could possibly be right for you.

Truth is far more interesting than fiction.

Obviously, the Sam Sage resume and the three cover letters are fictional. I made them up for *Rites of Passage.* They illustrate what I and many other executive-level recruiters have always *wished* executives would do...but not necessarily what very many—if any—were actually doing at that time.

Since then, of course, it's a different story. Plenty of real people are doing the real thing—and superbly—each in her or his own unique way, according to his or her own tastes, insights and accomplishments. You and I are both indebted to real people for letting us share their careers in the resume chapter. Here, again with permission, are a couple examples of real cover letters. Names, products, and some dates are changed, but performances and personal facts are true.

Andrew P. Thomlin
18 Darwin Road
Delham, New York 10803
Phone: 914 201-3629 Fax: 914 201-3911
apthomlin@metopia.net

(Date)

Ms. Madeleine R. Deane
Managing Partner
Delphi & Deane Inc.
645 Fifth Avenue
New York, New York 10022

Dear Ms. Deane:

Does one of your clients need a CEO, COO, or head of a major division?

Since 1994 I've rejuvenated Brandall's core business (specialty fibers), which was seriously threatened by low-cost foreign competition. Decline was stemmed by '98, and since then sales have increased 26%; profits are up 95%; and labor productivity has improved 40% in this $360 million unit.

Simultaneously as Group President, I've led growth from $458 million in '98 to $720 million in '02. Operating income is up from $64 million to $136 million.

Part of this growth has been my personal project to create a new specialty plastics business. We began with $14 million in '97; grew to $110 million in 2000 (about half through acquisitions); and since then, through internal growth, to '02 sales of $260 million.

Working cooperatively with others whose units haven't reported to me, I've also expanded our small $6 million stake in the automotive market to $150 million.

Now, I've just lost out as one of two contenders to lead my NYSE-listed company. I could stay, but prefer an open-ended challenge.

Opportunity is my goal. But you should know that in recent years my compensation has been in the range of $550,000 to $780,000.

May we talk?

Sincerely,

Andrew Thomlin

Andrew P. Thomlin

Sylvia P. Dorrington
476 Stone Wall Road
Pleasant Hills, Illinois 60057
Phone: (708) 012-2347 Fax: (708) 012-3691
E-mail: sylviapd@inzanet.net

(Date)

Mr. Crandell P. Aspecue
Chairman
Aspecue, Conollay, & Steiner
1472 North LaSalle Street, Suite 1766
Chicago, IL 60604

Dear Mr. Aspecue:

Does one of your clients need a strong Chief Human Resources Officer?

I've built and led state-of-the-art Human Resources functions for first the International and now the U.S. operations of Preferred Consumer Brands, Inc. —with over $6 billion annual sales, one of the world's major consumer products companies.

Success in heading our International HR [18,000 people in 26 countries with $3.2 billion annual sales] ('93-'98) led to my heading HR for all of our U.S. activities [now 7,225 people, $3.0 billion annual sales] since 1991. A steady series of promotions during 16 years with PCBrands brought me to these senior management positions.

Over the years I've handled the comprehensive spectrum of Human Resources activity. Moreover, as an African-American woman, I've also had notable success in managing a diverse U.S. workforce and in relating the company to employees—and even customers—from foreign cultures.

Now having succeeded as #2 in Human Resources responsibility to an outstanding person only a few years beyond my age, I've decided to seek a larger challenge outside of PCBrands...an ambitious personal goal understood by PCB's senior management, who will be pleased to tell you about me.

Challenge means far more to me than cash. However, you should know that in recent years my total compensation has ranged from approximately $340,000 to $520,000.

Should we talk?

Sincerely,

Sylvia Dorrington

Sylvia P. Dorrington

What Superb People!

They really are. It's my pleasure to know them both.

But you, too, can sense how well things would be taken care of if you entrusted the running of a business or the handling of its people to "Andrew" or "Sylvia." Your confidence comes partly from what they've told you...but partly, too, from the *way* they've told you. Straightforwardly in plain modest words and unequivocal numbers.

Wouldn't it be easy and pleasant to be their boss? You'd always know where things stood...and without having to sit through too many long, boring chart presentations or dig into lots of pretentiously worded memos and booklets. And their minds would be on the business—on what interests *you,* Ms. or Mr. CEO or Recruiter—not on their own desires. That you can assume, because these people have stayed objective and business-centered while writing something which causes many other people to wallow in subjectivity.

The Result?

Both of these people used their letters in a direct mail campaign exactly as described in *Rites of Passage.* Results were what you'd expect, given (1) the quality of the people and (2) the quality of what they sent. The CEO of a very large NYSE-listed corporation called up Mr. "Thomlin," had him in for a four-hour interview, and at the end of it offered him a job (which Mr. T wound up declining in favor of an even better one). And Ms. "Dorrington," despite already knowing dozens of America's top executive search people, wound up meeting a recruiter she did *not* know previously, and he introduced her to her current employer, where she is #1 in HR and there are more than 35,000 employees in 37 countries...a position she could have waited many years to achieve at "PCBrands."

And Now To Work!

To help focus your efforts in the same direction theirs took, there are "Design Sheets" for your cover letter, starting on the next page. So that you can scribble your way toward different jobs and/or problem-solutions, there are several worksheets.

As you've seen, the trick is to distill the most interesting and powerfully persuasive facts from your resume into a very few well-chosen words. Do that effectively, and your reader will be sufficiently intrigued to plunge into reading your resume to see if you can possibly be as good as those first few seconds of glancing at your cover letter have suggested you may be.

And whatever you write, *edit, EDIT, EDIT!* There's no other way to compress so much information into so few easy-to-read words. Fortunately, however, you already have all the facts sorted out and written up in your "sales representative" resume. Most of your *really* hard work is already done.

Cover Letter Design Sheet (**Strategy #1**)

What are you proposing the employer USE you for? (see pp. 7-12; 93-95; "central theme" p.140 &145)

What types of proof will you offer that, if hired, you will deliver what you're promising? ("size and scope" of what you've done and "major achievements" will be listed below; is there anything else? see "measurements" pp. 98-102.)

Size and Scope of what you've done.

Major Achievements (proof you are a superior performer...probably better than the other candidates who will be competing against you).

MAJOR ACHIEVEMENTS (CONTINUED).

QUALIFIERS (PROOF YOU'VE DONE THE WORK EVERYONE SEEKING THE POSITION SHOULD HAVE DONE. IF POSSIBLE, FULFILLMENT OF ALL REQUIREMENTS SHOULD BE IMPLICIT IN YOUR MAJOR ACHIEVEMENTS; SEE PP. 96-97).

REASON YOU'RE LOOKING (SHOULD BE AS POSITIVE—OR AT LEAST NON-NEGATIVE—AS POSSIBLE, AND PROBABLY SHOULD BE DEALT WITH HEAD-ON IN YOUR LETTER).

POTENTIAL NEGATIVES (REASONS—FAIR OR UNFAIR—PEOPLE MIGHT BE DOUBTFUL ABOUT HIRING YOU; ALSO YOUR STRATEGY FOR DEALING WITH—OR IGNORING—THEM IN YOUR LETTER. SEE PP. 22-29; 103-104).

POTENTIAL SPONSORSHIP (EITHER TO OVERCOME A POTENTIAL NEGATIVE—OR FOR ANY OTHER REASON—SHOULD YOU CONSIDER HAVING A "SPONSOR" SEND SOME OR MOST OF YOUR LETTERS? IF SO, WHO? REVIEW PP. 16-21).

Cover Letter Design Sheet (**Strategy #2**)

What are you proposing the employer USE you for? (see pp. 7-12; 93-95; "central theme" p.140 &145)

What types of proof will you offer that, if hired, you will deliver what you're promising? ("size and scope" of what you've done and "major achievements" will be listed below; is there anything else? see "measurements" pp. 98-102.)

Size and Scope of what you've done.

Major Achievements (proof you are a superior performer...probably better than the other candidates who will be competing against you).

MAJOR ACHIEVEMENTS (CONTINUED).

QUALIFIERS (PROOF YOU'VE DONE THE WORK EVERYONE SEEKING THE POSITION SHOULD HAVE DONE. IF POSSIBLE, FULFILLMENT OF ALL REQUIREMENTS SHOULD BE IMPLICIT IN YOUR MAJOR ACHIEVEMENTS; SEE PP. 96-97).

REASON YOU'RE LOOKING (SHOULD BE AS POSITIVE—OR AT LEAST NON-NEGATIVE—AS POSSIBLE, AND PROBABLY SHOULD BE DEALT WITH HEAD-ON IN YOUR LETTER).

POTENTIAL NEGATIVES (REASONS—FAIR OR UNFAIR—PEOPLE MIGHT BE DOUBTFUL ABOUT HIRING YOU; ALSO YOUR STRATEGY FOR DEALING WITH—OR IGNORING—THEM IN YOUR LETTER. SEE PP. 22-29; 103-104).

POTENTIAL SPONSORSHIP (EITHER TO OVERCOME A POTENTIAL NEGATIVE—OR FOR ANY OTHER REASON—SHOULD YOU CONSIDER HAVING A "SPONSOR" SEND SOME OR MOST OF YOUR LETTERS? IF SO, WHO? REVIEW PP. 16-21).

Cover Letter Design Sheet (**Strategy #3**)

What are you proposing the employer USE you for? (see pp. 7-12; 93-95; "central theme" p.140 &145)

What types of proof will you offer that, if hired, you will deliver what you're promising? ("size and scope" of what you've done and "major achievements" will be listed below; is there anything else? see "measurements" pp. 98-102.)

Size and Scope of what you've done.

Major Achievements (proof you are a superior performer...probably better than the other candidates who will be competing against you).

MAJOR ACHIEVEMENTS (CONTINUED).

QUALIFIERS (PROOF YOU'VE DONE THE WORK EVERYONE SEEKING THE POSITION SHOULD HAVE DONE. IF POSSIBLE, FULFILLMENT OF ALL REQUIREMENTS SHOULD BE IMPLICIT IN YOUR MAJOR ACHIEVEMENTS; SEE PP. 96-97).

REASON YOU'RE LOOKING (SHOULD BE AS POSITIVE—OR AT LEAST NON-NEGATIVE—AS POSSIBLE, AND PROBABLY SHOULD BE DEALT WITH HEAD-ON IN YOUR LETTER).

POTENTIAL NEGATIVES (REASONS—FAIR OR UNFAIR—PEOPLE MIGHT BE DOUBTFUL ABOUT HIRING YOU; ALSO YOUR STRATEGY FOR DEALING WITH—OR IGNORING—THEM IN YOUR LETTER. SEE PP. 22-29; 103-104).

POTENTIAL SPONSORSHIP (EITHER TO OVERCOME A POTENTIAL NEGATIVE—OR FOR ANY OTHER REASON—SHOULD YOU CONSIDER HAVING A "SPONSOR" SEND SOME OR MOST OF YOUR LETTERS? IF SO, WHO? REVIEW PP. 16-21).

Cover Letter Design Sheet (**Strategy #4**)

What are you proposing the employer USE you for? (see pp. 7-12; 93-95; "central theme" p.140 &145)

What types of proof will you offer that, if hired, you will deliver what you're promising? ("size and scope" of what you've done and "major achievements" will be listed below; is there anything else? see "measurements" pp. 98-102.)

Size and Scope of what you've done.

Major Achievements (proof you are a superior performer...probably better than the other candidates who will be competing against you).

MAJOR ACHIEVEMENTS (CONTINUED).

QUALIFIERS (PROOF YOU'VE DONE THE WORK EVERYONE SEEKING THE POSITION SHOULD HAVE DONE. IF POSSIBLE, FULFILLMENT OF ALL REQUIREMENTS SHOULD BE IMPLICIT IN YOUR MAJOR ACHIEVEMENTS; SEE PP. 96-97).

REASON YOU'RE LOOKING (SHOULD BE AS POSITIVE—OR AT LEAST NON-NEGATIVE—AS POSSIBLE, AND PROBABLY SHOULD BE DEALT WITH HEAD-ON IN YOUR LETTER).

POTENTIAL NEGATIVES (REASONS—FAIR OR UNFAIR—PEOPLE MIGHT BE DOUBTFUL ABOUT HIRING YOU; ALSO YOUR STRATEGY FOR DEALING WITH—OR IGNORING—THEM IN YOUR LETTER. SEE PP. 22-29; 103-104).

POTENTIAL SPONSORSHIP (EITHER TO OVERCOME A POTENTIAL NEGATIVE—OR FOR ANY OTHER REASON—SHOULD YOU CONSIDER HAVING A "SPONSOR" SEND SOME OR MOST OF YOUR LETTERS? IF SO, WHO? REVIEW PP. 16-21).

Job-Hunting by Mail

As *Rites of Passage at $100,000 to $1 Million+* explains, there are only 5 main ways to look for or change jobs at the executive level: (1) through Personal Contacts (people you already know); (2) Networking (strangers but—*please*—not handled in the usual way); (3) Direct Mail; (4) Executive Recruiters; and (5) the Internet (used very cautiously).

The Workbook helps with your *paperwork* on *all* these activities. But it *doesn't* tell you how to go about them. If it did, it'd be 1,200 pages long! And if the Workbook were dumped into *Rites, Rites* would be unwieldy...no longer fast and fun to read.

You and I have just made a resume and letter strong enough to use in a mass mailing, but we purposely haven't covered direct mail's philosophy and practices. Reason: In *Rites* I present them in a special sequence that helps folks see what direct mail can and can't do...and realize that *they may not be appropriate subjects for it.* Everyone always needs the strongest possible resume and cover letter, even if they don't launch a mail campaign or if, instead, they deploy their skillfully written resume on the Internet (see detailed instructions in *Rites of Passage*).

The "Sponsored" Direct Mail Campaign

Yet the forms you just used asked you to consider whether you should be asking a "sponsor" to send out your letters. That assumes you *are* doing a mass mailing. There is absolutely no use for a letter from a third party "sponsor" unless (1) it's sent to people who *don't know you* and (2) in *very large numbers* that have statistical probability of generating inquiries. Which brings up the question of what a "sponsor's" letter should say. And also, how to get any kindly soul to do so much work (they don't; *you* do!).

Actually, there are ***two uses*** of sponsored direct mail: (1) to conduct a job-changing campaign ***in complete secrecy*** when you're *employed* and (2) to ***add credibility and overcome prejudice*** when you have *special problems.*

Just so you'll know the device exists, here's a sample from *Rites.* Please read it carefully. Afterward, I'll give you my list of 6 essential points that must be covered, so you can look back and see how they were woven in. But please, don't throw time or money into direct mail until you've carefully read pages 160 to 227 of *Rites of Passage.* A great many—probably most—executives handle direct mail very naively and, for that reason, are disappointed with their outcome.

I want you either to do it right (if it's appropriate in your situation)...or not at all!

MONOLITHIC FOODS CORPORATION

WHITE PLAINS, NEW YORK 11618

MAURICE MARKETIER
Vice President - Marketing
(914) 201-6667

(Date)

Mr. Cabot Carson
President
Family-Owned Candies, Inc.
10 Ginger Road
Scottsdale, Arizona 09099

Dear Mr. Carson:

As Vice President - Marketing of Monolithic Foods, I've seen hundreds of fine marketing executives over the years, and one of the very best is my former boss at MegaFoods, Joyce McKee, who taught me most of what I know.

Recently the company where she's been Vice President - Marketing, Yumm Foods, was acquired through an unfriendly tender offer. And now at an amazingly youthful age 59...Joyce ran the New York Marathon again this year...she's available for another assignment.

Although company and opportunity will be Joyce's main concerns, you should know that in recent years her total compensation has been in the range of $160,000 to $240,000.

Joyce is the calibre of person there's hardly ever a shot at hiring, and nothing would please me more than to bring her in here. Unfortunately, I can't do that without dealing an undeserved blow to either of the two executives who head my Marketing Department...or by giving up my own job.

So, on the chance that you may have need for an exceptionally dynamic, creative, and versatile marketing executive, I thought I'd bring Joyce to your attention.

Sincerely,

Maurice Marketier

Maurice Marketier

MM:jc
Enclosure

P.S.: With Joyce's exceptional knack for training and recruiting, you can count on her building a strong department, with excellent people to take over whenever it's time for Joyce to retire.

What a great way to attack a potential negative!

Joyce couldn't send out her *own* letters saying, "Don't worry, I'm not too old!"

And she probably needs to reach far more employers than she can through networking alone, in order to find an open-minded one *with an opening*, who'll go along with her scenario.

Moreover, even if networking *did* lead her to a person who'd consider Maurice Marketier's pitch, can you imagine Joyce walking in and saying those same things about *herself*?

Here are the essential elements of a "sponsor's" letter:

1. ***Credentials*** that make the sponsor a valid judge of executives like you;
2. ***Vantage point*** that enables him or her to endorse your on-the-job effectiveness;
3. ***Recommendation***;
4. ***Reason the sponsor is not employing you***;
5. ***Explanation of your need for secrecy*** (if that's a factor); and
6. ***Offer*** to put the interested reader in touch with you.

All the elements but number 5 are in the letter we just saw. Please go back and take a look. Sponsorship can give an enormous boost to a difficult job-hunt. Give it serious consideration, if there's any chance you may need it.

Just one example before we depart the subject: Shortly after the first edition of *RITES* appeared in 1988, I got a lovely letter from a CEO who'd used *RITES'* direct mail and targeted networking techniques to discover and land the presidency of a famous company. Almost immediately he tried to buy that company, losing his position in the process. Afterward, he twice again became CEO of companies whose names you'd also recognize, again using *RITES* techniques. Each time he let me (and all other recruiters) know where he went. Now, after three big jobs in less than six years, he needed a fourth. This man is a superb writer and, as you can imagine, interviews flawlessly. But this time, he didn't even attempt self-signed letters. Instead, he sent out a huge mailing from the CEO of one of America's very largest and most famous corporations (his boss 12 years ago). Result? Just before sending this WORKBOOK to the printer, I received his letter announcing another equally big job!

Don't let the "Big Shots" monopolize the best techniques!

You might readily wonder from the last few examples, whether the techniques of this WORKBOOK and of *Rites* are somehow mainly for the person already established at the high end of the executive job market. Not so at all!

The same techniques have worked fully as well for folks at every level and at every stage of their career...even including the son of the CEO I just described, who recently graduated from college. Take a moment to look again at the note on page 83.

The executive-level job market fluctuates from overheated to deadly dull as the overall U.S. economy surges and recedes. That's an inescapable fact of business and career life.

But you only need one job! And with all the sophisticated techniques at your disposal, vastly more than just that one are well within your reach. Read *RITES* (be sure it's a current edition freshly tuned to the fast-changing Internet dimension of executive job-changing) and pursue all five main job-hunting techniques simultaneously. Expect to wind up with several opportunities to choose from. Most folks do.

Which brings us to the WORKBOOK'S help with your Networking...another of the five main job-hunting methods dealt with in *RITES OF PASSAGE.* Turn the page to begin using techniques we executive recruiters have been relying on for many years.

To Help With Your

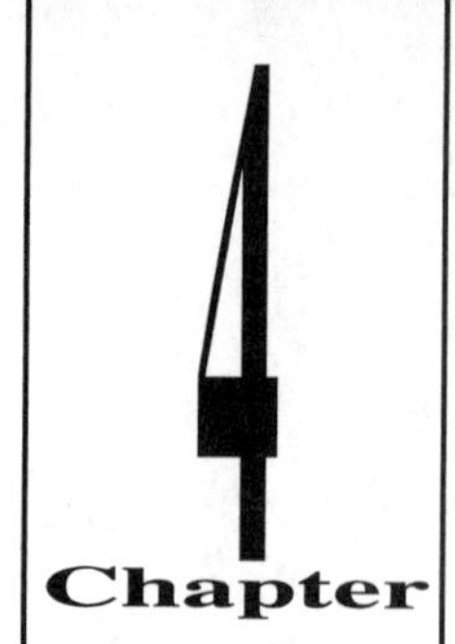

Networking

Speed your search and make it far more successful by using the tool executive search professionals use.

Introducing: "S&P Sheets." And much more!

The search process—yours and the executive recruiter's—is exactly the same. He or she looks for candidates to fit an opening. You look for openings to fit a candidate. And the main method you both use is the same:

Networking!

You and the recruiter both get in touch with lots of people. Most, unfortunately, don't solve the problem. But each supplies new information. Each suggests new people to contact. Those new folks *may* solve the problem. But even when they don't, they provide further information and additional names.

That's Networking. It's the single most powerful executive recruiting—and job-hunting—tool.

But it can be mighty frustrating, because it brings in bushels of new and unfamiliar names you've got to keep track of.

> *Who told you to call whom? What were you supposed to say? Or **not** say? When did you call? Was there a conversation or did you merely leave word? On a machine or with whom? When was the latest conversation? How was it left? What follow-up? When were you supposed to call back? Did you send a thank you note? Who else suggested calling the same key person? Which referral would be more likely to get a response? And on and on.*

Fortunately a very simple and effective method for staying on top of this process was invented over forty years ago at the management consulting firm of Booz Allen &

Hamilton. Today Booz doesn't do recruiting. But several of their early alumni went on to found some of America's top search firms. Those firms spawned others. Finally, almost the entire profession adopted the same clever but simple form to speed and track their searches.

The "S&P Sheet"

What the wheel is to on-the-ground transportation the S&P concept is to managing a series of referrals.

"S" stands for "Source" and "P" is for "Prospect." The source is the person who identifies someone who might be appropriate to fill a position, a prospect. If, when contacted, the prospect is both appropriate and interested, he or she becomes a candidate. If not, he or she usually becomes a source...a supplier of further names to contact. On and on the classic process goes...always conveniently noted on an "S&P sheet."

"Where do computers come in?"

We'll talk a bit more about that later. For now, let's absorb the classic on-paper method of record-keeping as invented and used by recruiters. Today—just like you and me—they apply desk-top, lap-top, and hand-held computers to their work. Some use both electronic and on-paper "S&Ps." Others use no papers at all. Either way, they are employing the same time-tested principles of their profession, which operate as we are about to see.

Using the Classic "S&P Sheet" Method

Before you turn the page and look at an executive recruiter-style S&P sheet in the midst of being used, please read this summary of what's happening:

> The search is for a Chief Technology Officer. Frank First recommended Sally Seconde. Frank considered her a *prospect*, not merely a *source,* so "P" rather than "S" was circled.
>
> Unfortunately, Sally said, "No." But she suggested Nathan Nue as a prospect (P is circled), and Sue Seesum as a source (S is circled). Note Sally's warning to screen Sue's recommendations; also that Sally permits the use of her name with Sue and suggests calling Sue at home. Sally knows Sue is cultivating recruiters, likes at-home calls, and may be more helpful there than in her hectic office.
>
> You and I are not doing this search. Yet after reading these scribbled S&Ps, either of us could instantly take over. We'd call Constantine for the first time, and renew the call to Nathan if he hasn't called our firm within a couple days after he returns on February 12.
>
> Indeed, "Researchers" in many search firms pick up and drop the work of phoning for candidates on their firm's searches on a moment's notice. Using S&Ps, they don't need to know or remember any prior contacting on the project...and may not have personally done any.
>
> Note that "S/O" in the "Contact" column means "Sign Off." Quality search firms always send "thank-you" notes when the search is completed.

From

Executive Recruiting...

SOURCE AND PROSPECT SHEET

DATE			
Contact 2/7 S/O	Sally Seconde VP R&D Symbiotic Software 77 Silicon Circle Sunnyvale CA 94086 Home 408-999-3986 office 408-764-4000 Source: Frank First	P (circled) S	"Perfect if she'd move." Better than her boss Adam Amos Sr. V.P Technology per Frank DO NOT MENTION FRANK! Sounds great on phone. Can't move. Will get $2 million on their IPO next year. After that wants CEO job. 2 Great ideas!
Contact 2/9 Left Word Back 2/12 S/O	Nathan Nue Dir Software Engineering Mega-Maxi Technology Corp. Reading MA 617-090-6620 Source: Sally Seconde	P (circled) S	Young (29?) But outstanding per Sally, who has tried to hire him! Supervises 30 PhD's older than he is "Brilliant & great with people" OK to Mention Sally
Contact 2/9 left word on vacation til 2/20 S/O	Sue Seesum Exec. Director International Software Scientists Association office 703-009-3240 Home 703-601-0110 Source: Sally Seconde	P S (circled)	"Knows everyone internationally" says Sally. But BE CAREFUL. "Can't tell if good or not." Praises the charming [illegible] to the skies. MENTION SALLY! Close friends. Call her at home evenings. "Loves headhunter calls & wants to move herself" per Sally.
Contact S/O	Constantine Klinor Goes by "CONNOR" Was V.P. Technology at Dynadyne Home 503-622-0014 Source: Dom Domino	P (circled) S	Out of work since Dynadyne/Mega-Maxi merger in Sept. But extremely able per Dr. Adams! (Cal Tech). Dom says he's "making big money now consulting for AT&T - but might be interested." Would know others
Contact		P	

Your Job-Hunting **S&Ps**
...the **Networking Contacts** *Pages*

For four decades, S&Ps were absolutely indispensible to the networking recruiters do. Now, with appropriate changes, similar pages can help you search for your new job:

1. ***The "S" and "P" are gone!*** *Everyone* you talk to will be a *source* of information. Unlike the recruiter, you're looking for a position, not a person.

2. ***"Mention Yes / No."*** This is a central issue to track, regardless of whether you use the classic on-paper method or you adapt it to your own preferred methods of computerization.

   Skilled recruiters break down barriers by saying, "Of course ***I won't use your name*** with anyone you mention ***unless you tell me to***. So, on that basis, who do you feel are absolutely the best people for the job?" Now folks who've stayed silent begin to speak up. Afterward, the recruiter asks name-use permission on each person discussed, marking the S&Ps accordingly.

   As you network, try prefacing your queries with a promise not to use your informant's name without permission. You'd prefer an introduction, of course. And you can always ask for one as you end the conversation. But, above all, you want *information.* Try the technique. If you like and use it, then "Mention YES Mention NO" will keep your permissions straight. These days people are just as nervous about having their name used by job-hunters as by headhunters. So find out the *names* of the people most likely to have or know of a job for you, and *then* ask with whom you may and may not use your informant's name.

3. ***Phone/E-mail, Visit, Letter.*** Retainer recruiters troll for names largely by phone, with a few lunch dates, e-mails and mailings thrown in. You, on the other hand, will do lots of your networking face-to-face and will send different and highly personalized letters at various times. Hence, I've added separate "boxes" for tracking your three types of contacts.

4. ***Larger Size Entries.*** For some reason, classic recruiting firm S&Ps are always very stingy with space. Usually there are six or more mini-entries per page. I've enlarged the "slots" to only four per page. You'll find them a lot more convenient than the traditional headhunter S&Ps would be.

More Information on Special People ...the Key Networking Contacts *Pages*

The on-paper search management system that begins at the end of this Workbook includes an ample supply of the modified S&Ps (described above and shown on p. 168). And every third page captures far more detailed information. Use these for any contact—old friend or new networking acquaintance—who merits in-depth attention.

These folks are either highly prominent and well-connected or very impressed with you and eager to help...hopefully both. So, besides capturing lots of information, this form prompts you to think what these people can do for you. What introductions? What reconnaissance? Who do they know in search firms? Recruiters will pay far more attention when you're referred by someone with "clout" (see *Rites* for specifics).

Classic On-paper Tools
for your networking campaign...

NETWORKING CONTACTS

DATES PERSON: TITLE, CO., ADDRESS, PHONE, E-MAIL COMMENTS & FOLLOW-UP

PHONE/ E-MAIL

VISIT

LETTER

SOURCE MENTION YES ☐ MENTION NO ☐

PHONE

VISIT

LETTER

SOURCE MENTION YES ☐ MENTION NO ☐

PHONE

VISIT

LETTER

SOURCE MENTION YES ☐ MENTION NO ☐

PHONE

VISIT

LETTER

SOURCE MENTION YES ☐ MENTION NO ☐

KEY NETWORKING CONTACT

Person/Title: ______________________________

Company: ______________________________

Address: ______________________________ **E-mail** ______________
STREET CITY STATE/ZIP

Phones/Fax: #1 (   ) ____-______ ☐ SWITCHBOARD ☐ PRIVATE #2 (   ) ____-______ ☐ SWITCHBOARD ☐ PRIVATE FAX (   ) ____-______ ☐ GENERAL ☐ PERSONAL/SECURE

Assistant(s): ______________ ______________ FAX (   ) ____-______ ☐ GENERAL ☐ PERSONAL/SECURE

Spouse: ____________ **Home Address:** ______________________________
STREET ADDRESS CITY STATE/ZIP

Home Phones: #1 (   ) ____-______ ☐ FAMILY PHONE ☐ HOME OFC. #2 (   ) ____-______ ☐ FAMILY PHONE ☐ HOME OFC. FAX (   ) ____-______ ☐ FAMILY ☐ HOME Office

Introduced by: ______________ **Connection:** ______________

CONTACTS	DATE: LETTER/PHONE/MTG./E-MAIL	WHAT ABOUT?	MY FOLLOW-UP	HIS / HER FOLLOW-UP	DATE THANKED
	1st				
	2nd				
	3rd				
	4th				
	5th				

COMMENTS:

OFFERS OF SEARCH FIRM INTRODUCTIONS:

RECRUITER / FIRM/ CITY ———— RELATIONSHIP WITH RECRUITER ———— FOLLOW-UP / DATE

RECRUITER / FIRM/ CITY ———— RELATIONSHIP WITH RECRUITER ———— FOLLOW-UP / DATE

What's happening with these people?

Karl Katz: Karl's a "source." He's told us about several people (on a prior page) and Audrey, his last suggestion, is at the top of 171. Information on Karl is a few pages earlier. Note Karl's permission to tell Audrey he identified her and told us to call...a big help in gaining her confidence.

Audrey Able: Since we were referred by Karl, whom Audrey *highly* respects, she's been surprisingly open and helpful...even revealing the deeply confidential fact that Mack Bigi is dissatisfied with his CFO and has offered her his job. He told Audrey, "I'd rather keep the guy I've got than bring in some stranger. But if you're ever ready to move, just let me know." Her relationship with Mack could be destroyed if he knew she'd told a stranger. ***We've marked "Mention NO" and will be careful!***

Meanwhile, since she's so willing, we've mailed her 4 resumes along with our "thank you" note (which does **NOT** mention the number enclosed or what we'd like done with them). We don't expect Audrey to send them to Mack and Dawn—*we'll* do that, although there's no harm if she does too. Since she's "sold" on us, we want her to have some handy if a recruiter happens to call her for suggestions or she thinks or hears of someone else who may need us. Many folks feel guilty about throwing away resumes. If we don't "high-pressure," they'll often try to forward the extras, rather than dump them. ***Page 171 shows at-a-glance everything we've done with Audrey and when we did it!***

Mack Bigi: Without Audrey's all-out endorsement (which she doesn't know us well enough to give under these delicate circumstances), we've had to place several calls (1/21, 1/26, 2/1, & 2/5) to get Mack on the wire...and then we've had to be ultra-persuasive to get him merely to say "I'm *not* interested personally, but send me your resume; I'll look at it and maybe send it along to someone *else*." Despite his dissembling, we know Mack's a valid prospect. So we send him just one copy by Federal Express, ensuring its arrival while he remembers our upbeat phone conversation.

Dawne Daley: Another excellent lead from Audrey. We left word on the 21st, called again and got her on the 25th, and FAXed a resume 5 minutes after we hung up the phone. Her office is nearby, and she called right back asking us to "drop in" Tuesday, February 15 at 2:00. Nothing more for now! We jot down the additional "Comments and Follow-up" on her entry in our S&Ps, and "quit while we're ahead."

Sheldon Salt: We'll wait until Wednesday of the week of February 18, to place our call. Permission to mention Mark may help us get through at a time when Sheldon will obviously be very busy catching up after his trip.

DATES	PERSON: TITLE, COMPANY, ADDRESS, PHONES	COMMENTS & FOLLOW-UP
PHONE Jan 11 VISIT LETTER 4 Res Jan 18	Audrey Able Sr. VP-Finance Advanced New Waves Inc. 1192 Orion S.W. Sarasota FL 34204 office 813-206-4444 HOME 813-016-3724 use home SOURCE Karl Katz	Karl worked with her at Diamond Energy. Saw her at Wharton lunch & she asked suggestions in case her Controller gets a job he's interviewing on. NICE! Would be great to work for. WOW! Extremely helpful - Too bad the guy didn't get the job. Great idea! MENTION YES ☑ MENTION NO ☐
PHONE Jan 21 26 Feb 1 5 VISIT LETTER 2/5 Resume by Fed Ex	Mack Bigi Scrub Pine Corporation (He owns it) 11 Scrub Pine Trail Sarasota FL 34231 office 813-069-9300 home 813-260-3281 SOURCE Audrey Able	Owns lots of McDonalds, KFC's & Midas Mufflers - Audrey thinks $50 million sales. She goes to same church. Asked her to join him. So "can't be too happy with the guy he has." Don't tell him she told me Finally Got him. Tough! But wound up great! RESUME BY FED EX 2/5. MENTION YES ☐ MENTION NO ☑
PHONE Jan 21 25 VISIT Feb 15 LETTER Res by FAX	Dawne Daley Managing Partner Creativity Capital Corp. 1194 Route 22 Dawson NJ 07974 office 201-001-9000 SOURCE Audrey Able	Dawne & Partners are refinancing failed LBO's. "She's always looking for CFOs that will work cheap & take a chance on future." Reached her on 1/25 & sent resume By FAX. Date to meet 2:00 on 2/15 MENTION YES ☑ MENTION NO ☐
PHONE Jan 24 away to Feb 18 VISIT LETTER	Sheldon Salt President Credit Cards Division Mega Bank Holdings 2142 Gulph Road King of Prussia PA 19406 office: 717-029-5000 home: 215-334-3912 SOURCE Mark Miller	Sheldon is one of 3 new division heads brought in by New CEO. Told Mark (his brother-in-law) of "lots of changes still coming." Mark that Sheldon or others might want new CEO. CALL HIM FEB. 20!!! MENTION YES ☑ MENTION NO ☐

What's happening with Kathryn?

Why is Kathryn a "KEY NETWORKING CONTACT"? Karl Katz prefaced his remarks by saying, *"This is my very best suggestion...an extremely well-connected person who's also exceptionally kind and helpful. She knows tons of people—many of them very high-level—all over the world! And she's Ann's and my closest friend; when we tell her about you, she'll go out of her way to help."* So, on a hunch, we flipped ahead in our ATTACHE PAGES to the next unused full-page form. "KEY NETWORKING" sheets are on every third page. With chronological indexing (which we'll soon discuss) you're free to skip ahead and use these—or any other pages—out of sequence.

Who are your "KEY NETWORKING CONTACTS"? Look back over pages 16-21. Pick out the small handful of *people you already know* who are your very most enthusiastic and prominent supporters. They're glad to help...and you want to be as efficient and nonbothersome as possible in asking and aiding them to help. A few special people you'll *newly* meet—as Karl has introduced us to Kathryn—may also merit special attention.

More Space for More Information: At any time during your search when you find yourself wanting to keep comprehensive information on your dealings with anyone, use one of these pages. Someone originally "squeezed" into an ordinary NETWORKING CONTACT slot can always be upgraded to a full page when you see the need, and chrono indexing will keep all your information sorted and handy.

Potential Recruiter Introductions: Some of your "Key Contacts" will know and perhaps have done business with executive search firms you'd like to make aware of your availability and the high regard your widely respected contact has for you. The concise grid at the bottom of the page is a convenient reminder to ask about potential introductions.

Kathryn, Will, and Buddy

Kathryn, Will, Buddy, and the major search firm of Gordon, Rossi & Boodles are, of course, fictitious. They're among the many folks you'll meet in the 70-page novella that is Appendix I of *RITES OF PASSAGE AT $100,000 TO $1 MILLION+*...a behind-the-scenes view of the executive recruiting and job-search process.

There you'll see some executives performing brilliantly...and others making serious but unseen mistakes in handling their campaigns. Kathryn is one who handles networking and recruiters exceptionally well...getting the best from both, without ever losing sight of her own best interests and personal agenda.

KEY NETWORKING CONTACT

ATTACHE PAGE 173

Person/Title: Kathryn Keane, President

Company: Colorado Colonnade Inc. (subsidiary of Cato-Carlo International)

Address: 1 First Terrace, Colorado Colonnades CO 80303
TITLE / STREET ADDRESS / CITY / STATE/ZIP

Phones/Fax: #1 (303) 021-7000 ☐ Switchboard ☐ Private #2 ( ) ___-____ ☐ Switchboard ☐ Private FAX ( ) ___-____ ☐ General ☐ Personal/Secure

Assistant(s): ________ ________ FAX ( ) ___-____ ☐ General ☐ Personal/Secure

Spouse: ________ **Home Address:** (same as above)
STREET ADDRESS / CITY / STATE/ZIP

Home Phones: #1 ( ) ___-____ ☐ Family Phone ☐ Home Ofc. #2 ( ) ___-____ ☐ Family Phone ☐ Home Ofc. FAX ( ) ___-____ ☐ Family ☐ Home Office

Introduced by: Karl Katz **Connection:** Runs Condo where Karl is an owner.

CONTACTS	Date: Letter/Phone/Mtg.	What About?	My Follow-Up	His / Her Follow-Up	Date Thanked
1st	1/10 - I phoned	Network	10 Resumes by Fed Ex	She'll send to search firms	Note Enclosed
2nd	1/22 I phoned	Thanks for Recruiter Calls Coming in		—	—
3rd	2/14 She called	Send Res to Summit & Bean at ISC			Note 2/15
4th					
5th					

COMMENTS: Kathryn completed job search a year ago. Was a top Marketing person at Parker Labs. Decided to leave. Got several offers. "Knows lots of search people" per Karl. Great friends with Karl & Anna Katz (their former neighbor). OK to call her at home, which is same as office, because she's building & running a huge new ski resort "almost from the bare land." 1/15. Spoke by phone 1/10. She'll send resumes to "5 or 6 of the biggest search firms where she knows people." Told me to call Will Pickham at Gordon Rossi & Boodles directly & just mention her — "My best headhunter friend" she says. Sent her 10 resumes by Fed Ex. Called her 1/22 to thank for calls coming in from Headhunters & tell her Will Pickham set me up with Buddy Young at his firm & I'm a candidate on Magna Edison CFO. She called 2/14 to say send resumes to Sherm Summit CEO & Bill Bean Pres. at Integrated Standard Corp. They own condos & she told them of me.

OFFERS OF SEARCH FIRM INTRODUCTIONS:

Will Pickham NY office of Gordon Rossi & Boodles — Appointment 1/20
RECRUITER / FIRM / CITY — RELATIONSHIP WITH RECRUITER — FOLLOW-UP/DATE

She'll send letters with resume to other top firms — Copies to me for follow-up.
RECRUITER / FIRM / CITY — RELATIONSHIP WITH RECRUITER — FOLLOW-UP/DATE

Networking: The Total System

Up to now we've been discussing the ideal on-paper record-keeping system for a series of information-gathering contacts...each providing not only facts and ideas but also the names of further contacts. That's Networking, and now you have the tools to manage it.

But they're not located at the end of this chapter. To use them, just flip this book upside down, so that the back cover becomes a front cover. Behind it there's a special INDEX, plus plenty of the sheets we've just looked at. Also the INTERVIEW DE-BRIEFERS and the TAX / EXPENSE record-keepers, which we'll cover in the next couple chapters.

Together, these elements make a sophisticated total system for speeding and tracking your search.

And it's portable!

Moreover, you can carry it wherever you go. Finish this chapter and the next two, and you'll see where this book ends and another—your ATTACHE PAGES—begins. There, just take a scissors and cut the spine of this big heavy book. Presto! You've got a streamlined volume with nothing in it but your search record-keeping materials. It's half as heavy and half as thick. It has all the contact information you need to manage your search and push it forward. If you're keeping your records on paper, don't leave home without it!

"Attache Page Numbers"

Your newly streamlined book has its own set of page numbers. The back cover is its front. Pages proceed upward from "1" and are marked "ATTACHE PAGE NUMBER xxx" in bold figures. It's no accident that the numbers are this big:

As an executive recruiter, I know the feeling of panic when the phone rings...and suddenly someone you think you've never heard of is "returning your call." Then, if you're like me, you just can't cope with itty-bitty numbers like the one at the top of this page, as you hunt for the S&P that will get you up-to-speed with this caller. Like a sports car, you've got to go "from zero to 60 MPH in less than 6 seconds!" These oversized numbers will zoom you ahead, not hold you back.

And the Key to Everything:

Chronological Indexing!

Obviously, the index just inside the back (now front) cover is the key to the entire system.

The name and page number of every "GENERAL" or "KEY" "NETWORKING CONTACT" you've phoned or met should be promptly written in. ***Do not, however, clutter the index with every name that is suggested to you and finds its way into your S&Ps.*** You'll receive many suggestions you decide *not* to follow up. Indexing them would merely bloat the index and slow you down when you're looking for people you urgently *want* to find.

Trust me on this. After many years of using indexed S&Ps as an executive recruiter, I know the importance of only indexing the contacts you've already made or intend to make very soon. Personally, I wouldn't index anyone until ***after I've actually placed a call to them*** (whether they answered or not). That way, the index grows in strict chronological order. The people I've phoned or met most recently appear on the last few filled-in pages of my index. And those are the pages I conveniently scan when the phone rings and someone says, "Hello, this is Marilyn Smith; I'm returning your call."

The index must grow chronologically.

The process works best, however, if it's casual and informal. Don't waste lots of time keeping the index—or any of the other pages—neat. Nobody but you will ever see or use them! And please don't try to organize it by subject matter (recruiters, networking, etc.). Just let it be a...

Mixed Bag!

Chronology is the grid. But don't be dogmatic. If you have a strong referral to a recruiter you want to be sure you don't forget to call, feel free to break the rules and index him or her even before you've called. Also, don't hesitate to list the same person and page number more than once. Maybe somebody you first contacted weeks or months ago will suddenly loom large in importance, and you'll expect to hear from him or her again soon. If so, just repeat the name and page number in your index, so you'll find it quickly among your recent entries if and when that person calls.

Here's what the index looks like. ***Last name first***, and ***boldly printed***...because that's what you'll be looking for when the phone rings. But notice too, that there's room for a few key descriptive words before you get to the page number in the right hand column. Condense some key hints into the middle slot, and you may not have to look any further to be reminded who Philip Jones is, when he belatedly calls back.

PERSON	COMPANY / CONNECTION	PAGE NUMBER
KATZ, Karl	Chrysler - Asst. Treasurer - Dave Doe's friend	154
ABLE, Audrey	Advanced New Waves - Sr. V.P. - Finance (Karl Katz)	171
BIGI, Mack	Owns franchises - From Audrey Able's Church	171 219
DARWIN, Charles	Enviro-Fit - CFO - Pres. Fla. Financial Roundtable	122
DALEY, Dawne	Mg. Partner - Creativity Capital (Audrey Able)	171
KEANE, Kathryn	Pres. Colorado Colonnades - Karl Katz's friend	173
PICKHAM, Will	Partner - Gordon Rossi & Boodles - Kathryn Keane	175
YOUNG, Buddy	" " " " Doing MAGNA EDISON Search	176 223
STERN, Si	Stern & Finnegan: Mack Bigi's Attorney interview	227
CALLAN, Gene	Bigi's Accountant WILL CALL ME WEEK of FEB 18	176
RAPHAEL, Ramon	U. of Chicago Bus. School - Finance Prof. GIVES SEMINARS (P. DAVIS)	152
MILLER, Mark	Sr. V.P. Citibank - Handles Chrysler Account (Karl Katz)	156

Sample Entries

Katz, Able, Daley, Keene and Pickham: Just the usual listings for people recently contacted and entered.

Bigi and Young: Two page numbers. The first mark original contacts. The second tag INTERVIEW DE-BRIEFERS. Apparently our persuasive resume arriving at the opportune time melted Mr. Bigi's reticence. After another warm phone conversation we met, and now he's having us meet his lawyer and his accountant.

Stern: No early contact; only an INTERVIEW DE-BRIEFER.

Callan: Here's a networking entry to remember the name and firm of Bigi's accountant, who's supposed to call next week. It's a good example of the rare instance when it pays to enter someone in the current chrono index even before actual contact.

Darwin, Raphael and Miller: Earlier people have become currently important, so they're re-listed here. Now we don't have to scan back 5 pages to find them. That's not a major task, but why not avoid it?

Tips on the System

Last names first...and bold! There are 25 names on a page...100 on four pages...200 on eight. In mere seconds you can run your thumb down the left margin and locate any "McCarthy" or "Davis" you've called in recent weeks and even months.

Latest contacts last. And no entry until you've called! Observe those simple rules and your index will be powerfully ***chronological***. Don't enter anyone until you've at least called and left word. Then every entry will be relevant and in a sequence that orients you quickly. Never will you flub your response to a ringing phone or lose track of anyone you've dealt with thus far.

Index people from all your activities! Your ATTACHE PAGES contain more tools than just NETWORKING CONTACTS pages. Chrono-index *everyone's* page...recruiters' and corporate interviewers' too.

Update continually! Whenever you meet with someone *or* phone—whether you talk *or* leave word, always make a brief note on their NETWORKING CONTACTS entry (see pp. 171 & 173). You won't change your index, of course, if they're already in it, because information on them is still in the same place.

Check before calling! You'll be making too many contacts to remember exactly when you did what with whom. Calling too soon and frequently can make you appear anxious and unbusinesslike. Not following up appropriately can seem inept and disinterested. Timing is important. Here you have the tools to keep your timing perfect with everyone.

Convenience above all! Neatness doesn't count. Scribble. Scratch out. Add marginal notes and reminders. And if someone from long ago becomes important now, don't hesitate to index him or her again.

Blanks and gaps don't matter! Skip ahead or back to reach an empty KEY NETWORKING page. Bypass partly unused NETWORKING pages in order to cluster certain people on a fresh one. Put latest contacts into empty slots on ancient pages. Why not? With chrono-indexing there's no problem.

Mass mailings don't count! If you send out a flood of letters to corporate people and recruiters you don't know, don't clutter this index with their names. Only index the rare few who call you (or who write and you call them).

Move rather than houseclean! When any entry's clogged, start another.

About Computers and Networking

By now you have probably formed your own personal plan as to how far you intend to personalize the record keeping you do with respect to your networking activities. Your approach will depend on your own level of comfort and expertise with computers and on whatever computerized database systems you (1) prefer and (2) currently have available.

Everybody will keep track of their networking contacts differently, depending on their circumstances, expertise, and equipment.

Maybe you'll work entirely on-paper and use only the tools this workbook provides for you.

Perhaps, on the other hand, you'll use highly sophisticated information handling techniques and equipment that are already a dominant factor in your business and personal life.

Or you may use this workbook's handy notation forms in conjunction with your PC, lap top, or hand-held unit...possibly writing down your information as it arises and later inserting it into a more formal structure on your computer whenever you have the time to do so.

No matter how you proceed, the principles we've just covered should be at the core of your strategy. Implementing—or supplementing—it on a computer is easy. Use any database program. Type in all of your information on all of your contacts. Then pull up your data on any person by typing their name, or by choosing to view your entire database either alphabetically or by date...or by any number of further criteria you wish to add to your program. This option is especially appealing if you're a fast and accurate typist. Otherwise, keying all of your data into the computer can be far more work than just relying on the notes you've jotted on your S&Ps.

And me? What do I do? Both at home and in the office I have top-of-the-line-Macintoshes, each with a 21-inch color monitor; also a couple "notebooks." Yet I still scribble on-paper S&Ps when doing my executive recruiting. Why? Am I a Luddite, lazy, or just a lousy typist? Maybe all three. But above all, I hate to spend my time typing up existing data, when I could be making new calls and scribbling new data that bring me closer to the results I seek.

Let Your Computer Help You Find Lost Networking Contacts

You can't network with people you've lost track of. Let your computer help you find them. Your Internet browser is almost certainly Internet Explorer or Netscape Navigator. Both have default search engines that immediately perform any function shown on the browser's home page.

For example, I use Netscape. To look for someone, I click "People Finder." On Internet Explorer, you'll click "White Pages." Now we have an engine ready to search the white page listings of every listed phone in the U.S. and Canada. Just fill in the blanks on the questionnaire.

You may need some creativity and experimentation to find your lost person. For example, confronted by a simple questionnaire, I input the name of my high school classmate Dick Vanner, plus WI, our state in those days. Nothing. Then I try *Richard* Vanner. Bingo!

But when I input Ralph Lauren and NY...nothing. Why? Unlisted residential phone. But then I try the business listings. Bingo! Of course. His name's included in the name of his firm. Might your lost person now be in business as an independent consultant?

You get the idea. There are over 60 pages of very specific information on how to use the Internet in executive-level job-searching and career development in *RITES OF PASSAGE.* Do take advantage of it.

Interview De-Briefers

Clustered behind the GENERAL NETWORKING and KEY NETWORKING pages is an ample supply of INTERVIEW DE-BRIEFERS (which we'll discuss in the next chapter). These 4-page questionnaires are designed to prompt you to write down absolutely everything you learned—or even sensed—during the interview. Fill one in as soon as possible after you talk to each person you meet during a potential employer's interviewing process. Also fill one in immediately after an executive recruiter interviews you for a particular job (but not after a mere "courtesy" interview). List these too (by person's last name) in your chronological index. Here's the top of page 1:

INTERVIEW DE-BRIEFER — ATTACHE PAGE 157

NOTE: THIS COMPREHENSIVE 4-PAGE QUESTIONNAIRE DEBRIEFS YOU AFTER *EMPLOYMENT INTERVIEWS*, NOT CASUAL NETWORKING VISITS. IT PROMPTS YOU TO JOT DOWN EVERYTHING YOU FIND OUT, AND HELPS PREPARE YOU FOR FUTURE SELLING, INQUIRING, NEGOTIATING, AND DECISION-MAKING. IF YOU SOAK UP EVERYTHING YOU LEARN FROM EVERYONE YOU TALK TO WITHIN THE COMPANY (AND PERHAPS CLOSE OUTSIDE OBSERVERS AND FORMER INSIDERS AS WELL), YOU CAN ACCUMULATE TREMENDOUS KNOWLEDGE IN A SITUATION WHERE "KNOWLEDGE IS POWER!" (**FILL OUT AFTERWARD; DON'T REVEAL AT INTERVIEW.**)

Company: ____________________

Person Seen: ____________________

Exact Title (query secretary by phone): ____________________

Date of Meeting: ____________________ **Thank You Sent:** ____________________

Time: ____________________

After each interview, you'll fill out an INTERVIEW DE-BRIEFER (covered in Chapter 5). What did you learn about the company and the job from this person? What "vibes" did you pick up that may, if remembered, help you see how this person perceives—and feels about—the company, the position, and the person to fill it? By fortifying yourself with a clear—and permanent (written)—record of everything you've heard from everyone you've met, you'll seem a lot more impressive than other, less knowledgeable candidates during subsequent rounds of interviews.

Moreover, by rereading your impressions of prior visits, you'll be far more able to spot inconsistent stories, promises, and attitudes that can warn you away from a bad situation which has been shrewdly shrouded in smiles and handshakes.

But for now, the INTERVIEW DE-BRIEFER is just another item to index. Interviews on a particular job may occur at various times. Chrono-index the initial page number of each DE-BRIEFER, and a quick scan will point out all the ones you should study in order to come out ahead in the next—and hopefully final—round of interviews.

An Important New Skill

Sophisticated executive recruiter-style networking, which you track with chronologically indexed "S&Ps" is a universally useful skill. Once you've mastered it, you'll use it whenever you need information and/or cooperation for any purpose...business or personal. The same techniques you're about to use to find employment will be just as powerful in helping you find anyone or anything else you ever need...an ideal subordinate, or a good housepainter, landscaper, personal-fitness trainer, dermatologist, nanny, school, HMO...the possibilities are endless!

To Help With Your

Interviews

Several candidates are seen. Only one is chosen.

That's the nature of interviewing. Our job here is to make sure you survive the weeding out...continually gain strength and stature...and emerge #1 at the end.

You can always say "No" to them. Let's make sure they don't say "No" to you.

Making a Sales Call...and Demonstrating the Product

Face it. When you go to an interview, a ***purchase decision*** is being made. The employer...whether one decision-maker or a group...is seeing you and others to determine who will be acquired and who won't.

Chances are your resume, sent by you or a recruiter, has been read. Now a salesperson is coming in with the actual product. Get ready. The employer won't just look at the paint job and kick the tires. He or she will take a test drive!

You're the salesperson. And you're also the ***product***.

Moreover, because it's an interview...not just a social call...your host has permission to probe deeply. She can ask tougher and more personal questions than she'd ask at any other time. And she can examine your analysis and strategy in solving business problems...yours and hers...far more frankly than she would under any other circumstances.

You've got to be prepared for a really penetrating inquiry, if your interviewer takes that approach. If he doesn't, you've got to reveal yourself to him. And if the interview fails to display your merits, that's your problem, not his.

Ideally, your potential employer will wind up wanting to buy the car...or at least to drive it again, after seeing and trying others. If so, you'll be offered the job...or at least invited back for another round of interviews.

In the end, you may decide that this employer's opportunity is not for you. But what we'll work on here is ***making sure that the employer doesn't conclude you're not for her or him.***

Working Together

I've talked to many outplacement counselors who use *Rites of Passage,* and virtually every one has brought up the interviewing chapter. "If I have to make them read it in my office while I watch," says one woman, "then that's what I do." And several senior executives who've surely interviewed and hired hundreds of people themselves have told me—to my continuing surprise—that they've reread the entire chapter every time they've had an interview.

Why? Usually they say, "I feel more in control." One man I recruited into a big job about 10 years ago, who's been merged out of that and another job since, told me, "After I've reread the chapter I feel I know everything they want me to do wrong, and I just damn well don't do it for them!"

The fact, of course, is that deep down everyone interviewing you—employer or recruiter—wants the opposite. They hope you'll do absolutely everything to their total satisfaction. They want their job filled. Now. By someone they've no qualms about. That's NOT hoping you'll fail. That's wanting you—or at least somebody—to succeed!

On the other hand, if there's anything negative, they're hoping to see it up-front... *before* they hire you, not later.

All of which has to do with how we'll proceed. I'll include every word on interviewing from *Rites*...and keep it in sequence. But since we have the luxury of working together on these large pages, I'll interrupt for comments and tools. You'll note the switch as we go from *Rites'* book-sized type, back to this style. And now to *Rites*:

Bear in mind that you're proving yourself on two levels:

1. **as a *fine person*, and**
2. **as someone obviously *able to do the job*.**

Your behavior and appearance will be scrutinized far more critically when you show up for an interview, than on any ordinary workday in the next ten years.

The person who's thinking of hiring you wants to be sure that you're someone he'll enjoy working with. And also someone who can walk around inside and outside the organization as a favorable reflection on the company and on him. Only if he's satisfied on these "***fine person***" points, will he concern himself with whether he thinks you can handle the job, as indicated by your experience and track record. He's hoping to find you:

Intelligent, and also "street smart," with abundant common sense;

Analytical, logical, goal-oriented, and a planner;

A skilled communicator...good at listening, speaking, and writing;

Unmistakably a leader...but also a "team player," cooperative, and congenial;

Healthful, attractive, and well-groomed;

Tasteful in dress and decorum;

Poised, courteous, and cultured;

Sensitive to the feelings of others...not pushy, pig-headed, or obnoxious;

Honest, loyal, and straightforward;

Politically aware, but not a political operator;

Committed, responsible, and diligent;

Cheerful and optimistic, with a "can-do" attitude;

And overall, an *interesting person*, with curiosity, enthusiasm...and maybe even a sense of humor!

Virtually all of the attributes listed above will help you to do the job, once you land it. And in interviewing to get the job, don't underestimate the seemingly superficial aspects that are more "image" than "essence." Appearance and behavior are first to be noticed. And if they're deficient, you may flunk the "***fine person***" test, even though you score plenty of "but-he-could-probably-do-the-job" points.

That's why I included those tips on "buffing-to-a-rich-luster" at the end of Chapter 14 (of *Rites*). You probably didn't need them. But some readers did. And interviewing is the time of maximum scrutiny, and therefore greatest need. For that reason, this chapter is just as concerned with interviewing behavior as with answering questions. At the end I've even included a "flight plan" for your interview.

But for now, let's forget "image," and go straight to "essence." This is a sales call. And, like any other salesperson, you've got to deliver *enough persuasive information to convince the prospect that your product can* ***do the job***.

Interviewing is a difficult form of selling for two reasons:

1. **It's a "package deal," where the salesperson comes with the product; and**

2. **The customer, not the salesperson, controls the unfolding of the sales presentation.**

Ordinarily a customer can take the product and leave the salesperson. Unfortunately, you're a "package deal." Therefore you must sell with great finesse. Much as you'd like to, you can't just make a well-organized presentation, and afterward deal with questions and objections.

The interview is a unique ritual drama, in which a sales call is played as if it's a social call.

Which it's not. One of the two parties is totally in command. He's the buyer. He's the decision-maker at the end. And he's in charge all along the way. By controlling the use of time and the choice of topic in a Q-and-A format, he determines which features are brought up, and in what order, and how thoroughly or superficially each one is discussed.

And the fact that *your* sociability is part of what's being sold prevents you from saying what a regular salesperson would say:

> "That's a very good question. But *let's hold it* until I've finished explaining how the machine works."
>
> "No, that's really not a problem with this machine. *Ours is the only one* which doesn't have that disadvantage."

Politeness, modesty, loyalty, confidentiality. You must display these and many other attributes, because you're "the product." Unfortunately, having to do so handicaps your sales presentation.

The first principle of interview salesmanship: forgo the monologue ...at the outset, and all the way to the end.

Because the format of the interview is ritualistically conversational, you can't give a too-long answer to any question. You can't sell yourself as socially polished, if you monopolize the conversation.

So don't use any question...no matter how broad...as a springboard for a monologue. Instead, give a concise answer that hits the highlights in clear and specific terms, including numbers ("a little under $25 million in sales and about 150 employees") and approximate dates ("as I recall, that was in late '99").

Don't ever talk longer than one or two minutes. Finished or not, wind up your sentence, shut your mouth, and look at your interviewer to see if she wants more on the same topic...or would rather switch to something else. If she wants elaboration, she'll say so. What's more, she'll point you in the right direction:

> "Interesting, and I certainly agree with your strategy. But when we tried something along those lines, we ran into trouble with the unions. How'd you make out on that score?"

Now you've got her eating out of your hand! How much better than if you'd bored her with a full explanation before "coming up for air."

Learn "newspaper style."
Written and oral, it will make you an outstanding communicator.

...And it's a lifesaver in the interview format.

Do me a favor. Next time you pick up a newspaper, notice the way every item is written:

1. The headline sums up the article.

2. The first paragraph lays out the entire story.

3. The first sentence of every paragraph tells what the whole paragraph is about.

4. And the major facts of every story always come earliest. Lesser, more detailed points come later, and the most trivial are at the end.

There's good reason for this "big-picture"-first format. It allows you, the reader, to get what you want out of the paper very quickly and efficiently. You can stop reading any article after a paragraph or two and still know the gist of the story. And when an article really interests you, you can dig deeper and deeper into the details, by reading further.

See the analogy to what you're trying to achieve in an interview? Just like you reading the paper, your interviewer always has the prerogative to dig deeper, or switch to a different topic. You can drop any article after just a headline or a paragraph. And he can divert you to a different subject, just by asking another question.

Therefore, all of your answers must be organized in "newspaper style." You've got to state your main point in the first sentence or two of each answer. You can't wallow in detail, "setting the stage" for your main point. Because if you do, a new question may cut you off before you *get* to your main point. Then you'll appear petty, illogical, and detail-oriented...even if you're not.

Surprisingly few people...even senior executives...have learned what their newspapers show them every day. Study and master newspaper style. Use it orally and in writing. Every bit of your business communication will improve...not just interviews, but memos and presentations, too.

Make your point...and move on!

Few things will help you more with interviewing than what we'll do now. Let's attack the number-one cause of an unimpressive interview...the difficulty almost everyone has in stating their main thoughts on any subject in just one to two minutes.

Why do we all have the same problem?

Because normally there's no need to be so clear and succinct. But in an interview you can't be sure of getting more than 20 to 40 minutes...*only half for you.* And much of that may be frittered away by an unskilled interviewer. Meanwhile, you want lots of "Q&As" both ways. Ironically, the candidate who covers his or her successes in the first 20 minutes may be given four more hours and offered the job, while someone with a far better record who fails to convey it quickly is ushered out when the big clock chimes.

And the answer?

Newspaper style. You've got to master it!

The whole trick is to start with a quick summary. That becomes the headline and first sentence or two. The whole story is sketched out. From then on, the reader—or interviewer—can dig for details...or move on. Folks who can think and talk like the newspaper are light years ahead in interviews.

With an hour's practice you'll be one of them.

Use a watch or clock with a sweep-second hand, and answer these open-ended questions aloud (there isn't a "yes" or "no" among them). You'll ***never*** *be asked any of these on a job interview, so you won't get emotionally tangled up in having said the right or wrong thing. All you have to do is master a surprisingly simple skill: (1) State a quick summary. (2) Tag on a few details. (3) Shut up! All in less than two minutes. Do that with these questions right now.*

Then, a few times in the next several days, make up your own questions and answer them, maybe while in the shower or driving your car. That's it. Just as in riding a bicycle, you'll develop reflexes. Every question will get a clear, crisp answer conveying the core of what you wanted to say. You'll be "world class" at interviewing, no matter what you're asked.

1. TELL ME ABOUT YOUR COLLEGE YEARS AND WHAT YOU GOT OUT OF THEM.

2. HOW DID YOU GET YOUR SPOUSE TO MARRY YOU?

3. WHAT'S YOUR PHILOSOPHY OF LIFE AND HOW DOES IT DIFFER FROM MOST OTHERS?

4. WHAT THREE CHARACTERISTICS DO YOU LOOK FOR IN A FRIEND...AND WHY?
5. WHAT COULD BE DONE TO IMPROVE SERVICE AT YOUR BANK?
6. HOW DID YOUR TWO FAVORITE TEACHERS OR PROFESSORS HELP YOU MOST?
7. WHY DO YOU EAT OUT AS OFTEN OR AS LITTLE AS YOU DO?
8. WHAT TWO CARS YOU'VE OWNED HAVE BEEN THE BIGGEST HEADACHES?
9. IF YOU HAD TO BE AN ANIMAL IN THE ZOO, WHICH WOULD IT BE AND WHY?
10. IF YOU COULD DO ONE NICE THING FOR 20 STRANGERS, WHAT WOULD IT BE?
11. WHAT HAVE YOU DONE FOR YOUR CHILDREN THAT YOUR PARENTS DIDN'T DO FOR YOU?
12. IF FORCED TO TAKE A GOVERNMENT JOB, WHAT WOULD IT BE AND WHY?
13. HOW COULD THE POSTAL SERVICE BE IMPROVED?
14. EXPLAIN THE TWO THINGS YOU LIKE MOST ABOUT YOUR SPOUSE?
15. WHAT DID YOU LEARN AS A TEENAGER THAT YOU'D LIKE OTHER KIDS TO LEARN?
16. TELL ME THE DISHES YOU PREPARE BEST AND YOUR MAIN COOKING SECRET.
17. WHY DO YOU KEEP RETURNING TO THE RESTAURANT YOU LIKE BEST?
18. WHICH AMERICAN POLITICIAN HAVE YOU RESPECTED MOST AND WHY?
19. TELL ME ABOUT THE TWO HAPPIEST DAYS OF YOUR LIFE.
20. TELL ABOUT ANOTHER HOUSE YOU'D PREFER TO THE ONE YOU HAVE?
21. YOU CAN REVERSE ONE U.S. FOREIGN POLICY MISTAKE. WHICH ONE AND WHY?
22. TELL ME HOW DOING THIS HAS BECOME EASIER THAN WHEN YOU FIRST STARTED?
23. IF MONEY WERE NO OBJECT, HOW WOULD YOU SPEND YOUR NEXT VACATION?
24. YOU MUST PACK A LUNCH YOU'LL EAT FOR THE NEXT 2 YEARS. WHAT IS IT?

Before We Leave "Newspaper Style"...

Just a few words about "newspaper style" and answering—in under two minutes—agonizingly open-ended questions. These days, interviewers are trained to throw you tough ones like you just dealt with...never anything you can just say "yes" or "no" to, and go on to explain.

Why?

Because tossing you complexity reveals how clearly you think...and often that's far more interesting than your actual answer. Also, the pressure may cause you to reveal things you'd hold back otherwise. All true! But, you'll be prepared by what you've just done and a little further practice. If that's their game, you'll blow them away!

Notice this about shaping an instant summary that becomes the headline and lead sentence of your interview answer cum newspaper story. Often you can do what the tabloids do so effectively. Use just one or two words. Or a couple facts. They say it all! Afterward, you can settle into a comfortable groove. Just add details until time is up. Here are a few sample answers to the prior questions:

1. ***"I had lots of fun. But mainly I began thinking more deeply about almost everything.*** Nothing has ever seemed quite as simple since then"...etc.

2. ***"I hugged her and kissed her."*** (Or *him.*) This could be your entire answer. There's nothing wrong with a little humor. And *occasionally* returning a serve with a smash rather than a volley wakes up an interviewer and says "Somebody special is here!" (This is just an example, *not* an interviewing question.)

8. ***"My '82 Mercedes and the MG I had in college"***...followed by an anecdote about each. Whenever you're asked for any specific number of things, it's usually good to begin by listing them. That's an early and complete answer; from then on, you can coast downhill on details until time is up. Handling each item separately is hardly ever as easy.

11. ***"Nothing.*** We didn't have much money, but we did have a loving home. I hope I've given my kids the same sense of security and personal self-worth we all had"...etc., coasting to time.

Thinking of Your Own Practice Questions

My practice questions were purposely ones you'd *never* be asked in a job interview, because I wanted you to think only about technique, not subject matter. But now you've learned the technique. Why not do your in-the-shower-and-car practicing on the sorts of questions you *are* likely to be asked? For example, ask yourself the reason-for-leaving on every job you've had...also your reason for joining, your greatest achievements while there, and so on.

Better still, why not go beyond merely responding to cliché questions you're likely to be asked? Why not take time out now to think specifically about the ideal face-to-face selling presentation you could possibly make for yourself. As *RITES* points out:

Just because you can't deliver a salesman's monologue is no reason not to prepare one.

Analyze your product and your customer's needs, and develop the sales message you *wish* you could deliver in a 15-minute monologue.

Then divide it into brief topical capsules. Believe it or not, almost every interviewer... no matter how inept...will ask questions that allow you to present everything you have clearly in mind.

That's right. The questions you receive *will* relate to what you want to say, if you *know* what you want to say. That's because your interviewer really does want to find out how your background and achievements fit his needs, and how they guarantee you'll perform as well for him as you have for others.

Fundamentally, he wants to hear what you want to communicate. Not necessarily, however, in the order you'd like to present it. And, of course, with more attention devoted to your failures and gaps in background than you'd prefer.

So prepare as if you could deliver a salesperson's monologue. If you've figured out what you should present, then you'll hear it asked for. And when each "appropriate" query comes along, you can drop in the right one- or two-minute capsule. Unprepared, you'd have found those same questions "irrelevant," and "not leading anywhere." But knowing where the conversation *should* be going, you'll more readily see the interviewer's questions as a path to get there.

How often have you been asked a question in an important meeting and given a "so-so" answer, only to realize afterward that you had a perfect opening to say something really favorable? That's an experience we all have almost every day. Prepare yourself. Don't let it happen in a potentially career-making job interview.

So grab your thoughts...and your pen. Imagine the best opportunity any interviewer could ever give you to cover everything you'd most like to communicate. What do you *want* to say? What are your high-priority topics? What do your most important selling points sound like in "newspaper style" under-2-minute "capsules"?

NOTES ON: OVERALL SELLING MESSAGE

WHO ARE YOU AND WHAT'S SPECIAL ABOUT YOU?

INTERVIEWING'S FLEXIBILITY AND CONVERSATIONAL NATURE NOW GIVE YOU FREEDOM TO SAY WHATEVER YOU WISH AND USE FAR MORE WORDS THAN THE RESUME AND COVER LETTER HAVE ALLOWED. NOW YOU'RE FREE TO THINK AND SPEAK IN TERMS OF YOUR FINEST "ABILITIES," "SKILLS," "STRENGTHS," "EXPERTISE." CHARACTERIZE YOUR NATURE AND WHAT'S SPECIAL ABOUT YOU IN ANY WAY YOU WISH. HOWEVER, YOU STILL CAN'T RELY ON FLATTERING SELF-ASSESSMENTS AND ADJECTIVES AS YOUR PROOF.

WRONG FOR EXAMPLE, YOU CANNOT SAY, "I'M AN OUTSTANDING SELECTOR AND DEVELOPER OF PEOPLE, AND I'M ALSO VERY GOOD AT DESIGNING EFFECTIVE ORGANIZATIONAL STRUCTURES, AND..., AND..., AND..., ETC.

RIGHT YOU *CAN* SAY, "I THINK I HAVE A TALENT FOR PICKING AND TRAINING PEOPLE. FOR EXAMPLE, 3 OF THE 7 DIVISION MANAGERS OF THE X COMPANY (YOUR EMPLOYER BEFORE THE MERGER) ARE PEOPLE I RECRUITED INTO OUR SALES FORCE IN THE LATE '90S. AND Y COMPANY, WHICH BOUGHT US AND LET ME GO BECAUSE THEY DIDN'T NEED *TWO* GENERAL MANAGERS, HAS KEPT ALL 5 OF MY REGION MANAGERS AND LET 2 OF THEIR OWN MANAGERS GO."

YOU GET THE IDEA. USE THESE TWO PAGES TO SKETCH OUT WHAT YOU'D LOVE TO CONVEY IN AN INTERVIEW. SUBSEQUENT PAGES PROMPT NOTES FOR 3 CATEGORIES OF "CAPSULES": (1) SPECIAL AREAS OF STRENGTH/ABILITY/ EXPERTISE, (2) KEY JOBS AND THEIR ACHIEVEMENTS, AND (3) COMPETENCIES WITH ILLUSTRATIONS/PROOFS.

NOTES ON: OVERALL SELLING MESSAGE

WHO ARE YOU AND WHAT'S SPECIAL ABOUT YOU?

Interview Performance ***DESIGN*** Sheet

(CAPSULES) STRENGTHS / ABILITIES / EXPERTISE

STRENGTH / ABILITY / EXPERTISE ______________________________

ILLUSTRATIONS / PROOFS

STRENGTH / ABILITY / EXPERTISE ______________________________

ILLUSTRATIONS / PROOFS

STRENGTH / ABILITY / EXPERTISE ______________________________

ILLUSTRATIONS / PROOFS

STRENGTH / ABILITY / EXPERTISE ______________________________

ILLUSTRATIONS / PROOFS

Interview Performance *DESIGN* Sheet

(CAPSULES) STRENGTHS / ABILITIES / EXPERTISE

STRENGTH / ABILITY / EXPERTISE ______________________________

ILLUSTRATIONS / PROOFS

STRENGTH / ABILITY / EXPERTISE ______________________________

ILLUSTRATIONS / PROOFS

And Now a Different Mirror...

Your career is the same. So are your achievements, recognitions, and other measurements.

However, interviews can unfold in any number of ways. Different lines of questioning can trigger your opportunity to display your advantages for the "use" the employer has in mind.

Turn the page and jot down your selling points according to the company at which—and/or the major position/title/time in which—you accomplished them.

Interview Performance ***DESIGN*** Sheet

(CAPSULES) COMPANIES AND / OR MAJOR POSITIONS

COMPANIES AND/OR MAJOR POSITIONS ______________________________

ACHIEVEMENTS / PROOFS

COMPANIES AND/OR MAJOR POSITIONS ______________________________

ACHIEVEMENTS / PROOFS

COMPANIES AND/OR MAJOR POSITIONS ______________________________

ACHIEVEMENTS / PROOFS

COMPANIES AND/OR MAJOR POSITIONS ______________________________

ACHIEVEMENTS / PROOFS

Interview Performance *DESIGN* Sheet

(CAPSULES) COMPANIES AND / OR MAJOR POSITIONS

COMPANIES AND/OR MAJOR POSITIONS ______________________________

ACHIEVEMENTS / PROOFS

COMPANIES AND/OR MAJOR POSITIONS ______________________________

ACHIEVEMENTS / PROOFS

And Yet Another Mirror...

Still the same career, achievements, recognitions, and other measurements.

But one more way of viewing them. This time as the basic requirements of experience and expertise for anyone seeking the position and level you're looking for. The question now is, "Have you touched all the bases?" "Have you got experience in X?"

Turn the page and jot down your selling points according to the basic requirements to be a professional at your level in your field.

Interview Performance ***DESIGN*** Sheet

(CAPSULES) BASIC REQUIRED COMPETENCY

COMPANIES AND/OR MAJOR POSITIONS ____________________

ILLUSTRATIONS / PROOFS

COMPANIES AND/OR MAJOR POSITIONS ____________________

ILLUSTRATIONS / PROOFS

COMPANIES AND/OR MAJOR POSITIONS ____________________

ILLUSTRATIONS / PROOFS

COMPANIES AND/OR MAJOR POSITIONS ____________________

ILLUSTRATIONS / PROOFS

Interview Performance ***DESIGN*** Sheet

(CAPSULES) BASIC REQUIRED COMPETENCY

COMPANIES AND/OR MAJOR POSITIONS ______________________________

ILLUSTRATIONS / PROOFS

COMPANIES AND/OR MAJOR POSITIONS ______________________________

ILLUSTRATIONS / PROOFS

COMPANIES AND/OR MAJOR POSITIONS ______________________________

ILLUSTRATIONS / PROOFS

COMPANIES AND/OR MAJOR POSITIONS ______________________________

ILLUSTRATIONS / PROOFS

So much for looking at various ways of viewing your selling message...and organizing and "capsulizing" it differently according to different approaches that interviewers are likely to take. Your offensive game is in good shape. It's time now to think of defensive strategy. Let's return to *RITES:*

What about questions specifically designed to give you trouble?

The possibilities are endless...too many to discuss. But almost all such zingers aim for a relatively few slips and wrong answers. Those I can identify for you.

As I said before, your interviewer is on your side. She wants to find out that you are the person she's looking for. If so, her staffing problem is solved. But if you're not as good as you appear to be, hiring you could cause far more difficulty than it resolves.

Therefore, she'll ask lots of questions aimed at revealing your flaws. Even your answers to the most bland and casual queries will be scrutinized for damaging admissions. And chances are, those revelations won't have much to do with your resume-stated background. Instead, they'll relate to your personality and your management techniques...the kinds of shortcomings behavioral psychologists probe. So here are some wrong answers to watch out for...both with the employer, and with the company's psychologist, if you consent to meet him:

WRONG ANSWER: There's more bad than good.

Of all the "wrong answers," this one fits more questions than any other. So many, in fact, that I can't even begin to think up enough examples to suggest its vast possibilities. However, the minute you're about to list attributes of anyone, anything, or any situation, be sure to ask yourself:

"How many good ones should I mention and how many bad ones?"

Decide shrewdly. Sometimes there should be lots of bad ones and hardly any good ones, as in the list of probable results you mention when your interviewer gets your reaction to an operating policy that verges on the unethical and illegal.

But suppose he asks how you feel about your current job. Obviously, it fails to utilize your prodigious talents and energy level. But don't slip. There's more good than bad; otherwise, the interviewer will expect you to be malcontent in his job, too. And in describing your current boss, there's probably a lot that's admirable, not just shortcomings; otherwise your interviewer envisions you talking negatively about him. Same with your reaction to the overall management of your current company. Some policies and approaches (which you will list) make lots of sense. However, certain *key* ones have serious disadvantages (obvious to any thinking person, including your interviewer).

Needless to say, you also see far more advantages relative to disadvantages when asked how the job you're interviewing for fits your talents and aspirations, and how you fit the job. Same, too, when it comes to balancing the opportunities in contrast to the obvious problems facing the industry and company you're being interviewed for. Same goes for the U.S. and its industrial and other institutions, and on and on.

You're no Pollyanna. You can see defects and problems, analyze them accurately, and conceive and execute realistic and creative strategies for dealing with them. However, you're absolutely not one of those "nattering nabobs of negativism" Spiro T. Agnew warned us about.

WRONG ANSWER: You'd live your life differently if you could.

This is the wrong answer to all those "if" questions. If you could be anyone other than yourself, who would you be? If you could go back and change an earlier career decision, what would you be doing today? Don't accept any offer to rewrite your personal history. You're basically a happy and highly functional person, who has high self-esteem and is busy producing and enjoying...not fretting and regretting.

Also bear this "wrong answer" in mind when faced with "if" questions about the future. If you can be anything you wish five years from now, it will be something that represents fine progress along the path you're on right now.

With respect to your current and past marriages, outstanding or difficult children, and other highly personal facets of your life, probably the less said the better...at least until you're sure that your values and circumstances clearly correspond to those of your interviewer. You can't possibly gain anything by being either ahead of, or behind, him on these points.

And of course if you're asked whether you "consider yourself successful," the answer is "Yes" and briefly why...not, "Well, sort of, and I'd have been more so, if it weren't for..."

WRONG ANSWERS: Illustrations of your greatest talents and achievements that:

1. don't relate to the job you're interviewing for

and/or

2. happened long ago.

Not surprisingly, your strongest attributes and the achievements you're proudest of are work-related and correlate amazingly well with the requirements of the job you're interviewing for. The fact that, after eighteen years of avid competition, you recently bred, trained, and groomed a Dalmatian that won Best-In-Show at the Grand National Competition of the American Kennel Club is hardly worth mentioning. Especially when compared with the fact that last month your Division's hemorrhoid remedy scored the highest market share in the 64-year history of the brand.

Don't be confused. When asked for your "*best*" achievements, always give your *latest* ones. Only when specifically asked about early phases of your career will you trot out the corresponding long-ago achievements...thus demonstrating that you've always been an overachiever. The greatest days of your career are now and in the future, not in the past.

A variation on this theme has to do with what you *like* most and least in your current job or the one under discussion. Your preferences will match the job you're interviewing for just as neatly as your talents do.

WRONG ANSWERS: You've failed to develop non-business interests.

AND

You spend time on non-business interests.

These wrong answers are bookends; they come as a matched pair. You're apt to be asked what your avocational interests are. Better have some ready to mention. Active sports are always good. Intellectual and artistic interests begin to look fairly respectable when you get comfortably over $100,000...and they take on great luster when you get over $1 million. Charitable and "cause" interests also gain respectability and ultimately cache, as you soar into the corporate stratosphere.

However, until you're being considered for a position high enough to be corporately ornamental as well as useful, don't let on that your wide-ranging interests take any significant amount of time away from work. Chances are your potential boss wants you "hungrier" for corporate performance bonuses than for intellectual and humanitarian nourishment.

By the way, there's a chance you may be asked what interesting books you've read lately. Anyone who asks won't worry about your time, since reading is usually done when and where you can't work. Don't bring up the subject. But do prepare. If you seldom read, you should pick up a critically-praised *non*business volume...perhaps a biography or a spy novel...from the current bestseller list. Comment knowledgeably. And if pressed further, mention a couple other books you'd like to read but haven't had time for. That's enough. You're joining a business, not a literary society.

WRONG ANSWER: Your aspirations for the future don't springboard from the job you're discussing.

"What-would-you-like-to-be-when-you-grow-up?" questions are just a variation of the "if" questions we discussed earlier. Make sure your stated objectives are consistent with getting the job you're interviewing for and pursuing it as whole-heartedly as the company could wish.

WRONG ANSWER: Anything but the frank truth about when and why you're leaving.

If you were FIRED, say so. Reference checking will surely reveal the fact, even if you still have an office and phone message service at your former company. Any attempt at cover-up will seem dishonest, unintelligent, and emotionally immature. Give a short, simple explanation, objectively avoiding bitterness and complaint. Show you can rise above temporary setbacks. Your forthrightness and maturity in comparison with most people, who fidget, fiddle, and fume, will come off favorably. More about this later.

WRONG ANSWER: The too-vague answer.

For every job you've held, know and be able to state without hesitation your title, whom you reported to, what size and type unit you commanded (in people, facilities, budgets, sales, profit, market share, etc). Know too in approximate numbers the size and situation of the overall organization of which your unit was a part. You absolutely must know what you're doing now...and you should also know what you've done in the past.

Remember JFK? Most of the nation became convinced he could cope with our problems...in large part because he could speak about them so succinctly, and yet so specifically in facts and figures. It takes no more time to say "a $110 million division in Akron" than it does to say "a medium-sized division located in the Midwest." Yet the former avoids raising several unnecessary questions in the interviewer's mind:

> "I wonder what she means by 'medium-sized.' "
>
> "*Where* in the Midwest?"
>
> "Why didn't she just give me the specifics? Maybe she's afraid I'll know somebody who was there when she was."

WRONG ANSWER: "Confidentiality prevents me..."

Use common sense when it comes to confidentiality. Don't be a blabbermouth. But if the competitor who's interviewing you frankly discusses his business with you, then reciprocate. Knowing the other person's figures won't make them your figures, and vice versa. If you've been responsible for something very brilliant and very recent, which must be screened from your competitor, just give a definite but nonspecific comparison he's undoubtedly already guessed:

> "With the new line included, sales for the first quarter are more than double what they were in the same period last year. *Much* more than double."

The sparkle in your eyes and your smile of pride and achievement will communicate your accomplishment just as well as if you'd stated the exact figure for the new line standing alone.

Remember: A lot of people who've done a poor job use confidentiality as a cover-up, which is what you'll be suspected of if you "take the Fifth Amendment." People who've done a great job are eager to tell about it.

WRONG ANSWER: More than was asked for.

One rather tricky question is to ask for your "four greatest achievements"...or your "three strongest talents"...or some other number of something favorable. Give exactly the number asked for, *and no more*. The test is to see if you'll plunge right past the requested number, piling on achievement after achievement, in a binge of self-praise. If so, you'll be revealed as a braggart, psychologically suffering from low self-esteem. At the very minimum, you'll seem to be someone who doesn't listen and follow instructions alertly.

WRONG ANSWER: A too-long answer.

This wrong answer is asked for by every agonizingly open-ended question...one of the commonest headaches of the interviewing process. Here the remedy is one of those *capsules* that I suggested you create out of the fifteen-minute salesperson's monologue you're not being allowed to deliver. That highly refined quarter-hour of mandatory product description and product advantages nicely fills anywhere from seven to ten 1½- to 2-minute capsules, which can be administered as requested throughout the interview.

Suppose you're zapped with this frequently thrown open-ender:

> "Tell me about yourself."

Don't be wimpy and grasp for help:

> "Well, what particular aspect would you like to know about?"

Instead, just plunge in and *cope!* Take no more than one to two minutes and hit the highlights, covering everything from childhood to now. Include a few words about where you grew up, because this question is usually asked to evoke a broad-brush personal portrait. To prove it can be done, I'll give you my own:

> "I was born and grew up in Reedsburg, Wisconsin, a small town of 5,000 people, where my father was a partner in the Ford car and tractor business. Worked my way through the University of Wisconsin and the University of Wisconsin Law School as a radio announcer and taught Legal Writing at the Law School for a year. Came to New York City in 1960 as Radio-TV Contract Administrator at J. Walter Thompson Advertising Agency and later became an Account Executive on various consumer products. Joined Bristol-Myers Products in '65 as a Product Manager and ultimately became Director of New Product Marketing. Next I was Director of Marketing for the Sheaffer Pen Company, and then General Manager of the Tetley Tea Division of Squibb-BeechNut. In '71 I got into executive recruiting with Heidrick & Struggles, where I became a Vice President and one of the firm's top producers of fee income. And in 1977 I started The John Lucht Consultancy Inc., specializing in the selection of high-level executives for major corporations...the same firm I operate today.

That's way under two minutes, and yet it certainly covers "Tell me about yourself." If this were an interview, anything else of interest could be asked about.

Capsules: The Interview Pain-Reliever

Gapingly *open-ended questions* are one of the worst headaches of the interviewing process. They're painful as you grope for an answer that's appropriate, clear, and succinct. And if not handled well, they can lead to the serious complication of bogged-down monologuing, which can demonstrate that you're innately a poor communicator, disorganized, less-than-candid...and more. Indeed, open-ended questions are asked, in part, because they *are* troublesome to insecure, fuzzy-thinking people, who don't communicate well under pressure...people the interviewer wants to weed out.

I just administered a capsule for "Tell me about yourself." You may not need yours, but be sure you take it with you to your interview. Indeed, take along plenty of capsules. Like the Lomotil®, Dramamine®, Tetracycline®, Acromycin®, Alka-Seltzer®, and Pepto-Bismol® you take on your foreign travels, you'll feel better knowing they're on hand, whether you wind up using them or not.

Most *RITES* readers I've talked to have found the capsule concept very helpful. Not only did they prepare capsules to show off their achievements, as we've done, they concentrated particular attention on the defensively oriented capsules and the ones on sure-to-be-asked questions. Here in the WORKBOOK we have the luxury of working together in letter-sized pages...and plenty of them. So I've added note-scribbling space after each one that you probably haven't yet dealt with. Please don't pass up this opportunity to polish your responses to these almost inevitable questions. As *RITES* continues:

Your interview pharmacopoeia should include:

A "Tell-Me-About-Yourself" Orientation (CAPSULE)

Already prescribed.

Really work on this, using my example on the opposite page as your model. Until they actually do, most folks don't believe they can sum up their entire lives in less than two minutes. However, if you read my capsule aloud at conversational speed, you'll find it runs closer to one minute than two. You can do just as well, and you're sure to impress any interviewer when you do.

More space for this important work on the next page.

"Tell-me-about-yourself" continued.

Key Segments of Experience and Achievement (CAPSULE)

These are the topically-organized segments of the fifteen-minute "salesperson's monologue" you'd love to deliver but can't in the conversational format of an interview. Have your selling points of experience and achievement clearly in mind, with specific figures stapled into your memory. Nothing minimizes an achievement more than failing to remember precisely what it was. (*Already done pp. 192-197.*)

Achievements in Rank Order (CAPSULE)

This one prepares you for any "Top Three" or "Top Five" question. Since your greatest achievements should also tend to be your most recent, you'll ponder the importance/time tradeoffs in preparing this list. If there's nothing major to report from your most recent briefly held job, don't feel you have to make something up, just to "represent" the ill-fated career move.

Maybe you have one monumentally large achievement sure to command awe and respect...and clearly attributable to your being there as the instigator and not merely one soldier in the platoon; but it happened too long ago to be one of your "latest-and-greatest." Prepare it succinctly, and deliver it *last*...third out of three, or fifth out of five, depending on how many you're asked for.

Try to have something quite recent topping your list—if possible from the past 2 or 3 years—and keep the rest of your main list no more than 8 years old. No interviewer will ask for more than 6 examples at a time, so 8 slots on your "contemporary" list should be plenty. But also have a second list of your 8 "all-time earlier" bests. You can easily "mix-'n-match" according to your quick good judgment in the interview, but plenty of careful thought now **will** *pay dividends.*

Contemporary List

1.
2.
3.
4.
5.
6.
7.
8.

All-time Earlier List

1.
2.
3.
4.
5.
6.
7.
8.

Strengths and Weaknesses (CAPSULE)

Give this one some real thought. Your strengths are at the heart of your sales pitch, and they ought to be the right ones for this job...or you'll be better off not getting it. Be ready to name and...if asked... illustrate several. Include your high energy level.

Come up with a proper "more-good-ones-than-bad-ones" answer; the ratio should be overwhelming ...maybe 4 to 1. But, within the boundaries of enlightened self-interest, also try to be honest. The standard formula for an interview-confessed "weakness" is "*A strength carried to a fault.*"

Examples:

> "Sometimes I may drive my people a little *too* hard. Since I'm a bit of a workaholic, I tend to expect others are, too."
>
> "Sometimes I can be *too* supportive of my people...hanging on to them, still trying to train and coach, when perhaps I should just pull the plug a few months sooner."

And how's this for a reverse-spin on a weakness?

> "I'm the broad overall conceptualist...the strategist, the planner, the schemer...and also the enthusiastic motivator of the team. But I'm not the down-to-the-nitty-gritty implementer. I always make sure to have an operations officer I can absolutely depend on to see that things don't slip between the cracks...and also a meticulous controller, to make sure that there are no financial surprises. Without both of those people doing their jobs, I couldn't do mine."

Obviously, this approach will work only if you're discussing a big job in a big company. But you get the idea and can adapt it to many situations.

*This is an inevitable question..and potentially very troubling in an interview. Give it plenty of time and attention now, and it need never bother you again. Whenever you mention a strength, always parenthetically link it with achievements that illustrate and prove it. Fortunately you did the basic work needed for this on pages 192 and 193. Pick your 6 favorites (preferring ones that your most impressive achievements illustrate). Rank them below in priority order, because they may be requested that way ("**Greatest** Strengths and Weaknesses"). Time you spend on this will pay off splendidly as you interview.*

Strengths

(Ranked from #1 on Down)

1.

2.

3.

4.

5.

6.

Giving serious thought now to your "weaknesses" will pay off just as handsomely. Try to be original. Interviewers are nauseated by the cliché, "Sometimes I work too hard." That just makes you sound slick and conniving and casts doubt on everything else you've said. And pushing ***other*** *people (the* Rites *example on the prior page) is only slightly better. Yet you want to seem cooperative and interested in self-improvement. Maybe you can attack a prejudice saying, "My biggest weakness is a popular misconception that has truth in it, but* NOT IN MY CASE. *Many people think that because I'm from a big company like GM, I'm not..." (see pp. 22-29). In a particular context, you might even stonewall, "After X years of working on them, I think I've pretty much succeeded; here are my references..." Whatever you choose, administer an antidote along with the poison (you've "worked on it for years and now get an occasional compliment"). You don't need many "weaknesses," but please make it or them interesting, not really harmful, and seemingly somewhat spontaneous and honest. Surely you can't fill more than the 3 slots below. Don't neglect the mitigating "spin." Good luck!*

Weaknesses

(With Mitigating "Spin")

1.

(Mitigation)

2.

(Mitigation)

3.

(Mitigation)

Reason for Leaving (CAPSULE)

It's not enough just to avoid the "wrong answer" of saying you quit...or worse yet that you're still doing your job...when everyone who's likely to be asked knows you've been fired. Prepare an accurate capsule on what happened and what your current status is. And *keep it brief and simple!*

If the new CEO brought along his own person for your job, no harm in saying so. Add, if true, that you too might have brought along someone you knew and trusted if you were in the CEO's shoes and had such a limited time to effect such a major turnaround. Indeed, you went out of your way to cooperate with the woman who's now your successor, during those first awkward weeks when you were both on the payroll and she hadn't yet been named to your job. As you see it, what she has to do to be successful is to finish installing this-and-this program which you were putting into place when the upheaval occurred, and she seems to be taking basically that approach (if true).

There wouldn't be room in this entire book for the enormous smorgasbord of familiar firing scenarios ...one of which may have happened to you. A great many, like the one above and all sorts of consolidation and staff-cutting measures, can be frankly stated and endorsed. "Personality clash" with your boss, however, normally should *not* be the diagnosis. Say instead, "Fundamental policy differences," and cite some concrete examples. You simply can't afford to be categorized as someone who can't get along with people.

The trick in discussing firing is to take an open-minded dispassionate, managerial stance. Observe, comment, and react as an informed, objective observer, who's also a very skilled manager...not as someone subjectively involved, wronged, and wounded. You're willing to stand and be judged on the wisdom of your programs and the next administration may have to continue them. On the other hand, if you tried something that failed and you were in the process of changing course, say so. You'll be judged far more on the calibre and comprehension you demonstrate, than on the fact that you were fired. Chances are, your interviewer has also been fired at least once in his or her career.

Really work on this. Try at least three different ways of stating what happened and write them out. Keep crossing out unessential words, until you can read it in about one minute...no more than two. Memorize it. Were you caught in an acquisition, merger, or downsizing? Describe it. Was there a "window of opportunity" on terms the company may not repeat? Mention it fondly, even though you were forced to accept. Were you and your former boss discussing off-and-on for months that you might no longer be needed? Is there a bit of not-unfriendly mutuality that he or she may go along with? The more prepared you are to answer briefly and nondefensively, the better.

1.

2.

3.

Your Management Style (CAPSULE)

For your answer to ring the bells on this issue, you'd better know what style the company feels *it* has. Check in advance and also watch for clues dropped by your interviewer. The "participative" style is currently in vogue, whereby your door is open to your subordinates and their ideas, and you get results through motivation and delegation.

But for some companies you should hedge your bet..."On the other hand, nobody wonders who the boss is or where the buck stops." Other possibilities include: "Problem solving"..."I enjoy analyzing what's wrong, figuring out a solution, and implementing it." And "results-oriented"..."My decisions are highly concerned with how the result will impact the bottom line." You might add, "On the other hand, I also care a lot about my people; training and developing them and seeing they're fairly treated is extremely important." A pragmatic pastiche, plus taking the pulse of your interviewer, will you get you safely past this issue.

The above suggestions are the only way through this wicket. However, here's something you can do to spice up your answer. Talk to a few former colleagues who are also good friends, and collect two or three favorable (and maybe humorous) quotes about your "style." Jot them below, so you won't forget them. They'll lend a refreshing note of believability and charm to a classic question that everyone else always answers in the dullest, safest (and thus least convincing) possible way.

What Appeals to You About Our Job and Our Company? (CAPSULE)

Capsule or no capsule, you absolutely must study the company prior to your interview. Devour its Internet site. Read the last two annual reports and the latest 10-K and proxy statement. If they're not available on the company's Web site, phone the Investor Relations Department and arrange to pick up copies by messenger or have them sent FedEx. Also read the company's latest news releases and up to two years of past releases as archived on the site. Check, too, the latest news summaries on the company put out by *Value Line* and *Standard & Poor* (available at your stock broker's office). Also, what have the major business periodicals have been saying? Check the *Reader's Guide & Index to Periodical Literature* and on-line services such as *Hoover's* and *Dow Jones Information Service*.

Knowing what's going on at the company not only helps you prepare an answer to the cliché question of what you like about the company; it also gets you thinking on your interviewer's wavelength long before you're in his or her office and on the spot.

This question is inevitable at every company you meet. The trick is not to be strictly self-centered. Talk first about the bright future the ***company*** *has, and only afterward nail the more selfish advantages. You want your future to be with a winner and you believe they* ***are*** *a winner. Be prepared to voice the following sorts of issues (and try to think of others), not just the short commute, and the stock options that will soar as soon as the IPO is cleared: Examples:*

Great Company

Strong present. *What are the specific strengths of the current business?*

Bright future. *What trends favor the company? Today? And potentially later on?*

Prestigious past. *Is there a reputation for quality? Strong customer base to build on?*

Financial solidity. *Good cash flow? New strength/expertise from a new corporate parent?*

Promising new products. *Which have you heard of? Ask if more are on the way.*

Fine corporate values. *Any enlightened HR policies? Commendable civic activities?*

Fine people. *Respect the ones you've met? Detect their enthusiasm? Contagious?*

Great Opportunity

Ideal use of your training and skills. *Nothing wasted?*

Professional growth and development. *Logical next step along career path?*

Opportune timing. *Turn-around? Imminent IPO? (Money angle is company's AND yours.)*

Apparent opportunity for future promotions.

Entry into new field you've wanted to get into. *Why?*

Fine location. *Great city/climate, fine education/culture/recreation for your FAMILY and you.*

Not *To Be Cited*

Liberal vacations, company car, medical (unless none up to now), retirement, etc.

Current Status and Long-Range Trends of Your Speciality and the Overall Industry (CAPSULE)

If you know anything at all about your present field, you certainly have some good ideas on where the action is now and where the future may lead. Marshal them. Don't just pull them together on the way *home* from an interview where the CEO of a conglomerate had more thought-provoking insights into your specialty than you did.

Here's your opportunity to shine...or "fade to black," as they say in the television industry. What are the most important waves of change sweeping over your field today. Any glimmers of potential new trends on the horizon? Is there any likely conversation topic in your field on which you're less than up-to-the-minute? Marshal your thoughts here. Jot down the major themes you know "cold" and want to remember. Jot down the others you need to investigate. Don't expect to win any job you interview for, unless you're #1 among all the candidates in this area.

What Would You Like To Know About Us? (CAPSULE)

The easiest or the hardest of questions. Ironically, the more you want the job, the tougher the question is. If you're skeptical about whether the job will advance your career, you're loaded with questions that have to be resolved to your satisfaction.

But suppose you're thrilled to be considered for the job. It's with an impeccable company, and represents a career breakthrough in responsibility. Then what do you ask? Certainly not about benefits and retirement. Maybe about what they see as the key problems and opportunities to be addressed by the person who gets the job, willingness to invest in the business, and whether it's central to the company's future growth or a candidate for "harvest" and possible divestment. But be careful. Shouldn't you *know* what the problems and opportunities are? Check for a *common view* of such issues; but don't imply you can't see without being told, what some of the key ones probably are.

The invitation to ask questions is inevitable. Be prepared for it.

This question requires great subtlety, but it can be very useful. Here's your "mopping-up" opportunity. What do you wish had been brought out, but wasn't? You can't say, "You should have asked about my international work." You CAN *say, "What's your international setup? I've had lots of success in that area." Don't ask about retirement and vacations. But do ask how they recognize and reward superior performance, pointing out you've usually made maximum bonus. Grab your pen. Jot down questions that aren't obnoxious, self-centered, greedy, or threatening (not easy!) and demonstrate your self confidence. They're a tactful* SALES MESSAGE! *You expect to perform exceedingly well, and would like to know how their top performers are measured and move up.*

Reading...and Writing...Between the Lines

You know darn well that your interviewer will be trying to "read between the lines" of your answers... looking for accidental unspoken nuances that may be even more revealing than your carefully worded statements.

So, since he's *reading*, you may as well make sure you're *writing*.

For example, when you're asked about your creativity, give some instances where you thought up a great idea that worked out well. But also give some samples of outstanding creativity within the unit you're responsible for, but which you personally did *not* think up. Give credit to the lower-echelon research subordinate whose "far-out" idea you backed with some money from your "Venture Fund," and to your CEO whose unpopular idea worked out sensationally well after you and your subordinates removed the kinks from it, and to the advertising agency that came up with the winning campaign after you asked them to give it "just one last try."

Incidentally, that until-recently junior scientist now has her own sizable section of the laboratory to run. And, far from being fired, you were able to help that ad agency win a client relationship with another division of the conglomerate you work for.

We see, of course, that you're creative. But we also read what you've written between the lines. You care about, and listen to, what others around you are thinking...*even your boss*! With you in charge, the company isn't limited to your own personal creativity. You recognize anyone's good idea when you see it. Moreover, you probably get along well with others, commanding their respect and loyalty, because you reward them for a job well done.

You get the idea. When answering questions about talents and triumphs, you have a perfect opportunity to write between-the-lines messages about your other fine characteristics and management techniques.

The "Pregnant Pause"...and How to Deal with It

The "pregnant pause" is a gimmick some interviewers use to unnerve candidates, and to force them to reveal personal insecurity, and hopefully to voice unguarded statements.

Here's how it works. After you've finished answering her question, the interviewer says absolutely nothing to move her side of the conversation forward. Dead silence. No question, no comment. She just looks you in the eye, waiting for you to panic and rush in to fill the awkward pause.

This startling stoppage may come at random...or possibly when the interviewer suspects, or wants you to *worry* that she suspects, that you're not telling the truth, or at least not the whole story. One recruiter I know loves this gimmick so much, he tries to use it on his co-workers at lunch.

The only way to deal with this behavior is to nip it in the bud. The first time your interviewer breaks the rhythm of the conversation this way, pause with him long enough to make absolutely sure he's "pregnant pausing" and to make sure he knows that *you* know that's what he's doing...maybe 20 seconds or more. Then say, kindly and helpfully, as if perhaps he seems to have lost track of the rather complex discussion you've been having:

> "Is there anything else you'd like to know about...(the question you just finished answering)?"

Treating the pregnant pause as a case of Alzheimer's Disease is the only way to deal with it. If you knuckle under to even one "cross-examination by silence," you'll signify that you're the insecure sort of person who submits to interrogation in this arch, smug fashion. If so, you're in for a tense, defensive interview. On the other hand, by kindly and inoffensively calling the interviewer's bluff, you create unspoken recognition and respect. If, by chance, your interviewer decides to try again, repeat the treatment.

Coping with the "Stress Interview"

Let's hope you never run into it, but there was a fad many years ago, which still hasn't completely died out, of giving a "stress interview." Pioneered by an executive recruiter who'd been a prisoner in one of the Nazi death camps, the idea was to discover what he called the "counterfeit executive"...the one who can't take pressure...by applying great pressure and tension during the interview. Seat the candidate with the sun in his eyes, hide the ashtrays (a lot more people smoked in those days), quickly interrupt his answers, telling him he obviously didn't understand the question, "pregnant pause," imply knowledge of information contrary to his statements. The possibilities for rude, challenging, inhospitable behavior are endless.

You'll almost certainly never get the full treatment. Even the guy who invented the process quit operating that way after achieving a few years of notoriety for inventing the concept. But you may run into someone who kicks off the interview by throwing down the gauntlet:

> "I can't see how you're qualified for this job!"

He goes on from there with argumentative, demeaning, and perhaps embarrassingly personal questions. Maybe he deliberately misinterprets your answers. And probably he avoids looking at you...gazing over your head, thumbing through his calendar, and shuffling papers. You're getting an up-dated version of the stress interview.

What to do? You have to call his bluff. That may be all he wants. Say:

> "I'd appreciate it if you'd look at me when I'm talking to you. If we can get this conversation on a more cordial basis, we'll communicate much better."

Maybe just saying something like that will pass his "test." If not, I suggest you get up to leave, turning back as you get to the door:

> "I'd still be willing to have a good conversation with you, but this session doesn't really seem worthwhile."

Chances are, he'll call you back, say you passed his "test," and continue the interview on a new and more cordial footing. By then, however, you wonder whether you should even consider working for this guy or the company he represents. So do I.

Who's in Charge of the Interview ...You or the Interviewer?

No question who's responsible for the outcome of the interview. You are. You've got to get your message across. If your appropriateness, your ability, and what a fine person you are fail to register, it's your loss. And it's your fault, not the interviewer's.

But who's *in charge*? Now that's a different question. Believe it or not, some people think that you should take charge. Go in, say "Hello," and see if the interviewer asks the questions that draw out the information you want to convey. If not, begin answering different questions from the ones she asks, and twist and lengthen your answers to make sure you cover all the important points that support your candidacy. Be poised and pleasant, but don't be afraid to demonstrate aggressiveness and leadership... crucial qualities in an executive.

If you're interviewing for Vice President - Marketing of a company that sells vacuum cleaners door-to-door, that's probably good advice. Barge in and take over. But for any other job, in my opinion, a much more polite and sensitive approach is absolutely mandatory.

First of all, you're selling yourself as a "***fine person***"...polite, socially poised, and someone who, if hired, will wear well as a coworker over the years. Somehow, the pushy vacuum cleaner salesperson doesn't fit that description.

Secondly, and equally important, if you try to take charge and control what information is covered, you may *not* convey what your interviewer wants to know. You may bore her with a persuasive pitch on points she was willing to concede...meanwhile, failing to address the doubts and concerns you would have discovered if you'd sensitively followed her lead.

Moreover, since the interview is a *demonstration* of how you think and operate, there's a good chance your interviewer may conclude that you're a "hip-shooter"...a superficial thinker, who plunges ahead before gathering information and checking pre-conceived assumptions. After all, that's the way you behaved in your interview.

Therefore, all things considered, *don't try to grab control*. In terms of personal image, you can't afford to dominate the interview. And in terms of accomplishing your objectives, you don't really want to.

Steering the Interview with Questions and "Red-Flagged" Answers

Only your own good judgment during the actual interview can determine to what extent you can and should try to influence the direction it takes.

If you're willing to become overtly pushy and aggressive, you can cover whatever you wish. But if you want to stay within the ritual boundaries of a social conversation in which the employer has the prerogative of asking most of the questions, there are really only two techniques by which you can gently guide him toward matters you'd like covered.

Questions

You can always ask a question to see if he's interested in a subject you want to talk about:

> "Is the development and marketing of internally generated new products a major factor in your growth plans? That's an area where I've had a lot of successful experience."

Nothing impolite or too pushy about that approach.

He may say:

> "Absolutely! Tell me about it."

Or he may say:

> "We're not entirely opposed to internally generated new products. But over the years we've become skeptical. We find we get a lot more for our money by acquiring under-developed products someone else has pioneered. Have you ever tried that approach?"

Well, now you know where he stands. Maybe you've also got success stories of the type he's more interested in. In any event, you didn't waste time and suggest future philosophical differences by giving a long recitation of exploits he's not looking for.

Red-Flagged Answers

Sometimes you can wave a red flag at the bull and he'll run for it... sometimes not. Even professional TV interviewers are often unbelievably nearsighted. The famous actress winds up her answer:

> "Of course, that was back when I was still stealing cars for a living..."

And the oblivious interviewer moves right along with:

> "Tell me...looking back on all the films you've made...which hairdresser has influenced you most?"

Nonetheless, a valuable technique for attempting to steer an interview along more promising lines is to wind up an answer with a provocative statement that cries out for a follow-up question, if the interviewer is interested:

> "...which is why, of course, I then completely changed our approach to incentive compensation."

Your interviewer ought to be tempted to ask what kinds of changes you made and what resulted. But if she's not, at least you haven't been rude or boring, and you haven't wasted time on a topic she's apparently not interested in. The bull doesn't always run after the red flag.

And that's it. Questions and flagged answers are the two polite ways you can attempt to steer an interview toward topics you'd like to discuss. The advantage of both is that they merely suggest...they don't force...a change of direction. They both leave control of the interview in the hands of the interviewer, which is what you will normally want anyway.

QUESTIONS AND RED-FLAGGED ANSWERS

PRACTICE IN POLITELY STEERING AN INTERVIEW

Here's your chance to become really good at steering an interview...or any other conversation you don't control and are too fine a person to dominate. Pick up your pen. Get proficient in using QUESTIONS and RED-FLAGGED ANSWERS to swing any discourse the way you want it to go.

You're preparing for important conversations right now. So use your Achievements in Rank Order from page 205 as the subjects you're turning attention toward...the 8 Achievements from your Contemporary List and the 8 from your All-time Earlier List.

For convenience as you use this tool, each slot employs the same lead-in words for every question and for every red-flagged answer. Others, of course, are possible and you'll soon be thinking of lots of them.

*But now, for **QUESTIONS**, it's **ARE YOU / DO YOU**... For example, "**ARE YOU** planning to increase your international business? I've had a lot of success overseas." Or, "**DO YOU** see Eastern Europe as a market for your new lines? I've just come back from Prague, where I did some consulting for their second-largest bank."*

*For **RED-FLAGGED ANSWERS**, it's **WHICH IS WHY**... As corresponding examples: "**WHICH IS WHY** I then shifted our investments overseas, where I was able to earn twice as... Or, "**WHICH IS WHY** when I was in Prague last month doing some consulting for their second-largest bank I also..." And on and on. "**WHICH IS WHY** we won several President's Cups while I..." "**WHICH IS WHY** I've often been chosen for interdepartmental task forces..." "**WHICH IS WHY** I increased spending on..." "**WHICH IS WHY** we've added training seminars to...*

You get the idea.

The direct question should turn things your way if there's any interest at all. If not, that's essential to know too. Even the more subtle "which-is-why" virtually forces your interviewer to ask a follow-up question along the lines you've indicated. If he or she doesn't, that's virtually an unequivocal statement of "no interest."

ACHIEVEMENT 1. ____________________

QUESTION: ARE YOU / DO YOU ____________________

____

FLAGGED ANSWER: WHICH IS WHY ____________________

____

ACHIEVEMENT 2. ______________________________

QUESTION: ARE YOU / DO YOU ______________________________

____

FLAGGED ANSWER: WHICH IS WHY ______________________________

____

ACHIEVEMENT 3. ______________________________

QUESTION: ARE YOU / DO YOU ______________________________

____

FLAGGED ANSWER: WHICH IS WHY ______________________________

____

ACHIEVEMENT 4. ______________________________

QUESTION: ARE YOU / DO YOU ______________________________

____

FLAGGED ANSWER: WHICH IS WHY ______________________________

____

ACHIEVEMENT 5. ______________________________

QUESTION: ARE YOU / DO YOU ______________________________

____

FLAGGED ANSWER: WHICH IS WHY ______________________________

____

ACHIEVEMENT 6. ______________________________

QUESTION: ARE YOU / DO YOU ______________________________

____

FLAGGED ANSWER: WHICH IS WHY ______________________________

____

ACHIEVEMENT 7. ______________________

QUESTION: ARE YOU / DO YOU ______________________

____

FLAGGED ANSWER: WHICH IS WHY ______________________

____

ACHIEVEMENT 8. ______________________

QUESTION: ARE YOU / DO YOU ______________________

____

FLAGGED ANSWER: WHICH IS WHY ______________________

____

ACHIEVEMENT 9. ______________________

QUESTION: ARE YOU / DO YOU ______________________

____

FLAGGED ANSWER: WHICH IS WHY ______________________

____

ACHIEVEMENT 10. ______________________

QUESTION: ARE YOU / DO YOU ______________________

____

FLAGGED ANSWER: WHICH IS WHY ______________________

____

ACHIEVEMENT 11. ______________________

QUESTION: ARE YOU / DO YOU ______________________

____

FLAGGED ANSWER: WHICH IS WHY ______________________

____

ACHIEVEMENT 12. ______________________

QUESTION: ARE YOU / DO YOU ______________________

____

FLAGGED ANSWER: WHICH IS WHY ______________________

____

ACHIEVEMENT 13. ______________________

QUESTION: ARE YOU / DO YOU ______________________

____

FLAGGED ANSWER: WHICH IS WHY ______________________

____

ACHIEVEMENT 14. ______________________

QUESTION: ARE YOU / DO YOU ______________________

____

FLAGGED ANSWER: WHICH IS WHY ______________________

____

ACHIEVEMENT 15. ______________________

QUESTION: ARE YOU / DO YOU ______________________

____

FLAGGED ANSWER: WHICH IS WHY ______________________

____

ACHIEVEMENT 16. ______________________

QUESTION: ARE YOU / DO YOU ______________________

____

FLAGGED ANSWER: WHICH IS WHY ______________________

____

What have we been doing?

Believe it or not, most of what we've worked on in this chapter so far has been to hand you just two main keys to interviewing success:

Brevity and <Advance Knowledge>

Remember the main point *Rites* makes about interviewing: You must prove yourself on two criteria: (1) as a ***fine person*** (2) who can ***do the job***. If you fail either test, you're out.

Brevity is Power

Brevity is absolutely essential to success in the "***fine person***" department, because the interview, while truly a selling situation is treated as a social one. You can't possibly emerge as "the sort of *person* we like" if you dominate the conversation. You can't be the pushy salesperson, steering the conversation, interrupting, and prolonging your answers until each sales point is fully registered.

Brevity comes to the rescue. Your short fact-packed answers don't grab control for more than a couple minutes at a time. "Fine person" is preserved. Also, short answers leave you time while it's still your "turn," to ask questions that (1) demonstrate your knowledge of the employer's business and the work to be done, (2) expand that knowledge, so that you can stress how perfectly you'd fit, and (3) help you steer the conversation, even though you don't—and don't *want* to—control it.

Moreover, short fact-packed newspaper-style answers do something else that's quite wonderful. They show how you *think*...clearly, logically, succinctly. And, by implication, what smart and effective work you'd do. And, too, what a pleasure it would be to have you as a subordinate, because it would always be quick and easy to find out from you the status of whatever you were responsible for.

Advance Knowledge is Power

Knowing what's coming is always a huge advantage. Then the right preparation usually yields victory. And by now, you're well armed. You've studied yourself and your career, and you've polished your selling message.

You also know the interviewing process. You know in detail what will happen...and how to turn those events to your advantage.

Here, as we begin to wind up our work on interviewing, is the last and most vital area of reconnaissance. What is the employer looking for? What's wanted? What's needed? Those may be different things!

Get ready to meet the employer...and score points!

Clearly the more you know ahead of time about the company, its markets, its problems and opportunities, its competitors, and its internal situation, the better (1) you can focus your answers to prove that you—of all the candidates—are most appropriate. And (2) you can ask questions that (a) demonstrate you're an alert, thorough person and (b) help you grasp the company's current key issues. That's especially vital if you're from outside the industry and may seem a "long shot."

Here's the reconnaissance you'll want and suggestions on the easiest ways to get it:

Annual Report, 10-K, Proxy Statement. *Also, any relevant* ***Product Literature.*** If a retainer recruiter is involved, he or she will volunteer these, usually leaving out the Proxy. If you're on your own, the company's Web site may provide what you need. Otherwise phone Shareholder Relations (which does *not* discuss inquiries with anyone you'll meet) as described on page 210. Do get the "Proxy / Notice of Annual Meeting," a thin booklet that profiles the Directors and the compensation (including option and incentive plans) they and the top people in the company receive. Phone for product literature from the Marketing Departments of the appropriate divisions. If you may bump into their people on interviews, have someone else order.

The Job Specifications. The executive recruiter, if one is involved, will have these and should share them with you. Ask, if they're not volunteered.

Directories and Industry Reference Books. The most comprehensive listing of these books is in your hands. Flip to page 257.

Value Line Sheet; *also* ***brokerage write-ups*** *and recent* ***articles in periodicals***. When it's the overall company and not just a division you're interested in, Value Line gives lots of quite up-to-date information on a single page. Your broker will supply it. Your local librarian can point you toward articles in major media. Use the phone to penetrate a more obscure trade publication. Ask for its librarian, or the editor covering a certain industry and find out what they've published lately on your target company and industry; also how you can get a copy.

What are knowledgeable people on the outside saying? Network your way to well-informed people in major competitive companies to find out the strengths, weaknesses, problems, opportunities, trends, and reputation of the firm you're seeing. Don't reveal there's a job opening and you're in contention (why stir up competition?); merely ask about *all* the major players, including your target. Learn lots; reveal little.

What are folks inside the company saying? This is more ticklish to explore. But as you network to get general information on the industry, somebody may mention rumors they've heard from within the company. Perhaps they'll even mention someone who's recently left, and give you permission to call him or her as a further source *on the industry*. Stay away, if there's any chance the person will realize you're interviewing at his or her former company. The wires will burn with the speed that information flashes back!

What have you found out at prior interviews? Here the WORKBOOK provides a powerful tool, the ***Interview Debriefing Form***, which will put you way ahead in the game. It helps you remember and use every clue you get from everyone you meet at every stage...from the headhunter's first phone call and interview, through all your sessions at the company. Before each new encounter, restudy everything you found out earlier. Other finalists won't be doing this. So, with a little work and luck, you'll seem by far the best prepared and the *smartest* participant in the selection process...the one who clearly remembers prior conversations and best understands the issues the company faces and what it intends to do about them.

And in *Certain Situations...* A Surprising Last-Minute Source of Information: Your Interviewer as the Interview Begins

Consider this strategy when your first contact with any company is a screening interview in their HR Department. Probably their on-staff recruiter has found you by running an advertisement or by placing multiple listings with *contingency* recruiters.

If so, you (and your competitors) usually won't be armed with all the nuances a *retainer* recruiter would have found out and told you. Rather than fly "blind" through the interview, here's a maneuver you can try. It's very hazardous and must be executed with great sensitivity. But it may alter the outcome of a screening interview. Ask right at the outset—very subtly and politely—something like this:

> "It's a pleasure to meet you, and I appreciate your inviting me in. I've admired the Jones Company for years. As we begin, if you don't mind, I'd really appreciate it if you might let me have just a little background on what you're hoping to accomplish in filling this position. That way I can focus on what I've done that you may need, and try to help you see if I might fit."

See the danger?

Every interviewer—whether Personnel Specialist or CEO—is in charge and doesn't want you barging in and taking over. (The "*fine person*" issue.) But if your inquiry can be so friendly, helpful and unthreatening as to to do no damage on that score, and if he or she responds with the lowdown on what's sought and why, then you can "spin" your answers in the proper direction. That might get you marked "the background we're looking for," when you'd otherwise have been labeled "not quite right."

If, on the other hand, a *retainer* recruiter has sent you, he or she knows the nuances and has briefed you and the other candidates. In that case, ***forget this gambit!*** It could make you seem less intelligent and confident than the candidates who walk in and proceed straightforwardly. Also be far, ***far!*** more cautious if you've gotten straight to a decision-maker, rather than a screener in the HR Department.

Seeking Information as a Way of Selling: the *"Consultative Sale"* and *"Where Does it Hurt?"*

These are methods I as a retainer executive recruiter and other types of management consultants are always taught in "New Business" seminars at our national conventions.

We're often asked to compete against other firms by potential clients who want to meet and choose among several recruiters. The trainers tell us, "When that happens, use the ***"Consultative Sale"*** technique. "Do *not* push competitive superiority. Instead, *ask lots of penetrating questions.* They will show you know the client's problems and how to find the ideal person to solve them. *Demonstrate* you're best; don't *merely claim* you are."

Armed with the advance information you'll have assembled, you can do the same thing. Ask the decision-maker lots of questions. Show you're well-acquainted with the field, you listen well, you care about what you're hearing, and you would probably soon (but don't hazard them yet!) be coming up with very constructive suggestions.

"Where does it hurt?" is the classic approach used successfully forever by all kinds of consultants (and others in the oldest profession) and should work very well for you too. It's similar to the "Consultative Sale" without the high-priced buzz word. Just keep asking surprisingly prescient questions about possible corporate ills and opportunities for improvement (symptoms already indicated by advance knowledge). Spice up your questioning with examples of how you've cured similar diseases in the past. Your skillful bedside manner may get you appointed attending physician.

THE INTERVIEW DE-BRIEFER

TURN THE PAGE FOR A POWERFUL TOOL. COPIES ARE ON ATTACHE PAGES 173-258 AT THE BACK OF THIS WORKBOOK. DE-BRIEF WITH THEM AS SOON AS YOU'RE ALONE AFTER EACH JOB INTERVIEW...WHETHER YOU'VE MET A RECRUITER OR AN EMPLOYER DECISION-MAKER.

MUCH INFORMATION IS IMPARTED DURING AN INTERVIEW THAT THE SPEAKER WILL NOT REMEMBER PROVIDING DAYS, OR EVEN HOURS, LATER. BY PROMPTLY USING THIS COMPREHENSIVE 4-PAGE QUESTIONNAIRE TO PROBE YOUR MEMORY, YOU CAN PRESERVE FOR FUTURE STUDY VIRTUALLY EVERYTHING YOU FIND OUT FROM EVERYONE YOU MEET.

IN EACH SUBSEQUENT INTERVIEW YOU'LL BE SAYING FAR MORE OF WHAT THE EMPLOYER WANTS TO HEAR THAN ANY OF THE OTHER CANDIDATES PARTICIPATING IN THE PROCESS. UNLESS THEY'RE DOING EXACTLY WHAT YOU'RE DOING, THEY CAN'T POSSIBLY ACHIEVE YOUR IMPRESSIVE KNOWLEDGE OF THE EMPLOYER'S BUSINESS, MARKETPLACE, PROBLEMS, OPPORTUNITIES, STRATEGIES, AND THE CIRCUMSTANCES, OBJECTIVES AND INTENTIONS SURROUNDING THE POSITION TO BE FILLED.

BEYOND YOUR OBVIOUS EDGE IN COMPETING FOR THE POSITION, YOU'LL ALSO BE FIGURING OUT ITS POLITICAL CONTEXT, AS YOU TALK TO THE EMPLOYER'S MANAGEMENT TEAM. THEREFORE, YOUR DE-BRIEFERS MAY EVEN WARN YOU AWAY FROM A BAD SITUATION YOU'D NEVER HAVE IDENTIFIED OTHERWISE.

READ THIS TOOL CAREFULLY. SEE HOW VERY VALUABLE IT WILL BE.

INTERVIEW DE-BRIEFER

NOTE: THIS COMPREHENSIVE 4-PAGE QUESTIONNAIRE DEBRIEFS YOU AFTER *EMPLOYMENT INTERVIEWS*, NOT CASUAL NETWORKING VISITS. IT PROMPTS YOU TO JOT DOWN EVERYTHING YOU FIND OUT, AND HELPS PREPARE YOU FOR FUTURE SELLING, INQUIRING, NEGOTIATING, AND DECISION-MAKING. IF YOU SOAK UP EVERYTHING YOU LEARN FROM EVERYONE YOU TALK TO WITHIN THE COMPANY (AND PERHAPS CLOSE OUTSIDE OBSERVERS AND FORMER INSIDERS AS WELL), YOU CAN ACCUMULATE TREMENDOUS KNOWLEDGE IN A SITUATION WHERE "KNOWLEDGE IS POWER!" (**FILL OUT AFTERWARD; DON'T REVEAL AT INTERVIEW.**)

Company: ____________________

Person Seen: ____________________

Exact Title (query secretary by phone): ____________________

Date of Meeting: ____________________ **Thank You Sent:** ____________________

Time: ____________________

Place: ____________________

Address & Phone: **OFFICE** **HOME**

OFFICE	HOME
____________________	____________________
____________________	____________________
____________________	____________________
____________________	____________________
( )__________ Switchboard	( )__________ Home Office
( )__________ Private	( )__________ Home Fax
( )__________ Fax	( )__________ Family Phone
( )__________ Fax (Secure)	( )__________ Vacation Home
( )__________ Secy./Asst.	( )__________ Home Office
E-mail__________	Personal E-mail__________

Assistant(s) / **Secretary**(ies): __________ __________ __________

Spouse (if met or mentioned): __________ **Children** (if met): __________

Introduced by: __________ (of what company?) __________

Introducer's Relationship: ____________________

Interviewer Reports to: ____________________

Interviewer's Subordinates: ____________________

____

____

Interviewer's Identifying Appearance: ____________________

____

Interviewer's Manner / Rapport / Possible Subjective Agenda: ____________________

____

____

____

____

INTERVIEW DE-BRIEFER

(Continued, page 2 of 4)

Seemed to Like about Me / Sold on: ____________________

Seemed *Not* to Like / Doubted: ____________________

Hobbies / Interests / Family / Personal Concerns and Social Causes (Don't voluntarily enter hazardous territory, but don't forget anything you happen to learn)**:** ____________________

About the Job:

Company or Business Unit (Name / Description / Location / Annual Sales / No. of Employees / Product Lines / Market Shares, etc.)**:** ____________________

Title: ____________________

Position reports to: ____________________

Subordinates reporting to this position:

	Title	# Subordinates	Doing What	$ Volume / Product Lines
1				
2				
3				
4				
5				
6				
7				
8				
9				
10				
11				
12				

INTERVIEW DE-BRIEFER

Position being re-filled? Newly created? ______

What happened to the incumbent? ______

Are there inside candidates? ______ **Their positions/names:** ______

What abilities and experience are lacking among insiders that cause outsiders to be considered? ______

What are the #1 and #2 make-or-break skills or talents on which success in the job depends? ______

What are the #1 and #2 make-or-break achievements the person is expected to accomplish? ______

On what timetable? ______

With what resources? ______

What is the likely scenario for advancement? ______

What are the company's overall long-range and near-term strategies? ______

What are the long-range and near-term strategies for the particular division, business unit, department or function? ______

Is this the kind of place I'd like to work? ______ **Positive indications:** ______

Negative Indications: ______

Are their business ethics and human values consistent with mine? ______ **Specific matches and mismatches:** ______

What is the corporate culture? ______

Will I enjoy it? Fit in? ______

INTERVIEW DE-BRIEFER

Any discussion or clues with respect to money for this job? For other jobs in the company (a clue for later bargaining)**? Base? Bonus? Stock options, grants, etc? Perks and benefits** (don't inquire until job is landed and other particulars are nailed down)**?**

Will there be an Employment Contract? A *multi-year* contract? An 18-month (or other) **termination arrangement** (see Chapter 16 of *Rites*)**? Or will an Offer Letter incorporate basic understandings** (don't go ahead without it)**?**

What particulars that should be in a Contract or Offer Letter were covered in this meeting, i.e., responsibility, reporting relationship, location, title, compensation, employment security? What key items haven't been covered?

Anything else I learned at this meeting?

How & When To Use

Use DE-BRIEFERS only for serious employment interviews, not for casual networking visits or recruiter get-acquainted sessions.

Use a separate form for each member of the employer's management team you meet; also the recruiter who contacts and introduces you.

For major players—your potential boss, the CEO, etc.—you may need a separate one for each meeting. For the recruiter and other secondary players, you'll merely add new information from later contacts to that person's original DE-BRIEFER.

You'll find an ample supply beginning at ATTACHE PAGE 173.

Should they be outlawed?

An executive who filled out INTERVIEW DE-BRIEFERS after each of his interviews in becoming President of a division of a big consumer products company told me:

> "John, those interview DE-BRIEFERS should be outlawed! They're lethal weapons! I figure I spent at least 35 hours interviewing...two sessions with the recruiter, lunches and dinners with the EVP and the CEO, and two solid days in their offices. I met with everyone but the janitor. Well, my new boss the EVP told me, 'We talked to four others just like we did to you, and there's no comparison. The Chairman says it's as if you already work here, and they're just visiting. If you want us, we want you!'"

This fellow said he felt he "memorized just by writing," which jibes with what psychologists tell us about how learning works. And he reread his notes before each major new meeting. The result:

> "John, I'm convinced that filling in those forms gave me a 'killer' advantage. Here I am reciting back to the Chairman and the EVP what they and their people told me, and they think I'm a genius! I pity those other candidates. I'm not *that* much smarter than they are. But there was a game going on, and they didn't even know they were playing!

Now back to *Rites:*

Out of Town Tryouts

Most people find that, in interviewing, "practice makes perfect." By the time they're in their third or fourth interview, they're very effective. But what if you haven't interviewed for quite awhile and you suddenly face an unexpected "biggie"? Or if you look forward to a series of interviews and don't want to waste the first one or two? Then try your show in Philadelphia and Boston prior to opening night on Broadway.

"Role playing," of course, is the answer. A social friend or your spouse can sit in for the interviewer, perhaps asking questions from a random list you've prepared. Better yet, try to set up a real grilling by a business friend from the right industry. Choose someone who can come up with his or her own tough questions, and who will give you a clear-eyed critique afterward.

The Danger of Being Prepared

There's no such thing as being overprepared. There always is, however, the danger of being over-eager to play back what you've worked on. And by recommending—and helping you develop—"capsules," I certainly don't mean to encourage that tendency.

Occasionally I come across people so anxious to deliver the thinking they've developed that they don't listen carefully to the question and conform their answer to it. These people are extremely rare...only one of them for every 50 or 75 who fail to come up with clearly focused, brief, and factually explicit answers to questions they certainly should have anticipated.

You're too alert to make either mistake.

Answering the Unasked Questions

No interviewer these days is going to invite legal action by asking:

> "Do you really think a woman can handle this job?"
>
> "Aren't you a little too old for a grueling position like this?"
>
> "Do people respond to you just like everyone else, even though you only have one eye?"
>
> "With that brace on your leg, I don't suppose you get out to visit the companies in your group very often, do you?"

In an ideal world, these questions would not only be unasked, they would also be unthought. But our present world is far from ideal. If you vary much from the norm...if you're an ethnic or racial minority, physically handicapped, noticeably younger or older than most executives, considerably heavier or shorter...there may be unspoken questions in the mind of the interviewer about your ability to handle the job because of your "difference." The best course is to rebut these objections, even though they're not voiced.

But you must communicate *indirectly*. You can't simply pipe up and say, "Don't worry about my age; I'm more effective at 59 than I ever was at 30 or 40." If by chance the interviewer *wasn't* thinking of your age as a problem, he'll wonder why you're being so defensive. And if he *was* thinking about it: (1) he'll be offended that you caught him, (2) he'll be unconvinced by your self-serving assertion, and (3) he'll worry that you may already be hinting at legal action if he doesn't give you the job.

Just as in writing your resume, you can answer such unspoken questions with offsetting information. If you're probably a lot older than the other candidates, casually mention spending your vacation as an instructor for Outward Bound...or that you're leaving in August for two weeks of mountain climbing in Nepal (if true!). Or maybe just mention your interest in finding a challenging partner for a few good sets of tennis while you're in town. Make the interviewer think of you as healthy, vigorous, and in your prime. Don't talk about something you watched on television, or how hard you were hit by the flu that's going around. Everyone watches TV and gets sick occasionally, but you can't afford to raise image problems with someone who doesn't know you.

Shatter your stereotype.

Offset *youth* with civic and business responsibilities normally reserved for someone more mature... president of a stodgy country club, trustee of a college, outside director of a bank. (For this purpose, forget "when-do-you-have-time-for-it?" concerns.) Fight the *age* problem with evidence of vigorous physical activity and a fast-paced schedule. And if you're a *woman*, stress the fact that you're accustomed to extensive travel and to coping with business demands that require personal flexibility. And throw in an anecdote that makes it clear that your household is organized accordingly.

If you belong to a racial or ethnic *minority*, be warm, self-confident, friendly and informal...thus demonstrating (1) that you'll fit right in, and (2) that you don't have any doubt or insecurity about fitting in.

If you're *physically challenged*, stress your ability to function effectively in the mainstream of everyday life; mention a party you went to recently, grumble about a speeding ticket, talk about your participation in active sports. And if you're *overweight*, stress the fact that you lead a highly disciplined and energetic life...that you adhere to demanding self-imposed schedules...that you work for long-term goals.

Engines Ready...Contact!

Prepared as you are, you have absolutely nothing to fear as you take off into the sunrise. If you've got anything close to the right stuff, your interview will demonstrate it.

However, let's run through a preflight checklist of practical tips:

Check the forecast. If your interview has been arranged by a recruiter, call her in the morning or the afternoon before. She may have new information since you saw her last, regarding job content, what's looked for, how long other interviews have lasted, what line of questioning was pursued, and what mistakes other candidates made. Don't betray nervousness by asking about all these items. Just say: "Anything I should know before I go over there tomorrow morning?"

Pack your flight case. Into your elegant attache go extra copies of your resume (just in case your host has misplaced his or wants to pass some along), a yellow pad and a *quality* pen, any charts of figures you may need to refresh your memory if questioning gets detailed, and a *Wall Street Journal* to pull out and read if your host is interrupted or you have to wait a few minutes.

Arrive early and check the equipment. Get there five minutes ahead of time and ask to use the lavatory before being announced. That way you can check for lint on your collar and parsley on your teeth. You'll perform best knowing you feel and look perfect.

Return your salute from the crew. The interview begins in the corridor as your host's secretary greets you and maybe offers to shake hands (be alert for this). He, and through him possibly the receptionist too, will probably be consulted for a report on your poise and personality. Your corridor conversation with him...cordial but not presumptuous...is the start of your interview.

Don't land prematurely. After your *firm* handshake, I hope your host doesn't feign a landing and then pull up, leaving you discourteously plopped for an awkward minute or two. But he might. It's a fairly common maneuver. Circle gracefully until you get landing instructions, or you clearly see where he's landing.

Warning. There's advice going around...maybe via a book or a psychologically oriented outplacement firm...not to sit where the interviewer first suggests and, wherever you land, to *move your chair*. This odd behavior is supposed to connote an aggressive personality. I merely find it obnoxious. Unless you've got a bad back, or the sun's in your eyes, why not just sit down where indicated, and relax?

Five-minute warning. Don't go all-business all at once. Get off to a positive, upbeat start on a relatively personal note. Admire something in the office, or the company's convenient location, or the fine weather. Do *not* start off with the lousy weather, a bad commute, or any other "downer."

Hazardous terrain. Enter the Bermuda Triangle with extreme caution, if at all. Avoid such obviously hazardous topics as politics, religion, and sexually and racially oriented issues. Beware of trick questions aimed at exposing your negative attitudes on these matters by implying in advance that the interviewer has such feelings. Even sports can be a hazardous topic until you know your host's opinions. Believe it or not, some interviewers will see your failure to share their views on player trades as an indication that you're probably not a very shrewd analyst in the world of business either.

Keep an eye on the radar. Read the interviewer's body language. Leaning back signals a smooth leisurely ride; tapping fingers, fidgeting, and checking the clock call for crisper answers. "Closed position" (tightly crossed arms and legs) says you're meeting resistance, whereas open, loose limbs say "all clear." And hand-to-face says she...and you...are uncertain, possibly untruthful. Body language can be overrated, but shouldn't be ignored. If you haven't read a book on the subject, you ought to.

Don't go on autopilot. No matter how well things seem to be going, don't let your guard down. The most skilled and subtle interviewer is never the one who treats you roughly. The one who puts you totally at ease is the one who'll find out even more than you'd prefer to tell.

Debrief promptly. If a recruiter is involved, call soon afterward to debrief. The client will also call, and if the recruiter can play back your favorable comments, they will reinforce the client's good feelings about you. Don't be a sappy sycophant. But don't be coy, either. People tend to like people who obviously like them. And recruiters are more inclined to support candidates who probably will accept, than those who might not.

File your flight report. Why not send a brief "thank you"...two to four paragraphs, using "Monarch" (7 1/4" x 10 1/2") personal stationery if you have it, otherwise "regular size." While you may refer in some way to what was discussed, this note is ***not*** a parting salvo of hard sell. Instead, it's a courtesy that says ***fine person***...and differentiates you from the vast majority of candidates, who don't bother with amenities. Even more importantly, write down for future reference everything you found out at your interview. (Use an INTERVIEW DE-BRIEFER.) Most candidates won't do this either. Therefore, you'll be more on the employer's wave length than they will, at "second round" interviews three or four weeks later.

What the Interview *Can't* Do for You

For years one of the leading literary agents has been trying to get me to write a book which ought to be called How to Package and Pretend Your Way Into a Big Job You're Not Qualified For. Naturally that's not the title he proposes, but it perfectly describes his premise.

Such a concept is not only dishonest, it's ridiculous. No combination of slick resume and glib interviewing can enable you to defeat an array of really excellent candidates and win a job you're not qualified for.

And you shouldn't want such a job. Get it, and your life will be miserable until you lose it...and even more miserable afterward!

However, armed with the information in this book and in *Rites of Passage at $100,000 to $1 Million+* and the willingness to work as hard as necessary to obtain the position you do deserve, you should be able to fight off the other fine candidates competing against you for any job you fully deserve and can perform.

Good luck. I hope you do.

Please do not be misled. The Workbook's comprehensive set of tools for improving your interviewing skills has dealt with interviewing in general ...supplying and supplementing Chapter 16 of *Rites of Passage*. The Workbook has not gone into any of the specialized interviewing information in *Rites*, such as obtaining and participating in interviews with retainer and contingency executive recruiters...information which figures substantially in chapters 6 through 10 of *Rites of Passage*.

To Help With Your

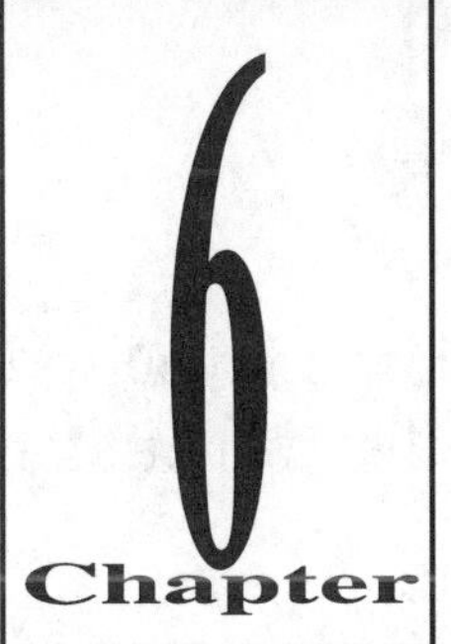

Tax / Expense Records

You'll pay taxes when your new job produces income. Therefore, your expenses in finding that job while unemployed are tax-deductible.

Check with your Tax Advisor for final determinations before you file. Meanwhile this discussion, plus keeping day-by-day records in the "attache pages," will help make sure you don't shortchange yourself.

Fairness

How unfair it would be if you couldn't deduct from your taxable income the money you spend looking for employment so you can pay more taxes.

You and I as taxpayers, however, are generally *not* allowed to deduct the expenses of striving—through education or otherwise—to get a *different* (and we hope better) job. However, we're sometimes allowed to deduct certain costs of *continuing in our current job and moving upward by doing it better;* for example, some of the professional dues and "continuing education" required by law or by the regulatory arms of some professions, including the medical field, law, accounting, teaching, etc.

So the bottom line as a practical matter—although always "Check with your Tax Advisor"—seems to be that you *can deduct quite a few expenses when you don't have a job and are looking for one.* You cannot deduct money spent to qualify yourself for a different position, but you may be able to deduct the most glaringly mandatory costs of keeping the job you have.

Good Records Are Essential

The *"why"* of good record-keeping is obvious. And the "how" can be quite painless, if you use the forms you'll find on Attache Pages 259 to 287. Each double-page layout provides convenient slots for jotting down a whole month's expenses as they occur. Save your receipts...and tax irritation on your job-search is scratched.

The 10 Slots on the Attache Pages

To keep things simple and handy, your expenses are slotted into 10 categories, and an entire month's spending is visible at a glance on just two pages. But once again this caveat: Federal and state laws and IRS rulings are constantly changing. Get final clearance on each deduction from your Tax Advisor. Meanwhile, these observations on each of the record-keeping slots:

1. ***Mileage.*** If you have a car, you'll surely be using it in your search...going to and from networking appointments and interviews, the post office and FedEx, the office supply store and print/copy store, etc. The IRS allows 32.5¢ per mile if you own your car. If you lease, you have the choice of deducting (1) your actual cost or (2) 32.5¢ per mile. Consult your Tax Advisor before filing. Meanwhile, if you prefer, you can merely write each day's miles into this column and not bother figuring the money until you go over year-end numbers with your TA.
2. ***Car Rental, Gas and Tolls.*** When you're away from home and have to rent a car to pursue your search activities, that cost is equally deductible. Also, don't forget any tolls and/or parking you pay, whether the car is rented or your own.
3. ***Taxi Cabs.*** Nothing to explain. Good luck getting one when you need it!
4. ***Air Fares.*** Tickets bought for your job search are deductible...although obviously ***not*** if reimbursed by a prospective employer or a recruiter. So are rail fares, including your usual commutation tickets, if your trips are now to seek employment.
5. ***Telephone.*** Do your telephone image and your sanity a favor. Have a separate line installed to be used for no other purpose than your job search. The cost is probably way under $20 per month, and the benefits are major. Folks who call the number on your resume will never get a busy signal because family members are using it; you won't waste time poring over the family bill to sort out your deductible calls; and you'll have perfect tax documentation. Incidentally, don't forget to log the pocket change you're continually dropping into pay-phone slots.
6. ***Hotels.*** Deductible if for your job-search...and unreimbursed.
7. ***Meals.*** Your food while away from home on job-search trips appears—under most circumstances—to be deductible. Lunches in your hometown that weren't deductible when you were working aren't now either. However, lunches you host to obtain help from networking contacts and references may be deductible... although only to the extent of 50% of what you spend on your guest and yourself. Keep receipts and write down the name and relevance of the person and what was discussed/accomplished. Here too, check with your TA!
8. ***Supplies, Equipment and Software.*** You ought to have a separate phone with voice

mail, call waiting, and call forwarding to use as your job-hunting line...and possibly a separate cell phone too. I personally believe a FAX machine is also almost mandatory for a well-conducted job search. So is a good program of computerized word-processing.

If you have to buy equipment, it will have a lifespan beyond your job search, so you can't deduct its entire cost all at once. On the other hand, the actual value of computers, printers, and software rapidly plunges to near-zero, whether a corporation or an individual is depreciating it. So besides fast depreciation—almost certainly 5 years or less—you may be advised to write off a very large chunk in the first year. Also, of course, there is always the option of donating equipment to a charity. Then your deduction plus your charitable gift might conceivably equal 100% of what you paid and the total cost might become history. But, again, ask your TA.

9. ***Printing and Secretarial Services.*** You can't get resumes and nice stationery for nothing. But you can probably write off all your resumes, even if you don't use them up. Same with all of the stationery, if you have to relocate for your new job. If you remain where you are and have stationery left over, deduct the value of what you've used. Word-processing you hire others to do for your search is, of course, deductible.

10. ***Postage and Overnight Delivery Services.*** Obviously deductible. However, don't forget to ask for and save a receipt, if you lay out substantial sums at the Post Office. FedEx and UPS don't let you leave without one.

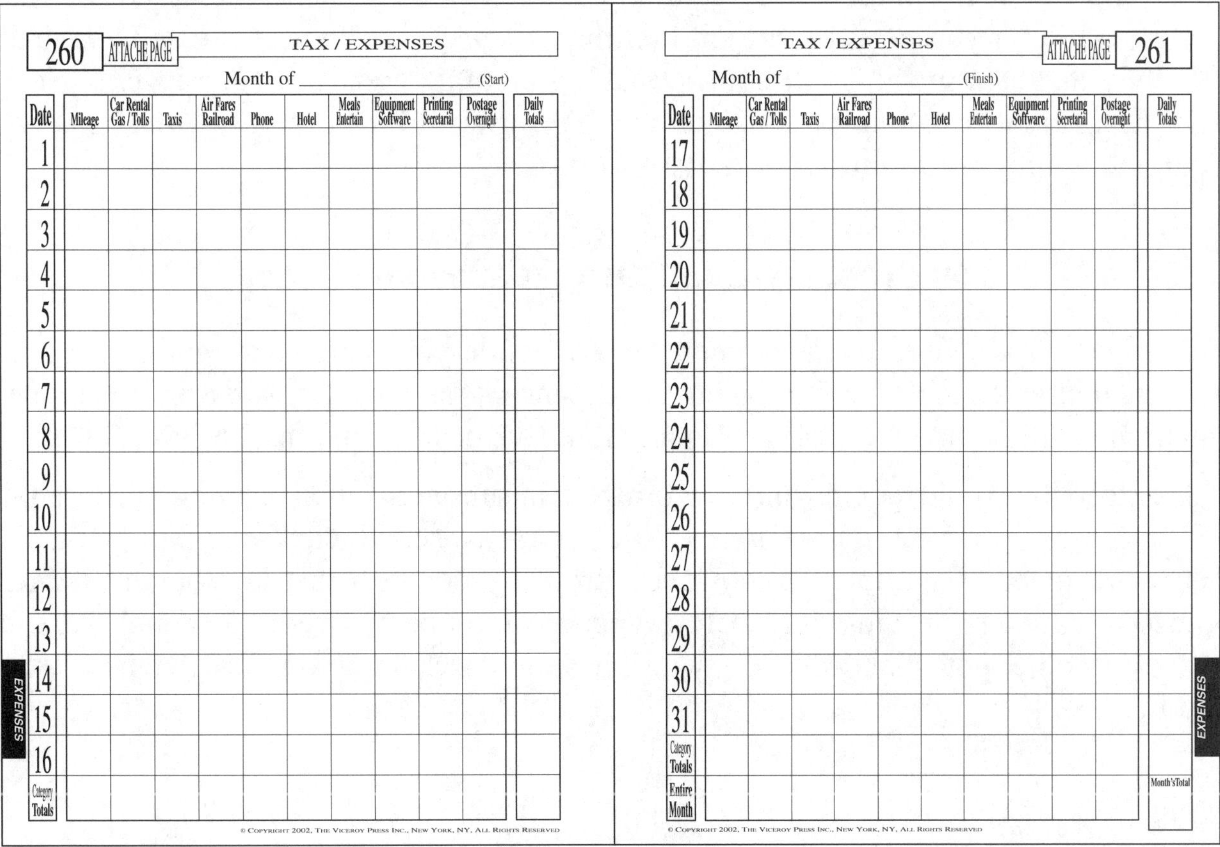

260 ATTACHE PAGE — TAX / EXPENSES

Month of ____________(Start)

Date	Mileage	Car Rental Gas / Tolls	Taxis	Air Fares Railroad	Phone	Hotel	Meals Entertain	Equipment Software	Printing Secretarial	Postage Overnight	Daily Totals
1											
2											
3											
4											
5											
6											
7											
8											
9											
10											
11											
12											
13											
14											
15											
16											
Category Totals											

EXPENSES

TAX / EXPENSES — ATTACHE PAGE 261

Month of ____________(Finish)

Date	Mileage	Car Rental Gas / Tolls	Taxis	Air Fares Railroad	Phone	Hotel	Meals Entertain	Equipment Software	Printing Secretarial	Postage Overnight	Daily Totals
17											
18											
19											
20											
21											
22											
23											
24											
25											
26											
27											
28											
29											
30											
31											
Category Totals											
Entire Month											Month's Total

EXPENSES

Moving Expenses

When you're switching jobs and must relocate, you may have a deduction. However, your expenses must be reasonable, your new place of employment must be at least 50 miles farther from your old residence than that residence was from your previous workplace, and you must be employed full time in the new job for at least 39 weeks. Check with your Tax Advisor to make sure you are qualifying yourself for this deduction. Tax rules are not simple and they *do* keep changing.

The 2% Rule

As in everything about taxes, each person's situation is different. Everyone should consult with a Tax Advisor when determining deductions. Moreover, even with good record-keeping, the outcome may be disappointing. Here's the "catch" in deducting the expenses of your search for employment:

> Job-hunting expenses are deductible only as "Miscellaneous Itemized Deductions," and then only to the extent that your total "MIDs" exceed 2% of your Adjusted Gross Income. Fortunately, other unreimbursed deductible expenses in the production of income will help get you over the 2% hurdle; for example, professional organization dues or union dues (too bad there's no executive's union!).

If you're already over the 2% in MIDs for this year, then 100% of what you spend on your job search this year will be deductible (except, of course, the 50% limit on food and drinks mentioned above). If you're sure your job-hunting expenses *can't possibly* reach above the 2%, then maybe you shouldn't bother tracking them. Otherwise, ***keep track!*** Never was the ancient McDonald's jingle truer than now, *"You deserve a break today!"* Your handy tool begins on ATTACHE PAGE 260.

You Probably Can't Deduct a "Home Office"

If some spot at home becomes your "office" while you search for another one, you quite naturally itch to deduct "home office" expense. Ask your Tax Advisor. Everyone's situation is different, but in many instances that I've heard about the TA has said "No!"

An exception would require you to be bringing in substantial income through consulting and/or other work done in a separate area of your manse, which would then become a true work-place. That income, however, probably couldn't just be your investment proceeds that were arriving even before you became unemployed. Although here, as with every other potential deduction, you'll have to check with your Tax Advisor before you file.

To Help You With

Retainer Executive Search Firms

Executive recruiters are a surprisingly complex and fascinating subject...far beyond the scope of this WORKBOOK. In the current edition of *RITES OF PASSAGE AT $100,000+ ...THE INSIDER'S LIFETIME GUIDE TO EXECUTIVE JOB-CHANGING AND FASTER CAREER PROGRESS* six chapters and a novella—231 pages (more than 1/3 of the book)—show you how executive searchers work and how best to deal with them to achieve your objectives.

The Two Types of Recruiters

There are only two types of headhunters, and the difference is strictly in how they're paid by the employer.

"Contingency recruiters" are paid ***only if someone they identify is hired***. They're **brokers.** Just as real estate brokers try to list as many properties as possible and show them to as many potential buyers as possible, the contingency recruiters try to get resumes from as many attractive job-seekers as possible and show them to as many potential employers as possible...always hoping that "lightning will strike," someone will get hired, and they'll get paid.

"Retainer recruiters" are paid ***regardless of whether anyone they identify is hired or not.*** They're **consultants**...paid for their time and expertise in trying to fill the position. Paid ***while they work*** to look for exactly the type of person the employer seeks, they should submit people only when paid to look for them. Moreover, their slate of only a few carefully selected people should be right on target.

The employer pays both types; you do not. However, the retainer-compensated searchers are the ones who do the overwhelming majority—although not all—of executive-level searches.

Here, from *RITES,* is a uniquely helpful list of over 350 outstanding U.S. and Canadian firms. Included are North America's largest, plus particularly outstanding medium-sized and smaller firms. Because they work only "on retainer," every one of these firms is filling a completely different list of jobs than any of the others. Therefore, you'll have the best and broadest (and entirely nonoverlapping) exposure if you contact many of the listed firms. Note that some specialize (or are generalists with special concentrations), so don't bother contacting ones that don't fit your background and interests.

An increasing number of firms can now accept resumes by e-mail and insert them into a searchable database. Where available, use this option, with a "Dear Recruiters" e-mail cover letter not addressed to any particular person. When submitting by mail, send to the home office and *do* address your cover letter to a specific person. If a firm has multiple offices, the address given *is* the home office.

Cities having branch offices are also listed, each with phone number and the name of the local manager or another prominent local member. Locally and nationally you can, if you wish, phone and ask who specializes in your field. However, unless you're trying to target a personal appointment, there's virtually no advantage. Inside-the-firm procedures will normally redistribute your inquiry appropriately.

Although *unnecessary*, there's no harm in sending an on-paper letter and resume to one person in each of two or three different offices. If only an electronic file is kept, the papers will be superfluous, and if papers are kept, the filer will merely discard the extras. They won't occasion notice, notation, or comment.

Many of these firms (marked by †) are members of the Association of Executive Search Consultants (AESC), a trade association of retainer-compensated recruiters.

Of course, it's beyond the scope of this book to provide any assurances, but all firms selected for this list should deal with you in a first-class manner. To the best of our knowledge, they all work only on retainer, and almost all accept searches for nearly every management function in virtually any industry. A few outstanding specialists are also included, and their specialties are clearly noted.

You may wish to phone-check before mailing to a recruiter. Information on recruiters changes even faster than on companies.

AEGIS GROUP
(SPECIALIZE IN HEALTH CARE)
23875 Novi Road
Novi, MI 48375-3243
(248) 344-1450
http://www.aegis-group.com/
resume@aegis-group.com
Timothy J. Ignash, President

ALLERTON HENEGHAN & O'NEILL
Three First National Plaza
70 West Madison, Suite 2015
Chicago, IL 60602
(312) 263-1075
aho@interaccess.com
Donald T. Allerton, Donald A. Heneghan & Donald Wilson, Partners

ANDERSON & ASSOCIATES†
(SPECIALIZE IN NON-PROFIT, MANUFACTURING, GRAPHIC COMMUNICATIONS, FINANCIAL SERVICES, HEALTHCARE)
112 South Tryon St., Suite 800
Charlotte, NC 28284
(704) 347-0090
http://www.andersonexecsearch.com/
info@andersonexecsearch.com
Douglas K. Anderson, Chairman

THE ANDRE GROUP INC.
(SPECIALIZE IN HUMAN RESOURCES)
500 North Gulph Road, Suite 210
King of Prussia, PA 19406
(610) 337-0600
info@theandregroup.com
Larry Cozzillio, Vice President & General Manager
Also:
Atlanta, GA (770) 698-8000
Randi Nelson, Regional Manager
Palm Beach Gardens, FL (561) 630-7800
Richard B. Andre, President

ARIAIL & ASSOCIATES
(SPECIALIZE IN FURNITURE MANUFACTURING)
210 West Friendly Avenue, Suite 200
Greensboro, NC 27401
(336) 275-2906

http://www.ariailassoc.com/
information@ariailassoc.com
Randolph C. Ariail, Principal

William B. Arnold Associates, Inc.

Cherry Creek Plaza
600 South Cherry Street, Suite 1105
Denver, CO 80246
(303) 393-6662
William B. Arnold, President
Sheridan J. Arnold, Vice President

Ast/Bryant†

(Specialize in Non-profit)
2716 Ocean Park Boulevard, Suite 3001
Santa Monica, CA 90405
(310) 314-2424
http://www.astbryant.com/
Chris Bryant, President
Also:
Stamford, CT (203) 975-7188
Steven Ast, Chairman

Aubin International, Inc.

(Specialize in High Tech & Communications)
30 Rowes Wharf
Boston, MA 02110
(617) 443-9922
http://www.aubin.com/
info@aubin.com
Richard E. Aubin, Chairman & CEO

Avery James, Inc.†

(Specialize in Engineering & Information Technology)
6601 Center Drive West, Suite 500
Los Angeles, CA 90045
(310) 342-8224
http://www.averyjames.com/
itsyourmove@averyjames.com
Michele James, President

The Badger Group

(Specialize in High Tech)
4125 Blackhawk Plaza Circle, Suite 270
Danville, CA 94506
(925) 736-5553
http://www.badgergroup.com/
resumes@badgergroup.com
Fred Badger, President

Baker, Parker & Associates, Inc.

5 Concourse Parkway, NE, Suite 2440
Atlanta, GA 30328
(770) 804-1996
http://www.bpasearch.com/
confidential@bpasearch.com
Jerry H. Baker & Daniel F. Parker, Partners

The Baldwin Group

(Specialize in Information Technology)
P.O. Box 158
Arlington Heights, IL 60006-0158
(847) 612-1294
thebaldgrp@aol.com
Keith Baldwin, President

Barger & Sargeant, Inc.†

131 Windermere Road, Suite A
Post Office Box 1420-L
Center Harbor, NH 03226-1420
(603) 253-4700
H. Carter Barger, President

Barnes Development Group, LLC†

1017 West Glenn Oaks Lane, Suite 108
Mequon, WI 53092
(262) 241-8468
http://www.barnesdevelopment.com/
Richard E. Barnes & Roanne L. Barnes, Presidents & Co-Owners

Jonathan C. Barrett & Co., Inc.

P.O. Box 247
Hawthorne, NJ 07507-0247
(973) 423-4111

A. John Gorga, President

Bartholdi & Company, Inc.

(Specialize in High Technology)
1860 Blake Street, Suite 415
Denver, CO 80202
(303) 383-2130
http://www.bartholdisearch.com/
tmalouf@bartholdisearch.com
Terry Malouf & Carol J. Fanning, Partners
Also:
Boulder, CO (303) 664-5088
J. Fred Henderson, Vice President
Reston, VA (703) 476-5519
Carol Holt, Partner
San Diego, CA (619) 881-2664
Tom Courbat, Vice President
Scottsdale, AZ (480) 502-2178
Theodore G. Bartholdi, Managing Partner

Barton Associates, Inc.

One Riverway, Suite 2500
Houston, TX 77056
(713) 961-9111
http://www.BartonA.com/
tflores@bartona.com
Gary R. Barton, Partner

Sunny Bates Associates†

345 7th Avenue
8th Floor
New York, NY 10001
(212) 691-5252
http://www.sunnybates.com/
info@sunnybates.com
Sunny Bates, Cheif Executive Officer
Janet Muir, Cheif Operations Officer
Marilyn Byrd, Vice President
Also:
Los Angeles, CA (310) 229-5760
Mark Brooke, Managing Director

Battalia Winston International, Inc.†

International Affiliation - The Accord Group
555 Madison Avenue , 19th Floor
New York, NY 10022
(212) 308-8080
http://www.battaliawinston.com/
info@battaliawinston.com
Dale Winston, Chairman & CEO
Jo A. Bennett, Partner & Executive Vice President
Also:
Chicago, IL (312) 704-0050
James F. McSherry, Sr. Vice President-Midwest
Edison, NJ (732) 549-8200
Terry Gallagher, President
Los Angeles, CA (310) 284-8080
Michael McClain, Partner
San Francisco, CA (212) 308-8080
Dale Winston, Chairman & CEO
Wellesley Hills, MA (781) 239-1400
Steven M. Garfinkle, Managing Director

Martin H. Bauman Associates, LLC†

375 Park Avenue, Suite 2002
New York, NY 10152
(212) 752-6580
mhb@baumanassociates.com
Martin H. Bauman, President
Also:
Chicago, IL (312) 751-5407
Audrey W. Hellinger, Vice President

The Bedford Consulting Group Inc.†

(Specialize in Technology, Life Sciences, Mining and Heavy Industy, Food Services, Manufacturing)
The Bedford House, 60 Bedford Road
Toronto, ON M5R 2K2
(416) 963-9000
http://www.bedfordgroup.com/
search@bedfordgroup.com
Steven Pezim, President
Howard Pezim, Partner and Managing Director
Also:
Oakville, ON L6J 3K5
(905) 338-7008
Russ Buckland, Managing Partner

Belle Isle, Djandji, Brunet, Inc.

1555 Peel Street, Suite 1200
Montreal, QC H3A 3L8
(514) 844-1012
reception@bidi.com
Charles Belle Isle, Guy N. Djandji & Michele Brunet, Partners

Bender Executive Search

(Specialize in Marketing and Sales)
45 North Station Plaza, Suite 315
Great Neck, NY 11021
(516) 773-4300
http://www.marketingexecsearch.com/
benderexec@aol.com
Alan S. Bender, President

Bialecki Inc.†

(Specialize in Investment Banking)
780 Third Avenue, Suite 4203
New York, NY 10017-2024
(212) 755-1090
http://www.bialecki.com/
Linda Bialecki, President

Paul J. Biestek Associates, Inc.

PMB 101, Suite 700
800 East Northwest Highway
Palatine, IL 60074
(847) 825-5131

http://www.biestek-associates.com/
Paul J. Biestek, President

Bishop Partners†

(Specialize in Entertainment, Media & Communications)
708 Third Avenue, Suite 2200
New York, NY 10017
(212) 986-3419
http://www.bishoppartners.com/
info@bishopnet.com
Susan K. Bishop, President/CEO

Blake/Hansen, Ltd.

(Specialize in Aviation, Aerospace & Defense)
1920 Bayshore Drive
Englewood, FL 34223
(941) 475-1300
http://www.hansengroupltd.com/
Ty E. Hansen, President

BMF Reynolds, Inc.

(Specialize in Health Care, Nuclear Energy)
P.O. Box 157
Summerville, NJ 08876
(908) 704-9100
http://www.bmfr.com/
inquiry@bmfr.com
John H. Reynolds, President

Boardroom Consultants†

530 Fifth Avenue, Suite 2100
New York, NY 10036
(212) 328-0440
http://www.board-search.com/
info@board-search.com
Roger M. Kenny, Peter A. Kindler, William E. Tholke, John A. Coleman, Peter W. Eldredge & Sarah K. Stewart, Partners

Bonnell & Associates Ltd.

2960 Post Road South, Suite 200
Southport, CT 06490
(203) 319-7214
http://www.bonnellassociates.com/
info@bonnellassociates.com
William R. Bonnell, President

John C. Boone & Company

1807 Henley Street
Glenview, IL 60025
(847) 998-1905
John C. Boone, President

Bowden & Company, Inc.

P.O. Box 467
Medina, OH 44258
(330) 722-1722
http://www.bowdenandco.com/
Chester W. Dickey, President & Chief Executive Officer

Boyden†

364 Elwood Avenue
Hawthorne, NY 10532-1239
(914) 747-0093
http://www.boyden.com/
Christopher Clarke, President
Also:
Bloomfield Hills, MI (248) 647-4201
John Slosar, President - Boyden USA
Calgary, AB (403) 237-6603
Robert S. Travis, Managing Director
Chesterfield, MO (636) 519-7400
William Tunney Jr., Senior Partner
George B. Zamborsky, Managing Partner
Chicago, IL (312) 565-1300
Richard A. McCallister, Managing Director
Nicholaas VanHevelingen, Managing Partner
Houston, TX (713) 655-0123
Thomas C. Zay Jr., James N. J. Hertlein, Charles A. Rhoads & Cheryl R. Smith, Partners
Miami, FL (305) 476-1200
Alan Griffin, Managing Partner
Montreal, QC (514) 935-4560
Paul J. Bourbeau, Managing Director
Phoenix, AZ (602) 224-5000
Ingrid Murro, Managing Parter
Pittsburgh, PA (412) 820-7559
E. Wade Close Jr. & Thomas T. Flannery, Managing Directors
San Francisco, CA (415) 981-7900
Frederick J. Greene, Managing Director
Summit, NJ (973) 267-0980
Carlyle R. Newell, Managing Partner

Boyden Global Executive Search†

Redwood Tower
217 East Redwood Street, 16th Floor
Baltimore, MD 21202-3316
(410) 625-3800
http://www.boyden.com
stacy.cook@boyden.com
Martin Knott, Vice President
Timothy C. McNamara, Managing Director
Dale Legal, Partner

The Brand Company, Inc.

181 Shores Drive
Vero Beach, FL 32963
(561) 231-1807
J. Brand Spangenberg, President

Brenner Executive Resources, Inc.†

1212 6th Avenue, 3rd Floor
New York, NY 10036
(212) 391-4494
http://www.brennerresources.com/
resumes@brennerresources.com
Michael Brenner, President

Brooke Chase Associates, Inc.
(Specialize in Kitchen/Bath, Hardware, Automotive, IT)
1800 Ravine Place
Orland Park, IL 60462
(708) 873-0033
http://www.brookechase.com/
brookechase@brookechase.com
Joseph J. McElmeel, President
Also:
Gastonia, NC (704) 852-4050
Howard Sharpe, Managing Director
Livingston, NJ (973) 716-0088
Carolyn O'Brien, Managing Director

Brownson & Associates
5599 San Felipe, Suite 610
Houston, TX 77056
(713) 626-4790
http://www.brownson.com/
bbrown3848@aol.com
Bruce F. E. Brownson, Managing Director

Bullis & Company, Inc.
1097 Green Street , Suite #3
San Francisco, CA 94133
(415) 359-1508
rjbullis@cs.com
Richard J. Bullis, President

Burke, O'Brien & Bishop Associates, Inc.
301 North Harrison St., Suite 111
Princeton, NJ 08540
(609) 921-3510
James F. Bishop, President & Chief Executive Officer

Joseph R. Burns and Associates, Inc.
2 Shunpike Road
Madison, NJ 07940-2727
(973) 377-1350
Joseph R. Burns, President

Butterfass, Pepe & MacCallan, Inc.
(Specialize in Financial Services)
P.O. Box 721
Mahwah, NJ 07430
(201) 512-3330
http://www.bpmi.com/
staff@bpmi.com
Stanley W. Butterfass, Deirdre MacCallan & Leonida R. Pepe, Principals

The Caldwell Partners International†
64 Prince Arthur Avenue
Toronto, ON M5R 1B4
(416) 920-7702
http://www.caldwell.ca/
resumes@caldwell.ca
C. Douglas Caldwell, Founder, Chairman, & C.E.O
Ann Fawcett, Partner
Also:
Calgary, AB (403) 265-8780
Timothy J. Hamilton, Partner
Halifax, NS (902) 429-5909
Susan Letson, Partner
Montreal, QC (514) 935-6969
Richard Joly, Partner
Vancouver, BC (604) 669-3550
Donald Prior, Partner

Callan Associates, Ltd.
2021 Spring Road, Suite 175
Oak Brook, IL 60523
(630) 574-9300
http://www.callanassociates.com/
rcallan@callanassociates.com
Robert M. Callan, Robert M. Ward, James R. Stranberg, Elizabeth C. Beaudin & Marianne C. Ray, Partners

Canny, Bowen Inc.
280 Park Avenue West, 30th Floor
New York, NY 10017
(212) 949-6611
http://cannybowen.com/
main@cannybowen.com
David R. Peasback, Chief Executive Officer & President
Greg Gabel, Managing Director

The Capstone Group
99 Almaden Boulevard, 6th Floor
San Jose, CA 95113
(408) 292-0770
http://www.capstone-group.com
resumes@mgmtsolutions.com
Bob Tuvell, Managing Director

The Capstone Partnership
(Specialize in Investment Banking)
100 Park Avenue, 34th Floor
New York, NY 10017
(212) 843-0200
nyinfo@capstonepartnership.com
Allison Bush, Director

Carrington & Carrington Ltd.†
(Specialize in Diversity Executive Search)
39 South La Salle Street
Chicago, IL 60603-1557
(312) 606-0015
http://www.cclltd.com/
cclltd@cclltd.com
Marian H. Carrington, Principal

Caruthers & Company, LLC
(Specialize in Corporate Communications, Public Affairs, and Marketing)
19 Ludlow Road, Suite 302
Westport, CT 06880

(203) 221-3234
Robert D. Caruthers, Principal

Cejka & Company

(Specialize in Health Care)
222 South Central, Suite 400
St. Louis, MO 63105
(314) 726-1603
http://www.Cejka.com/
cwestfallcejka.com
Joseph A. Boshart, President & CEO
David W. Cornett, Senior Vice President

David Chambers & Associates, Inc.

2 Sound View Drive, Suite 100
Greenwich, CT 06830
(203) 622-1333
David E. Chambers, President

Christenson, Hutchison, McDowell, LLC

EMA Partners International
466 Southern Boulevard
Chatham, NJ 07928-1462
(973) 966-1600
http://www.chmsearch.com/
solutions@chmsearch.com
H. Alan Christenson, Founder & Managing Partner
William K. Hutchison, Robert McDowell & Paul H. Sartori, Partners
Also:
Providence, RI (401) 861-2550
John R. Sahagian, Managing Director

Christian & Timbers, Inc.†

One Corporate Exchange
25825 Science Park Drive, Suite 400
Cleveland, OH 44122
(216) 464-8710
http://www.ctnet.com/
resumes@ctnet.com
Jeffrey Christian, Chairman & CEO
Also:
Alpharetta, GA (770) 754-1198
Russell Gray, Managing Director
Burlington, MA (781) 229-9515
Stephen P. Mader, President & COO
Columbia, MD (410) 872-0200
William Houchins, Managing Director Mid-Atlantic
Cupertino, CA (408) 446-5440
David R. Mather, Vice President & Managing Director
Linda Mikula, Managing Director
Irvine, CA (949) 727-3400
Peter C. Santora, Vice President
Robert J. Lambert, Managing Partner
McLean, VA (703) 448-1700
Paul Unger, Managing Director
New York, NY (212) 588-3500
John Daily, Managing Director
Morgan McKeown, Principal
San Francisco, CA (415) 885-8004
Victoria Wayne, Managing Director
Stamford, CT (203) 352-6000
Mark Esposito, Managing Director
Toronto, ON (416) 628-5175
David Kinley, Managing Director - Canadian Operations
Upper Mount Claire, NJ (973) 746-7976
Leigh Marshall, Executive Director

Clarey & Andrews, Inc.†

1200 Shermer Road, Suite 108
Northbrook, IL 60062-4563
(847) 498-2870
http://www.clarey-andrews.com/
resumes@clarey-andrews.com
Jack R. Clarey & J. Douglas Andrews, Partners

Dean M. Coe & Associates†

(Specialize in Real Estate, Non-Profit)
32 Pine Street
Sandwich, MA 02563-2109
(508) 888-8029
dcoe@capecod.net
Dean M. Coe, President

Coe & Company

EMA Partners International
(Specialize in Technology, Industrial, Energy)
400 3rd Avenue, SW, Suite 2600
Calgary, AB T2P 4H2
(403) 232-8833
http://coeandcompany.com/
coe@coeandcompany.com
Karen J. Coe PhD., President & CEO

The Coelyn Group

(Specialize in Healthcare and Life Sciences)
1 Park Plaza, 6th Floor
Irvine, CA 92614
(949) 553-8855
TCGexecsearch@aol.com
Ronald H. Coelyn, Partner
Also:
Jacksonville, FL (904) 371-3566
Kathleen H. Fehling, Managing Director

Cole, Warren and Long, Inc.

2 Penn Center Plaza, Suite 312
Philadelphia, PA 19102-1703
(215) 563-0701
http://www.cwl-inc.com/
cwlserch@cwl-inc.com
Ronald J. Cole, President

Coleman Lew & Associates, Inc.†

326 West Tenth Street
Post Office Box 36489
Charlotte, NC 28202-6489
(704) 377-0362

http://www.colemanlew.com/
mail@colemanlew.com
Charles E. Lew, President

COLTON BERNARD INC.
(SPECIALIZE IN APPAREL & RETAIL)
870 Market Street, Suite 822
San Francisco, CA 94102
(415) 399-8700
http://www.coltonbernard.com/
hbernard@coltonbernard.com
Roy C. Colton, President/Partner/CEO
Harry Bernard, Executive Vice President/Partner/CMO

THE COLTON PARTNERSHIP, INC.
(SPECIALIZE IN FINANCIAL SERVICES)
44 Wall Street
New York, NY 10005
(212) 509-1800
W. Hoyt Colton, President

COLUMBIA CONSULTING GROUP, INC.†
The Sun Life Building
20 South Charles Street, 9th Floor
Baltimore, MD 21201-3220
(410) 385-2525
http://www.ccgsearch.com/
ccgbal@erols.com
Lawrence J. Holmes, President
Also:
Jupiter, FL (561) 748-0232
Larry D. Mingle, Managing Principal
New York, NY (212) 832-2525
Ann Fulgham McCarthy, Managing Director

COMPASS GROUP LTD.†
THE HEVER GROUP
401 South Old Woodward Avenue, Suite 460
Birmingham, MI 48009-6613
(248) 540-9110
http://www.compassgroup.com/
executivesearch@compassgroup.com
Paul W. Czamanske, President & CEO
Christina L. Balian, Katherine T. Slaughter, Peter M. Czamanske & James W. Sturtz, Vice Presidents
Also:
Oak Brook, IL (630) 645-9110
Richard A. McDermott & Jerold L. Lipe, Managing Directors

CONEX, INC./INTERSEARCH
150 East 52nd Street, 2nd Floor
New York, NY 10022
(212) 371-3737
http://www.intersearch.org/
conexny@aol.com
Fred Siegel, President-USA

ROBERT CONNELLY & ASSOCIATES, INC.
(SPECIALIZE IN COMMERCIAL REAL ESTATE, ARCHITECTURE, ENGINEERING, CONSTRUCTION, AGRIBUSINESS)
5200 Willson Road, Suite 150
Minneapolis, MN 55424
(952) 925-3039
http://www.robertconnelly.com/
robtconn@aol.com
Robert F. Olsen, President

THE COOPER EXECUTIVE SEARCH GROUP, INC.
P.O. Box 375
Wales, WI 53183
(262) 968-9049
cesgroup@aol.com
Robert M. Cooper, President

THE CORPORATE SOURCE GROUP, INC.
One Cranberry Hill
Lexington, MA 02173
(781) 862-1900
http://www.csg-search.com/
csglex@csg-search.com
Dana Willis, Sr. Vice President
Also:
Tampa, FL (813) 286-4422
Mark Hausherr, Senior Vice President

CORSO, MIZGALA & FRENCH
INTERSEARCH
90 Eglinton Avenue East, Suite 404
Toronto, ON M4P 2Y3
(416) 488-4111
http://www.InterSearchCanada.com/
resumes@intersearchcanada.com
John J. Corso, Tony Mizgala, Guy French & Ralph Hansen, Partners

CRAWFORD DE MUNNIK, INC.
130 Adelaide Street West, Suite 2000
Toronto, ON M5H 3P5
(416) 863-0153
toronto@crawforddemunnik.com
John D. Crawford & N. Lynne DeMunnik, Parters

CROWE-INNES & ASSOCIATES, LLC†
1120 Mar West, Suite D
Tiburon, CA 94920
(415) 435-6211
http://www.croweinnes.com/
resumes@croweinnes.com
Jenny Crowe-Innes, President

CSI SEARCH†
(SPECIALIZE IN HEATHCARE)
201 Midwest Road, Suite 310
Oak Brook, IL 60523
(630) 916-1166
http://www.csisearch.com/
jobs-il@csistaff.com

Kathleen Ballein, Vice President and Practice Leader
Also:
Milwaukee, WI (414) 224-8181
Jim Hader, Branch Manager

M. J. Curran & Associates, Inc.

(Specialize in Biotechnology, Investment Management, Real Estate, Non-Profit)

304 Newberry, Suite 509
Boston, MA 02108
(617) 723-7002
Martin J. Curran, President

Curran Partners, Inc.

One Landmark Square, 18th Floor
Stamford, CT 06901
(203) 363-5350
http://www.curranpartners.com/
research@curranpartners.com
Michael Curran, President

Judith Cushman & Associates, Inc.

(Specialize in Public Relations)

1125 12th Avenue NW, Suite B-1A
Issaquah, WA 98027-3271
(425) 392-8660
http://www.jc-a.com/
info@jc-a.com
Judith Cushman, President

The Dalley Hewitt Company

1401 Peachtree Street, NE, Suite 500
Atlanta, GA 30309-3000
(404) 885-6642
http://www.DalleyHewitt.com/
rives@dalleyhewitt.com
Rives D. Hewitt, Principal

John J. Davis & Associates, Inc.

(Specialize in Information Technology)

521 Fifth Avenue, Suite 1740
New York, NY 10175
(212) 286-9489
http://www.johnjdavisandassoc.com/
jackdavis@comcastwork.net
John J. Davis, President

Deloitte & Touche Management Consultants

1 Place Ville-Marie, Room 3000
Montreal, QC H3B 4T9
(514) 393-7115
Paul Atrice Simard, Managing Partner

Denney & Company, Inc.

Gateway Center
Post Office Box 22156
Pittsburgh, PA 15222-0156
(412) 441-9636
Thomas L. Denney, President

DHR International, Inc.

10 South Riverside Plaza, Suite 2220
Chicago, IL 60606
(312) 782-1581
http://www.DHR-Intl.com/
resumes@dhrintl.net
David H. Hoffmann, Chairman & Chief Executive Officer
Robert E. Reilly Jr., President
Also:
Atlanta, GA (770) 730-5900
Jerry Franzel, Executive Vice President and Managing Director
Austin, TX (512) 469-6388
Ted Balistreri, Executive Vice President & Managing Director
Boca Raton, FL (561) 447-0561
Conrad Lee, President, International
Boston, MA (617) 742-5899
Christopher P. Dona, Vice Chairman
Brookfield, WI (262) 879-0850
Robert Stanislaw, Executive Vice President & Managing Director
Dennis Hood, Vice Chairman & Managing Director
Burbank, CA (818) 729-3803
Bob Kayhs, Executive Vice President
Charlotte, NC (704) 442-2503
Alan Stafford, Executive Vice President & Managing Director
Cincinnati, OH (513) 762-7874
Harry Rolfes, Senior Vice President & Managing Director
Columbus, OH (614) 785-6464
Jack Warren, Executive Vice President & Managing Director
Concord, MA (978) 369-1350
John L. Alexanderson, Managing Director
Denver, CO (303) 629-0730
Martin Pocs, Vice Chairman
East Greenwich, RI (401) 884-1695
Stephen P. Bartlett, Senior Vice President and Managing Director
Fort Myers, FL (941) 466-9899
Phil Jackson, Executive Vice President
Garden City, NY (516) 739-0010
Michael Carey, Executive Vice President
Hutchinson, KS (316) 728-1100
Jim Wright, Executive Vice President and Managing Director
Indianapolis, IN (317) 684-6948
James K. Doan, Executive Vice President & Managing Director
Irvine, CA (949) 852-1700
Ronald E. LaGrow, Senior Vice President & Managing Director
Irving, TX (214) 574-4044
Victor Arias Jr., Executive Vice President and Regional Managing Director
Issaquah, WA (425) 557-3681
James L. Black, Executive Vice President & Managing Director
Lansing, MI (517) 886-9010
Gordon S. White Jr., Senior Vice President & Managing

Director
Lansing, MI (517) 886-9010
Merritt Norvell, President Education
Lewiston, ME (207) 783-8834
Bill Klouthis, Executive Vice President
Lincoln, NE (402) 464-0566
Ted Balistreri, Executive Vice President & Managing Director
Los Angeles, CA (310) 789-7333
Bruce Babashan, Executive Vice President & Managing Director
Los Angeles, CA (310) 789-7333
John Wasley, Executive Vice President & Managing Director
Minnetonka, MN (952) 449-6015
Curt Hedeen, Executive Vice President
Mississauga, ON (905) 276-3667
Douglas Colling, President - DHR Canada
Mount Pleasant, SC (843) 856-3470
Dan Doherty & Rich Miller, Executive Vice Presidents
New York, NY (212) 883-6800
Deborah DeMaria, Executive Vice President
Frank T. Spencer, Vice Chairman
Terence J. McCarthy, Managing Director - Global
Oakland, CA (510) 273-2305
Tim Russi, Executive Vice President
Orchard Park, NY (716) 648-9260
Patrick Crotty, Executive Vice President
Oregonia, OH (513) 934-1667
Wayne Anglin, Executive Vice President
Overland Park, KS (913) 317-1600
Mike Klockenga, Executive Vice President & Managing Director
Pebble Beach, CA (831) 658-0700
William Manby, Executive Vice President
Philadelphia, PA (215) 665-5683
Michael E. Volpe, Executive Vice President & Managing Director
Phoenix, AZ (602) 953-7810
David Bruno, Vice Chairman
Pittsburgh, PA (412) 331-4700
John Thomburgh, Executive Vice President & Managing Director
David Smith, Executive Vice President
Pleasanton, CA (925) 468-4121
David Kurrasch, Executive Vice President & Managing Director
Ponte Vedra Beach, FL (904) 273-9660
William S. Elston, Executive Vice President & Managing Director
Salt Lake City, UT (801) 350-9101
Richard Hill, Executive Vice President & Managing Director
San Diego, CA (619) 792-7654
Joel T. Grushkin, Executive Vice President & Managing Director
San Francisco, CA (415) 439-5213
Gerald E. Parsons, Senior Vice President & Managing Director
Schaumburg, IL (847) 490-6450
Michael Setze, Executive Vice President
Short Hills, NJ (973) 912-4444
Hayes Reilley, Executive Vice President
Southbury, CT (203) 264-0810
Ralph DeCristoforo, Executive Vice President
St. Louis, MO (314) 205-2115
Steven Wood, Senior Vice President & Managing Director
Stamford, CT (203) 359-9700
Lawrence Noble, Executive Vice President & Managing Director
Tampa, FL (813) 348-0931
John T. Watters, Vice President & Managing Director
Townson, MD (410) 494-6500
Ken Miller, Executive Vice President/Managing Director
Tucson, AZ (520) 299-5608
Jerry Coon, Executive Vice President
Washington, DC (202) 822-9555
Stephen A. Hayes, Vice Chairman

The Dieck Group, Inc.

(Specialize in Forest Products, Chemical, Printing, Packaging, Food)
102 East Green Bay Street, Suite 101
Shawano, WI 54166-2444
(715) 524-5000
http://www.dieckgroup.com/
execsearch@dieckgroup.com
Daniel W. Dieck, President & CEO

Dieckmann & Associates, Ltd.†

2 Prudential Plaza, Suite 5555
180 North Stetson Avenue
Chicago, IL 60601-3708
(312) 819-5900
http://dieckmann-associates.com/
dieckmann@dieckmann-associates.com
Ralph E. Dieckmann & Donald R. Utroska, Principals

DiMarchi Partners

7107 La Vista Place, Suite 200
Niwot, CO 80503
(303) 415-9300
mail@dimarchi.com
Paul M. DiMarchi, President
Patricia A. McKeown, Partner

Robert W. Dingman Company, Inc.†

650 Hampshire Road, Suite 116
Westlake Village, CA 91361-4211
(805) 778-1777
http://www.dingman.com/
info@dingman.com
H. Bruce Dingman, President
Robert W. Dingman, Chairman

The Diversified Search Companies†

One Commerce Square
2005 Market Street, Suite 3300
Philadelphia, PA 19104
(215) 732-6666

http://www.divsearch.com/
diversified@divsearch.com
Judith M. von Seldeneck, President & Chief Executive Officer
Burton A. MacLean Jr., Managing Director
Also:
Atlanta, GA (404) 262-1049
W.H. Peter Keesom, Managing Director
Boston, MA (617) 523-6870
Joan Lucarelli, Managing Director
Charlotte, NC (704) 370-3110
Jeffrey Siegrist, Managing Director
New York, NY (212) 661-3220
Elaine Burfield, Managing Director
San Francisco, CA (415) 352-0418
W.H. Peter Keesom, Managing Director

DMG Maximus
(Specialize in Health Care, Education, Public Sector, Utilities & Transportation)
1800 Century Park East, Suite 430
Los Angeles, CA 90067-1507
(310) 552-1112
http://www.dmgmaximus.com/
searchla@dmg.maximus.com
Norman C. Roberts, Vice President

Dougan & Associates
EMA Partners International
333 North Sam Houston Parkway East, Suite 400
Houston, TX 77060-2403
(281) 999-7209
http://www.emapartners.com/
David Dougan, President

Dromeshauser & Associates
(Specialize in High Tech)
70 Walnut Street
Wellesley Hills, MA 02181
(508) 358-9600
Peter Dromeshauser, President

J. H. Dugan & Associates, Inc.
(Specialize in Plastics Industry)
225 Crossroads Boulevard, Suite 416
Carmel, CA 93923
(831) 655-5880
http://www.jhdugan.com/
resumes@jhdugan.com
John H. Dugan, Chairman

E Search Group
30 Tower Lane
Avon, CT 06001
(860) 677-6770
http://www.esearchgroup.com/
info@esearchgroup.com
Ronald R. Evans, Managing Director
Also:
Dallas, TX (972) 960-8640
Mark W. Hardwick Ph.D., Director of Southwest Region

Earley Kielty & Associates, Inc.
Two Pennsylvania Plaza, Suite 1990
New York, NY 10121
(212) 736-5626
http://www.earleykielty.com
resumes@earleykielty.com
Eugene J. Herman, President
John C. Sterling, Senior Vice President

Early Cochran & Olson, LLC
(Specialize in Lawyers)
401 North Michigan Avenue, Suite 515
Chicago, IL 60611-4205
(312) 595-4200
http://www.ecollc.com
Corinne Cochran & B. Tucker Olson, Principals

Eastman & Beaudine, Inc.
5700 West Plano Parkway, Suite 2800
Plano, TX 75093
(972) 267-8891
http://www.eastman-beaudine.com/
Robert E. Beaudine, President
Also:
Atlanta, GA (770) 390-0801
Frank R. Beaudine Jr., Senior Vice President & Managing Director

EFL Associates/TranSearch
7101 College Boulevard, Suite 550
Overland Park, KS 66210-1891
(913) 451-8866
http://transearch.com/
eflinfo@eflkc.com
Peter K. Lemke, Chairman & Chief Executive Officer
Also:
Englewood, CO (303) 779-1724
Jeffrey K. Riley, Senior Vice President & Managing Partner

EFL International
8777 East Via de Ventura, Suite 300
Scottsdale, AZ 85258
(480) 483-0496
http://www.eflinternational.com/
jeff@eflinternational.com
William R. Franquemont, President
Jeffrey D. Franquemont, Senior Vice President

Elwell & Associates, Inc.
3100 West Liberty Street, Suite E
Ann Arbor, MI 48103
(734) 662-8775
http://www.elwellassociates.com/
elwellas@elwellassociates.com
Richard F. Elwell, President
Steve Elwell & David Gilmore, Vice Presidents

Enns Hever, Inc.†
South Tower, Suite 601
100 University Avenue, Post Office Box 134
Toronto, ON M5J 1V6
(416) 598-0012
http://www.ennshever.com/
info@ennshever.com
George R. Enns, Jock McGregor, Alan Burns, Morris Tambor & Rita Eskudt, Partners

ExecuCounsel, Inc.
(Specialize in Health Care)
2 Bloor Street West, Suite 700
Toronto, ON M4W 3R1
(416) 928-3025
Richard Marty, Managing Director

Executive Bridge Inc.
(Specialize in High Tech)
9900 Clayton Road
St. Louis, MO 63124-1102
(314) 872-8800
http://www.executivebridge.com/
resume@executivebridge.com
Cynthia J. Kolhbry, President and CEO
Stephen J. Robin, Principal

Executive Manning Corporation
3000 NE 30th Place, Suite 405
Fort Lauderdale, FL 33306
(954) 561-5100
http://www.exmanning.com/
emc@exmanning.com
Richard L. Hertan, President & Chief Executive Officer

Executive Resource Group, Inc.
(Specialize in Publishing Industry)
29 Oakhurst Road
Cape Elizabeth, ME 04107
(207) 871-5527
http://www.mediahunter.com/
Sibyl Masquelier, President

The Executive Source†
2201 11th Avenue, Suite 401
Regina, SK S4P 0J8
(306) 359-2550
search@theexecutivesource.com
Holly Hetherington, President

Leon A. Farley Associates
31 Laderman Lane
Greenbrae, CA 94904
(415) 989-0989
Leon A. Farley, Managing Partner

Ferneborg & Associates, Inc.†
160 Bovet Road, Suite 210
San Mateo, CA 94402
(650) 577-0100
http://www.execsearch.com/
resume@execsearch.com
John R. Ferneborg, President
Jay W. Ferneborg, Partner

Finnegan & Associates
P.O. Box 1183
Palos Verdes Estates, CA 90274
(310) 375-8555
Richard G. Finnegan, President & Chief Executive Officer

Howard Fischer Associates, Inc./*ITP Worldwide*
(Specialize in Information Technology)
1800 Kennedy Boulevard, Suite 700
Philadelphia, PA 19103
(215) 568-8363
http://www.hfischer.com/
search@hfischer.com
Howard M. Fischer, President and CEO
Adam J. Fischer, Partner
Also:
Houston, TX (713) 974-2300
Beth Shapiro, Vice President & Managing Director

Fisher Personnel Management Services
1219 Morningside Drive
Manhattan Beach, CA 90266-4766
(310) 546-7507
http://fisheads.net
HookMe@Fisheads.net
Neal Fisher & Judy Gibson, Principals

The Flagship Group
(Specialize in Investment Management)
185 Devenshire Street, Suite 350
Boston, MA 02110
(617) 728-0220
Anna Coppola, President

Robert M. Flanagan & Associates, Ltd.
39 Fields Road
North Salem, NY 10560
(914) 277-7210
Robert M. Flanagan, President

Fleming Associates of New Orleans
3900 North Causeway Boulevard, Suite 770
Metairie, LA 70002
(504) 836-7090
David W. McClung, Managing Partner

Foley Proctor Yoskowitz
(Specialize in Health Care)
One Cattano Avenue
Morristown, NJ 07960-6820
(973) 605-1000
http://www.fpysearch.com/
fpy@fpysearch.com
Thomas J. Foley, Senior. Partner

Richard Proctor & Reggie Yoskowitz, Partners

L. W. Foote Company
110 - 110th Avenue, NE, Suite 603
Bellevue, WA 98004-5840
(425) 451-1660
http://www.lwfoote.com/
email@lwfoote.com
Leland W. Foote, President

The Ford Group, Inc.
485 Devon Park Drive, Suite 110
Wayne, PA 19087
(610) 975-9007
http://www.thefordgroup.com/
Info@thefordgroup.com
Sandra D. Ford, CEO & Managing Director

D. E. Foster Partners, Inc.
570 Lexington Avenue, 14th Floor
New York, NY 10022
(212) 893-2300
http://www.fosterpartners.com/
recruiting@fosterpartners.com
Dwight E. Foster, Chairman & Chief Executive Officer
Also:
Chicago, IL (312) 453-9410
Ken Daubenspeck, Managing Director
Dallas, TX (214) 880-0432
William D. Rowe II, Vice Chairman & Managing Director
Minneapolis, MN (652) 222-4420
Christopher P. Johnson, Managing Director
Bellevue, WA (425) 637-2993
Mr. William Reffett, Managing Partner
Washington, DC (202) 223-9112
J. Chris Dowell, Managing Director

Foy, Schneid & Daniel, Inc.
555 Madison Avenue, 12th Floor
New York, NY 10022
(212) 980-2525
fsd1brd@aol.com
James Foy & Beverly R. Daniel, Partners

Francis & Associates†
6923 Vista Drive
West Des Moines, IA 50266
(515) 221-9800
http://francisassociates.com/
FranSearch@aol.com
Dwaine Francis, Managing Partner
Kay Francis, Partner

KS Frary & Associates
One Salem Green, Suite 403
Salem, MA 01970
(978) 741-5201
http://www.ksfrary.com/
ksfrary@tiac.net
Kevin S. Frary, President

Furst Group/MPI
(Specialize in Health Care)
555 South Perryville Road
Rockford, IL 61108-2509
(815) 229-9111
http://www.furstgroup.com/
furstgroup@furstgroup.com
Sherrie L. Barch, J. Robert Clarke & Tyler P. Pratt, Principals
Also:
Minneapolis, MN (612) 339-8500
Brad J. Frischmon, Vice President
Woodridge, VA (703) 580-1737
Deanna Banks, Vice President
Wylie, TX (972) 429-4610
William J. Fosick, Vice President

Jay Gaines & Company, Inc.†
(Specialize in Finance & MIS)
450 Park Avenue, Suite 500
New York, NY 10022
(212) 308-9222
jgandco@jaygaines.com
Jay Gaines, President

Gardiner, Townsend & Associates†
101 East 52nd Street, 25th Floor
New York, NY 10022
(212) 838-0707
http://www.gardinertownsend.com/
E. Nicholas P. Gardiner, President
John W. Townsend, Partner

Gilbert Tweed Associates Inc.
415 Madison Avenue, 20th Floor
New York, NY 10017-1111
(212) 758-3000
http://www.gilberttweed.com/
hrdept@gilberttweed.com
Stephanie L. Pinson, President
Janet Tweed, Chief Executive Officer

Gilreath Consultantcy
(Specialize in Manufacturing, Venture Capital)
50 B Brook Street, Post Office Box 1483
Manchester by the Sea, MA 01944
(978) 526-8771
http://www.gwisearch.com/
jim@gilreathsearch.com
James M. Gilreath, President

The Glazin Group
(Specialize in Real Estate & Hospitality)
2300-1066 West Hasting Street
Vancouver, BC V6E 3X2
(604) 687-3875
Lynne Glazin, Partner

Goodrich & Sherwood Associates, Inc.
521 Fifth Avenue, 19th Floor

New York, NY 10175
(212) 697-4131
http://www.goodrichsherwood.com/
rycunningham@goodrichsherwood.com
Andrew Sherwood, Chairman
Charles Wright, Senior Vice President
Also:
Norwalk, CT (203) 899-7900
Richard E. Spann, Executive Vice President
Parsippany, NJ (973) 455-7100
http://www.goodrichsherwood.com/
William Heald, Principal
Princeton, NJ (609) 452-0202
Frank Dees, Senior Vice President
Rochester, NY (716) 262-4277
Art Brent, Managing Director
Shelton, CT (203) 944-2828
John Schegg, Principal

Goodwin & Company

1150 Connecticut Avenue, NW, Suite 200
Washington, DC 20036
(202) 785-9292
Tom L. Goodwin, President

Gould, McCoy & Chadick, Inc.†

300 Park Avenue, 20th Floor
New York, NY 10022
(212) 688-8671
http://www.gmcsearch.com/
resumes@gmcsearch.com
Susan L. Chadick, Managing Director and CEO
William E. Gould, Millington M. McCoy & Janice Reals Ellig, Managing Directors

A. Davis Grant & Company

(Specialize in MIS & Information Technology)
295 Pierson Avenue
Edison, NJ 08837-3118
(732) 494-2266
http://www.adg.net/
mail@adg.net
Allan D. Grossman, Senior Partner

Grant Cooper & Associates

9900 Clayton Road
St. Louis, MO 63124-1102
(314) 567-4690
http://www.grantcooper.com/
resume@grantcooper.com
Cynthia J. Kolhbry, Managing Principal/ President and CEO
Stephen H. Loeb, Chairman
J. Dale Meier, Principal

Grantham, Griffin & Buck, Inc.

161 Weaver Dairy Road
Chapel Hill, NC 27514
(919) 932-5650
http://www.integritycareers.com/
grantham@nc.rr.com
John D. Grantham, President
Charlie Griffin & John Buck, Vice Presidents

Annie Gray Associates, Inc.

516 South Hanley
St. Louis, MO 63105
(314) 721-0205
http://www.anniegray.com/
resume@anniegray.com
Annie Gray, President & Chief Executive Officer

Grossberg & Associates

(Specialize in Manufacturing & Distribution)
1100 Jorie Boulevard, Suite 221
Oak Brook, IL 60523
(630) 574-0066
bobgsearch@aol.com
Robert M. Grossberg, Managing Partner

Gundersen Partners†

230 W. 17th Street, 6th Floor
New York, NY 10011
(212) 675-2300
http://www.gundersenpartners.com/
Steven Gundersen, President & Chief Executive Officer
Also:
Bloomfield Hills, MI (248) 258-3800
John Bissell, Partner

Hailes & Associates†

(Specialize in High Tech)
400 Colony Square, Suite 200
1201 Peachtree Street
Atlanta, GA 30361
(404)-877-9185
http://www.hailes.com/
recruiter@hailes.com
Brian Hailes, President

Halbrecht Lieberman Associates, Inc.†

(Specialize in Information Technology)
1200 Summer Street
Stamford, CT 06905-5573
(203) 327-5630
http://www.hlassoc.com/
info@hlassoc.com
Beverly Lieberman, President

W. L. Handler & Associates

2255 Cumberland Parkway NW, Building 1500
Atlanta, GA 30339
(770) 805-5000
http://www.wlhandler.com/
resume@wlhandler.com
William Handler, President

Handy Partners

380 Lexington Avenue, Suite 2125
New York, NY 10168
(212) 697-5600

http://www.handypartners.com/
info@handypartners.com
Patrick Brennan, Managing Partner
Gaffney J. Feskoe & R. Kevin Hughes, Partners

Bente Hansen Associates
1207 High Bluff Drive, Suite 200
San Diego, CA 92130
(858) 350-4331
Bente Hansen, Managing Director

Harvard Aimes Group
(Specialize in Corporate Risk Management & Safety Claims Management)
6 Holcomb Street, Post Office Box 16006
West Haven, CT 06516
(203) 933-1976
http://www.riskmanagementsearch.com/
James J. Gunther, Principal

Haskell & Stern Associates Inc.
380 Madison Avenue, 7th Floor
New York, NY 10017
(212) 856-4451
Allan D. R. Stern, Managing Director

Hayden Group, Inc.
(Specialize in Financial Services)
One Post Office Square
Suite 3830
Boston, MA 02109
(617) 482-2445
Harry B. McCormick & Robert E. Hawley, Partners

Heath/Norton Associates, Inc.
545 Eighth Avenue, 7th Floor
New York, NY 10018
(212) 695-3600
Richard S. Stoller, President
Richard Rosenow, Senior Vice President

Heidrick & Struggles International, Inc.†
Sears Tower, Suite 7000
233 South Wacker Drive
Chicago, IL 60606-6402
(312) 496-1000
http://www.heidrick.com/
William J. Bowen, Chairman
Linda H. Heagy, Office Managing Partner
Caroline B. Ballantine & P. Frederick Kahn, Partners
Also:
Atlanta, GA (404) 577-2410
Patrick S. Pittard, President & CEO
Dale E. Jones, Office Managing Partner
Boston, MA (617) 737-6300
Robert E. Hallagan, Vice Chairman
Chuck W.B. Wardell III, Office Managing Partner
Charlotte, NC (704) 335-1953
Gerry P. McNamara, Office Managing Partner
Cleveland, OH (216) 241-7410
Bonnie W. Gwin, Office Managing Partner
Dallas, TX (214) 706-7700
David R. Pasahow, Office Managing Partner
Denver, CO (303) 295-7000
Fred Ley, Principal
Emeryville, CA (510) 420-8650
Mark K. Yowe, Office Managing Partner
Foster City, CA (650) 234-1500
Mark W. Lonergan, Office Managing Partner
Greenwich, CT (203) 862-4600
Dona E. Roche-Tarry, Office Managing Partner
Houston, TX (713) 237-9000
David A. Morris, Office Managing Partner
Irvine, CA (949) 475-6500
Judy L. Klein, Office Managing Partner
Jacksonville, FL (904) 355-6674
Charles R. Hoskins, Office Managing Partner
Lexington, MA (781) 862-3370
Donald R. Gordon, Office Managing Partner
Los Angeles, CA (213) 625-8811
Thomas M. Mitchell, Office Managing Partner
McLean, VA (703) 848-2500
Kevin A. McNerney, Office Managing Partner
Menlo Park, CA (650) 234-1500
John T. Thompson, Vice Chairman
Mark W. Lonergan, Office Managing Partner
Miami, FL (305) 262-2606
Bernard S. Zen Ruffinen, Managing Partner
Montreal, QC (514) 285-8900
Guy Hebert, Office Managing Partner
New York, NY (212) 699-3000
Barry I. Bregman, Office Managing Partner
New York, NY (212) 867-9876
Gerard R. Roche, Senior Chairman
Marvin B. Berenblum, North America Area Managing Partner
Philadelphia, PA (215) 988-1000
Kenneth L. Kring, Office Managing Partner
San Francisco, CA (415) 981-2854
Laurence O'Neil, Office Managing Partner
Seattle, WA (206) 839-8686
Jason Hancock, Office Managing Partner
Toronto, ON (416) 361-4700
Jack H.B. Nederpelt, Office Managing Partner-Canada
Washington, DC (202) 289-4450
Kevin A. McNerney, Managing Partner

G. W. Henn & Company
9420 Route 37 East
Sunbury, OH 43074
(740) 965-9912
gwhenn@aol.com
George W. Henn Jr., President

The Hetzel Group
157K Helm Road
Barrington, IL 60010
(874) 776-7000

William G. Hetzel, President

Heyman Associates, Inc.

(Specialize in Communications & PR)
11 Penn Plaza, Suite 1105
New York, NY 10001
(212) 784-2717
http://www.heymanassociates.com/
resume@heymanassociates.com
William C. Heyman, President & CEO

Hodge-Cronin & Associates, Inc.

P.O. Box 309-0309
Des Plaines, IL 60016-0309
(847) 803-9000
Richard J. Cronin, President
Kathleen A. Cronin, Vice President

Harvey Hohauser & Associates, LLC

5600 New King Street, Suite 355
Troy, MI 48098
(248) 641-1400
http://www.hohauser.com/
information@hohauser.com
Harvey Hohauser, President
Also:
Gibsonia, PA (724) 449-3320
Joseph F. Schatt, Senior Vice President
Okemos, MI (517) 349-7007
Kenneth S. Glickman, Senior Vice President

The Holman Group, Inc.†

(Specialize in CEOs, Venture Capital Partners, Information Technology)
1592 Union Street, Suite 239
San Francisco, CA 94123
(415) 751-2700
http://www.holmangroup.net/
Jonathan S. Holman, President

J. B. Homer Associates Inc.

(Specialize in Information Technology)
420 Lexington Avenue, Suite 2328
New York, NY 10170-0002
(212) 697-3300
http://www.JBHomer.com/
resumes@JBHomer.com
Judy B. Homer, President & Principal

Horton International, Inc.†

10 Tower Lane
Avon, CT 06001
(860) 674-8701
http://www.horton-intl.com/
avon@horton-intl.com
Larry C. Brown, Managing Director
Also:
Atlanta, GA (404) 459-5950
Sally Baker, Director Of Admission
Austin, TX (512) 494 9443
Michael Boxberger, Chief Executive Officer
Chicago, IL (312) 332-3830
Dirk A. Himes, Managing Director
New York, NY (212) 973-3780
Franklin K. Brown, Managing Director
Palm Harbor, FL (727) 945-0803
Linda Kearschner

Howe-Lewis International

(Specialize in Health Care)
521 Fifth Avenue, 36th Floor
New York, NY 10175
(212) 697-5000
Anita Howe-Waxman, Chairman
Patricia Greco & Esther Rosenberg, Co-Managing Directors

HR/RH Inc.

3545 Cote-des-Meiges, Suite 024
Montreal, QC H3H 1V1
(514) 932-6500
info@hrrhinc.com
Jean S. Morrissette, Senior Partner

HRD Consultants, Inc.†

(Specialize in Human Resources)
60 Walnut Avenue, Suite 100
Clark, NJ 07066-1647
(732) 815-7825
http://www.hrdconsultants.com/
hrd@aol.com
Marcia Glatman, President

E. A. Hughes & Company†

(Specialize in Apparel & Home Fashion)
146 East 37th Street
New York, NY 10016
(212) 689-4600
http://www.eahughes.com/
general@eahughes.com
Elaine A. Hughes, Founder & President

Hunt & Howe Partners LLC†

One Dag Hammarskjold Plaza, 34th Floor
New York, NY 10017
(212) 758-2800
http://www.hunthowe.com/
info@hunthowe.com
James E. Hunt, William S. Howe, Helga M. Long, Carol A. McCullough & Robert B. Whaley, Partners

Hutchinson Group, Inc.

250 Consumers Road, Suite 603
Toronto, ON M2J 4V6
(416) 499-6621
http://www.hutchgroup.com/
resumes@hutchgroup.com
Hamilton B. Hutchinson, President
H. David Hutchinson, Vice President

HVS International†
(Specialize in Hospitality Industry)
372 Willis Avenue
Mineola, NY 11501
(516) 248-8828
http://www.hvsinternational.com/
Stephen Rushmore, President & Founder
Also:
Boulder, CO (303) 443-3933
Gregory Hartmann, Managing Director
Miami, FL (305) 378-0404
Kathleen Conroy, Managing Director
N. Vancouver, BC (604) 988-9743
Betsy McDonald, Managing Director
San Francisco, CA (415) 896-0868
Suzanne R. Mellen, Managing Director
Toronto, ON (416) 686-2260
Jon Lantz & Lorenzo Palumbo, Managing Directors

Hyde Danforth & Company
5950 Berkshire Lane, Suite 1040
Dallas, TX 75225
(214) 691-5966
http://www.hydedanforth.com/
resume@hydedanforth.com
W. Michael Danforth, President
W. Jerry Hyde, Executive Vice President

Ingram & Aydelotte, Inc.
430 Park Avenue, Suite 700
New York, NY 10022
(212) 319-7777
http://www.iasearch.com/
D. John Ingram, Senior Partner
G. Thomas Aydelotte, Partner

International Management Advisors, Inc.
Member, International Search Associates, Inc.
FDR Station, P.O. Box 174
New York, NY 10150
(212) 758-7770
Constance W. Klages, President

Isaacson, Miller
334 Boylston Street, Suite 500
Boston, MA 02116
(617) 262-6500
http://www.imsearch.com/
info@imsearch.com
Arnie Miller, Founder & Partner
John Isaacson, Managing Director

J: Blakslee International
(Specialize in Pharmaceuticals, Biotechnology & Medical)
49 Hillside Avenue
Mill Valley, CA 94941
(415) 389-7300
resumes@jblakslee.com
Jan H. Blakslee, President
Joyce Mustin, Partner

January Management Group
432 East Rich Street, Suite 2F
Columbus, OH 43215
(614) 463-1820
Bruce M. Bastoky, President

Jonas, Walters & Associates, Inc.
1110 N. Old World Third Street, Suite 510
Milwaukee, WI 53203-1184
(414) 291-2828
jwa@execpc.com
William F. Walters, President
John Kuhn, Executive Vice President

Jones-Parker/Starr
(Specialize in Consulting Industry)
207 South Elliot Road, Suite 155
Chapel Hill, NC 27514
(919) 542-5977
http://www.jonesparkerstarr.com/
info@jonesparkerstarr.com
Janet Jones-Parker & Jonathan Starr, Managing Directors
Also:
New York, NY (212) 280-6464
Louise Young, Senior Vice President

Kaludis Consulting Group, Inc.
(Specialize in Higher Education)
1055 Thomas Jefferson Street N.W., Suite 400
Washington, DC 20007
(202) 298-2800
http://www.kcg.com/
info@kcg.com
George Kaludis, President & Chairman
John A. Stephens, Senior Vice President & COO

Gary Kaplan & Associates
201 South Lake Avenue, Suite 600
Pasadena, CA 91101
(626) 796-8100
http://www.gkasearch.com/
resumes@gkasearch.com
Gary Kaplan, President

Karr & Associates Inc.†
(Specialize in Finance)
1777 Borel Place, Suite 408
San Mateo, CA 94402-3513
(650) 574-5277
http://www.karr.com/
search@karr.com
Howard L. Karr, President
Cynthia L. Karr & Liz Karr, Vice Presidents

A. T. Kearney Executive Search†
222 West Adams Street

Chicago, IL 60606
(312) 648-0111
http://www.atkearney.com/
Charles W. Sweet, President
Also:
Atlanta, GA (404) 760-6600
Richard Citarella, Vice President & Managing Director
Cleveland, OH (216) 241-6880
David Lauderback, Vice President & Managing Director
Dallas, TX (214) 969-0010
Rocky Johnson, Vice President & Managing Director
Los Angeles, CA (213) 689-6800
Jack Groban, Vice President & Managing Director
Miami, FL (305) 577-0046
John T. Mestepey, Vice President & Managing Director
Minneapolis, MN (952) 921-8436
David A. McQuoid, Vice President
New York, NY (212) 751-7040
Emmet Kelly, Vice President & Managing Director
Redwood Shores, CA (650) 637-6600
Maggie Yen, Director
San Diego, CA (858) 646-3066
Susan Major, Vice President & Managing Director
Stamford, CT (203) 969-2222
Mark J. McMahon, Vice President & Managing Director
Toronto, ON (416) 947-1990
Rosemary Duff, Office Manager

KENZER CORPORATION
777 Third Avenue
New York, NY 10017
(212) 308-4300
http://www.kenzer.com/
ny@kenzer.com
Robert D. Kenzer, Chairman
Eric B. Segal, President
Also:
Atlanta, GA (770) 955-7210
Marie Powell, Vice President
Chicago, IL (312) 266-0976
Barbara Kauffmann, Vice President
Dallas, TX (972) 620-7776
Don Jones, Vice President
Los Angeles, CA (310) 417-8577
Robert Armstrong, Vice President
Minneapolis, MN (612) 332-7700
Mary Jeanne Scott, Vice President

KETCHUM, INC.
(SPECIALIZE IN NON-PROFIT & FUNDRAISING)
12770 Merit Drive, Suite 900
Dallas, TX 75251
(412) 281-1481
Robert E. Carter, President

KINCANNON & REED†
(SPECIALIZE IN FOOD, AGRIBUSINESS, LIFE SCIENCES)
2106-C Gallows Road
Vienna, VA 22182
(703) 761-4046
http://www.krsearch.com/
office@krsearch.com
Kelly Kincannon, President & CEO

KINSER & BAILLOU, LLC†
515 Madison Avenue, 36th Floor
New York, NY 10022
(212) 588-8801
http://www.kinserbaillou.com/
search@kinserbaillou.com
Richard E. Kinser, President

KNAPP CONSULTANTS
(SPECIALIZE IN AEROSPACE, HIGH TECH)
184 Old Ridgefield Road
Wilton, CT 06897
(203) 762-0790
Ronald A. Knapp, President

KORN/FERRY INTERNATIONAL†
1800 Century Park East, Suite 900
Los Angeles, CA 90067-1593
(310) 552-1834
http://www.kornferry.com/
Paul C. Reilly, Chairman & CEO
Richard M. Ferry, Chairman
Peter L. Dunn, Vice Chairman & COO
John Moxley, Managing Director
Caroline Nahas, Managing Director-Southwest Region
Also:
Atlanta, GA (404) 577-7542
Craig Dunlevie, Managing Director
Austin, TX (512) 236-1834
Bill Funk, Managing Director
Boston, MA (617) 345-0200
Mark L. Smith, Vice President & Office Manager
Kevin Conley, Managing Director
Calgary, AB (403) 269-3277
Micheal Honey & John McKay, Managing Directors
Chicago, IL (312) 466-1834
Scott Kingdom, Vice President & Managing Director
Dallas, TX (214) 954-1834
Robert William Funk, Managing Director
Denver, CO (303) 542-1880
Scott Kingdom, Managing Director
Houston, TX (713) 651-1834
Greg Barnes, Managing Director
Irvine, CA (949) 851-1834
Elliot Gordon, Managing Director
McLean, VA (703) 761-7020
Micheal Kirkman, Managing Director
Miami, FL (305) 377-4121
Bonnie Crabtree, Managing Director
Minneapolis, MN (612) 333-1834
Jeremy Hanson, Vice President
Montreal, QC (514) 397-9655
Jean-Pierre Bourbonnais, Managing Director
New York, NY (212) 687-1834

Windle B. Priem, Founder Chairman
Robert E. Kerson, President & Global Retail Practice
Greg Coleman, VP Financial Services & Managing Director
Tim Friar, Managing Director - New York Office
Philadelphia, PA (215) 496-6666
David Shabot, Managing Director
Princeton, NJ (609) 452-8848
Richard Arons, Managing Director
Redwood City, CA (650) 632-1834
David Nosal, Managing Director
San Francisco, CA (415) 956-1834
Bill Caldwell, Managing Director
San Francisco, CA (415) 956-1834
James N. Heuerman, Managing Director
Seattle, WA (206) 447-1834
Hershel V. Jones, Vice President & Managing Director
Stamford, CT (203) 359-3350
Terence P. McGovern, Managing Director
Toronto, ON (416) 365-1841
Elan Pratzer, President - Canada
Vancouver, BC (604) 684-1834
Grant Spitz, Managing Director
Washington, DC (202) 822-9444
Mike Kirkman, Managing Director

KORS MONTGOMERY INTERNATIONAL
(SPECIALIZE IN GLOBAL ENERGY & HIGH TECH)
14811 Saint Mary's Lane, Suite 280
Houston, TX 77079
(713) 840-7101
http://www.korsmontgomery.com/
research@korsmontgomery.com
R. Paul Kors, President

KRECKLO CONSULTANTS INTERNATIONAL
(SPECIALIZE IN MIS & TECHNOLOGY)
1250 Boulevard Rene-Levesque Ouest, Suite 2200
Montreal, QC H3B 4W8
(514) 989-3163
http://www.krecklo.com/
info@krecklo.com
Brian D. Krecklo, President

KREMPLE & MEADE INC.
P.O. Box 426
Pacific Palisades, CA 90272
(310) 459-4221
Thomas M. Meade, President & CEO

KREUTZ CONSULTING GROUP, INC.†
585 North Bank Lane, Suite 2000
Lake Forest, IL 60045
(847) 234-9115
Gary L. Kreutz, President

KRISTOPHERS CONSULTANTS
(SPECIALIZE IN HEALTH CARE, CONSUMER PRODUCTS & AUTOMOTIVE)
5551 North Osceola
Chicago, IL 60656
(773) 594-1301
Kevin Cabai, President

KUNZER ASSOCIATES, LTD.
1415 West 22nd Street, Suite 1180
Oak Brook, IL 60521
(630) 574-0010
William J. Kunzer, President

THE LAPHAM GROUP, INC.
80 Park Avenue, Suite 3-K
New York, NY 10016-2533
(212) 599-0644
llapham@thelaphamgroup.com
Lawrence L. Lapham, President

LARSEN, WHITNEY, BLECKSMITH, AND ZILLIACUS
888 West Sixth Street, Suite 500
Los Angeles, CA 90017
(213) 243-0033
lwbz1@mindspring.com
Richard F. Larsen, William A. Whitney, Edward L. Blecksmith, & Patrick W. Zilliacus, Principals

LAUER, SBARBARO ASSOCIATES†
EMA PARTNERS INTERNATIONAL
30 North LaSalle Street, Suite 4030
Chicago, IL 60602-2588
(312) 372-7050
http://www.lauersbarbaro-ema.com/
SBARBS@AOL.com
Richard D. Sbarbaro, Chairman
William J. Yacullo, Executive Vice President

LAWRENCE-LEITER & COMPANY
4400 Shawnee Mission Parkway, Suite 208
Shawnee Mission, KS 66205
(913) 677-5500
lleiter@sky.net
David Bywaters, President
William B. Beeson, Vice President

LOCKE & ASSOCIATES
4144 Carmichael Road, Suite 20
Montgomery, AL 36106
(334) 272-7400
gopruitt@mindspring.com
Glen Pruitt, Vice President
Also:
Charlotte, NC (704) 372-6600
Fred Locke Jr., President

THE JOHN LUCHT CONSULTANCY INC.†
641 Fifth Avenue
New York, NY 10022
(212) 935-4660
John Lucht, President

M/J/A PARTNERS, INC.
(SPECIALIZE IN EXECUTIVE MANAGEMENT)
1100 Jorie Boulevard, Suite 301
Oak Brook, IL 60521
(630) 990-0033
Manuel J. Alves, President
Victor R. Lindquist, Vice President

THE MACDONALD GROUP, INC.
301 Route 17, Suite 800
Rutherford, NJ 07070
(201) 939-2312
macdgrp@aol.com
G. William Macdonald, President

MACKENZIE GRAY MANAGEMENT INC.†
444 Fifth Avenue, SW, Suite 1500
Calgary, AB T2P 2T8
(403) 264-8906
macgray@cadvision.com
Douglas G. MacKenzie, Principal

THE MADISON GROUP
342 Madison Avenue, Suite 1060
New York, NY 10173
(212) 599-0032
David Soloway, Managing Director

MARK ADAM ASSOCIATES
(SPECIALIZE IN INFORMATION SYSTEMS, FINANCE & GENERAL MANAGEMENT)
256 Canterbury Road
Westfield, NJ 07090-1905
(908) 654-8999
http://www.markadamassociates.com
mpizzi@markadamassociates.com
Donald A. Pizzi, Principal

J. L. MARK ASSOCIATES, INC.
2000 Arapahoe Street, Suite 505
Denver, CO 80205
(303) 292-0360
jlmark@jlmark.com
John L. Mark, President
Lynne Mark, Senior Recruiter

MARRA PETERS & PARTNERS
Millburn Esplanade
Millburn, NJ 07041
(973) 376-8999
http://www.marrapeters.com/
marrapeters@aol.com
John V. Marra Jr., President

MARSHALL CONSULTANTS, INC.
(SPECIALIZE IN CORPORATE COMMUNICATIONS)
360 East 65th Street, Penthouse B
New York, NY 10021
(212) 628-8400
http://www.marshallconsultants.com/
Larry Marshall, President & CEO

MARTIN PARTNERS, LLC†
(SPECIALIZE IN EBUSINESS, FINANCIAL SERVICES, HEALTHCARE, BIOTECHNOLOGY)
224 South Michigan Avenue, Suite 620
Chicago, IL 60604
(312) 922-1800
http://www.martinptrs.com/
webmaster@martinpartners.com
Theodore B. Martin, Founder & Managing Partner
Sally Frantz & Thomas Jagielo, Partners

MASCHAL/CONNORS, INC.
(SPECIALIZE IN INDUSTRIAL PRODUCTS)
306 South Bay Avenue
Beach Haven, NJ 08008
(609) 492-3400
Charles E. Maschal Jr., President

MASON & ASSOCIATES
Building 1, Suite 155
3000 Sand Hill Road
Menlo Park, CA 94025
(650) 322-5288
cfmsearch@volcano.net
Robert G. Mason, President

THE MCAULAY FIRM†
Bank of America Corporate Center
100 North Tryon Street, Suite 5220
Charlotte, NC 28202
(704) 342-1880
http://www.mcaulay.com
info@mcaulay.com
Albert L. McAulay Jr., President

MCBRIDE ASSOCIATES, INC.†
1742 N Street NW
Washington, DC 20036-2907
(202) 452-1150
Jonathan E. McBride, President

MCCORMACK & ASSOCIATES†
(SPECIALIZE IN NONPROFIT & DIVERSITY EXECUTIVE SEARCH)
5042 Wilshire Boulevard, Suite 505
Los Angeles, CA 90036
(323) 549-9200
http://www.mccormackassociates.com/
jmsearch@earthlink.net
Joseph A. McCormack, Managing Partner
Also:
New York, NY (212) 481-3220
Robert Ankerson, Senior Associate

MCCORMACK & FARROW
695 Town Center Drive, Suite 660

Costa Mesa, CA 92626-1981
(714) 549-7222
http://www.mfsearch.com/
resumes@mfsearch.com
Helen Friedman, Kenneth Thompson, Jim Wade, Jeff McDermott & Steven Treibel, Partners
Also:
Peoria, AZ (623) 566-2124
Gene L. Phelps, Partner

G. E. McFarland & Company
535 Colonial Park Drive
Roswell, GA 30075
(770) 992-0900
Charles P. Beall, Managing Partner

Clarence E. McFeely, Inc.†
39 Brinker Road
Barrington, IL 60010
(847) 381-0475
Clarence E. McFeely, President

McNichol Associates
(Specialize in Architecture, Engineering, & Construction)
54 West Willow Grove Road
Philadelphia, PA 19118
(215) 922-4142
John McNichol, President

Jon McRae & Associates, Inc.
(Specialize in Presidential & Cabinet Searches for Universities)
1930 North Druid Hills Road NE, Suite 200
Atlanta, GA 30319
(404) 325-3252
http://www.jonmcrae.com/
jma@jonmcrae.com
O. Jon McRae, President

MDR Associates
(Specialize in Health Care)
9485 S.W. 72nd Street, Suite A265
Miami, FL 33173
(305) 271-9213
http://www.mdrsearch.com/
jberger@mdrsearch.com
Judith Berger, President
Stephen Schoen, Executive Director

James Mead & Company
(Specialize in Consumer Packaged Goods)
15 Old Danbury Road, Suite 202
Wilton, CT 06897-2524
(203) 834-6300
mailbox@jmeadco.com
James D. Mead, President
Arthur S. Brown, Executive Vice President & Partner

Meng, Finseth & Associates, Inc.
Del Amo Executive Plaza
3858 Carson Street, Suite 202
Torrance, CA 90503
(310) 316-0706
mengfinseth@aol.com
Charles M. Meng, President
Carl L. Finseth, Executive Vice President & Partner

Messett Associates, Inc.
Partner in International Executive Search, Inc.
7700 North Kendall Drive, Suite 304
Miami, FL 33156
(305) 275-1000
http://www.messett.com/
messett@messett.com
William J. Messett III, President

Herbert Mines Associates, Inc.†
375 Park Avenue, Suite 301
New York, NY 10152
(212) 355-0909
http://www.herbertmines.com/
Herbert Mines, Chairman
Harold D. Reiter, President & CEO
Jane Vergari, Senior Vice President

Mirtz Morice, Inc.
One Dock Street, 3rd Floor
Stamford, CT 06902-5836
(203) 964-9266
P. John Mirtz & James L. Morice, Partners

Montgomery West/MSI
99 Almaden Boulevard, 6th Floor
San Jose, CA 95113
(408) 292-9876
http://montgomerywest.com/
careers@montgomerywest.com
Gregg Goodere, Vice President & Managing Director

Morris & Berger, Inc.
(Specialize in Nonprofit)
201 South Lake Avenue, Suite 700
Pasadena, CA 91101
(626) 795-0522
http://www.morrisberger.com/
Kristine A. Morris & Jay V. Berger, Partners

Moyer, Sherwood Associates†
(Specialize in Communications, Public Relations & Investment Relations)
1285 Avenue of the Americas, 35th Floor
New York, NY 10019
(212) 554-4008
http://www.moyersherwood.com/
research@moyersherwood.com
David S. Moyer, President

Mruk & Partners
EMA Partners International
230 Park Avenue, 10th Floor
New York, NY 10017
(212) 808-3076
http://www.emapartners.com/
Edwin S. Mruk, Senior Partner

MTA Partners
(Specialize in Health Care)
2828 West Parker Road, Suite 207
Plano, TX 75075
(972) 758-8646
Michael Tucker & Brian Ehringer, Partners

P. J. Murphy & Associates, Inc.
735 North Water Street, Suite 915
Milwaukee, WI 53202
(414) 277-9777
http://www.pjmurphy.com/
cszaff@pjmurphy.com
Patrick J. Murphy, Chairman

Nadzam, Horgan & Associates, Inc.†
(Specialize in High Tech)
3211 Scott Boulevard, Suite 205
Santa Clara, CA 95054-3091
(408) 727-6601
http://www.nhexecutivesearch.com/
Richard J. Nadzam & Thomas F. Horgan, Partners

Nagler, Robins & Poe, Inc.
(Specialize in High Tech)
65 William Street
Wellesley Hills, MA 02181-3802
(781) 431-1330
http://www.nrpinc.com/
Leon G. Nagler, Jeri N. Robins & James B. Poe, Managing Directors

Nordeman Grimm, Inc.†
717 Fifth Avenue, 26th Floor
New York, NY 10022
(212) 935-1000
http://www.nordemangrimm.com/
resume@nordemangrimm.com
Jacques C. Nordeman, Chairman
Peter G. Grimm, Vice Chairman

Norman Broadbent International Inc.
(Specialize in New Media, Technology, Communications & Financial Services)
200 Park Avenue, 20th Floor
New York, NY 10166-0011
(212) 953-6990
http://www.normanbroadbent.com/
Leah Peskin, Managing Director
Also:
Atlanta, GA (770) 955-9550
Charles J. Chalk, Managing Director
Chicago, IL (312) 876-3300
Thomas Higgins, COO

O'Brien & Bell
812 Huron Road, Suite 535
Cleveland, OH 44115
(216) 575-1212
http://www.obrienbell.com/
Timothy O'Brien, President

O'Shea, Divine & Corporation
4 Civic Plaza, Suite 350
Newport Beach, CA 92660
(949) 720-9070
Robert S. Divine, Principal

Dennis P. O'Toole & Associates, Inc.†
(Specialize in Hospitality & Leisure)
1865 Palmer Avenue, Suite 210
Larchmont, NY 10538
(914) 833-3712
Dennis P. O'Toole, President

Ober & Company
11777 San Vicente Boulevard, Suite 860
Los Angeles, CA 90049
(310) 207-1127
Lynn W. Ober, President

Oliver & Rozner Associates, Inc.
823 Walton Avenue
Mamaroneck, NY 10543-4535
(914) 381-6242
Burton L. Rozner, President

The Onstott Group†
60 William Street, Suite 250
Wellesley, MA 02181-3803
(781) 235-3050
http://www.onstott.com/
Joseph E. Onstott & Bentley H. Beaver, Managing Directors
Also:
Los Altos, CA (650) 917-8317
Mary Dean, Vice President - California

Oppedisano & Company, Inc.
(Specialize in Investment Management)
370 Lexington Avenue, Suite 1200
New York, NY 10017
(212) 696-0144
oppsearch@aol.com
Edward A. Oppedisano, Chairman & CEO

Opportunity Resources, Inc.†
(Specialize in Nonprofit & Cultural Organizations)
25 West 43rd Street, Suite 1017
New York, NY 10036
(212) 575-1688
Freda Mindlin, President

Ott & Hansen, Inc.

136 South Oak Knoll, Suite 300
Pasadena, CA 91101
(626) 578-0551
George W. Ott, President & CEO
David G. Hansen, Executive Vice President

D. P. Parker & Associates Inc.†

(Specialize in High Tech)
372 Washington Street
Wellesley, MA 02481
(781) 237-1220
http://www.dpparker.com/
David P. Parker, President

Parker, Sholl and Gordon, Inc.

9 LaChance Drive, Post Office Box 10
Rindge, NH 03461
(603) 899-3267
Calvin K. Sholl, Chairman & CEO

The Partnership Group

(Specialize in Management Consulting and Human Resources)
7 Becker Farm Road
Roseland, NJ 07068
(973) 535-8566
http://www.partnershipgroup.com/
Peter T. Maher, President
Raymond Schwartz, Partner

People Management International, Ltd.

Avon Park South, One Darling Drive
Avon, CT 06001
(860) 678-8900
Steven M. Darter, President & CEO - People Management Northeast
Also:
Nashville, TN (615) 463-2800
Tommy Thomas, President & CEO - People Management Midsouth
Stillwater, MN (651) 351-7214
Robert T. Stevenson, President & CEO - People Management Minnesota

Picard International, Ltd.

(Specialize in Finance, Technology & Health Care)
125 East 38th Street
New York, NY 10016
(212) 252-1620
http://www.picardintl.com/
Daniel A. Picard, President
Georgina Lichtenstein, Cheif Operating Officer

Rene Plessner Associates

(Specialize in Cosmetics & Fragrances)
375 Park Avenue
New York, NY 10152
(212) 421-3490
Rene Plessner, President

Plummer & Associates, Inc.

(Specialize in Retail, Direct Marketing, Food Service & E-Commerce)
65 Rowayton Avenue
Norwalk, CT 06853
(203) 899-1233
http://www.plummersearch.com/
resume@plummersearch.com
John Plummer, President
Also:
Marietta, GA (770) 429-9007
Susan Gill, Managing Director

Poirier, Hoevel & Company

12400 Wilshire Boulevard, Suite 915
Los Angeles, CA 90025
(310) 207-3427
http://www.phandco.com/
submissions@phandco.com
Roland Poirier, Michael J. Hoevel, & Kristina Hoevel, Principals

David Powell, Inc.

(Specialize in High Tech & Biotechnology)
2995 Woodside Road, Post Office Box 620109
Woodside, CA 94062
(650) 851-6000
http://www.davidpowell.com/
David L. Powell Sr., President

The Prairie Group

(Specialize in Finance, Marketing & Human Resources)
One Westbrook Corp Center, Suite 300
Westchester, IL 60154
(708) 449-7710
James W. Kick & Mark Scott, Principals

Preng & Associates, Inc.†

(Specialize in Energy and Natural Resources)
2925 Briar Park, Suite 1111
Houston, TX 77042-3734
(713) 266-2600
http://www.preng.com/
David E. Preng, President

PricewaterhouseCoopers, LLP†

Toronto-Dominion Centre Royal Trust Tower
77 King Street West, Suite 3000
Post Office Box 82
Toronto, ON M5K 1G8
(416) 863-1133
http://www.pwcglobal.com/
B. Keith McLean, Paul F. Crath, & Bill McFarland, Senior Vice Presidents
W. Tom Sinclair, Principal-Executive Search
Also:

Calgary, AB (403) 509-7500
Kerry McBrine, Director - Executive Search
Montreal, QC (514) 205-5000
Joseph Beaupre, Principal
St. John's, NB (506) 632-1810
Donald Moors, Partner
Vancouver, BC (604) 806-7000
Robert McMillin, Vice President - Executive Search

PRINCEGOLDSMITH LLC†

420 Lexington Avenue, Suite 2048
New York, NY 10170
(212) 313-9891
recruit@princegoldsmith.com
Marylin L. Prince, Megan Murray, & Joseph B. Goldsmith, Partners

RAINES INTERNATIONAL INC.†

250 Park Avenue, 17th Floor
New York, NY 10177
(212) 997-1100
http://www.rainesinternational.com/
Bruce R. Raines, President

RAY & BERNDTSON†

301 Commerce Street, Suite 2300
Fort Worth, TX 76102
(817) 334-0500
http://www.rayberndtson.com/
Paul R. Ray Sr., Chairman Emeritus and Senior Partner
Paul R. Ray Jr., Chairman & Chief Executive Officer
Breck Ray, Managing Partner
John N. Hobart, Renee Baker Arrington & Jay R. Kizer, Partners
Also:
Atlanta, GA (404) 215-4600
Kathleen Maloney, Clarke Collins, Robert P. Collins, Stephen A. Dezember, Noel A. Follrath, William T. Gilbert & John P. Schreitmueller, Partners
Chicago, IL (312) 876-0730
John P. Doyle, Peter J. Sweeney, Jane C. Beatty, Paul E. Came, Lynn K. Charney, Donald B. Clark, Henry C. Deaver, Charles C. Ratigan, Alvin H. Spector, Robert H. Tate, Larry Taylor & Timothy Wujcik, Partners
Dallas, TX (214) 969-7620
Stephen T. Jordan Jr., David M. Love II, Jerry D. Pham & Linus D. Wright, Partners
Halifax, NS (902) 421-1330
Mark Surrette, Managing Partner
Jamie Baillie, Partner
Houston, TX (713) 309-1400
Kathleen A. Johnson & W. Randall Lowry, Partners
Los Angeles, CA (310) 557-2828
Scott D. Somers, Managing Partner
John B. Bohle, Kathryn Foreman & Shelly F. Fust, Partners
Montreal, QC (514) 937-1000
Bernard F. Labrecque, Managing Partner
Roger Lachance & Jean E. Laurendeau, Partners
New York, NY (212) 370-1316
Kenneth M. Rich, Managing Partner
Frederic M. Comins Jr., Lucienne de Mestre, Mary Helen Dunn, Lisa C. Hooker, Penny Simon, Judy K. Weddle, Jacques P. Andre, Pammy Brooks, Kenneth Chase, Abram Claude Jr., Patrick A. Delhougne & William H. Weed, Partners
Ottawa, ON (613) 749-9909
Ronald Robertson, Managing Partner
Richard S. Morgan, Partner
Palo Alto, CA (650) 494-2500
James A. McFadzean, Managing Partner
John A. Holland, Kirsten Smith & Geraldine Whitaker, Partners
Toronto, ON (416) 366-1990
Paul R. A. Stanley, Senior Partner
W. Carl Lovas, Managing Partner
Sue Banting, David R. Murray, Larry Ross, James H. Stonehouse, Christine S. Thomas, Elizabeth B. Wright & Joseph E. Zinner, Partners

RAY & BERNDTSON/TANTON MITCHELL†

710-1050 West Pender Street
Vancouver, BC V6E 3S7
(604) 685-0261
http://www.rayberndtson.com/
vancouver@raybern.ca
John E. Tanton & Kyle R. Mitchell, Managing Partners
Craig P. Hemer, Caroline Jellinck, Catherine Van Alstine & Alec Wallace, Partners

REDDEN & MCGRATH ASSOCIATES, INC.

427 Bedford Road
Pleasantville, NY 10570
(914) 725-5566
Mary Redden & Laura McGrath Faller, Partners

REEDER & ASSOCIATES, LTD.†

(SPECIALIZE IN HEALTH CARE)
1095 Old Roswell Road, Suite F
Roswell, GA 30076
(770) 649-7523
http://www.reederassoc.com/
Michael S. Reeder, President

REYNOLDS & PARTNERS

380 Madison Avenue, 7th Floor
New York, NY 10017
(212) 856-4466
Sydney Ann Reynolds, President

ROBERTS RYAN AND BENTLEY, INC.

1107 Kenilworth Drive, Suite 208
Baltimore, MD 21204
(410) 321-6600
Richard Cappe, President
Richard Dannenberg, Senior Vice President & Partner
Also:
Bethesda, MD (301) 469-3150
Gregory Reynolds, Vice President

Bruce Robinson Associates†

Harmon Cove Towers
A/L, Tower 1, Suite 8
Secaucus, NJ 07095
(201) 617-9595
Bruce Robinson, President
Eric B. Robinson, Vice President & Partner

Robinson, Fraser Group Ltd.

10 Bay Street, Suite 700
Toronto, ON M5J 2R8
(416) 864-9174
Stephen A. Robinson, President

Robison & Associates

128 South Tryon Street, Suite 1350
Charlotte, NC 28202
(704) 376-0059
John H. Robison Jr., Chairman & President

Ropes Associates, Inc.†

(Specialize in Real Estate)
333 North New River Drive, East 3rd Floor
Fort Lauderdale, FL 33301-2200
(954) 525-6600
jropes@ropesassociates.com
John Ropes, President

Rurak & Associates, Inc.†

1776 Massachusetts Avenue N.W., Suite 300
Washington, DC 20036
(202) 293-7603
resumes@rurakassociates.com
Zbigniew T. Rurak, President

Rusher, Loscavio & LoPresto†

142 Sansone Street, 5th Floor
San Francisco, CA 94104-4235
(415) 765-6600
http://www.rll.com/
resumes@rll.com
J. Michael Loscavio, President & Senior Partner
William H. Rusher Jr., Chairman & Chief Executive Officer/Managing Partner
Also:
Palo Alto, CA (650) 494-0883
Robert L. LoPresto, Vice President and Senior Partner
G. Kay Sullivan, Vice President and Partner
Southborough, MA (508) 624-7291
Elson Hung, Vice President

Russell Reynolds Associates, Inc.†

200 Park Avenue, Suite 2300
New York, NY 10166-0002
(212) 351-2000
http://www.russellreynolds.com/
Hobson Brown Jr., President & Chief Executive Officer
Gordon Grand lll, Managing Director-Area Manager
P. Clarke Murphy, James M. Bagley & Joseph A. Bailey III, Managing Directors
Also:
Atlanta, GA (404) 577-3000
Joseph T. Spence, Managing Director-Area Manager
Boston, MA (617) 523-1111
J. Nicholas Hurd, Managing Director-Area Manager
Calgary, AB (403) 205-3640
Irene E. Pfeiffer, Managing Director
Chicago, IL (312) 993-9696
Andrea Redmond & Charles Tribbett III, Area Co-ManagerS
Dallas, TX (214) 220-2033
David M. Love III, Managing Director-Area Manager
Steven Raben, Managing Director
Los Angeles, CA (213) 253-4400
Richard B. Krell, Managing Director-Area Manager
Menlo Park, CA (650) 233-2400
Barry S. Obrand, Managing Director-Area Manager
Minneapolis, MN (612) 332-6966
Robert W. Macdonald Jr., Managing Director-Area Manager
San Francisco, CA (415) 352-3300
Barry S. Obrand, Managing Director-Area Manager
Toronto, ON (416) 364-3355
Paul Cantor, Managing Director-Country Manager
Washington, DC (202) 628-2150
Eric L. Vautour, Managing Director-Area Manager

Saley Partners International

WaterPark Place
10 Bay Street, 14th Floor
Toronto, ON M5J 2R8
(416) 364-2020
Albert Saley, Chief Executive Officer

Norm Sanders Associates

(Specialize in Information Technology)
2 Village Court
Hazlet, NJ 07730
(732) 264-3700
http://www.normsanders.com/
mail@normsanders.com
Norman D. Sanders, Managing Director

Allan Sarn Associates, Inc.

(Specialize in Human Resources)
230 Park Avenue, Suite 1522
New York, NY 10169
(212) 687-0600
Allan G. Sarn, President

Sathe & Associates, Inc.

5821 Cedar Lake Road
Minneapolis, MN 55416
(952) 546-2100
http://www.sathe.com/
info@sathe.com
Mark Sathe, President
Greg Albrecht, Partner

Savoy Partners Ltd.
1620 L Street, NW, Suite 801
Washington, DC 20036
(202) 887-0666
Robert J. Brudno, Managing Director

Schuyler Associates, Ltd.
400 Perimeter Center Terraces Northeast, Suite 900
Atlanta, GA 30346
(770) 352-9414
http://www.Schuyler-Associates.com/
Lambert Schuyler, President

Schweichler Associates, Inc./ITP Worldwide
(Specialize in High Tech)
200 Tamal Vista Boulevard, Suite 100
Corte Madera, CA 94925
(415) 924-7200
http://www.schweichler.com/
search@schweichler.com
Lee J. Schweichler, President
Ann Peckenpaugh, Vice President

J. Robert Scott
255 State Street, 5th Floor
Boston, MA 02109
(617) 563-2770
http://www.j-robert-scott.com/
resumes@j-robert-scott.com
William A. Holodnak, President

Scott Executive Search
61 Woodbury Place, Suite 200
Rochester, NY 14618
(716) 264-0330
E. Ann Scott, President

The Search Alliance
(Specialize in Health Care, Banking, Manufacturing & Technology)
31 South Fourth Street
Amelia Island, FL 32034
(904) 277-2535
http://www.tsainc.net/
Tom Byrnes, Managing Partner
Also:
Greenwich, CT (203) 622-6903
Catherine deTuede, Managing Partner
West Hartford, CT (860) 232-2300
Bill Thomas, Managing Partner

Search America
(Specialize in Private Club Mgmt. & Hospitality)
5908 Meadowcreek Drive
Dallas, TX 75248-5451
(972) 233-3302
Harvey M. Weiner, President

Secura Burnett Company, LLC
555 California Street, Suite 3950
San Francisco, CA 94104
(415) 398-0700
http://www.securagroup.com/
Louis C. Burnett, Managing Partner

Seiden Krieger Associates
375 Park Avenue, Suite 1601
New York, NY 10152-3201
(212) 688-8383
Steven A. Seiden, President
Dennis F. Krieger, Managing Director

Seitchik Corwin and Seitchik
(Specialize in Textiles, Apparel, Footwear & Related Industries)
330 East 38th Street
Suite 5P
New York, NY 10016
(212) 370-3592
William Seitchik, Vice President
Also:
San Francisco, CA (415) 928-5717
Jack Seitchik, President
J. Blade Corwin, Vice President

Sensible Solutions, Inc.
239 W. Coolidge Avenue
Barrington, IL 60010-4211
(847) 382-0070
http://www.sensibleinc.com/
Patrick J. Delaney, Principal

M. B. Shattuck & Associates, Inc.
(Specialize in High Tech & General Manufacturing)
1904 Franklin Street, Suite 818
Oakland, CA 94612
(510) 663-8922
http://www.mbshattuck.com/
Merrill B. Shattuck, President

Shepherd Bueschel & Provus, Inc.†
401 North Michigan Avenue, Suite 3020
Chicago, IL 60611
(312) 832-3020
Daniel M. Shepherd, David A. Bueschel & Barbara L. Provus, Principals

David Shiplacoff & Associates
2030 Fairburn Avenue, Suite 200-L
Los Angeles, CA 90025-5914
(310) 474-3600
http://www.dsasearch.com/
David Shiplacoff, President

Michael Shirley Associates, Inc.
10709 Barkley, Suite B
Overland Park, KS 66211
(913) 341-7655

http://www.mshirleyassociates.com/
Michael Shirley, President

Shoemaker & Associates
1862 Independence Square, Suite A
Atlanta, GA 30338
(770) 395-7225
http://www.shoemakersearch.com/
Larry C. Shoemaker, President

M. Shulman, Inc
44 Montgomery Street, Suite 3085
San Francisco, CA 94104
(415) 398-3488
Melvin Shulman, President

John Sibbald & Associates, Inc.
7733 Forsyth Boulevard, Suite 2010
Saint Louis, MO 63105
(314) 727-0227
John R. Sibbald, President
Kathryn Costick, Vice President

Signature Search
338 West College Avenue, Suite 203
Appleton, WI 54911
(920) 749-9300
http://www.signaturesearch.com/
Michael S. Mueller, President & CEO

Signium International Group, Inc.†
44 North Virginia Street, Suite 3-B
Crystal Lake, IL 60014-4106
(815) 479-9415
http://www.signium.com/
Sue Spate & Dorothy Marquelles, Principals

Siler & Associates, LLC
11512 North Port Washington Road
Mequon, WI 53092
(262) 241-5041
David J. Siler, President

Daniel A. Silverstein Associates, Inc.
(Specialize in Health Care, Pharmaceuticals, Biotech, Medical Devices)
5355 Town Center Road, Suite 1001
Boca Raton, FL 33486
(561) 391-0600
Daniel A. Silverstein, President

Skott/Edwards Consultants
1776 On the Green
Morristown, NJ 07960
(973) 644-0900
http://www.skottedwards.com/
search@skottedwards.com
Skott B. Burkland, President
Charles R. Grebenstein, Senior Vice President

Slayton International, Inc./IIC Partners
181 West Madison Street
Suite 4510
Chicago, IL 60602
(312) 456-0080
http://www.slaytonintl.com/
Richard C. Slayton, Chairman
Richard S. Slayton, President
Thomas M. Hazlett & Terance N. Burns, Vice Presidents

Smith & Sawyer LLC
634 Ocean Road
Indian River Shores, FL 32963
(516) 234-0607
www.smithsawyer.com
resumes@smithsawyer.com
Robert L. Smith & Patricia L. Sawyer, Partners

Herman Smith Search Inc.
161 Bay Street, Suite 3860
Post Office Box 629
Toronto, ON M5J 2S1
(416) 862-8830
info@hermansmith.com
Herman Smith, President

Smith & Syberg, Inc.†
825 Washington Street, Suite 2A
Columbus, IN 47201
(812) 372-7254
http://www.smithandsyberg.com/
mail@smithandsyberg.com
Joseph E. Smith & Keith A. Syberg, Partners

Sockwell & Associates
(Specialize in Finance, Technology, Education, Healthcare, Real Estate)
227 West Trade Street, Suite 1930
Charlotte, NC 28202
(704) 372-1865
http://www.sockwell.com/
email@sockwell.com
J. Edgar Sockwell, Managing Partner
Susan Jernigan & Lyttleton Rich, Partners
Also:
Research Triangle Park, NC (919) 806-4450
Robert Sherrill, Partner

Solutions Group
1512 Valley Place
Birmingham, AL 35209
(205) 663-1301
http://www.solutiongroupsearch.com/
Hinky Verchot & Michael E. Wheless, Principals

Spencer Stuart†
277 Park Avenue, 29th Floor
New York, NY 10172-2998
(212) 336-0200

http://www.spencerstuart.com/
resumes@spencerstuart.com
Thomas J. Neff, Chairman-U.S.
David S. Daniel, CEO
Robert A. Damon, Co-Managing Director-U. S.
William B. Reeves, William B. Clemens Jr., Kevin Connelly & Robert Heidrick, Managing Directors
Also:
Coral Gables, FL (305) 443-9911
Ken Eckhart, Managing Director
Dallas, TX (214) 672-5200
O. Dan Cruse & Randy Kelley, Managing Directors
Houston, TX (713) 225-1621
Tom Simmons, Managing Director
Los Angeles, CA (310) 209-0610
Michael Bruce, Managing Director
Minneapolis, MN (612) 313-2000
Susan Boren & Matthew Christoff, Principals
Montreal, QC (514) 288-3377
Manon Vennat, Chairman-Canada
E. Peter McLean, Senior Director
Robert C. Nadeau & Jerome Piche, Directors
Philadelphia, PA (215) 814-1600
Dennis C. Carey, US Vice Chairman
Connie McCann, Managing Director
Pleasanton, CA (925) 738-4900
Phil Johnston, Managing Director
San Francisco, CA (415) 495-4141
Jonathan O. White, Managing Director
Joseph E. Griesedieck Jr., Director
San Mateo, CA (650) 356-5500
John Ware & Johnathon Visbal, Managing Directors
Stamford, CT (203) 324-6333
Dayton Ogden, Chairman & President
Claudia Lacy Kelly & Harry Somerdyk, Managing Directors
Toronto, ON (416) 361-0311
Andrew McDougall & Jeff Hauswirth, Managing Directors

SPLAINE & ASSOCIATES, INC.
(SPECIALIZE IN HIGH TECH)
15951 Los Gatos Boulevard, Suite 13
Los Gatos, CA 95032
(408) 354-3664
http://www.exec-search.com/
Charles E. Splaine, President

SPRIGGS & COMPANY, INC.
1701 E Lake Avenue, Suite 265
Glenview, IL 60025
(847) 657-7181
Robert D. Spriggs, Chairman
John Goldrick & William Billington, Partners

STANTON CHASE INTERNATIONAL
100 East Pratt Street, Suite 2530
Baltimore, MD 21202
(410) 528-8400
http://www.stantonchaseaccess.com/
H. Edward Muendel & James R. Piper Jr., Managing Directors
Also:
Dallas, TX (972) 404-8411
Ed Moerbe, Managing Director
Los Angeles, CA (310) 474-1029
Edward J. Savage, Managing Director

STAUB WARMBOLD ASSOCIATES INC.
575 Madison Avenue, 10th Floor
New York, NY 10022
(212) 605-0554
Robert A. Staub, President

STEPHENS ASSOCIATES, LTD., INC.
(SPECIALIZE IN HIGH TECH)
One German Village, 2nd Floor
480 South Third Street
Columbus, OH 43215
(614) 469-9990
Stephen A. Martinez, President & Managing Partner

MICHAEL STERN ASSOCIATES, INC.
70 University Avenue, Suite 370
Toronto, ON M5J 2M4
(416) 593-0100
http://www.michaelstern.com/
Michael Stern, President

STEWART, STEIN & SCOTT, LTD.
1000 Shelard Parkway, Suite 606
Minneapolis, MN 55426
(763) 545-8151
Jeffrey O. Stewart, President

LINFORD E. STILES ASSOCIATES
(SPECIALIZE IN MANUFACTURING COMPANIES, ALL FUNCTIONS)
46th Newport Road, Suite 210
New London, NH 03257-4240
(603) 526-6566
Linford E. Stiles, President

STONE MURPHY
5500 Wayzata Boulevard
Suite 1020
Minneapolis, MN 55416
(763) 591-2300
http://www.stonemurphy.com/
sm@stonemurphy.com
Toni M. Barnum & Gary J. Murphy, Partners

STRATEGIC EXECUTIVES, INC.
980 Michigan Avenue, Suite 1400
Chicago, IL 60611-4501
(312) 988-4821
http://www.strategicexecutives.com/
Randolph S. Gulian, President
Laurie R. Goldman, James A. Perry, Gil Smith & Harlan Harper, Senior Vice Presidents

Stratford Group
6120 Parkland Boulevard
Cleveland, OH 44124
(440) 869-4600
Larry S. Imley, President
Eric Peterson, Managing Director

W. R. Strathmann Associates
(Specialize in Financial Services)
150 Fifth Avenue, Suite 626
New York, NY 10011
(212) 353-2034
Winfried R. Strathmann, Senior Partner

Straube Associates, Inc.
855 Turnpike Street
North Andover, MA 1845
(978) 687-1993
http://www.straubeassociates.com/
Stanley H. Straube, President

Strawn, Arnold, Leech & Ashpitz, Inc.
(Specialize in Health Care)
11402 Bee Caves Road West
Austin, TX 78733
(512) 263-1131
http://www.salainc.com/
William M. Strawn, Jerry M. Arnold, David M. Leech & Jeff Ashpitz, Partners

Sullivan & Associates†
344 North Old Woodward Avenue, Suite 304
Birmingham, MI 48009
(248) 258-0616
http://www.sullivanassociates.com/
Dennis B. Sullivan, Founder
Jeffrey A. Evans, Kevin E. Mahoney, Dodie C. David & Douglas R. Allen, Partners

Sweeney, Harbert, Mummert & Gallagher
777 South Harbour Island Boulevard, Suite 130
Tampa, FL 33602
(813) 229-5360
James W. Sweeney, David O. Harbert, Dennis D. Mummert & David A. Gallagher, Partners

Synergistics Associates Ltd.†
(Specialize in Information Technology)
400 North State Street, Suite 400
Chicago, IL 60610
(312) 467-5450
Alvin J. Borenstine, President & Founder

Tarnow Associates
150 Morris Avenue
Springfield, NJ 07081-1306
(973) 376-3900
http://www.tarnow.com/
Emil Vogel, President

Thorndike Deland Associates
275 Madison Avenue, Suite 1300
New York, NY 10016-1101
(212) 661-6200
http://www.tdeland.com/
mcatalano@tdeland.com
Joseph J. Carideo, Managing Partner
Howard Bratches & William W. Venable, Partners

Thorne, Brieger Associates Inc.
11 East 44th Street, Suite 1502
New York, NY 10017
(212) 682-5424
Steven Brieger, Mike Jacobs & Jeffrey M. Stark, Principals

TMP Worldwide
225 West Wacker Drive, Suite 2100
Chicago, IL 60606-1229
(312) 782-3113
http://www.tmpsearch.com/
John S. Rothschild, Executive Vice President & Managing Partner
Also:
Atlanta, GA (404) 688-0800
David W. Gallagher, Managing Partner
Bethesda, MD (301) 941-1301
Kathy Epstein
Bloomfield Hills, MI (248) 858-9970
John Rothschild, Managing Partner
Boston, MA (617) 292-6242
Walter E. Williams, Managing Partner
Cleveland, OH (216) 694-3000
Mark P. Elliott, Cheif Administrative Officer
Dallas, TX (214) 754-0019
Judy Stubbs, Managing Partner
Frederick A. Halstead, Partner
El Segundo, CA (213) 688-9444
Robert S. Rollo & Peter Kelly, Managing Partners
Encino, CA (818) 905-6010
Neal L. Maslan, Managing Partner
Houston, TX (713) 843-8600
John Griffin, Managing Partner
New York, NY (212) 351-7100
Harold E. Johnson, Senior Partner
Michael Sullivan, Managing Partner
Palo Alto, CA (650) 424-9233
Bradley A. Stirn, Managing Partner
San Francisco, CA (415) 296-0600
Keith Anderson, Managing Partner
Stamford, CT (203) 324-4445
Michael Castine, Managing Partner
Toronto, ON (416) 862-1273
Rick C.E. Moore, Head of Canadian Search Operations

TNS Partners, Inc.
8140 Walnut Hill Lane, Suite 301
Dallas, TX 75231
(214) 369-3565
Craig C. Neidhart & John K. Semyan, Partners

Skip Tolette Executive Search
(Specialize in Financial Services and Information Technology)
577 West Saddle River Road
Upper Saddle River, NJ 7458
(201) 327-8214
http://www.tolettesearch.com/
Skip Tolette, President

Travis & Company
(Specialize in Medical, Biotechnology, Computer Hardware & Software)
325 Boston Post Road
Sudbury, MA 1776
(978) 443-4000
http://www.travisandco.com/
John A. Travis, President
Mary K. Morse & Michael J. Travis, Vice Presidents

Tyler & Company
(Specialize in Health Care)
1000 Abernathy Road , Suite 1400
Atlanta, GA 30328-5655
(770) 396-3939
http://www.tylerandco.com/
J. Larry Tyler , President & Cheif Executive Officer
Also:
Chaddsford, PA (610) 558-6100
Patti Hoffmeir, Senior Vice President
Charlotte, NC (704) 672-1662
George Linney Jr., MD, Vice President
St. Louis, MO (314) 569-9882
Mark Krinsky, Consultant

VanMaldegiam Associates, Inc.
500 Park Boulevard, Suite 800
Itasca, IL 60143
(630) 250-8338
Norman E. VanMaldegiam, President

VerKamp-Joyce Associates, Inc.
4320 Winfield Road, Suite 200
Warrenville, IL 60555
(630) 836-8030
Frank VerKamp & Sheila M. Joyce, Partners

The Verriez Group Inc.†
205 John Street
London, ON N6A 1N9
(519) 673-3463
http://www.verriez.com
verriez@verriez.com
Paul M. Verriez, President

Vlcek & Company, Inc.
(Generalists with Emphasis in Consumer Goods and Food Industry)
620 Newport Center Drive, Suite 1100
Newport Beach, CA 92660
(949) 752-0661
Thomas J. Vlcek, President

Wakefield Talabisco International
342 Madison Avenue, Suite 1702
New York, NY 10173
(212) 661-8600
http://www.wtali.com/
resumes@wtali.com
Barbara Talabisco, Partner/President/CEO
Also:
Mendon, VT (802) 747-5901
J. Alvin Wakefield, Partner

Walling, June & Associates
(Specialize in High Tech, Health Care & Financial Services)
716 Church Street
Alexandria, VA 22314
(703) 548-9660
w716@erols.com
Gregory J. Walling, Senior Partner

Ward Liebelt Associates, Inc.
Sales and Marketing
1175 Post Road East
Westport, CT 06880
(203) 454-0414
wlacaruso@aol.com
Anthony C. Ward, President

R. J. Watkins & Company, Ltd.
3104 Fourth Avenue
San Diego, CA 92103
(619) 299-3094
http://www.rjwatkins.com/
info@rjwatkins.com
Robert J. Watkins, Chairman
Tom Murphy, Vice President
Also:
Santa Clarita, CA (661) 284-7500
Gary Saenger, President

Webb, Johnson Associates, Inc.
280 Park Avenue, 43rd Floor
New York, NY 10017
(212) 661-3700
George H. Webb Jr., John W. Johnson Jr. & James K. Makrianes Jr., Directors

D. L. Weiss and Associates
18201 Von Karman Avenue, Suite 310
Irvine, CA 92612
(949) 833-5001
http://www.dlweiss.com/
mail@dlweiss.com
David L. Weiss, President
Wendy A. Worrell, Principal Consultant

Wellington Management Group
(Generalists with emphasis on High Tech, Telecommunications, Human Resources & Health Care)
1601 Market Street
Suite 2902
Philadelphia, PA 19103
(215) 569-8900
http://www.wellingtonmg.com/
Walter R. Romanchek, Robert S. Campbell & Donald H. Janssen, Principals

The Wentworth Company, Inc.
The Arcade Building
479 West Sixth Street
San Pedro, CA 90731-2656
(310) 519-0113
http://www.wentco.com/
John Wentworth, President

Westcott Thomas & Associates Ltd.
(Concentration in Government, Associations, Human Resources, Sales & Marketing)
5650 Yonge Street, Suite 1500
Post Office Box 2412
Toronto, ON M2M 4G3
(416) 481-4471
Michael J. Thomas, President & Chief Executive Officer

Western Reserve Search Associates, Inc.
(Emphasis in Reorganizations & Startups in Eastern Europe)
199 S. Chillicothe Road
Suite 200-6
Post Office Box 606
Aurora, OH 44202
(330) 562-4811
Darrell G. Robertson, President

Wheeler, Moore & Company
Building 3, Suite 100
701 Northcentral Expressway
Richardson, TX 75080
(972) 386-8806
drmark@msn.com
Mark H. Moore, Managing Partner

Whitehead Mann Pendleton James, Inc.†
200 Park Avenue, Suite 1600
New York, NY 10166
(212) 894-8300
http://www.wmann.com/
newyork@wmann.com
E. Pendleton James, Senior Partner
Also:
Boston, MA (617) 598-1200
Durant A. Hunter, Senior Partner
Los Angeles, CA (310) 575-4806
Daniela Beyrouti, Partner

K. L. Whitney Company
(Specialize in Investment Management)
6 Aspen Drive
Caldwell, NJ 7006
(973) 228-7124
Kenneth L. Whitney Jr., President

The Whitney Group†
850 Third Avenue, 11th Floor
New York, NY 10022
(212) 508-3500
http://www.whitneygroup.com/
recruiter@whitneygroup.com
Gary S. Goldstein, President & Chief Executive Officer
Also:
Chicago, IL (312) 587-3030
Mitchell Berman, Partner & Managing Director

Whittlesey & Associates, Inc.
300 South High Street
West Chester, PA 19382
(610) 436-6500
James G. Hogg Jr., President

Williams Executive Search, Inc.
4200 Wells Fargo Center
90 South Seventh Street
Minneapolis, MN 55402-3903
(612) 339-2900
http://www.williamsexec.com/
resumes@williams-exec.com
William P. Dubbs, President
Christina Borchers, Principal

Williams, Roth & Krueger, Inc.
911 North Elm Street
Suite 328
Hinsdale, IL 60521
(630) 887-7771
wrkinc@aol.com
Robert J. Roth & Alan Hanley, Partners

William Willis Worldwide, Inc.†
310 W Lyon Farm Drive, P.O. Box 4444
Greenwich, CT 06831-4356
(203) 532-9292
wwwinc@aol.com
William H. Willis, President & Managing Director

Patricia Wilson Associates
One Sansome, 21st Floor
San Francisco, CA 94104
(415) 984-3112
Patricia L. Wilson, Partner

Winguth, Grant & Donahue
417 Montgomery Street
Suite 910

San Francisco, CA 94104
(415) 283-1970
http://www.wgdsearch.com/
kark@wgdsearch.com
Susan G. Grant, President & Partner
Ed Winguth & Patrick D. Donahue, Vice Presidents & Partners

WITT/KIEFFER

(SPECIALIZE IN HEALTH CARE, HIGHER EDUCATION, NON-PROFIT, INSURANCE, ECOMMERCE)
2015 Spring Road, Suite 510
Oak Brook, IL 60523
(630) 990-1370
http://www.wittkieffer.com/
Jordan M. Hadelman, Chairman & Chief Executive Officer
John S. Lloyd, Vice Chairman
Michael F. Doody & J. Daniel Ford, Senior Vice Presidents
Also:
Atlanta, GA (404) 233-1370
Martha C. Hauser & Howard Jessamy, Vice Presidents
Burlington, MA (781) 272-8899
Anna Wharton Phillips, Senior Vice President
Dallas, TX (972) 490-1370
Keith Southerland, Senior Vice President
Emeryville, CA (510) 420-1370
Elaina Spitaels Genser, Senior Vice President
Houston, TX (713) 266-6779
Marvene M. Eastham, Senior Vice President
Irvine, CA (949) 851-5070
James W. Gauss, Senior Vice President
New York, NY (212) 686-2676
Alexander H. Williams, Vice President
Phoenix, AZ (602) 267-1370
Michael F. Meyer, Senior Vice President

WOJDULA & ASSOCIATES, LTD.

700 Rayovac Drive, Suite 204
Madison, WI 53711
(608) 271-2000
http://www.wojdula.com/
search@wojdula.com
Andrew G. Wojdula, President

M. WOOD COMPANY

(SPECIALIZE IN TECHNOLOGY)
10 North Dearborn Street, Suite 700
Chicago, IL 60602
(312) 368-0633
http://www.mwoodco.com/
resume@mwoodco.com
Milton M. Wood, President

DICK WRAY & CONSULTANTS, INC.

(SPECIALIZE IN RESTAURANT CONSULTING)
3123 Hannan Lane
Soquel, CA 95073
(408) 436-9729
http://www.dickwray.com/
dick.wray@dickwray.com
Dick Wray, President

JANET WRIGHT & ASSOCIATES†

(SPECIALIZE IN PUBLIC & NON-PROFIT)
21 Bedford Road, Suite 100
Toronto, ON M5R 2J9
(416) 923-3008
Janet Wright, President

WTW ASSOCIATES, INC./IIC PARTNERS

(SPECIALIZE IN ENTERTAINMENT, MEDIA, INTERNET, LAW SERVICES, FINANCIAL SERVICES)
675 Third Avenue, Suite 2808
New York, NY 10017
(212) 972-6990
http://www.wtwassociates.com/
Warren T. Wasp Jr., President

YELVERTON EXECUTIVE SEARCH

1925 Zanker Road
San Jose, CA 95112
(408) 453-1492
Jack R. Yelverton, President

ZAY & COMPANY INTERNATIONAL/IIC PARTNERS

Two Midtown Plaza, Suite 1740
1349 West Peachtree Street, NW
Atlanta, GA 30309
(404) 876-9986
http://www.zaycointl.com/
Thomas C. Zay Sr., President

EGON ZEHNDER INTERNATIONAL INC.

350 Park Avenue, 8th Floor
New York, NY 10022
(212) 519-6000
http://www.zehnder.com/
ezinewyork@ezi.net
A. Daniel Meiland, Chief Executive Officer
Also:
Atlanta, GA (404) 836-2800
Joel M. Koblentz, Managing Partner
Boston, MA (617) 535-3500
George L. Davis Jr., Managing Director
Chicago, IL (312) 260-8800
Louis J. Kacyn, Managing Partner
Dallas, TX (972) 728-5910
Brian C. Reinken, Office Leader
Los Angeles, CA (213) 337-1500
George C. Fifield, Managing Partner
Miami, FL (305) 329-4600
Ronald O. Tracy, Managing Partner
Montreal, QC (514) 876-4249
J. Robert Swidler, Managing Director-Canada
Palo Alto, CA (650) 847-3000
Jon F. Carter, Managing Partner

San Francisco, CA (415) 904-7800
Jennifer C. McElrath, Office Leader
Toronto, ON (416) 364-0222
Jan J. Stewart, Managing Partner

ZINGARO & CORPORATION
(SPECIALIZE IN HEALTH CARE)
21936 Briarcliff Drive
Briarcliff, TX 78669-2012
(512) 327-7277
http://www.zingaro.com/
search@zingaro.com
Ronald J. Zingaro, President & Chief Executive Officer

MICHAEL D. ZINN & ASSOCIATES, INC
601 Ewing Street, Suite C-8
Princeton, NJ 08540
(609) 921-8755
http://www.zinnassociates.com/
Michael D. Zinn, President
Also:
New York, NY (212) 391-0070
Michael D. Zinn, President

RiteSite.com

NOTE: For a continually updated list of the outstanding retainer-compensated search firms honored in ***RITES OF PASSAGE***, please visit **RiteSite.com**. There you can purchase ***Custom Career Service***...a wide-ranging package of online career development services for executives. One of the tools is the ability to download a freshly updated version of the above list in a variety of helpful formats that will speed and ease your contacting of these very highly regarded search firms.

Further on Recruiters...

Two publications are most frequently turned to for different types of information on executive recruiters:

RITES OF PASSAGE AT $100,000 TO $1 MILLION+...THE INSIDER'S GUIDE TO EXECUTIVE JOB-CHANGING AND FASTER CAREER PROGRESS provides comprehensive tactical advice on dealing successfully with recruiters in an executive job campaign. Recruiters are one of five central job-hunting topics covered in *RITES*. The others are use of Personal Contacts, Networking, Direct Mail, and the Internet. Six full chapters and a fascinating 70-page novella—231 pages in all (more than 1/3 of the book)—give you an ***insider's view of how*** executive searchers operate and how best to deal with them in order to ***achieve your own personal objectives***. The novella takes you behind-the-scenes as a fictionalized search is conducted. You see executives moving adroitly and clumsily among the headhunters and you witness the advantages of being well-informed about a much misunderstood area of business activity. 627 pp. VICEROY PRESS / HENRY HOLT & CO. $29.95 HARDCOVER

THE DIRECTORY OF EXECUTIVE RECRUITERS Annually revised, this ***comprehensive listing*** of recruiting firms includes both retainer and contingency firms, has a 10-word self-description of each, and names one or more staff members at each...identifying a total of over 13,200 people in 5,320 executive search firms. It is extensively cross-indexed...alphabetically, by function and industry of activity, and also geographically. 1331 pp. KENNEDY PUBLICATIONS, Fitzwilliam NH 03447 $47.95 plus $5.00 shipping PAPERBACK

Index

About the Author

John Lucht is one of America's foremost executive recruiters.

Since 1971 he has been bringing senior executives into major corporations in the U.S. and overseas...as head of The John Lucht Consultancy Inc. in New York City since 1977, and for six prior years at Heidrick and Struggles, New York, where he was an officer. Earlier he was in general management and marketing with Bristol-Myers, J. Walter Thompson Co. and Tetley Tea.

Lucht is the author of *RITES OF PASSAGE AT $100,000 TO $1 MILLION+...THE INSIDER'S GUIDE TO ABSOLUTELY EVERYTHING ABOUT EXECUTIVE JOB-CHANGING AND FASTER CAREER PROGRESS*. Today *RITES* is—as it has been for over a decade—the world's #1 best-selling book on executive-level job-changing and career management. With over 300,000 copies in print, it has helped many thousands of executives find new and better jobs and/or move up in their current company.

Lucht's newest book is *INSIGHTS FOR THE JOURNEY...NAVIGATING TO THRIVE, ENJOY, AND PROSPER IN SENIOR MANAGEMENT.* This unusually succinct book delivers 47 "insights" on leadership and business management in just 104 pages and has been widely praised for its penetrating observations and elegant writing.

The *EXECUTIVE JOB-CHANGING WORKBOOK*, by John Lucht is, like *RITES*, the #1 best-seller in its field.

Lucht's books are supplemented by **RiteSite.com**, a no-advertising, entirely service-oriented Internet site.

In the past decade, Lucht has expanded his highly personalized practice to include not only executive search, but also outplacement and executive coaching at the senior levels of management. He is also an expert legal witness on executive careers and compensation.

John Lucht grew up in the Midwest. He earned his B.S. and law degrees from the University of Wisconsin and its Law School, where he also taught Legal Writing. For the past 40 years Lucht has lived and worked in New York City.

**RITES OF PASSAGE* has been in scores of publications (several times in many), including: Business Week, Wall Street Journal, Forbes, U.S.A. Today, New York Times, Working Woman, Self, Boston Globe, Denver Post, Chicago Tribune, The Philadelphia Inquirer, Los Angeles Times, Chief Executive, Black Enterprise, Seattle Times, American Way, Financial World, Portland Telegram, Dallas Morning News, Omaha World-Herald, New York Daily News, Savvy, Salt Lake City Tribune, American Banker, Women's Wear Daily, Psychology Today, Minneapolis Star & Tribune, Industry Week, Newsday, Success, Investor's Business Daily, St. Louis Post-Dispatch, Training, Publishers Weekly, San Antonio Express News, National Business Employment Weekly, Harper's Bazaar, Chicago Sun-Times, Board Room Reports, Newark Star-Ledger, Cleveland Plain Dealer, Baltimore Sun, El Paso Times, Wichita Eagle, Across the Board (The Conference Board), Men's Health, Personnel Executive, Training & Development Journal, Atlanta Journal/ Constitution, Indianapolis Star & News, Executive Female, Manchester Union Leader, Personnel Administrator, Worcester Telegram, Akron Beacon Journal, Brandweek, Human Resource Executive, Madison State Journal & Capitol Times, Albany Times Union, Career News (Harvard Business School Alumni Career Services), Corpus Christi Caller-Times, The Bricker Bulletin, Canadian Industrial Relations & Personnel Development, World Executive's Digest (serving Asia from Singapore), China Technology Market News (mainland China), and many more.

The RITES OF PASSAGE Program

...the ultimate resources for executive-level career development

Rites of Passage at $100,000 to $1 Million+

...the insider's guide to executive job-changing

Ever since it first appeared over a decade ago, *RITES OF PASSAGE* has been America's and the world's #1 bestselling and most used and respected book of job-changing and career advice for executives. Now comprehensively revised, updated and expanded, *RITES* covers every avenue of job-hunting and career development at the executive level, including cautious use of the Internet. You've seen *RITES* in *Business Week, The Wall Street Journal, The New York Times, USA Today, Working Woman* and virtually every other major newspaper and business publication in the U.S. and, increasingly, around the world as well. "If you're not using *RITES*, you're at a severe disadvantage, because you're probably competing with other executives who are," says John Drake, founder of Drake Beam Morin. "Very few people have John Lucht's knowledge of executive job-hunting and recruiting. None can match his uniquely practical way of sharing that know-how."

HARDCOVER, 640 pages, $29.95. Viceroy Press, ISBN No. 0-942785-30-4.

Executive Job-Changing *Workbook*

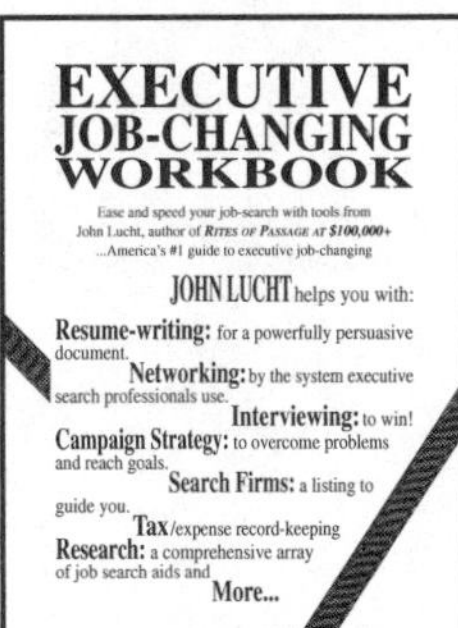

Here are unique tools to develop your thoughts and speed your work. Proceed confidently step-by-step under the personal guidance of John Lucht. By means of pen-and-paper fill-ins, he helps you figure out how best to present yourself...what to emphasize and de-emphasize, and what to write, say, and do to surmount the most daunting obstacles of an executive-level job search...planning your campaign, writing your resume and cover letter, networking, and interviewing. The challenging need to present yourself effectively on-paper and in interviews is greatly eased by the *WORKBOOK'S* templates and techniques. There's also a carefully selected list of outstanding retainer-compensated executive search firms.

PAPERBACK, 576 pages, $29.95. Viceroy Press, ISBN No. 0-942785-22-3.

Insights for the Journey...Navigating to Thrive, Enjoy, and Prosper in Senior Management

Here is John Lucht's latest and most intimately personal sharing of his many years of experience in consulting to—and coaching of—senior executives. Experts are extravagant in their praise of this unique new guide to achieving success, enjoyment, recognition, and financial rewards by excelling in a senior executive career. Yvonne Jackson, Chief Human Resources Officer of Compaq says, "*INSIGHTS FOR THE JOURNEY* is, by far the best book I've ever read on senior executive leadership, performance, and strategy. Here are truths you've never seen before, plus the basics we all should live my...now together in one book *INSIGHTS* can elevate your performance while lowering stress and tension." Gerard Roche, Senior Chairman of Heidrick and Struggles says, "Profound and important...yet fun to read. Once won't be enough!"

HARDCOVER, 104 pages, $19.95. Viceroy Press, ISBN No. 0-942785-31-2.

To Purchase: **Most local and online bookstores carry all 3 books.**
If you prefer to order by phone, call **1 800 JANUARY**.

To Make the WORKBOOK Portable!

For your convenience the WORKBOOK is in two parts.

The front is "at home" activity. But the ATTACHE PAGES can be a lot more helpful if you can slip them inconspicuously into your attache. Then in your first private moments after a networking appointment and after every job interview, you can jot notes while they're fresh-in-mind. You can also refresh your memory immediately prior to any meeting. And you'll always have all the names, addresses, phone numbers, and current status of everyone involved in your search at your fingertips, no matter where you are.

To achieve this goal, we've used America's highest-quality producer of large size paperbacks, and have had them bind in 2 sheets of cardboard (this is one) between the front and back sections. Their adhesive is extremely strong and resilient. Hence, (1) if you're careful you've got a good chance—though no guarantee—of winding up with *two* books...a bit corner-frayed, perhaps, but still together solidly enough to carry. But (2) unless you aggressively stretch, flex, and bend the parts over against themselves as shown here, you'll have a hard time severing them.

Caution!

1. Separate the Workbook on the ***other*** side of this cardboard (the severed parts will have plain unprinted back covers).

2. Flex/bend repeatedly until you've really broken and stretched the spine at the point between the cardboards. See illustration.

3. Use a tough kitchen or garden ***shears***, not granny's antique sewing scissors or your long sleek bond-clipping ones.

4. Work on a table (preferably protected by a couple fat newspapers), ***not*** on your lap.

5. Cut only with a tough shears, ***not*** with any kind of knife, razor blade or any other keen-unshielded instrument.

6. Cut with the book opened downward (the glossy outside covers will face upward toward you as in the illustration). This will result in a far easier and much neater cut than if you work with the book opened to face you in the usual way.